Memory and the
Computational Brain

Memory and the Computational Brain

Why Cognitive Science Will
Transform Neuroscience

C. R. Gallistel and Adam Philip King

WILEY-BLACKWELL

A John Wiley & Sons, Ltd., Publication

Blackwell Publishing was acquired by John Wiley & Sons in February 2007. Blackwell's publishing program has been merged with Wiley's global Scientific, Technical, and Medical business to form Wiley-Blackwell.

Registered Office
John Wiley & Sons Ltd, The Atrium, Southern Gate, Chichester, West Sussex, PO19 8SQ, United Kingdom

Editorial Offices
350 Main Street, Malden, MA 02148-5020, USA
9600 Garsington Road, Oxford, OX4 2DQ, UK
The Atrium, Southern Gate, Chichester, West Sussex, PO19 8SQ, UK

For details of our global editorial offices, for customer services, and for information about how to apply for permission to reuse the copyright material in this book please see our website at www.wiley.com/wiley-blackwell.

Library of Congress Cataloging-in-Publication Data
Gallistel, C. R., 1941–
    Memory and the computational brain : why cognitive science will transform neuroscience / C. R. Gallistel and Adam Philip King.
        p. cm.
    Includes bibliographical references and index.
    ISBN 978-1-4051-2287-0 (alk. paper) — ISBN 978-1-4051-2288-7 (pbk. : alk. paper)
    1. Cognitive neuroscience. 2. Cognitive science. I. King, Adam Philip. II. Title.
    QP360.5G35 2009
    612.8'2—dc22
                                                                        2008044683

A catalogue record for this book is available from the British Library.

Set in 10/12.5pt Sabon by Graphicraft Limited, Hong Kong
Printed and bound in Singapore by Fabulous Printers Pte Ltd

1   2009

Contents

Preface

This is a long book with a simple message: there must be an addressable read/write memory mechanism in brains that encodes information received by the brain into symbols (writes), locates the information when needed (addresses), and transports it to computational machinery that makes productive use of the information (reads).

Such a memory mechanism is indispensable in powerful computing devices, and the behavioral data imply that brains are powerful organs of computation. Computational cognitive scientists presume the existence of an addressable read/write memory mechanism, yet neuroscientists do not know of, and are not looking for, such a mechanism. The truths the cognitive scientists know about information processing, when integrated into neuroscience, will transform our understanding of how the brain works.

An example of such a transformation is the effect that the molecular identification of the gene had on biochemistry. It brought to biochemistry a new conceptual framework. The foundation for this new framework was the concept of a code written into the structure of the DNA molecule. The code concept, which had no place in the old framework, was foundational in the new one. On this foundation, there arose an entire framework in which the duplication, transcription, translation, and correction of the code were basic concepts.

As in biochemistry prior to 1953, one can search through the literature on the neurobiology of memory in vain for a discussion of the coding question: How do the changes wrought by experience in the physical structure of the memory mechanism encode information about the experience? When experience writes to memory the distance and direction of a food source from a nest or hive, how are that distance and that direction represented in the experientially altered structure of the memory mechanism? And how can that encoded information be retrieved and transcribed from that enduring structure into the transient signals that carry that same information to the computational machinery that acts on this information? The answers to these questions must be at the core of our understanding of the physical basis of memory in nervous tissue. In the voluminous contemporary literature on the neurobiology of memory, there is no discussion of these questions. We have written this book in the hope of getting the scientific community that is interested in how brains compute to focus on finding the answers to these critical questions.

In elaborating our argument, we walk the reader through the concepts at the heart of the scientific understanding of information technology. Although most students know the terminology, the level of their understanding of the conceptual framework from which it comes is often superficial. Computer scientists are, in our view, to some extent to be faulted for this state of affairs. Computer science has been central to cognitive science from the beginning, because it was through computer science that the scientific community came to understand how it was possible to physically realize computations. In our view, the basic insights taught in computer science courses on, for example, automata theory, are a more secure basis for considering what the functional architecture of a computational brain must be than are the speculations in neuroscience about how brains compute. We believe that computer science has identified the essential components of a powerful computing machine, whereas neuroscience has yet to establish an empirically secured understanding of how the brain computes. The neuroscience literature contains many conjectures about how the brain computes, but none is well established. Unfortunately, computer scientists sometimes forget what they know about the foundations of physically realizable computation when they begin to think about brains. This is particularly true within the neural network or connectionist modeling framework. The work done in that tradition pays too much attention to neuroscientific speculations about the neural mechanisms that supposedly mediate computation and not enough to well-established results in theoretical and practical computer science concerning the architecture required in a powerful computing machine, whether instantiated with silicone chips or with neurons. Connectionists draw their computational conclusions from architectural commitments, whereas computationalists draw their architectural conclusions from their computational commitments.

In the first chapter, we explicate Shannon's concept of communication and the definition of information that arises out of it. If the function of memory is to carry information forward in time, then we have to be clear about what information is. Here, as in all of our chapters on the foundational concepts in computation, we call attention to lessons of fundamental importance to understanding how brains work. One such lesson is that Shannon's conception of the communication process requires that the receiver, that is, the brain, have a representation of the set of possible messages and a probability distribution over that set. Absent such a representation, it is impossible for the world to communicate information to the brain, at least information as defined by Shannon, which is the only rigorous definition that we have and the foundation on which the immensely powerful theory of information has been built. In this same chapter, we also review Shannon's ideas about efficient codes, ideas that we believe will inform the neuroscience of the future, for reasons that we touch on repeatedly in this book.

Informative signals change the receiver's probability distribution, the probability of the different states of the world (different messages in a set of possible messages). The receiver's representation after an information-bearing signal has been received is the receiver's posterior probability distribution over the possible values of an empirical variable, such as, for example, the distance from the nest to a food source or the rate at which food has been found in a given location. This conception puts Bayes' theorem at the heart of the communication process, because it is a theorem about the normative (correct) way in which to update the receiver's representation of the probable state of the world. In Chapter 2, we take the reader through the Bayesian updating process, both because of its close connection to Shannon's conception of the communication process, and because of the ever growing role of Bayesian models in contemporary cognitive science (Chater, Tenenbaum, & Yuille, 2006). For those less mathematically inclined, Chapter 2 can be skipped or skimmed without loss of continuity.

Because communication between the brain and the world is only possible, in a rigorous sense, if the brain is assumed to have a representation of possible states of the world and their probabilities, the concept of a representation is another critical concept. Before we can explicate this concept, we have to explicate a concept on which it (and many other concepts) depends, the concept of a function. Chapter 3 explains the concept of a function, while Chapter 4 explains the concept of a representation.

Computations are the compositions of functions. A truth about functions of far-reaching significance for our understanding of the functional architecture of the brain is that functions of arbitrarily many arguments may be realized by the composition of functions that have only two arguments, but they cannot be realized by the composition of one-argument functions. The symbols that carry the two values that serve as the arguments of a two-argument function cannot occupy physically adjacent locations, generally speaking. Thus, the functional architecture of any powerful computing device, including the brain, must make provision for bringing symbols from their different locations to the machinery that effects the primitive two-argument functions, out of which the functions with many arguments are constructed by composition.

A representation with wide-ranging power requires computations, because the information the brain needs to know in order to act effectively is not explicit in the sensory signals on which it depends for its knowledge of the world. A read/write memory frees the composition of functions from the constraints of real time by making the empirically specified values for the arguments of functions available at any time, regardless of the time at which past experience specified them.

Representations are functioning homomorphisms. They require structure-preserving mappings (homomorphisms) from states of the world (the represented system) to symbols in the brain (the representing system). These mappings preserve aspects of the formal structure of the world. In a functioning homomorphism, the similarity of formal structure between symbolic processes in the representing system and aspects of the represented system is exploited by the representing system to inform the actions that it takes within the represented system. This is a fancy way of saying that the brain uses its representations to direct its actions.

Symbols are the physical stuff of computation and representation. They are the physical entities in memory that carry information forward in time. They become, either directly or by transcription into signals, the arguments of the procedures that implement functions. And they embody the results of those computations; they carry forward in explicit, computationally accessible form the information that has been extracted from transient signals by means of those computations. To achieve a physical understanding of a representational system like the brain, it is essential to understand its symbols as physical entities. Good symbols must be distinguishable, constructible, compact, and efficacious. Chapter 5 is devoted to explicating and illustrating these attributes of good symbols.

Procedures, or in more contemporary parlance algorithms, are realized through the composition of functions. We make a critical distinction between procedures implemented by means of look-up tables and what we call compact procedures. The essence of the distinction is that the specification of the physical structure of a look-up table requires more information than will ever be extracted by the use of that table. By contrast, the information required to specify the structure of a mechanism that implements a compact procedure may be hundreds of orders of magnitude less than the information that can be extracted using that mechanism. In the table-look-up realization of a function, all of the singletons, pairs, triplets, etc. of values that might ever serve as arguments are explicitly represented in the physical structure of the machinery that implements the function, as are all the values that the function could ever return. This places the table-look-up approach at the mercy of what we call the infinitude of the possible. This infinitude is merciless, a point we return to repeatedly.

By contrast, a compact procedure is a composition of functions that is guaranteed to *generate* (rather than *retrieve*, as in table look-up) the symbol for the value of an *n*-argument function, for any arguments in the domain of the function. The distinction between a look-up table and a compact generative procedure is critical for students of the functional architecture of the brain. One widely entertained functional architecture, the neural network architecture, implements arithmetic and other basic functions by table look-up of nominal symbols rather than by mechanisms that implement compact procedures on compactly encoded symbols. In Chapter 6, we review the intimate connection between compact procedures and compactly encoded symbols. A symbol is compact if its physical magnitude grows only as the logarithm of the number of distinct values that it can represent. A symbol is an encoding symbol if its structure is dictated by a coding algorithm applied to its referent.

With these many preliminaries attended to, we come in Chapter 7 to the exposition of the computer scientist's understanding of computation, Turing computability. Here, we introduce the standard distinction between the finite-state component of a computing machine (the transition table) and the memory (the tape). The distinction is critical, because contemporary thinking about the neurobiological mechanism of memory tries to dispense with the tape and place all of the memory in the transition table (state memory). We review well-known results in computer science about why this cannot be a generally satisfactory solution, emphasizing the infinitude of *possible* experience, as opposed to the finitude of the *actual* experience. We revisit the question of how the symbols are brought to the machinery that returns the values of the functions of which those symbols are arguments. In doing so, we explain the considerations that lead to the so-called von Neumann architecture (the central processor).

In Chapter 8, we consider different suggestions about the functional architecture of a computing machine. This discussion addresses three questions seldom addressed by cognitive neuroscientists, let alone by neuroscientists in general: What are the functional building blocks of a computing machine? How must they be configured? How can they be physically realized? We approach these questions by considering the capabilities of machines with increasingly complex functional structure, showing at each stage mechanical implementations for the functional components. We use mechanical implementations because of their physical transparency, the ease with which one can understand how and why they do what they do. In considering these implementations, we are trying to strengthen the reader's understanding of how abstract descriptions of computation become physically realized. Our point in this exercise is to develop, through a series of machines and formalisms, a step-by-step argument leading up to a computational mechanism with the power of a Turing machine. Our purpose is primarily to show that to get machines that can do computations of reasonable complexity, a specific, minimal functional architecture is demanded. One of its indispensable components is a read/write memory. Secondarily, we show that the physical realization of what is required is not all that complex. And thirdly, we show the relation between descriptions of the structure of a computational mechanism at various levels of abstraction from its physical realization.

In Chapter 9, we take up the critical role of the addressability of the symbols in memory. Every symbol has both a content component, the component of the symbol that carries the information, and an address component, which is the component by which the system gains access to that information. This bipartite structure of the elements of memory provides the physical basis for distinguishing between a variable and its value and for binding the value to the variable. The address of a value becomes the symbol for the variable of which it is the value. Because the addresses are composed in the same symbolic currency as the symbols themselves, they can themselves be symbols. Addresses can – and very frequently do – appear in the symbol fields of other memory locations. This makes the variables themselves accessible to computation, on the same terms as their values. We show how this makes it possible to create data structures in memory. These data structures encode the relations between variables by the arrangement of their symbols in memory. The ability to distinguish between a variable and its value, the ability to bind the latter to the former, and the ability to create data structures that encode relations between variables are critical features of a powerful representational system. All of these capabilities come simply from making memories addressable. All of these capabilities are absent – or only very awkwardly made present – in a neural network architecture, because this architecture lacks addressable symbolic memories.

To bolster our argument that addressable symbolic memories are required by the logic of a system whose function is to carry information forward in an accessible form, we call attention to the fact that the memory elements in the genetic code have this same bipartite structure: A gene has two components, one of which, the coding component, carries information about the sequence of amino acids in a protein; the other of which, the promoter, gives the system access to that information.

In Chapter 10, we consider current conjectures about how the elements of a computing machine can be physically realized using neurons. Because the suggestion that the computational models considered by cognitive scientists ought to be neurobiologically transparent[1] has been so influential in cognitive neuroscience, we emphasize just how conjectural our current understanding of the neural mechanisms of computation is. There is, for example, no consensus about such a basic question as how information is encoded in spike trains. If we liken the flow of information between locations in the nervous system to the flow of information over a telegraph network, then electrophysiologists have been tapping into this flow for almost a century. One might expect that after all this listening in, they would have reached a consensus about what it is about the pulses that conveys the information. But in fact, no such consensus has been reached. This implies that neuroscientists understand as much about information processing in the nervous system as computer scientists would understand about information processing in a computer if they were unable to say how the current pulses on the data bus encoded the information that enters into the CPU's computations.

In Chapter 10, we review conventional material on how it is that synapses can implement elementary logic functions (AND, OR, NOT, NAND). We take note of the painful slowness of both synaptic processes and the long-distance information transmission mechanism (the action potential), relative to their counterparts in an electronic computing machine. We ponder, without coming to any conclusions, how it is possible for the brain to compute as fast as it manifestly does.

Mostly, however, in Chapter 10 we return to the coding question. We point out that the physical change that embodies the creation of a memory must have three aspects, only one of which is considered in contemporary discussions of the mechanism of memory formation in neural tissue, which is always assumed to be an enduring change in synaptic conductance. The change that mediates memory formation must, indeed, be an enduring change. No one doubts that. But it must also be capable of encoding information, just as the molecular structure of a gene endows it with the capacity to encode information. And, it must encode information in a readable way. There must be a mechanism that can transcribe the encoded information, making it accessible to computational machinery. DNA would have no function if the information it encodes could not be transcribed.

We consider at length why enduring changes in synaptic conductance, at least as they are currently conceived, are ill suited both to encode information and, assuming that they did somehow encode it, make it available to computation. The essence of our argument is that changes in synaptic conductance are the physiologists' conception of how the brain realizes the changes in the strengths of associative bonds. Hypothesized changes in the strengths of associative bonds have been at the foundation of psychological and philosophical theorizing about learning for centuries. It is important to realize this, because it is widely recognized that associative bonds make poor symbols: changes in associative strength do not readily encode facts about the state of the experienced world (such as, for example, the distance from a hive to food source or the duration of an interval). It is, thus, no accident that associative theories of learning have generally been anti-representational (P. M. Churchland, 1989; Edelman & Gally, 2001; Hoeffner, McClelland, & Seidenberg, 1996;

---

[1] That is, they ought to rest on what we understand about how the brain computes.

Hull, 1930; Rumelhart & McClelland, 1986; Skinner, 1938, 1957; Smolensky, 1991). If one's conception of the basic element of memory makes that element ill-suited to play the role of a symbol, then one's story about learning and memory is not going to be a story in which representations figure prominently.

In Chapter 11, we take up this theme: the influence of theories of learning on our conception of the neurobiological mechanism of memory, and vice versa. Psychologists, cognitive scientists, and neuroscientists currently entertain two very different stories about the nature of learning. On one story, learning is the process or processes by which experience rewires a plastic brain. This is one or another version of the associative theory of learning. On the second story, learning is the extraction from experience of information about the state of the world, which information is carried forward in memory to inform subsequent behavior. Put another way, learning is the process of extracting by computation the values of variables, the variables that play a critical role in the direction of behavior.

We review the mutually reinforcing fit between the first view of the nature of learning and the neurobiologists' conception of the physiological basis of memory. We take up again the explanation of why it is that associations cannot readily be made to function as symbols. In doing so, we consider the issue of distributed codes, because arguments about representations or the lack thereof in neural networks often turn on issues of distributed coding.

In the second half of Chapter 11, we expand on the view of learning as the extraction from experience of facts about the world and the animal's relation to it, by means of computations. Our focus here is on the phenomenon of dead reckoning, a computational process that is universally agreed to play a fundamental role in animal navigation. In the vast literature on symbolic versus connectionist approaches to computation and representation, most of the focus is on phenomena for which we have no good computational models. We believe that the focus ought to be on the many well-documented behavioral phenomena for which computational models with clear first-order adequacy are readily to hand. Dead reckoning is a prime example. It has been computationally well understood and explicitly taught for centuries. And, there is an extensive experimental literature on its use by animals in navigation, a literature in which ants and bees figure prominently. Here, we have a computation that we believe we understand, with excellent experimental evidence that it occurs in nervous systems that are far removed from our own on the evolutionary bush and many orders of magnitude smaller.

In Chapter 12, we review some of the behavioral evidence that animals routinely represent their location in time and space, that they remember the spatial locations of many significant features of their experienced environment, and they remember the temporal locations of many significant events in their past. One of us reviewed this diverse and large literature at greater length in an earlier book (Gallistel, 1990). In Chapter 12, we revisit some of the material covered there, but our focus is on more recent experimental findings. We review at some length the evidence for episodic memory that has been obtained from the ingenious experimental study of food caching and retrieval in a species of bird that, in the wild, makes and retrieves food from tens of thousands of caches. The importance of this work for our argument is that it demonstrates clearly the existence of complex experience-derived, computationally accessible data structures in brains much smaller than our own and far removed from ours in their location on the evolutionary bush. It is data like these that motivate our focus in an earlier chapter (Chapter 9) on the architecture that a memory system must have in order to encode data structures, because these data are hard to understand within the associative framework in which animal learning has traditionally been treated (Clayton, Emery, & Dickinson, 2006).

In Chapter 13, we review the computational considerations that make learning processes modular. The view that there are only one or a very few quite generally applicable learning processes (the general process view, see, for example, Domjan, 1998, pp. 17ff.) has long dominated discussions of learning. It has particularly dominated the treatment of animal learning, most particularly when the focus is on the underlying neurobiological mechanism. Such a view is consonant with a non-representational framework. In this framework, the behavioral modifications wrought by experience sometimes make animals look as if they know what it is about the world that makes their actions rational, but this appearance of symbolic knowledge is an illusion; in fact, they have simply learned to behave more effectively (Clayton, Emery, & Dickinson, 2006). However, if we believe with Marr (1982) that brains really do compute the values of distal variables and that learning is this extraction from experience of the values of variables (Gallistel, 1990), then learning processes are inescapably modular. They are modular because it takes different computations to extract different representations from different data, as was first pointed out by Chomsky (1975). We illustrate this point by a renewed discussion of dead reckoning (aka path integration), by a discussion of the mechanism by which bees learn the solar ephemeris, and by a discussion of the special computations that are required to explain the many fundamental aspects of classical (Pavlovian) conditioning that are unexplained by the traditional associative approach to the understanding of conditioning.[2]

In Chapter 14, we take up again the question of how the nervous system might carry information forward in time in a computationally accessible form in the absence of a read/write memory mechanism. Having explained in earlier chapters why plastic synapses cannot perform this function, we now consider in detail one of the leading neural network models of dead reckoning (Samsonovich & McNaughton, 1997). This model relies on the only widely conjectured mechanism for performing the essential memory function, reverberatory loops. We review this model in detail because it illustrates so dramatically the points we have made earlier about the price that is paid when one dispenses with a read/write memory. To our mind, what this model proves is that the price is too high.

In Chapter 15, we return to the interval timing phenomena that we reviewed in Chapter 12 (and, at greater length, in Gallistel, 1990; Gallistel & Gibbon, 2000; Gallistel & Gibbon, 2002), but now we do so in order to consider neural models

---

[2] This is the within-field jargon for the learning that occurs in "associative" learning paradigms. It is revelatory of the anti-representational foundations of traditional thinking about learning. It is called conditioning because experience is not assumed to give rise to symbolic knowledge of the world. Rather, it "conditions" (rewires) the nervous system so that it generates more effective behavior.

of interval timing. Here, again, we show the price that is paid by dispensing with a read/write memory. Given a read/write memory, it is easy to model, at least to a first approximation, the data on interval timing (Gallistel & Gibbon, 2002; Gibbon, Church, & Meck, 1984; Gibbon, 1977). Without such a mechanism, modeling these phenomena is very hard. Because the representational burden is thrown onto the conjectured dynamic properties of neurons, the models become prey to the problem of the infinitude of the possible. Basically, you need too many neurons, because you have to allocate resources to all possible intervals rather than just to those that have actually been observed. Moreover, these models all fail to provide computational access to the information about previously experienced durations, because the information resides not in the activity of the neurons, nor in the associations between them, but rather in the intrinsic properties of the neurons in the arrays used to represent durations. The rest of the system has no access to those intrinsic properties.

Finally, in Chapter 16, we take up the question that will have been pressing on the minds of many readers ever since it became clear that we are profoundly skeptical about the hypothesis that the physical basis of memory is some form of synaptic plasticity, the only hypothesis that has ever been seriously considered by the neuroscience community. The obvious question is: Well, if it's not synaptic plasticity, what is it? Here, we refuse to be drawn. We do not think we know what the mechanism of an addressable read/write memory is, and we have no faith in our ability to conjecture a correct answer. We do, however, raise a number of considerations that we believe should guide thinking about possible mechanisms. Almost all of these considerations lead us to think that the answer is most likely to be found deep within neurons, at the molecular or sub-molecular level of structure. It is easier and less demanding of physical resources to implement a read/write memory at the level of molecular or sub-molecular structure. Indeed, most of what is needed is already implemented at the sub-molecular level in the structure of DNA and RNA.

1

Information

Most cognitive scientists think about the brain and behavior within an information-processing framework: Stimuli acting on sensory receptors provide information about the state of the world. The sensory receptors transduce the stimuli into neural signals, streams of action potentials (aka spikes). The spike trains transmit the information contained in the stimuli from the receptors to the brain, which processes the sensory signals in order to extract from them the information that they convey. The extracted information may be used immediately to inform ongoing behavior, or it may be kept in memory to be used in shaping behavior at some later time. Cognitive scientists seek to understand the stages of processing by which information is extracted, the representations that result, the motor planning processes through which the information enters into the direction of behavior, the memory processes that organize and preserve the information, and the retrieval processes that find the information in memory when it is needed. Cognitive neuroscientists want to understand where these different aspects of information processing occur in the brain and the neurobiological mechanisms by which they are physically implemented.

Historically, the information-processing framework in cognitive science is closely linked to the development of information technology, which is used in electronic computers and computer software to convert, store, protect, process, transmit, and retrieve information. But what exactly is this "information" that is so central to both cognitive science and computer science? Does it have a rigorous meaning? In fact, it does. Moreover, the conceptual system that has grown up around this rigorous meaning – information theory – is central to many aspects of modern science and engineering, including some aspects of cognitive neuroscience. For example, it is central to our emerging understanding of how neural signals transmit information about the ever-changing state of the world from sensory receptors to the brain (Rieke, Warland, de Ruyter van Steveninck, & Bialek, 1997). For us, it is an essential foundation for our central claim, which is that the function of the neurobiological memory mechanism is to carry information forward in time in a computationally accessible form.

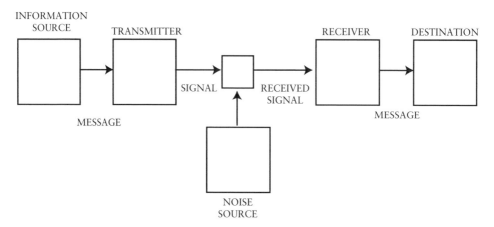

Figure 1.1   Shannon's schematization of communication (Shannon, 1948).

Shannon's Theory of Communication

The modern quantitative understanding of information rests on the work of Claude Shannon. A telecommunications engineer at Bell Laboratories, he laid the mathematical foundations of information theory in a famous paper published in 1948, at the dawn of the computer age (Shannon, 1948). Shannon's concern was understanding communication (the transmission of information), which he schematized as illustrated in Figure 1.1.

The schematic begins with an information *source*. The source might be a person who hands in a written message at a telegraph office. Or, it might be an orchestra playing a Beethoven symphony. In order for the message to be communicated to you, you must receive a *signal* that allows you to reconstitute the message. In this example, you are the *destination* of the message. Shannon's analysis ends when the destination has received the signal and reconstituted the message that was present at the source.

The *transmitter* is the system that converts the messages into transmitted signals, that is, into fluctuations of a physical quantity that travels from a source location to a receiving location and that can be detected at the receiving location. Encoding is the process by which the messages are converted into transmitted signals. The rules governing or specifying this conversion are the code. The mechanism in the transmitter that implements the conversion is the encoder.

Following Shannon, we will continue to use two illustrative examples, a telegraphic communication and a symphonic broadcast. In the telegraphic example, the source messages are written English phrases handed to the telegrapher, for example, "Arriving tomorrow, 10 am." In the symphonic example, the source messages are sound waves arriving at a microphone. Any one particular short message written in English and handed to a telegraph operator can be thought of as coming from a finite *set of possible messages*. If we stipulate a maximum length of, say, 1,000 characters, with each character being one of 45 or so different characters (26 letters, 10 digits, and punctuation marks), then there is a very large but finite number of possible messages. Moreover, only a very small fraction of these messages are intelligible English, so the size of the set of possible messages – defined as intelligible English messages of 1,000 characters or less – is further reduced. It is less clear that the sound waves generated by an orchestra playing Beethoven's Fifth can be conceived of as coming from a finite set of messages. That is why Shannon chose this as his second example. It serves to illustrate the generality of his theory.

In the telegraphy example, the telegraph system is the transmitter of the messages. The signals are the short current pulses in the telegraph wire, which travel from the sending key to the sounder at the receiving end. The encoder is the telegraph operator. The code generally used is the Morse code. This code uses pulses of two different durations to encode the characters – a *short mark* (dot), and a *long mark* (dash). It also uses four different inter-pulse intervals for separations – an intra-character gap (between the dots and dashes within characters), a short gap (between the letters), a medium gap (between words), and a long gap (between sentences).

In the orchestral example, the broadcast system transmitting radio signals from the microphone to your radio is the transmitter. The encoder is the electronic device that converts the sound waves into electromagnetic signals. The type of code is likely to be one of three different codes that have been used in the history of radio (see Figure 1.2), all of which are in current use. All of them vary a parameter of a high-frequency *sinusoidal* carrier signal. The earliest code was the AM (amplitude modulated) code. In this code, the encoder modulates the amplitude of the carrier signal so that this amplitude of the sinusoidal carrier signal varies in time in a way that closely follows the variation in time of the sound pressure at the microphone's membrane.

When the FM (frequency modulated) code is used, the encoder modulates the frequency of the carrier signal within a limited range. When the *digital* code is used, as it is in satellite radio, parameters of the carrier frequency are modulated so as to implement a binary code, a code in which there are only two characters, customarily called the '0' and the '1' character. In this system, time is divided into extremely short intervals. During any one interval, the carrier signal is either low ('0') or high ('1'). The relation between the sound wave arriving at the microphone with its associated encoding electronics and the transmitted binary signal is not easily described, because the encoding system is a sophisticated one that makes use of what we have learned about the statistics of broadcast messages to create efficient codes. The development of these codes rests on the foundations laid by Shannon.

In the history of radio broadcasting, we see an interesting evolution (Figure 1.2): We see first (historically) in Figure 1.2a a code in which there is a transparent (easily comprehended) relation between the message and the signal that transmits it (AM). The code is transparent because variation in the amplitude of the message is converted into variation in the amplitude of the carrier signal that transmits the message. This code is, however, inefficient and highly vulnerable to noise. It is low tech. In Figure 1.2b, we see a code in which the relation is somewhat less transparent, because variation in the amplitude of the message is converted into

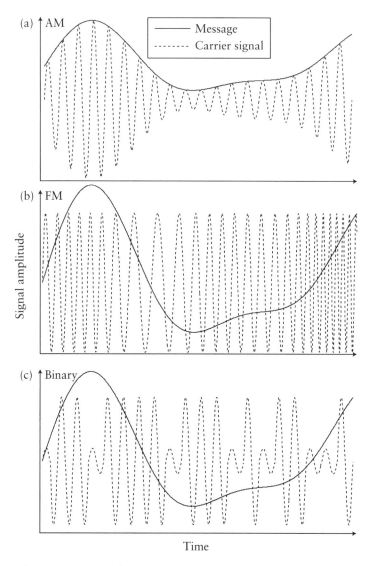

Figure 1.2 The various ways of encoding sound "messages" into broadcast radio signals. All of them use a carrier frequency and vary parameters of that carrier frequency. (a) In the AM encoding, the amplitude of the message determines the amplitude of the carrier frequency. This makes for a transparent (easily recognized) relation between the message and the signal that transmits it. (b) In the FM encoding, the amplitude of the message modulates the frequency of the carrier. This makes for a less transparent but still recognizable relation between message and signal. (c) In digital encoding, there is binary (two-values only) modulation in a parameter of the carrier signal. In this purely notional illustration, the amplitude of any given cycle has one of two values, depending on whether a high or low bit is transmitted. In this scheme, the message is converted into a sophisticated binary code prior to transmission. The relation between message and signal is opaque.

variation in the frequency of the carrier signal that transmits it (FM). This code is no more efficient than the first code, but it is less vulnerable to noise, because the effects of extraneous noise tend to fall mostly in frequency bands outside a given FM band. Finally, in Figure 1.2c we see a high-tech code in which the relation between the message and the signal that transmits it is opaque. The encoding makes extensive use of advanced statistics and mathematics. The code is, however, both efficient and remarkably invulnerable to noise. That's why satellite broadcasts sound better than FM broadcasts, which sound better than AM broadcasts. The greater efficiency of the digital code accounts for the ability of digital radio to transmit more channels within a given bandwidth.

The evolution of encoding in the history of broadcasting may contain an unpalatable lesson for those interested in understanding communication within the brain by means of the action potentials that carry information from sources to destinations within the brain. One of neurobiology's uncomfortable secrets – the sort of thing neurobiologists are not keen to talk about except among themselves – is that we do not understand the code that is being used in these communications. Most neurobiologists assume either explicitly or tacitly that it is an unsophisticated and transparent code. They assume, for example, that when the relevant variation at the source is in the amplitude or intensity of some stimulus, then the information-carrying variation in the transmitted signal is in the firing rate (the number of action potentials per unit of time), a so-called *rate code*. The transparency of rate codes augurs well for our eventually understanding the communication of information within the brain, but rate codes are grossly inefficient. With more sophisticated but less transparent codes, the same physical resources (the transmission of the same number of spikes in a given unit of time) can convey orders of magnitude more information. State-of-the-art analysis of information transmission in neural signaling in simple systems where we have reason to believe that we know both the set of message being transmitted and the amount of information available in that set (its entropy – see below) implies that the code is a sophisticated and efficient one, one that takes account of the relative frequency of different messages (source statistics), just as the code used in digital broadcasting does (Rieke et al., 1997).

A signal must travel by way of some physical medium, which Shannon refers to as the signal-carrying channel, or just channel for short. In the case of the telegraph, the signal is in the changing flow of electrons and the channel is a wire. In the case of the symphony, the signal is the variation in the parameters of a carrier signal. The channel is that carrier signal.[1] In the case of the nervous system, the axons along which nerve impulses are conducted are the channels.

In the real world, there are factors other than the message that can also produce these same fluctuations in the signal-carrying channel. Shannon called these *noise*

---

[1] In digital broadcasting, bit-packets from different broadcasts are intermixed and travel on a common carrier frequency. The receivers sort out which packets belong to which broadcast. They do so on the basis of identifying information in the packets. Sorting out the packets and decoding them back into waveforms requires computation. This is why computation and communication are fused at the hip in information technology. In our opinion, a similar situation obtains in the brain: Computation and communication are inseparable, because communication has been optimized in the brain.

sources. The signal that arrives at the *receiver* is thus a mixture of the fluctuations deriving from the encoding of the message and the fluctuations deriving from noise sources. The fluctuations due to noise make the receiver's job more difficult, as the received code can become corrupted. The receiver must reconstitute the message from the source, that is, change the signal back into that message, and if this signal has been altered, it may be hard to decode. In addition, the transmitter or the receiver may be faulty and introduce noise during the encoding/decoding process.

Although Shannon diagrammatically combined the sources of noise and showed one place where noise can be introduced, in actuality, noise can enter almost anywhere in the communication process. For example, in the case of telegraphy, the sending operators may not code correctly (use a wrong sequence of dots and dashes) or even more subtly, they might make silences of questionable (not clearly discernible) length. The telegraph key can also malfunction, and not always produce current when it should, possibly turning a dash into some dots. Noise can also be introduced into the signal directly – in this case possibly through interference due to other signals traveling along wires that are in close proximity to the signal-carrying wire. Additionally, the receiving operator may have a faulty sounder or may simply decode incorrectly.

Shannon was, of course, aware that the messages being transmitted often had *meanings*. Certainly this is the case for the telegraphy example. Arguably, it is the case for the orchestra example. However, one of his profound insights was that from the standpoint of the communications engineer, the meaning was irrelevant. What was essential about a message was not its meaning but rather that *it be selected from a set of possible messages*. Shannon realized that for a communication system to work efficiently – for it to transmit the maximum amount of information in the minimum amount of time – both the transmitter and the receiver had to know what the set of possible messages was and the relative likelihood of the different messages within the set of possible messages. This insight was an essential part of his formula for quantifying the information transmitted across a signal-carrying channel. We will see later (Chapter 9) that Shannon's set of possible messages can be identified with the values of an experiential variable. Different variables denote different sets of possible messages. Whenever we learn from experience the value of an empirical variable (for example, how long it takes to boil an egg, or how far it is from our home to our office), the range of a priori possible values for that variable is narrowed by our experience. The greater the range of a priori possible values for the variable (that is, the larger the set of possible messages) and the narrower the range after we have had an informative experience (that is, the more precisely we then know the value), the more informative the experience. That is the essence of Shannon's definition of information.

The thinking that led to Shannon's formula for quantifying information may be illustrated by reference to the communication situation that figures in Longfellow's poem about the midnight ride of Paul Revere. The poem describes a scene from the American revolution in which Paul Revere rode through New England, warning the rebel irregulars that the British troops were coming. The critical stanza for our purposes is the second:

> He said to his friend, "If the British march
> By land or sea from the town to-night,
> Hang a lantern aloft in the belfry arch
> Of the North Church tower as a signal light, –
> One if by land, and two if by sea;
> And I on the opposite shore will be,
> Ready to ride and spread the alarm
> Through every Middlesex village and farm,
> For the country folk to be up and to arm."

The two possible messages in this communication system were "by land" and "by sea." The signal was the lantern light, which traveled from the church tower to the receiver, Paul Revere, waiting on the opposite shore. Critically, Paul knew the possible messages and he knew the code – the relation between the possible messages and the possible signals. If he had not known either one of these, the communication would not have worked. Suppose he had no idea of the possible routes by which the British might come. Then, he could not have created a set of possible messages. Suppose that, while rowing across the river, he forgot whether it was one if by land and two if by sea or two if by land and one if by sea. In either case, the possibility of communication disappears. No set of possible messages, no communication. No agreement about the code between sender and receiver, no communication.

However, it is important to remember that information is always about something and that signals can, and often do, carry information about multiple things. When we said above that no information was received, we should have been more precise. If Paul forgot the routes (possible messages) or the code, then he could receive no information about how the British might come. This is not to say that he received no information when he saw the lanterns. Upon seeing the two lanterns, he would have received information about how many lanterns were hung. In the simplest analysis, a received signal always (baring overriding noise) carries information regarding which signal was sent.

Measuring Information

Shannon was particularly concerned with *measuring* the amount of information communicated. So how much information did Paul Revere get when he saw the lanterns (for two it was)? On Shannon's analysis, that depends on his prior expectation about the relative likelihoods of the British coming by land versus their coming by sea. In other words, it depends on how uncertain he was about which route they would take. Suppose he thought it was a toss-up – equally likely either way. According to Shannon's formula, he then received one bit[2] (the basic unit) of information when he saw the signal. Suppose that he thought it less likely that they

---

[2]   Shannon was the first to use the word *bit* in print, however he credits John Tukey who used the word as a shorthand for "binary digit."

would come by land – that there was only one chance in ten. By Shannon's formula, he then received somewhat less than half a bit of information from the lantern signal.

Shannon's analysis says that the (average!) amount of information communicated is the (average) amount of uncertainty that the receiver had before the communication minus the amount of uncertainty that the receiver has after the communication. This implies that information itself is the reduction of uncertainty in the receiver. A reduction in uncertainty is, of course, an increase in certainty, but what is measured is the uncertainty.

The discrete case

So how did Shannon measure uncertainty? He suggested that we consider the *prior probability* of each message. The smaller the prior probability of a message, the greater its information content but the less often it contributes that content, because the lower its probability, the lower its relative frequency. The contribution of any one possible message to the average uncertainty regarding messages in the set of possible messages is the information content of that message times its relative frequency. Its information content is the log of the reciprocal of its probability $\left(\log_2 \frac{1}{p_i}\right)$. Its relative frequency is p_i itself. Summing over all the possible messages gives Shannon's famous formula:

$$H = \sum_{i=1}^{i=n} p_i \log_2 \frac{1}{p_i}$$

where H is the amount of uncertainty about the possible messages (usually called the *entropy*), n is the number of possible messages, and p_i is the probability of the ith message.[3] As the probability of a message in the set becomes very small (as it approaches 0), its contribution to the amount of uncertainty also becomes very small, because a probability goes to 0 faster than the log of its reciprocal goes to infinity. In other words, the fall off in the relative frequency of a message (the decrease in p_i) outstrips the increase in its information content $\left(\text{the increase in } \log_2 \frac{1}{p_i}\right)$.

In the present, simplest possible case, there are two possible messages. If we take their prior probabilities to be 0.5 and 0.5 (50–50, equally likely), then following Shannon's formula, Paul's uncertainty before he saw the signal was:

$$p_1 \log_2 \frac{1}{p_1} + p_2 \log_2 \frac{1}{p_2} = 0.5 \log_2 \frac{1}{0.5} + 0.5 \log_2 \frac{1}{0.5} \tag{1}$$

---

[3]   The logarithm is to base 2 in order to make the units of information bits, that is, to choose a base for the logarithm is to choose the size of the units in which information is measured.

Now, $1/0.5 = 2$, and the log to the base 2 of 2 is 1. Thus, equation (1) equals:

$$(0.5)(1) + (0.5)(1) = 1 \text{ bit.}$$

Consider now the case where $p_1 = 0.1$ (Paul's prior probability on their coming by land) and $p_2 = 0.9$ (Paul's prior probability on their coming by sea). The $\log_2 (1/0.1)$ is 3.32 and the $\log_2 (1/0.9)$ is 0.15, so we have $(0.1)(3.32) + (0.9)(0.15) = 0.47$. If Paul was pretty sure they were coming by sea, then he had less uncertainty than if he thought it was a toss-up. That's intuitive. Finding a principled formula that specifies exactly how much less uncertainty he had is another matter. Shannon's formula was highly principled. In fact, he proved that his formula was the only formula that satisfied a number of conditions that we would want a measure of uncertainty to have.

One of those conditions is the following: Suppose we have H_1 amount of uncertainty about the outcome of the roll of one die and H_2 amount of uncertainty about the outcome of the roll of a second die. We want the amount of uncertainty we have about the combined outcomes to be simply $H_1 + H_2$, that is, we want the amounts of uncertainties about independent sets of possibilities to be additive. Shannon's formula satisfies this condition. That's why it uses logarithms of the probabilities. Independent probabilities combine multiplicatively. Taking logarithms converts multiplicative combination to additive combination.

Assuming Paul trusted his friend completely and assuming that there was no possibility of his mistaking one light for two (assuming in other words, no transmission noise), then when he saw the two lights, he had no more uncertainty about which way the British were coming: p_1, the probability of their coming by land, was 0 and p_2, the probability of their coming by sea, was 1. Another condition on a formula for measuring uncertainty is that the measure should be zero when there is no uncertainty. For Paul, after he had seen the lights, we have: $0 \log_2 (1/0) + 1 \log_2 (1/1) = 0$ (because the $\lim_{p \to 0} p \log (1/p) = 0$, which makes the first term in the sum 0, and the log of 1 to any base is 0, which makes the second term 0). So Shannon's formula satisfies that condition.

Shannon defined the amount of information *communicated* to be the difference between the receiver's uncertainty before the communication and the receiver's uncertainty after it. Thus, the amount of information that Paul got when he saw the lights depends not only on his knowing beforehand the two possibilities (knowing the set of possible messages) but also on his prior assessment of the probability of each possibility. This is an absolutely critical point about communicated information – and the subjectivity that it implies is deeply unsettling. By subjectivity, we mean that the information communicated by a signal depends on the receiver's (the subject's) prior knowledge of the possibilities and their probabilities. Thus, the amount of information actually communicated is not an objective property of the signal from which the subject obtained it!

Unsettling as the subjectivity inherent in Shannon's definition of communicated information is, it nonetheless accords with our intuitive understanding of communication. When someone says something that is painfully obvious to everyone, it is not uncommon for teenagers to reply with a mocking, "Duh." Implicit in this mockery is that we talk in order to communicate and to communicate you have to change the hearer's representation of the world. If your signal leaves your listeners with the same representation they had before they got it, then your talk is empty blather. It communicates no information.

Shannon called his measure of uncertainty entropy because his formula is the same as the formula that Boltzmann developed when he laid the foundations for statistical mechanics in the nineteenth century. Boltzmann's definition of entropy relied on statistical considerations concerning the degree of uncertainty that the observer has about the state of a physical system. Making the observer's uncertainty a fundamental aspect of the physical analysis has become a foundational principle in quantum physics, but it was extremely controversial at the time (1877). The widespread rejection of his work is said to have driven Boltzmann to suicide. However, his faith in the value of what he had done was such that he had his entropy-defining equation written on his tombstone.

In summary, like most basic quantities in the physical sciences, information is a mathematical abstraction. It is a statistical concept, intimately related to concepts at the foundation of statistical mechanics. The information available from a source is the amount of uncertainty about what that source may reveal, what message it may have for us. The amount of uncertainty at the source is called the source entropy. The signal is a propagating physical fluctuation that carries the information from the source to the receiver.

The information *transmitted* to the receiver by the signal is the *mutual information* between the signal actually received and the source. This is an objective property of the source and signal; we do not need to know anything about the receiver (the subject) in order to specify it, and it sets an upper limit on the information that a receiver could in principle get from a signal. We will explain how to quantify it shortly. However, the information that is *communicated* to a receiver by a signal is the receiver's uncertainty about the state of the world before the signal was received (the receiver's prior entropy) minus the receiver's uncertainty after receiving the signal (the posterior entropy). Thus, its quantification depends on the changes that the signal effects in the receiver's representation of the world. The information communicated from a source to a receiver by a signal is an inherently subjective concept; to measure it we must know the receiver's representation of the source probabilities. That, of course, implies that the receiver has a representation of the source probabilities, which is itself a controversial assumption in behavioral neuroscience and cognitive psychology. One school of thought denies that the brain has representations of any kind, let alone representations of source possibilities and their probabilities. If that is so, then it is impossible to communicate information to the brain in Shannon's sense of the term, which is the only scientifically rigorous sense. In that case, an information-processing approach to the analysis of brain function is inappropriate.

The continuous case

So far, we have only considered the measurement of information in the discrete case (and a maximally simple one). That is to say that each message Paul could receive was distinct, and it should not have been possible to receive a message "in between" the messages he received. In addition, the number of messages Paul could receive was finite – in this case only two. The British could have come by land or by sea – not both, not by air, etc. It may seem puzzling how Shannon's analysis can be applied to the continuous case, like the orchestra broadcast. On first consideration, the amount of prior uncertainty that a receiver could have about an orchestral broadcast is infinite, because there are infinitely many different sound-wave patterns. Any false note hit by any player at any time, every cough, and so on, alters the wave pattern arriving at the microphone. This seems to imply that the amount of prior uncertainty that a receiver could have about an orchestral broadcast is infinite. Hearing the broadcast reduces the receiver's uncertainty from infinite to none, so an infinite amount of information has been communicated. Something must be wrong here.

To see what is wrong, we again take a very simple case. Instead of an orchestra as our source, consider a container of liquid whose temperature is measured by an analog (continuous) thermometer that converts the temperature into a current flow. Information is transmitted about the temperature to a receiver in a code that theoretically contains an infinite number of possibilities (because for any two temperatures, no matter how close together they are, there are an infinite number of temperatures between them). This is an analog source (the variation in temperature) and an analog signal (the variation in current flow). Analog sources and signals have the theoretical property just described, infinite divisibility. There is no limit to how finely you can carve them up. Therefore, no matter how thin the slice you start with you can always slice them into arbitrarily many even thinner slices. Compare this to the telegraphy example. Here, the source was discrete and so was the signal. The source was a text written in an alphabetic script with a finite number of different characters (letters, numbers, and various punctuation marks). These characters were encoded by Morse's code into a signal that used six primitive symbols. Such a signal is called a digital signal.

In the temperature case, there would appear to be an infinite number of temperatures that the liquid could have, any temperature from $0-\infty°$ Kelvin. Further thought tells us, however, that while this may be true in principle (it's not clear that even in principle temperatures can be infinite), it is not true in practice. Above a certain temperature, both the container and the thermometer would vaporize. In fact, in any actual situation, the range of possible temperatures will be narrow. Moreover, we will have taken into account that range when we set up the system for measuring and communicating the liquid's temperature. That is, the structure of the measuring system will reflect the characteristics of the messages to be transmitted. This is the sense in which the system will know the set of possible messages; the knowledge will be implicit in its structure.

However, even within an arbitrarily narrow range of temperatures, there are arbitrarily many different temperatures. That is what it means to say that temperature is a continuous variable. This is true, but the multiple and inescapable sources of noise in the system limit the attainable degree of certainty about what the temperature is. There is source noise – tiny fluctuations from moment to moment and place to place within the liquid. There is measurement noise; the fluctuations in the

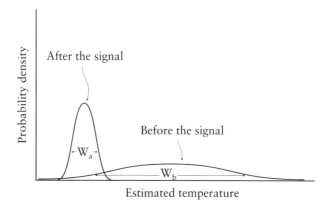

Figure 1.3   In analog communication, the receipt of a signal alters the receiver's probability density distribution, the distribution that specifies the receiver's knowledge of the source value. Generally (though not obligatorily), it narrows the distribution, that is, $\sigma_a < \sigma_b$, and it shifts the mean and mode (most probable value).

electrical current from the thermometer will never exactly mimic the fluctuations in the temperature at the point being measured. And there is transmission noise; the fluctuations in the current at the receiver will never be exactly the same as the fluctuations in the current at the transmitter. There are limits to how small each of these sources of noise can be made. They limit the accuracy with which the temperature of a liquid can in principle be known. Thus, where we went wrong in considering the applicability of Shannon's analysis to the continuous case was in assuming that an analog signal from an analog source could give a receiver information with certainty; it cannot. The accuracy of analog signaling is always noise limited, and it must be so for deep physical reasons. Therefore, the receiver of an analog signal always has a residual uncertainty about the true value of the source variable. This a priori limit on the accuracy with which values within a given range may be known limits the number of values that may be distinguished one from another within a finite range. That is, it limits resolution. The limit on the number of distinguishable values together with the limits on the range of possible values makes the source entropy finite and the post-communication entropy of the receiver non-zero.

Figure 1.3 shows how Shannon's analysis applies to the simplest continuous case. Before the receiver gets an analog signal, it has a continuous (rather than discrete) representation of the possible values of some variable (e.g., temperature). In the figure, this prior (before-the-signal) distribution is assumed to be a normal (aka Gaussian) distribution, because it is rather generally the case that we construct a measurement system so that the values in the middle of the range of possible (i.e., measured) values are the most likely values. Shannon derived the entropy for a normal distribution, showing that it was proportional to the log of the standard deviation, σ, which is the measure of the width of a distribution. Again, this is intuitive: the broader the distribution is, the more uncertainty there is. After receiving the signal, the receiver has less uncertainty about the true value of the temperature. In Shannon's analysis, this means that the posterior (after-the-signal) distribution is narrower and higher. The information conveyed by the signal is proportional to the difference in the two entropies: $k(\log \sigma_b - \log \sigma_a)$.

How does the simple case generalize to a complex case like the orchestral broadcast? Here, Shannon made use of the Fourier theorem, which tells us how to represent a continuous variation like the variation in sound pressure produced by an orchestra with a set of sine waves. The Fourier theorem asserts that the whole broadcast can be uniquely represented as the sum of a set of sinusoidal oscillations. If we know this set – the so-called Fourier decompositions of the sound – we can get back the sound by simply adding all the sinusoids point by point. (See Gallistel, 1980, for elementary explanation and illustration of how this works; also King & Gallistel, 1996.) In principle, this representation of the sound requires infinitely many different sinusoids; but in practice, there are limits on both the sensible range of sinusoidal frequencies and the frequency resolution within that range. For example, there is no point in representing the frequencies above 20 kHz, because humans cannot hear them. In principle, the number of possible amplitudes for a sinusoid is infinite, but there are limits on the amplitudes that broadcast sounds actually do have; and within that attainable range, there are limits on the resolution with which sound amplitude may be ascertained. The same is true for phase, the third and final parameter that defines a sinusoid and distinguishes it from other sinusoids. Thus, the space of possible broadcasts is the space defined by the range of hearable frequencies and attainable amplitudes and phases. Because there are inescapable limits to the accuracy with which each of these three space-defining parameters may be ascertained, there is necessarily some residual uncertainty about any broadcast (some limit on the fidelity of the transmission). Hence, odd as it seems, there is a finite amount of prior uncertainty about possible broadcasts and a residual amount of uncertainty after any transmitted broadcast. This makes the amount of information communicated in a broadcast finite and, more importantly, actually measurable. Indeed, communications engineers, following the guidelines laid down by Shannon, routinely measure it. That's how they determine the number of songs your portable music player can hold.

Mutual information

The mutual information between an information-conveying signal and its source is the entropy of the source plus the entropy of the signal minus the entropy of their joint distribution. Recall that entropy is a property of a probability (relative frequency) distribution over some set of possibilities. The source entropy is a quantity derived from the distribution of probability over the possible messages (the relative frequencies of the different possible messages). The signal entropy is a quantity derived from the distribution of probability over the possible signals (the relative frequencies of the different possible signals). A distribution is the set of *all* the probabilities (or relative frequencies), one probability for each possibility. Thus, the sum over these probabilities is always 1, because one or the other possibility must obtain in every case and the set contains all the possible cases (all the possible messages or all the possible signals). In computing the entropy of a distribution, we take each probability in turn, multiply the logarithm of its reciprocal by the probability itself, and sum across all the products. Returning to the Paul Revere example, if the probability, p_L, of their coming by land is 0.1 and the probability, p_S of their coming by sea is 0.9, then the source entropy (the basic uncertainty inherent in the situation) is:

$$p_L \log_2 \frac{1}{p_L} + p_S \log_2 \frac{1}{p_S} = (0.1)(3.32) + (0.9)(0.15) = 0.47.$$

If the two signals, one light and two lights, have the same probability distribution, then the signal entropy is the same as the source entropy.

The joint distribution of the messages and the signals is the probabilities of all possible co-occurrences between messages and signals. In the Paul Revere example, four different co-occurrences are possible: (1) the British are coming by land and there is one signal light; (2) the British are coming by land and there are two signal lights; (3) the British are coming by sea and there is one signal light; (4) the British are coming by sea and there are two signal lights. The joint distribution is these four probabilities. The entropy of the joint distribution is obtained by the computation we already described: multiply the logarithm of the reciprocal of each probability by the probability itself and sum the four products.

The entropy of this joint distribution depends on how reliably Paul's confederate carries out the assigned task. Suppose that he carries it out flawlessly: every time they come by land, he hangs one lantern; every time they come by sea, he hangs two. Then the four probabilities are $p_{L\&1} = 0.1$, $p_{L\&2} = 0$, $p_{S\&1} = 0$, $p_{S\&2} = 0.9$ and the entropy of this joint distribution is the same as the entropy of the source distribution and the entropy of the signal distribution; all three entropies are 0.47. The sum of the source and signal entropies (the first two entropies) minus the third (the entropy of the joint distribution) is 0.47, so the mutual information between source and signal is 0.47, which is to say that all the information available at the source is transmitted by the signal.

Suppose instead that Paul's confederate is terrified of the British and would not think of spying on their movements. Therefore, he has no idea which way they are coming, but, because he does not want Paul to know of his cowardice, he hangs lanterns anyway. He knows that the British are much more likely to go by sea than by land, so each night he consults a random number table. He hangs one lantern if the first digit he puts his finger on is a 1 and two lanterns otherwise. Now, there is no relation between which way the British are coming and the signal Paul sees. Now the four probabilities corresponding to the four possible conjunctions of British movements and the coward's signals are: $p_{L\&1} = 0.01$, $p_{L\&2} = 0.09$, $p_{S\&1} = 0.09$, $p_{S\&2} = 0.81$ and the entropy of this joint distribution is:

$$(0.01) \log_2 \left(\tfrac{1}{0.01}\right) + (0.09) \log_2 \left(\tfrac{1}{0.09}\right) + (0.09) \log_2 \left(\tfrac{1}{0.09}\right) + (0.81) \log_2 \left(\tfrac{1}{0.81}\right)$$
$$= (0.01)(6.64) + (0.09)(3.47) + (0.09)(3.47) + (0.81)(0.30) = 0.94.$$

The entropy of the joint distribution is equal to the sum of the two other entropies (more technically, the entropy of the joint distribution is the sum of the entropies of the marginal distributions). When it is subtracted from that sum, the difference is 0. There is no mutual information between the signal and the source. Whether Paul knows it or not, he can learn nothing about what the British are doing from monitoring his confederate's signal. Notice that there is no subjectivity in the computation of the mutual information between source and signal. That is why we can measure the amount of information transmitted without regard to the receiver's representation of the source and the source probabilities.

Finally, consider the case where Paul's confederate is not a complete coward. On half the nights, he gathers up his courage and spies on the British movements. On those nights, he unfailingly signals correctly what he observes. On the other half of the nights, he resorts to the random number table. Now, the probabilities in the joint distribution are: $p_{L\&1} = 0.055$, $p_{L\&2} = 0.045$, $p_{S\&1} = 0.045$, $p_{S\&2} = 0.855$ and the entropy of this joint distribution is:

$$(0.055) \log_2 \left(\tfrac{1}{0.055}\right) + (0.045) \log_2 \left(\tfrac{1}{0.045}\right) + (0.045) \log_2 \left(\tfrac{1}{0.045}\right) + (0.855) \log_2 \left(\tfrac{1}{0.855}\right)$$

$$= (0.055)(4.18) + (0.045)(4.47) + (0.045)(4.47) + (0.855)(0.23) = 0.83.$$

When this entropy is subtracted from 0.94, the sum of the entropies of the source and signal distributions, we get 0.11 for the mutual information between source and signal. The signal does convey some of the available information, but by no means all of it. The joint distribution and the two marginal distributions are shown in Table 1.1. Notice that the probabilities in the marginal distributions are the sums of the probabilities down the rows or across the columns of the joint distribution.

The mutual information between source and signal sets the upper limit on the information that may be communicated to the receiver by that signal. There is no way that the receiver can extract more information about the source from the signal received than is contained in that signal. The information about the source contained in the signal is an objective property of the statistical relation between the source and the signal, namely, their joint distribution, the relative frequencies with which all possible combinations of source message and received signal occur. The information communicated to the receiver, by contrast, depends on the receiver's ability to extract the information made available in the signals it receives (for example, the receiver's knowledge of the code, which may be imperfect) and on the receiver's representation of the possibilities and their probabilities.

Table 1.1 Joint and marginal distributions in the case where lantern signal conveys some information about British route

British route/Lantern signal	One lantern	Two lanterns	Marginal (route)
By land	0.055	0.045	0.1
By sea	0.045	0.855	0.9
Marginal (Signal)	0.1	0.9	

Efficient Coding

As illustrated in Figure 1.2c, in a digital broadcast, the sound wave is transmitted digitally. Typically, it is transmitted as a sequence of bits ('0' or '1') that are themselves segregated into sequences of eight bits – called a byte. This means that each byte can carry a total of 256 or 2^8 possible messages (each added bit doubles the information capacity). The coding scheme, the method for translating the sound into bytes, is complex, which is why a digital encoder requires sophisticated computational hardware. The scheme incorporates knowledge of the statistics of the sound waves that are actually produced during human broadcasts into the creation of an efficient code. Shannon (1948) showed that an efficient communication code could only be constructed if one knew the statistics of the source, the relative likelihoods of different messages.

An elementary example of this is that in constructing his code, Morse made a single dot the symbol for the letter 'E,' because he knew that this was the most common letter in English text. Its frequency of use is hundreds of times higher than the frequency of use of the letter 'Z' (whose code is dash, dash, dot, dot). Shannon (1948) showed how to measure the efficiency of a communication code, thereby transforming Morse's intuition into quantitative science.

The routine use of digital transmission (and recordings with digital symbols) of broadcasts is another example that the space of discernibly different broadcasts ultimately contains a finite and routinely measured amount of uncertainty (entropy). To a first approximation, the prior uncertainty (the entropy) regarding the sound-form of a broadcast of a specified length is measured by the capacity (often expressed in megabytes, that is, a million bytes) of the CD required to record it. The number of possible broadcasts of that length is the number of different patterns that could be written into that amount of CD space. If all of those patterns were equally likely to occur, then that number of megabytes would be the prior entropy for broadcasts of that length. In fact, however, some of those patterns are vastly more likely than others, because of the harmonic structure of music and the statistical structure of the human voice and instruments, among other things. To the extent that the sound-encoding scheme built into a recorder fails to take account of these statistics, the actual entropy is less than the entropy implied by the amount of disk space required.

It is, however, often possible to specify at least approximately the amount of information that a given signal could be carrying to a receiver. This is a critical point because efficient codes often do not reflect at all the intrinsic properties of what it is they encode. We then say that the code is indirect. An appreciation of this last point is of some importance in grasping the magnitude of the challenge that neuroscientists may face in understanding how the brain works, so we give an illustrative example of the construction of increasingly efficient codes for sending English words.

One way to encode English words into binary strings is to start with the encoding that we already have by virtue of the English alphabet, which encodes words as strings of characters. We then can use a code such as ASCII (American Standard

Code for Information Interchange), which specifies a byte for each letter, that is a string of eight '0's or '1's – A = 01000001, B = 01000010, and so on. The average English word is roughly 6 characters long and we have to transmit 8 bits for each character, so our code would require an average of about 48 bits each time we transmitted a word. Can we do better than that? We will assume about 500,000 words in English and 2^{19} = 524,288. Thus, we could assign a unique 19-bit pattern to each English word. With that code, we need send only 19 bits per word, better by a factor of 2.5. A code that allows for fewer bits to be transferred is said to be compact or compressed and the encoding process contains a compression scheme. The more successfully we compress, the closer we get to transmitting on average the number of bits specified by the source entropy. Can we make an even better compression scheme? This last code assumes in effect that English words are equally likely, which they emphatically are not. You hear or read 'the' hundreds of times every day, whereas you may go a lifetime without hearing or reading 'eleemosynary' (trust us, it's an English word, a rare but kindly one).

Suppose we arrange English words in a table according to their frequency of use (Table 1.2 shows the first 64 most common words). Then we divide the table in half, so that the words that account for 50% of all usage are in the upper half and the remaining words in the lower half. It turns out that there are only about 180 words in the top half! Now, we divide each of these halves in half, to form usage quartiles. In the top quartile, there are only about 15 words! They account for 25% of all usage. In the second quartile, accounting for the next 25% of all usage, are about 165 words; and in the third quartile, about 2,500 words. The remaining 500,000 or so words account for only 25% of all usage.

We can exploit these extreme differences in probability of occurrence to make a more highly compressed and efficient binary code for transmitting English words. It is called a Shannon-Fano code after Shannon, who first placed it in print in his 1948 paper, and Fano, who originated the idea and popularized it in a later publication. We just keep dividing the words in half according to their frequency of usage. At each division, if a word ends up in the top half, we add a 0 to the string of bits that code for it. Thus, the 180 words that fall in the top half of the first division, all have 0 as their first digit, whereas the remaining 500,000 odd words all have 1. The 15 words in the first quartile (those that ended up in the top half of the first two divisions), also have 0 as their second digit. The 165 or so words in the second quartile all have 1 as their second digit. We keep subdividing the words in this way until every word has been assigned a unique string of '0's and '1's. Table 1.2 shows the Shannon-Fano codes for the first 64 most commonly used English words, as found in one source (The Natural Language Technology Group, University of Brighton) on the Internet.

As may be seen in Table 1.2, this scheme insures that the more frequent a word is, the fewer bits we use to transmit it. Using the Shannon-Fano code, we only need to transmit *at most* 19 bits for any one word – and that only very infrequently. For 40% of all the words we transmit, we use 9 bits or fewer. For 25%, we use only 5 or 6 bits. With this code, we can get the average number of bits per word transmitted down to about 11, which is almost five times more efficient than the code we first contemplated. This shows the power of using a code that takes account

Table 1.2 Constructing a Shannon-Fano code for English words. Shannon-Fano codes for the first 64 most common words in the English language.* Also shown is the cumulative percent of usage. These 64 words account for roughly 40% of all usage in English text. Note that some words are repeated as they are considered separate usage.

Rank	Word	%	cum %	1	2	3	4	5	6	7	8	9
1	the	6.25%	6.25%	0	0	0	0	0				
2	of	2.97%	9.23%	0	0	0	0	1				
3	and	2.71%	11.94%	0	0	0	1	0				
4	a	2.15%	14.09%	0	0	0	1	1				
5	in	1.83%	15.92%	0	0	1	0	0	0			
6	to	1.64%	17.56%	0	0	1	0	1	1			
7	it	1.10%	18.66%	0	0	1	1	0	0			
8	is	1.01%	19.67%	0	0	1	1	1	0			
9	was	0.93%	20.60%	0	0	1	1	1	1			
10	to	0.93%	21.53%	0	0	1	0	0	0			
11	I	0.89%	22.43%	0	0	1	0	1	0			
12	for	0.84%	23.27%	0	0	1	0	1	1			
13	you	0.70%	23.97%	0	0	1	1	0	0			
14	he	0.69%	24.66%	0	0	1	1	1	0			
15	be	0.67%	25.33%	0	0	1	1	1	1			
16	with	0.66%	25.99%	0	1	0	0	0	0	0		
17	on	0.65%	26.64%	0	1	0	0	0	0	1	0	
18	that	0.64%	27.28%	0	1	0	0	0	0	1	1	
19	by	0.51%	27.79%	0	1	0	0	0	1	0	0	
20	at	0.48%	28.28%	0	1	0	0	0	1	1	0	
21	are	0.48%	28.75%	0	1	0	0	0	1	1	1	
22	not	0.47%	29.22%	0	1	0	0	1	0	0	0	
23	this	0.47%	29.69%	0	1	0	0	1	0	1	0	
24	but	0.46%	30.15%	0	1	0	0	1	0	1	1	
25	's	0.45%	30.59%	0	1	0	0	1	1	0	0	
26	they	0.44%	31.03%	0	1	0	0	1	1	0	1	
27	his	0.43%	31.46%	0	1	0	0	1	1	1	0	
28	from	0.42%	31.88%	0	1	0	0	1	1	1	1	
29	had	0.41%	32.29%	0	1	0	1	0	0	0	0	
30	she	0.38%	32.68%	0	1	0	1	0	0	0	1	
31	which	0.38%	33.05%	0	1	0	1	0	0	1	0	
32	or	0.37%	33.43%	0	1	0	1	0	0	1	1	
33	we	0.36%	33.79%	0	1	0	1	0	1	0	0	
34	an	0.35%	34.14%	0	1	0	1	0	1	0	1	
35	n't	0.34%	34.47%	0	1	0	1	0	1	1	0	
36	's	0.33%	34.80%	0	1	0	1	0	1	1	1	
37	were	0.33%	35.13%	0	1	0	1	1	0	0	0	
38	that	0.29%	35.42%	0	1	0	1	1	0	0	1	0
39	been	0.27%	35.69%	0	1	0	1	1	0	0	1	1
40	have	0.27%	35.96%	0	1	0	1	1	0	1	0	0
41	their	0.26%	36.23%	0	1	0	1	1	0	1	0	1
42	has	0.26%	36.49%	0	1	0	1	1	0	1	1	0
43	would	0.26%	36.75%	0	1	0	1	1	0	1	1	1
44	what	0.25%	37.00%	0	1	0	1	1	1	0	0	0
45	will	0.25%	37.25%	0	1	0	1	1	1	0	1	0

Table 1.2   (*cont'd*)

Rank	Word	%	cum %	1	2	3	4	5	6	7	8	9
46	there	0.24%	37.49%	0	1	0	1	1	1	0	1	1
47	if	0.24%	37.73%	0	1	0	1	1	1	1	0	0
48	can	0.24%	37.96%	0	1	0	1	1	1	1	0	1
49	all	0.23%	38.20%	0	1	0	1	1	1	1	1	0
50	her	0.22%	38.42%	0	1	0	1	1	1	1	1	1
51	as	0.21%	38.63%	0	1	1	0	0	0	0	0	0
52	who	0.21%	38.83%	0	1	1	0	0	0	0	1	0
53	have	0.21%	39.04%	0	1	1	0	0	0	0	1	1
54	do	0.20%	39.24%	0	1	1	0	0	0	1	0	0
55	that	0.20%	39.44%	0	1	1	0	0	0	1	0	1
56	one	0.19%	39.63%	0	1	1	0	0	0	1	1	0
57	said	0.19%	39.82%	0	1	1	0	0	0	1	1	1
58	them	0.18%	39.99%	0	1	1	0	0	1	0	0	0
59	some	0.17%	40.17%	0	1	1	0	0	1	0	0	1
60	could	0.17%	40.34%	0	1	1	0	0	1	0	1	0
61	him	0.17%	40.50%	0	1	1	0	0	1	0	1	1
62	into	0.17%	40.67%	0	1	1	0	0	1	1	0	0
63	its	0.16%	40.83%	0	1	1	0	0	1	1	0	1
64	then	0.16%	41.00%	0	1	1	0	0	1	1	1	1

* This list is not definitive and is meant only for illustrative purposes.

of the source statistics. Another important property of a Shannon-Fano code is that it is what is called a *prefix code*. This means that no word is coded by a bit pattern that is the prefix for any other word's code. This makes the code self-delimiting so that when one receives multiple words as a string of bits, there is no need for any form of punctuation to separate the words, and there is no ambiguity. Notice that this leads to a clarification of the efficiency of the ASCII encoding. The ASCII encoding of English text is not a prefix code. For example, if one received the text "andatareallastask," there would be no way to know with certainty if the intended words were "and at are all as task," or "an data real last ask." Because of this, the ASCII encoding scheme would actually require each word to end with a space character (another code of 8 bits), and the total expected bits per word increases to 7 bytes or 56 bits per word.[4]

Compact codes are not necessarily a win-win situation. One problem with compact codes is that they are much more susceptible to corruption by noise than non-compact codes. We can see this intuitively by comparing the ASCII encoding scheme to the each-word-gets-a-number scheme. Let's say we are trying to transmit one

---

[4] The Shannon-Fano prefix code, while efficient, is suboptimal and can result in less than perfect compression. The Huffman (1952) encoding scheme uses a tree-like structure formed from the bottom up based on the probabilities themselves, not just the rankings. It produces a prefix code that can be shown to be optimal with respect to a frequency distribution that is used irrespective of the text sent, that is, it does not take advantage of the statistics of the particular message being sent.

English word. In the ASCII scheme, roughly 48 bits encode each word. This is a total number of 2^{48} possible patterns – a number in excess of 36 quadrillion – 36,000,000,000,000,000. With our each-word-gets-a-number scheme, we send 19 bits per word, resulting in 2^{19} possible patterns or 524,288. If, for argument's sake, we assume that our lexicon contains 524,288 possible words, then if one bit is changed (from a '0' to a '1' or from a '1' to a '0') because of noise on the signal channel, then the word decoded will with certainty be another word from the lexicon (one of possibly 19 words), with no chance of knowing (without contextual clues) that the error occurred. On the other hand, with the ASCII scheme, regardless of the noise, we will have less than a 1 in 50 billion chance of hitting another word in our lexicon. Since this "word" will almost certainly not be found in the lexicon, it will be known that an error has occurred and the communication system can request that the word be re-sent or likely even correct the error itself. Clearly in a communication system with very noisy channels, using the ASCII scheme would be more costly in terms of bits, but more likely to get the right message across.

We can help this problem, however, by adding redundancy into our schemes. For example, with the each-word-gets-a-number scheme, we could send 3 bits for each 1 bit we sent before, each 3 bits simply being copies of the same bit. So instead of transmitting the 19 bits, 1001010001100110011, we would transmit 57 bits:

111000000111000111000000000111111000000111111000000111111

In this case, we have decreased the efficiency back to the ASCII scheme, however, the redundancy has resulted in certain advantages. If any one bit is flipped due to noise, not only can we detect the error with certainty, we can also correct it with certainty. If two bits are flipped, then with certainty we can detect it. We would also have a 55/56 chance of correcting it.

Information and the Brain

Clearly, the tradeoffs between efficiency, accuracy, error detection, and error correction can lead to tremendous complexities when designing efficient codes in a world with noise. These issues are made even more complex when one takes into account the relative frequencies of the messages, as is done with the Shannon-Fano coding scheme. Computer scientists must routinely deal with these issues in designing real-world communication schemes. It is almost certainly the case that that the brain deals with the same issues. Therefore, an understanding of these issues is crucial to understanding the constraints that govern the effective transmission of information by means of nerve impulses within the brain.

As noted in connection with Figure 1.2, insofar as the considerations of efficiency and noise-imperviousness have shaped the system of information transmission within the brain, the brain's signaling code may be indirect. That is, the signals may not reflect intrinsic properties of the things (source messages) that they encode for. For example, first consider an ASCII encoding of a word, such as 'dog.' Note that we are talking about the word 'dog', not the animal. The word is first encoded into letters, that is "dog." This code reflects inherent properties of the word 'dog', as the letters (to some degree) reflect phonemes in the spoken word ("d" reflects the 'd' sound). If we encode each letter by an ASCII symbol, we retain this coding property, as each character has a one-to-one mapping to an ASCII symbol. This coding scheme is quite convenient as it also has some direct relationships with many other features of words such as their frequency of usage (smaller words tend to be more common), their part of speech, their country of origin, and even their meaning. As we saw, however, this direct encoding comes at a price – the code is not compact and is not ideal for transmission efficiency.

On the other hand, consider the Shannon-Fano encoding scheme applied to words. Here, the letters are irrelevant to the coding process. Instead, the code generates the signals based on the words' rank order in a usage table, not from anything related to its sound or meaning (although there are strong and interesting correlations between meaning and relative frequency – something that code breakers can use to their advantage). Most efficient (compact) codes make use of such relative frequencies and are therefore similarly indirect.

In addition, in modern signal transmission, it is often the case that encoded into the signals are elements of redundancy that aid with the problem of noise. One common technique is to include what are called *checksum* signals to the encoding signal. The checksum refers not to what the symbol encodes for, but instead, the symbol itself. This allows the communication system to detect if a message was corrupted by noise. It is called a checksum, as it typically treats the data as packets of numbers, and then adds these numbers up. For example, let's take the ASCII encoding scheme. The word 'dog' (lower case) would be encoded as 01100100, 01101111, 01100111. Now, we can treat these bytes as binary numbers, giving us the sequence (in decimal), 100, 111, 103. If we sum these numbers, we get 314. Because this is a bigger number than can be encoded by one byte (8 bits), we take the remainder when divided by 255, which is 59. In binary, that is 00111011. If we prepend this byte to the original sequence, we can (with over 99% certainty), determine if the signal was corrupted. Such schemes involve computations at both the source and destination, and they can make the code harder to break.

If coding schemes in the nervous system are similarly indirect, then the neuroscientist's job is hard. We have no assurance that they are not. At present, with a few small and recent exceptions (Rieke et al., 1997), neurophysiologists are in the position of spies trying to figure out how a very complex multinational corporation functions by listening to phone conversations conducted in a communication code they do not understand. That is because, generally speaking, neuroscientists do not know what it is about trains of action potentials that carries the information, nor exactly what information is being communicated. We've been listening to these signals for a century, but we have only translated minute parts of what we have overheard.

This brings us to a brief consideration of how Shannon's analysis applies to the brain (Figure 1.4). The essential point is that the brain is a receiver of signals that, under the proper conditions, convey to it information about the state of the world. The signals the brain receives are trains of action potentials propagating down sensory axons. Neurophysiologists call these action potentials spikes, because they

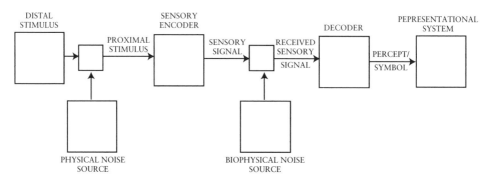

Figure 1.4   World-to-brain communication. The states of some delimited aspect of the world correspond to Shannon's messages. Perceptual psychologists call these states distal stimuli. Stimulus energy is either reflected off or emitted by the source. This energy together with contaminating energy from other sources (noise) impinges on sensory receptors in sensory organs (sensory encoders). Perceptual psychologists call the stimulus that actually impinges on the receptors the proximal stimulus. The encoders translate the proximal stimulus into sensory signals, streams of spikes in the sensory axons leading from sensory organs to the brain. Biophysical noise contaminates this neural signal, with the result that variations in the spike train are not due entirely to variations in the proximal stimulus. The sensory-processing parts of the brain are the decoder. Successive stages of sensory decoding translate incoming sensory signals into, first, a representation of aspects of the proximal stimulus, and then into a set of symbols that constitute what psychologists call a percept. This set of symbols represents the distal stimulus in the brain's subsequent information processing. The appropriate processing of these symbols, together with the communication chain that confers reference on them, makes the brain a representational system.

look like spikes when viewed on an oscilloscope at relatively low temporal resolution. Spikes are analogous to electrical pulses that carry information within electronic systems. Sensory organs (eyes, ears, noses, tongues, and so on) and the sensory receptors embedded in them convert information-rich stimulus energy to spike trains. The stimuli that act directly on sensory receptors are called proximal stimuli. Examples are the photons absorbed by the rods and cones in the retina, the traveling waves in the basilar membrane of the cochlea, which bend the underlying hair cells, the molecules absorbed by the nasal mucosa, and so on. Proximal stimuli carry information about distal stimuli, sources out there in the world. The brain extracts this information from spike trains by processing them. This is to say that much of the signal contains data from which useful information must be determined.

The problem that the brain must solve is that the information it needs about the distal stimulus in order to act appropriately in the world – the source information – is not reflected in any simple way in the proximal stimulus that produces the spike train. Even simple properties of the proximal stimulus itself (how, for example, the pattern of light is moving across the retina) are not reflected in a straightforward way in the spike trains in the optic nerve, the bundle of sensory axons that carries information from the retina to the first way-stations in the brain. The physical processes in the world that convert source information (for example, the reflectance of a surface) to proximal stimuli (the amount of light from that surface impinging on the retina) encode the source information in very complex ways. Many different, quite unrelated aspects of the world – for example, the reflectance of the surface and the intensity of its illumination – combine to determine proximal stimuli. To extract from the spike train useful facts about a specific source (for example, what the reflectance of a particular surface actually is), the brain must invert this complex encoding and separate the messages that are conflated in the signals it receives. This inversion and message separation is effected by a sequence of computational operations, very few of which are currently understood.

The modern approach to a neurobiological understanding of sensory transduction and the streams of impulses thereby generated relies heavily on Shannon's insights and their mathematical elaboration (Rieke et al., 1997). In a few cases, it has been possible to get evidence regarding the code used by sensory neurons to transmit information to the brains of flies and frogs. The use of methods developed from Shannon's foundations has made it possible to estimate how many bits are conveyed per spike and how many bits are conveyed by a single axon in one second. The answers have been truly revolutionary. A single spike can convey as much as 7 bits of information and 300 bits per second can be transmitted on a single axon (Rieke, Bodnar, & Bialek, 1995).

Given our estimates above of how many bits on average are needed to convey English words when an efficient code is used (about 10 per word), a single axon could transmit 30 words per second to, for example, a speech center.[5] It could do so, of course, only if the usage-frequency table necessary to decode the Shannon-Fano code were stored in the speech center, as well as in the source center. Remember that both Paul's confederate (the encoder) and Paul (the decoder) had to know the lantern code for their system to work. These encoding tables constitute knowledge of the statistical structure of English speech. Central to Shannon's analysis of communication is the realization that the structure of the encoding and decoding mechanisms must reflect the statistical structure of the source. To make a system with which the world can communicate efficiently, you must build into it implicit information about the statistical structure of that world. Fortunately, we know that English speakers do know the usage frequency of English words (even though they don't know they know it). The effects of word frequency in many tasks are among the more ubiquitous and robust effects in cognitive psychology (Hasher & Zacks, 1984; Hulme et al., 1997; Jescheniak & Levelt, 1994). The information-theoretic analysis provides an unusual explanation of why they ought to know these relative frequencies.[6]

Until the advent of these information-theoretic analyses, few neuroscientists had any notion of how to go about estimating how many axons it might in principle take to relay words to a speech center at natural speaking rates (2–8 words/second).

---

[5] Whether transmission rates of 300 bits per second are realistic for axons within the brain (as opposed to sensory axons) is controversial (Latham & Nirenberg, 2005).

[6] This knowledge is, of course, not built in; it is constructed in the course of learning the language.

No one would have guessed that it could be done with room to spare by a single axon. Understanding how the brain works requires an understanding of the rudiments of information theory, because what the brain deals with is information.

Digital and Analog Signals

Early communication and recording technology was often analog. Analog sources (for example, sources putting out variations in sound pressure) were encoded into analog signals (continuously fluctuating currents) and processed by analog receivers. For decades, neuroscientists have debated the question whether neural communication is analog or digital or both, and whether it matters. As most technophiles know, the modern trend in information technology is very strongly in the digital direction; state-of-the-art transmitters encode analog signals into digital signals prior to transmission, and state-of-the art receivers decode those digital signals. The major reason for this is that the effects of extraneous noise on digital communication and recording are much more easily controlled and minimized. A second and related reason is that modern communication and recording involves computation at both the transmitting (encoding) and receiving (decoding) stages. Much of this computation derives from Shannon's insights about what it takes to make a code efficient and noise resistant. Modern information-processing hardware is entirely digital – unlike the first computers, which used analog components. To use that hardware to do the encoding and decoding requires recoding analog signals into digital form. One of the reasons that computers have gone digital is for the same reason that modern information transmission has – noise control and control over the precision with which quantities are represented.

Our hunch is that information transmission and processing in the brain is likewise ultimately digital. A guiding conviction of ours – by no means generally shared in the neuroscience community – is that brains do close to the best possible job with the problems they routinely solve, given the physical constraints on their operation. Doing the best possible job suggests doing it digitally, because that is the best solution to the ubiquitous problems of noise, efficiency of transmission, and precision control.

We make this digression here because the modern theory of computation, which we will be explaining, is cast entirely in digital terms. It assumes that information is carried by a set of discrete symbols. This theory has been extensively developed, and it plays a critical role in computer science and engineering. Among other things, this theory defines what it means to say that something is computable. It also establishes limits on what is computable. There is no comparable theory for analog computation (and no such theory seems forthcoming). The theory we will be explaining is currently the only game in town. That does not, of course, mean that it will not some day be supplanted by a better game, a better theory of computation. We think it is fair to say, however, that few believe that analog computation will ultimately prove superior. There is little reason to think that there are things that can only be computed by an analog computer. On the contrary, the general, if largely unspoken, assumption is that digital computation can accomplish anything that analog computation can, while the converse may not be the case. As a practical matter, it can usually accomplish it better. That is why there is no technological push to create better analog computers.

Appendix: The Information Content of Rare Versus Common Events and Signals

Above, we have tacitly assumed that the British move out night after night and Paul's confederate spies on them (or fails to do so) and hangs lanterns (transmits a signal) every night. In doing so, we have rectified an implicit fault in the Paul Revere example that we have used to explicate Shannon's definition of information. The fault is that it was a one-time event. As such, Shannon's analysis would not apply. Shannon information is a property of probability (that is, relative frequency) *distribution*, not of single (unique) events or single (unique) signals. With a unique event, there is only one event in the set of messages. Thus, there is no distribution. Hence, there is no entropy (or, if you like, the entropy is 0, because the relative frequency of that event is 1, and the log of 1 is 0). The consequences of the uniqueness were most likely to have surfaced when he or she came to the case in which there was said to be a 0.1 "probability" of their coming by land and a 0.9 "probability" of their coming by sea. If by probability we understand relative frequency, then these are not intelligible numbers, because with a unique event, there is no relative frequency; it either happens or it doesn't.[7] If we ignore this, then we confront the following paradox: the information communicated by the lantern signal is the same whether Paul sees the low probability signal or the high probability signal, because the prior probability distribution is the same in both cases, hence the pre-signal entropies are the same, and the post-signal entropies are both 0. If, however, the event belongs to a set of events (a set of messages) with empirically specifiable relative frequencies, then when we compute the entropy per event or per signal we find that, for rare events, the entropy per event is higher than for common events, in accord with our intuitions. We get this result because the entropy is defined over the full set of events, that is, the entropy is a property of the relative frequency *distribution* (and only of that distribution, not of its constituents, nor of their individual relative frequencies). The source entropy in the case of the British movements (assuming they recur night after night) is a single fixed quantity, regardless of whether we consider the rare occurrences (coming by land) or the common ones (coming by sea). However, the common occurrences are nine times

[7] This is among the reasons why radical Bayesians reject the interpretation of probabilities as relative frequencies. For a radical Bayesian, a probability is a strength of belief. Although we are sympathetic to this position, considering how information theory would look under this construal of probability would take us into deeper philosophical waters than we care to swim in here. As a practical matter, it is only applied in situations where relative frequencies are in fact defined. Note that whether or not an event has a relative frequency depends on the set of messages to which it belongs and that in turn depends on how we choose to describe it. Any event has a relative frequency under at least some description. This issue of descriptions relates to the question of "aboutness," which we take up in a later chapter.

more frequent than the rare ones. Therefore, the amount of entropy per common event is nine times less than the amount of entropy per rare event, because the amount of entropy per type of event times the relative frequency of that type of event has to equal the total entropy of the distribution. As the rare events get rarer and rarer, the total entropy gets smaller and smaller, but the entropy per rare event gets larger and larger. This is true whether we are considering source entropy or signal entropy. The entropy per event, which is sometimes called the information content of an event, is $\log(1/p)$, which goes to infinity (albeit slowly) as p goes to 0. Thus, the entropy of a distribution is the average information content of the events (messages) over which the distribution is defined.

2

Bayesian Updating

Shannon's analysis of communication and the definition of information that emerges from it are rooted in a probabilistic conceptual framework. In this framework, there are no certainties; everything is true only with some probability. As we gain information about the world, our estimate of the probabilities changes. The information we gain is defined by the relation between the probabilities before we got the signal and the probabilities after we got it. Moreover, as the discussion of world–brain communication emphasized, the information-carrying signals themselves are only probabilistically related to the source states of the world, the states that the brain must determine with as much accuracy as it can if it is to act effectively in that world (Knill & Pouget, 2004). One may be led to ask whether there is an analytic relation between these various uncertainties, a relation that plays, or at least ought to play, a central role in mediating the updating of our probabilistic representation of the world. There is indeed: it's called Bayes' rule or Bayes' theorem, depending somewhat on the user's metamathematical perspective on what we should regard as the origin or logical foundation of the principle.

Bayes' rule specifies what ought be the relation between the probability that we assign to a state of the world after we get a signal (called the *posterior probability*), the probability that we assign to that state of the world before we get the signal (called the *prior probability*), the probability of getting that signal given that state of the world (called the *likelihood*), and the overall probability of getting that signal, regardless of the state of the world (the *unconditional probability* of the signal, which is sometimes called the *marginal likelihood* because it is the sum over the likelihoods under all possible states of the world). Bayes' rule brings together all the relevant uncertainties, specifying the analytic relation between them.

The rule follows directly from the frequentist definitions of probability and conditional probability, which is why it is often called simply a rule rather than a theorem, the honorific, "theorem," being reserved for relations that follow less directly and obviously from definitions and axioms. Let N_x be the number of times we have observed x (say, that a pool ball is black). And let N_o be the number of observations we have made (all the balls we have examined). The empirical probability of x is: $p(x) = N_x / N_o$. More technically, in the frequentist tradition, this observed ratio is an estimate of the true probability, which is the limit approached by N_x/N_o as the number of observations becomes indefinitely large. The same comment applies to all the "empirical" probabilities to be mentioned. Let $N_{x\&y}$ be the number of times we have observed both x and y (for example, a ball that is both black and has an '8' on it). The empirical *conditional* probability of our having observed a black ball, given that we have observed a ball with an '8' on it, is: $p(x \mid y) = N_{x\&y}/N_y$. This empirical conditional probability is the frequency with which we have observed x (that the ball was black), considering only those occasions on which we also observed y (that the ball had '8' on it). The '|' in the notation '$p(x \mid y)$' indicates that what follows is the limiting condition, the other observation(s) that restrict(s) the instances that we consider in defining a conditional probability. When there are two things we might observe (x and y), then there are two unconditional probabilities, $p(x)$ and $p(y)$, and two conditional probabilities, $p(x \mid y)$ and $p(y \mid x)$ – the probability of observing black given '8' and the probability of observing '8' given black. Bayes' rule is that:

$$p(x \mid y) = \frac{p(y \mid x)p(x)}{p(y)}. \tag{1}$$

It specifies the relation between the two probabilities and the two conditional probabilities. Thus, it tells us how to compute any one of them from the other three. We can see that the rule is analytically true simply by replacing the probabilities with their definitions:

$$\frac{N_{x\&y}}{N_y} = \frac{\dfrac{N_{x\&y}}{N_x} \dfrac{N_x}{N_o}}{\dfrac{N_y}{N_o}}. \tag{2}$$

On the right of the equals sign in equation (2) are the definitions of $p(y \mid x)$, $p(x)$ and $p(y)$ in terms of the numbers of observations of various kinds that we have made, substituted for the probabilities on the right of equation (1). As indicated, the N_x's and N_o's on the right of equation (2) cancel out, leaving the expression on the left of equation (2), which is the definition of $p(x \mid y)$, the conditional probability on the left of equation (1). Thus, from one perspective, Bayes' rule is a trivially provable analytic truth about the relation between the two probabilities and the two conditional probabilities that arise when we observe joint occurrences, such as the joint occurrence of British routes and lantern signals in the previous chapter.

   The Reverend Thomas Bayes, however, interpreted it as a law of logical or rational inference in the face of uncertainty. Under this interpretation, it is more controversial, because it requires us to specify *a priori* probabilities. That is often hard to do, or at least to justify rigorously, even though in some sense we do clearly do it when we reason about uncertain propositions. Moreover, this interpretation is connected to a debate within the theory of probability about the conceptual foundations of probability theory, a debate about what a probability in some metaphysical sense, is, or, more practically, how it ought to be defined. According to the frequentist school a probability *is* (or ought to be defined as) the limit approached by the ratio between the total number of observations, N_o, and the number of a subset of those observations, N_x, as the number of observations becomes indefinitely large. This definition assumes that the observations can be repeated indefinitely many times under some standard, unchanging conditions – an assumption that, if you think about it, is open to doubt on empirical grounds. On this view, probabilities have nothing inherently to do with our beliefs. According to strong Bayesians, however, a probability *is* (or ought to be defined as) a quantity representing strength of belief, which is constrained to behave so as not to violate a few common-sense constraints on rational belief and inference. In the words of Laplace (1819), an early proponent of this view, "Probability theory is nothing but common sense reduced to calculation" – a dictum that generations of students of statistics would probably not readily assent to.

The Bayesian approach to probability begins by noting that our empirically rooted beliefs are rarely if ever categorical; rather, they vary in strength. We doubt that some things are true; we think other things are rather likely to be true; we feel strongly that some things are almost certainly true (the less cautious would omit the "almost") and that still other things are very unlikely to be true. These beliefs are about distal stimuli, which, as we have already learned, is psychological jargon for states of the world that affect our sensory systems only indirectly. Distal stimuli affect our senses by way of proximal stimuli that bear a complex, noisy, and ambiguous relation to the states of the world about which we entertain beliefs. Given the modern understanding of sensory processes, anything other than a graded "probabilistic" treatment of our empirically rooted beliefs about distal stimuli (states of the world) would be foolish. It would ignore the manifest difficulties in the way of our obtaining true knowledge from sensory experience. These difficulties become ever more apparent as our understanding of sensory mechanisms and the stimuli that act on them deepens.

Classical symbolic logic, which specifies normative laws for reasoning – how we ought to reason – only considers categorical reasoning: *All men are mortal. Socrates is a man. Therefore, Socrates is mortal.* We need to extend it by making it quantitative so that it is capable of reflecting the graded nature of actual belief: *All crows are black. (At least all the crows I've ever seen.) The bird that ate the corn was almost certainly a crow. Therefore, the bird that ate the corn was probably black.* The Bayesian argues that we must recognize that beliefs are in fact – and, moreover, ought to be – accompanied by a graded internal (mental or brain) quantity that specifies our uncertainty regarding their truth. From a mathematical perspective, graded quantities are represented by real numbers. (Only quantities that get bigger in discrete steps can be represented by integers.) For a Bayesian, a probability *is* a continuously graded subjective quantity that specifies a subjective uncertainty about states of the world, in a receiver whose knowledge of the world comes from noisy and ambiguous signals. That is, of course, just what Shannon supposed in his analysis of communication. From this perspective (a radical Bayesian perspective), the theory of probability is the theory of how to handle the real numbers with which we represent subjective (receiver) uncertainties in a logically consistent and mathematically sound way (Cox, 1961; Jaynes, 2003; Jeffreys, 1931).

On the face of it, the Bayesian approach to probability, unlike the frequentist approach, does not sufficiently constrain the numbers that represent probabilities. If probabilities are relative frequencies, then it is obvious why they must be represented by real numbers between 0 and 1, because $\lim_{N_o \to \infty} N_x/N_o$ cannot be less than 0 nor more than 1, given that the x observations are a subset of the o observations. However, it turns out that the constraints imposed by common sense are more powerful than one might suppose. The common sense constraints are logical consistency, fairness, and coherence:

1 *Logical consistency:* If there is more than one reasoning path to the same conclusion, the conclusion should not vary with the path taken. It should not be possible to conclude "A" by one line of reasoning and "not A" by another line.
2 *Fairness:* All the available evidence must be taken into account.
3 *Coherence:* Equivalent uncertainties must be represented by the same number.

Unlikely as it may seem, these constraints suffice to deduce Bayes' formula for the updating of the strengths of belief, and they strongly motivate mapping strength of belief into the real numbers in such a way that: (1) possible numerical strengths range between 0 and 1, and (2) relative frequencies map to the same numbers they would map to under the frequentist definition of probability (Jaynes, 2003). When thus derived, Bayes' rule gets promoted to Bayes' theorem.

Bayes' Theorem and Our Intuitions about Evidence

As a formula for the updating of belief, Bayes' theorem nicely captures our intuitions about what does and does not constitute strong evidence. These intuitions turn on: (1) *the prior probability*: how probable we think something is *a priori*, on the basis of logic or extensive prior experience; and (2) *relative likelihood*: how likely the evidence is if that something is true versus how likely it is otherwise (see Figure 2.1).

Note first that when the prior probability of the hypothesis is 0, then the posterior must also be 0. If we think something (the hypothesized state of the world) is impossible, then it is not true no matter what the evidence (no matter how good or strong the signal, s).

Note secondly, and more interestingly, that if the experience (signal, s) offered as evidence is common (an everyday experience), it cannot be strong evidence for any hypothesis. To see this, consider the limiting case where $p(s) = 1$, that is, we consider it an absolute certainty that we will observe s no matter what. In that case, it must also be true that $p(s \mid h) = 1$, because $p(s) = 1$ means that no matter what else we may observe, we always observe s. But if both $p(s)$ and $p(s \mid h)$ are 1, then (as we see from scrutinizing Bayes' formula in Figure 2.1), the posterior probability must simply be the prior probability.[1] The evidence did not change our

[1] To see this, replace both the likelihood, $p(s \mid h)$, and $p(s)$ with 1 in the formula in Figure 2.1.

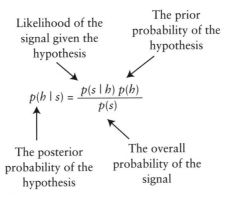

Figure 2.1 Bayes' rule, with names for the four probabilities involved.

belief at all. Strong evidence is evidence capable of producing a large change in our belief and weak evidence is evidence that can produce little or no change. As $p(s)$ approaches 1 (as the signal becomes very common), then $p(s \mid h)/p(s)$ cannot be much greater than 1, but $p(s \mid h)/p(s)$ is the factor relating the posterior probability to the prior probability, which means that the more common s becomes, the weaker it becomes as evidence. Thus, commonplace events are not evidence for interesting hypotheses about the state of the world. Only rare and unexpected events are. This is, of course, fully consistent with the fact that in Shannon's formula, the rarer an event is, the greater its information content, $\log (1/p)$.

Among other things, this suggests an explanation of why habituation to frequent and or unchanging stimuli is a ubiquitous phenomenon in sensory systems and in animal behavior. Common and/or persistent stimuli are not informative stimuli, and the information-processing machinery of nervous systems is constructed so as to discard uninformative signals. Only informative signals get converted into symbols in memory, because the function of memory is to carry information forward in time and only informative signals communicate information. Notice, once again, that the information *communicated* by a signal depends on what we already know (whereas the information *carried* by a signal does not).

If so-called evidence in fact has nothing to do with the hypothesis in question – if $p(s \mid h) = p(s)$, that is, if the truth or falsity of the hypothesis has no effect on the probability of observing s – then again $p(s \mid h)/p(s) = 1$, and the posterior probability is simply equal to the prior probability. More generally, if the truth or falsity of the hypothesis has little impact on the probability of s, then s cannot be strong evidence for that hypothesis. This captures our intuition that in order for something to be evidence for something else, there must be a connection of some kind between them. The evidence must be relevant.

If $p(h)$, the prior probability of the hypothesis, is high, then $p(h \mid s)$, the posterior probability, cannot be much higher. Thus, an experience that confirms a hypothesis already considered highly probable is not very informative. This directly reflects the subjectivity in Shannon's definition of the information communicated.

If $p(s \mid h) = 0$, then $p(h \mid s) = 0$. If the hypothesis says that s cannot occur, but it does in fact occur, then the hypothesis cannot be true. This is a powerful principle. It is the key to understanding the impact of many decisive scientific experiments.

If $p(s \mid h) = 1$, if the hypothesis says that s must occur, then the lower $p(s)$ is (the less likely that signal is otherwise), the stronger the evidence that the observation of s provides for h. In scientific reasoning, this corresponds to the principle that the confirmation of a counterintuitive prediction (the prediction of an observation that is judged to be otherwise improbable) is strong evidence in favor of a theory, provided, of course, that the theory does in fact make that prediction under all reasonable assumptions about other conditions of the experiment (that is, provided $p(s \mid h) \approx 1$).

In short, Bayes' rule encapsulates a range of principles governing how we think we reason. Whether in fact we regularly reason in *quantitative* accord with Bayes' rule is another matter. There are many cases in which we demonstrably do not (Kahneman, Slovic, & Tversky, 1982; Piattelli-Palmarini, 1994). However, that does not mean that we never do (Hudson, Maloney & Landy, 2006; Trommershäuser, Maloney & Landy, 2003). It is wrong to assume that there is a single, central reasoning mechanism that comes into play wherever what we might call reasoning occurs. We have no conscious access to the reasoning underlying our perception of the world, and information we get by way of recently evolved channels of communication, like language and print, may not have access to those mechanisms (Rozin, 1976). Introspection and verbal judgments are poor guides to much of what goes on in our brain. The non-verbal part may have a better appreciation of Bayes' theorem than does the verbal part (Balci & Gallistel, under review).

Using Bayes' Rule

Shannon's definition of the information communicated by a signal in terms of the change in the receiver's entropy (the change in subjective uncertainty about some state of the world) leads us to Bayes' rule. To see the rule in action, we expand our Paul Revere example. We whimsically and anachronistically suppose that there were four possible routes by which the British might have come – land, sea, air, and submarine – and that these were communicated by two successive signals, each consisting of 1 or 2 lights, according to the following code: <1, 1> = land; <1, 2> = sea; <2, 1> = air; <2, 2> = submarine. We do this, so that, by considering what is communicated by only one of the two successive signals (a partial signal), we have a situation in which more than one state of the world generates the same signal. This is essential in order to illustrate the critical role of the likelihood function, the function that specifies how likely a signal is for each different state of the world.

In this example, there are four different partial signals that Paul could get: <1, _>, <2, _>, <_, 1> and <_, 2>, where the blank indicates the missing half of the bipartite signal. Each partial signal leaves Paul less uncertain than he was, but still uncertain. That is exactly the state of affairs that the brain generally finds itself in after getting a sensory signal.

Figure 2.2 shows at top left the prior probability distribution, which is the same in every case, because it represents what Paul knows before he gets any signal. Below that are four rows, one for each possible partial signal. On the right are the likelihood functions for these different partial signals. On the left are the resulting posterior distributions, the state of belief after getting the partial signal. In each case, the difference in entropy between the posterior distribution and the prior distribution gives the information conveyed by the partial signal.

For each of the rows in Figure 2.2, Bayes' rule holds. Consider, for example, the first row, where the observed partial signal is <1, _>. The prior probabilities for the four possible states of the world are <0.25, 0.25, 0.25, 0.25>. The probability of the partial signal is 0.5, because in half of all signals the first signal will be a single light. The likelihoods of the different possible states of the world giving rise to that partial signal are <1, 1, 0, 0>. By Bayes' rule, the posterior probabilities for the four possible states of the world, after that signal has been seen, are:

$$\left\langle \frac{(0.25)(1)}{0.5}, \frac{(0.25)(1)}{0.5}, \frac{(0.25)(0)}{0.5}, \frac{(0.25)(0)}{0.5} \right\rangle = \langle 0.5, 0.5, 0, 0 \rangle$$

Note that the probabilities in the prior and posterior distributions in Figure 2.2 sum to 1, as they must in any probability distribution. A probability distribution ranges over mutually exclusive and exhaustive possibilities, specifying for each possibility its probability. Because the possibilities are mutually exclusive and exhaustive, one and only one of them obtains in every case. Thus, the sum of their probabilities must be 1.

Note, by contrast, that the likelihoods within a likelihood function do not sum to 1. A likelihood function, unlike a probability distribution, does not give the probabilities of a set of mutually exclusive and exhaustive possibilities. Rather, it gives the probabilities that different states of the world might produce the same signal (the same evidence). As in the present case, two different states of the world may both produce the same signal with likelihood 1, in which case the likelihoods sum to 2. It is also possible that no heretofore conceived of state of the world produces the signal in question. In that case, the likelihoods within the likelihood function for this "impossible" signal would sum to 0. (Then, if the "impossible" signal in question is in fact observed, we have to enlarge our conception of the possible states of the world to include a state that generates that signal with non-zero likelihood.) In short, the likelihoods in a likelihood function may sum to any finite positive value, because the probability with which one state of the world gives rise to a signal does not constrain the probability with which other states of the world give rise to the same signal.

Notice that the posterior probability distributions in Figure 2.2 are rescalings of the likelihood functions. They have the same shape (relative heights); only the numbers on the ordinate differ. The numbers on the ordinate are determined by the scale factor for the y-axis. In these examples, the posterior probability distributions and the likelihood functions look the same because (1) the prior probabilities are all the same, so the products of the prior probabilities and the likelihoods have the same profile (relative heights) as the likelihoods; and (2) more generally, the

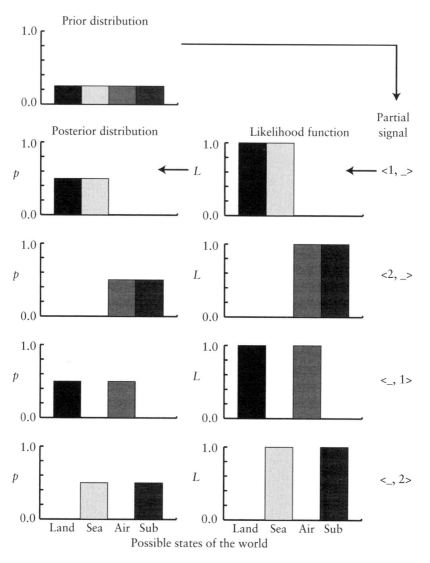

Figure 2.2 Bayesian updating. The distribution at the top left is the prior probability distribution, the probabilities assigned to the different possibilities before the partial signal is received. The functions on the right are the likelihood functions for each possible partial signal. They specify for each possible state of the world how likely that partial signal is. The distributions on the left are the posterior probability distributions. They specify how probable each state of the world is *after* a partial signal has been received and the information it carries integrated with the prior information. p = probability; L = likelihood.

posterior probability distribution is always related to the *posterior* likelihood function by a scale factor, which must be such as to make the probabilities in the posterior distribution sum to 1. This may be seen by examining Bayes' rule, where it will be noticed that the scale factor is $1/p(s)$. (That is to say, the rule can be rewritten $p(h \mid s) = (1/p(s))p(s \mid h)p(h)$.) In the example we have been considering $p(s) = 0.5$, so the scale factor $1/p(s) = 2$. The products of the two non-zero likelihoods and the corresponding probabilities are 0.25. These are the *posterior* likelihoods, as opposed to the simple likelihoods, which are shown on the right column of Figure 2.2. When these *posterior* likelihoods are scaled up by a factor of 2 to compose the posterior probability distribution, they sum to 1.

The product of the prior distribution and the likelihood function gives the *posterior* likelihood function, which specifies the relative likelihoods of the different states of the world after integrating (combining) the prior information and the information conveyed by the signal. The posterior likelihood function may always be converted to the posterior probability distribution by scaling it to make the probabilities sum to 1. Moreover, the odds favoring one state of the world relative to others may be derived directly from the posterior likelihood function, without first converting the likelihoods to probabilities. For that reason, the scale factor, $1/p(s)$, in Bayes' rule is often ignored, and the rule is rewritten as a proportion rather than an equation:[2]

$$p(h \mid s) \propto p(s \mid h)p(h), \qquad (3)$$

giving it a particularly simple and memorable form. Notice that now the terms $(p(h \mid s),\ p(s \mid h),\ p(h))$ no longer refer to individual probabilities and likelihoods. Now they refer to functions, that is, to mappings from the possible states of the world to the probabilities or likelihoods associated with those states. In shifting from individual probabilities and likelihoods to functions, we bring in the constraint that the probabilities within the probability functions must sum to 1. It is that constraint that allows us to ignore the scale factor $(1/p(s))$ in most Bayesian calculations. The formula in (3) is about as simple as it is possible to get. It says that one function, the posterior probability distribution, is proportional to the point-by-point (state-by-state) product of two other functions, the prior probability distribution, which gives the prior probabilities of different states of the world, and the likelihood function, which gives, for each of those states of the world, the likelihood (probability) that it will produce the observed signal.

Notice, finally, that the entropy of the prior distribution is 2 bits, $\sum_1^4 0.25 \log_2 (1/0.25) = (4)(0.25 \log_2 (4)) = (4)(0.25)(2)$, while the entropy of each posterior distribution is 1 bit, so the partial signal transmits 1 bit of information in each case.

Informative priors

In our first example, the prior probabilities are said to be uninformative because they were all equal. That is the state of maximum prior uncertainty (maximum prior entropy). Very often, we do not start in a state of complete uncertainty, because

---

[2] $\propto$ means 'is proportional to'.

we have evidence of a different kind from other sources (prior information). Consider, for example, reasoning from the results of diagnostic tests for medical conditions whose base rate is known from general surveys performed by the government health authorities. In such cases, absent any diagnostic test, and assuming we have appropriately identified the relevant population from which the person being diagnosed should be regarded as coming, the prior probability that they have the condition tested for is simply the base rate for that population. There are about 300,000,000 people in the US, of whom, by widely agreed on estimates, somewhat less than 1,000,000 are living with an HIV infection. Thus, for a person drawn at random from the population of the US, there are two possible states (HIV infected or not) with associated prior probabilities of about 0.003 and 0.997. We know this before we consider whether any particular person has been tested for AIDS.

Suppose next that there is a diagnostic test for HIV infection that has been shown to give a positive result in 99.5% of all cases in which the person tested is HIV positive and a negative result for 99% of all cases in which the person tested is HIV negative. By the standards governing medical diagnostic tests in general, such a test would be considered extremely reliable, an "almost certain" indicator (signal) of AIDS. Suppose we applied the test to the entire population of the US. How strongly should we believe that someone who tests positive has AIDS? The prior probability that they do is 0.003; the prior probability that they don't is 0.997. These two probabilities constitute the prior probability distribution (and, of course, they sum to 1). The likelihood of a positive test result if they do is 0.995; the likelihood of a positive test result if they don't is 0.01. Thus the likelihood function for a positive test result is <0.995, 0.01>, and, as usual, the likelihoods do not sum to 1.

The proportion form of Bayes' rule,

$$p(h \mid s) \propto p(s \mid h)p(h) = \frac{\langle 0.995,\ 0.01 \rangle}{\times \langle 0.003,\ 0.997 \rangle} = \langle 0.002985,\ 0.00997 \rangle,$$

gives us the relative post-test likelihoods that the person has AIDS (the likelihoods, 0.995 and 0.01, multiplied by the respective prior probabilities, 0.003 and 0.997). Despite the impressive reliability of the test, the odds are less than one in three (0.002985/0.00997 = 1/3.34) that a person who tests positive has AIDS. In this case, we have highly informative prior information, which has a huge impact on what we consider (or should consider) the most probable state of the world given a highly informative signal (an "almost certain" test).

Notice that the numbers that we got using the proportional form of Bayes' rule, 0.002985 and 0.00997, are likelihoods, not probabilities; they do not come anywhere near summing to 1. Without converting them to probabilities, we determined the *relative* likelihood (odds) of the two possible states, which is all we usually want to know. From the odds, we can, if we want, determine the probabilities: if the relative likelihoods (odds) for two mutually exclusive and exhaustive states of the world are 1:3, then their probabilities must be <0.25, 0.75>, because those are the unique probabilities that both sum to 1 and stand in the ratio 1:3 one to the other. This illustrates why the simpler proportional form of Bayes' rule is so often used – and it illustrates how to get the probabilities from the odds or from the relative likelihood function by imposing the constraint that the numbers sum to 1.

Parameter estimation

The two examples of Bayesian updating so far considered involved discrete states of the world and therefore discrete probabilities and likelihoods, which are represented by numbers that can be at most 1. In very many cases, however, we want to use a noisy signal to update our estimate of a continuous (real-valued) *parameter* of our situation in the world or, in less egocentric cases, just parameters of the environment. An example of such a parameter would be the width of the gap between two buildings, across which we contemplate jumping. Other relevant parameters of this same situation are the mean and variability of our jump distances (how far we can jump and how much that distance varies from one attempt to another). These three parameters determine the probability that our jump would fall short. This probability is highly relevant to what we decide to do.[3]

Another such parameter would be how long it has been since we arrived at a red traffic signal. A second relevant parameter of this situation is how long a *functioning* traffic light stays red and how much variability there is in that interval. These parameters play an important role in our deciding whether to chance advancing through the red light on the hypothesis that it is not functioning. (If you don't chance it sooner or later, the driver behind you will blow his or her stack.)

Another such parameter would be how far back we have come since we turned to head back home. A second relevant parameter in this situation would be how far we were from home when we started back. Estimates of these parameters are relevant to our deciding whether or not we have missed the turn into our street.

Still another example of world parameters that we might want to estimate is the amount of food per unit of time that appears in various locations where we might forage for food.

Later, we will consider learning mechanisms whose function it is to estimate these and other critical parameters of our environment and our situation in it. In every case, information relevant to estimating one or more of these parameters arrives in dribs and drabs over time. We suppose that each arrival of a bit of relevant information leads to a Bayesian update of our current estimate of that parameter. This is how our brain keeps up with the world (Knill & Pouget, 2004). That is why we need to understand how Bayes' rule applies to the case where the possible states of the world vary continuously rather than discretely.

Suppose we want to estimate the proportion of black balls in a huge urn containing small balls of many colors. This may sound like a discrete problem, because no matter how big the urn is, it contains a finite number of balls; therefore, the proportion is a rational number, a ratio between two integers. However, the case

---

[3] This is an example of why Bayesians think that the idea that probabilities and probabilistic reasoning come into play only in situations where we can reasonably imagine repeating the experiment a large number of times (the frequentist's definition of a probability) is a joke.

we are considering is a toy version of estimating the concentration of, say, CO_2 in the atmosphere, in which case we want to know the number of CO_2 molecules relative to the total number of molecules in the atmosphere. The point is that for practical purposes, we assume that the parameter, P (for proportion of black balls), that we seek to estimate is a real number (a continuous variable).

Suppose that a friend with a reputation for reliability has told us that, while they don't know at all precisely what the proportion of black balls is, it is unlikely to be more than 50% or less than 10%. How to translate this vague prior information into a frighteningly specific prior probability distribution is not clear, which is why Bayesian methods arouse so much unease when first used. But one learns that, provided some care and thought is used in setting up the priors, the details will not in the end matter much. The most important thing is not to assume a prior distribution that makes some possibility impossible, because, as we already saw, if the prior probability is truly zero, then so is the posterior. There is a critical difference between assuming a zero prior and assuming a very low prior. The latter allows the low probability value of a parameter to be saved by the data. (Notice that now possible values of the parameter take the place of possible hypotheses.) Given good enough data, any prior possibility becomes probable, no matter how improbable it was once taken to be, as we will see shortly.

With that in mind, we plunge ahead and assume a normal prior probability distribution centered at 30% (half way between the limits our friend specified) and with a standard deviation of 7%, which means that the limits specified by our friend lie almost 3 standard deviations away from the mean. Thus, we judge *a priori* that the chances of the proportion being less than 10% are on the order of one in a thousand, and similarly for the chances of its being greater than 50%. That seems to pay sufficient respect to our friend's reputation for truth telling. At the same time, however, it does not rule out any proportion, because the normal distribution assigns non-zero probability to every number between minus and plus infinity. In fact, that is a reason why we might have decided not to use it here, because the parameter we are estimating cannot be less than 0 nor greater than 1. If we wanted to be really sophisticated, we would choose a prior distribution that was non-zero only on the interval between zero and 1 (the beta distribution, for example). However, the total probabilities that the normal distribution we have naively assumed assigns to values below 0 and above 1 are very small, so we won't worry about this technicality just now.

The prior distribution we have just so boldly and naively assumed is shown at the top left of Figure 2.3. Note that the numbers on the ordinate are greater than 1, which a probability can never be. This tells us that we have moved from the realm of discrete probability to the realm of continuous probability. In the latter realm, our distribution functions specify *probability densities* rather than probabilities. Probability density distributions share with discrete probability distributions the critical property that they must integrate to 1. That means that the area under the curve must equal 1. You can see at a glance that the area under the prior probability curve in Figure 2.3 must be less than the area of the superposed rectangle that is as high and wide as the curve. The width of this rectangle is 0.4, because it spans from 0.1 to 0.5 on the abscissa. The area of the rectangle is its width times its height. If the height of the distribution were less than 1, the area of the rect-angle would be less than 0.4, and the area under the curve even less than that, in which case the curve could not be a probability distribution. You can see that in order for the area under the curve to be equal to 1, the height of the curve must be substantially greater than 1, as in fact it is. Thus, probability densities, unlike probabilities, can be greater than 1. A probability density is the derivative (slope) at a point of the cumulative probability function, and this derivative can have any value between 0 and plus infinity. The height of a probability density curve spe-cifies the maximum rate at which the cumulative probability increases as we move along the x-axis (the axis specifying the value of the parameter). The cumulative probability is the probability that the parameter *is less than or equal to* a given value on this axis. Whereas probability itself cannot be more than 1, the rate at which probability increases can be any value up to plus infinity.

Now that we have a prior distribution to represent more or less the knowledge with which we started (such as it was), we proceed to draw balls from the urn, note their color, and update/improve our estimate of the proportion of black balls on the basis of the proportions we have actually observed. Figure 2.3 shows four stages in the progress of this updating: when we have only a little evidence (from the first 5 balls drawn), somewhat better evidence (from the first 10), rather good evidence (from the first 50), and good evidence (from the first 100).

At each stage, we use the evidence we have obtained up to that point to com-pute a likelihood function (see right side of Figure 2.3). This computation brings out again the distinction between a likelihood function and a probability distribu-tion, because we use a *discrete* distribution function, the binomial distribution func-tion, to compute a *continuous* likelihood function. The binomial distribution function gives the probability of observing k outcomes of a specified binary kind (e.g., heads in a coin flip) in N observations (flips) when the probability of such an outcome is assumed to be p. Because the observed outcome must always be an integer (you can't get 4.3 heads), the associated probabilities are discrete (that is, they are probabilities, not probability densities). But we do not now use this func-tion to calculate the discrete probabilities for different numbers of a specified out-come. Rather, we use it to calculate how likely a specified outcome – for example, 4 heads in 5 flips – is for different values of p. The values of p vary continuously (unlike the numbers of possible outcomes). Moreover, the likelihoods that we get as we let p range across the infinitesimally minute gradations in its possible values do not integrate (sum) to 1. That is why we call them likelihoods rather than prob-abilities, even though we use the binomial distribution function in both cases and it does not, so to speak, know whether it is computing a probability or a likelihood.

Using the binomial distribution in reverse, so to speak, we get the likelihood func-tions that we show on the right side of Figure 2.3. We don't give numbers on the likelihood ordinate, because it is only relative likelihoods that matter (how high the curve is at one point relative to other points; in other words, the shape of the curve). Recall that when we are done multiplying a likelihood function point-by-corresponding-point with the prior distribution function, we scale the ordinate of the resulting posterior distribution function so as to make the function integrate to 1.

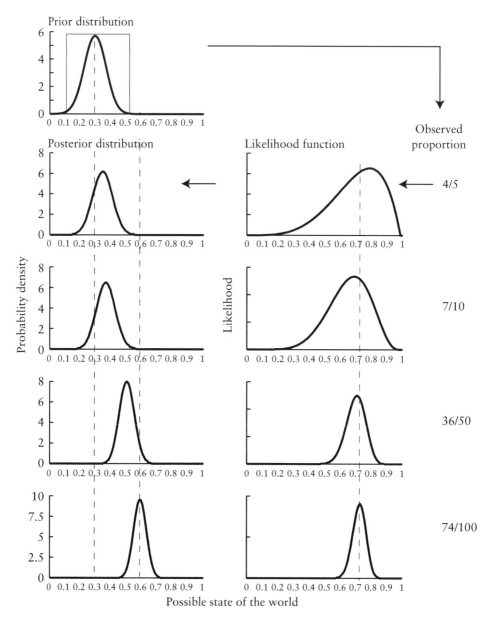

Figure 2.3 Computing posterior distribution functions through point-by-point multiplication of the prior distribution by the likelihood function for the observed proportion. (Both the numerator and the denominator of the observed proportion are arguments of the binomial distribution function used to compute the likelihood function.) For explanation of the light rectangle enclosing the prior distribution function, see text. The dashed vertical lines are to aid in comparisons.

In Figure 2.3 we see that, despite his reputation for reliability, our friend misled us. Judging by the posterior distribution after 100 balls have been observed, the true proportion of black balls appears to be nearer 60% than 30%. It is in a range our friend thought was very unlikely. However, the more important thing to see is the power of the data, the ability of the likelihood function, which is based purely on the data, to overcome a misleading prior distribution. Bayesian updating, which integrates our friend's information, bad as it may in retrospect have been, into our own beliefs about the proportion, does not prevent our arriving at a more or less accurate belief when we have good data. When our prior belief is in the right ballpark, when our friends do not lead us astray, integrating the prior knowledge with such new evidence as we have gets us close to the true state of affairs faster. When the prior belief is considerably off the mark, integrating it into our current estimate will not prevent our getting reasonably close to the mark when we have good data. Already, after only 100 observations, the data have moved us to within about 10% of what looks to be the true proportion (roughly 70%), when we judge by the data alone, ignoring the prior distribution. As anyone who follows opinion polling knows, a sample of 100 is small when you are trying to estimate a binary proportion. Notice that even a sample of 5, which is pathetically small ("anecdotal"), moves the mode (what we believe to be the most likely proportion) a noticeable amount away from its prior location. By the time we get to a sample of 50, the mode of the posterior is approaching what our friend thought was the upper limit on plausible values. At that point, we have good evidence that our friend must have been mistaken. It would not be unreasonable at that point to jettison our prior, in which case we will now have as good an estimate as if we had not started with a misleading prior. (Jettisoning the prior is justified whenever the prior becomes unlikely in the light of the data. In a changing world, this is often the case.) It is because of the power of the data that Bayesians do not worry too much about details of the prior distributions they sometimes have to assume in the face of murky evidence.

Summary

Bayesian updating provides a rigorous conceptual/mathematical framework for understanding how the brain builds up over time a serviceably accurate representation of the behaviorally important parameters of our environment and our situation in it, based on information-carrying signals of varying reliability from different sources that arrive intermittently over extended periods of time. It is natural in this framework to have several different Bayesian data-processing modules, each working with a different kind of data, for which likelihood functions are derived in different ways, but all updating a common "prior" distribution. It is also natural to have hierarchically structured belief networks, in which lower-level modules provide evidence to higher-level modules, which in turn structure the prior hypothesis space of the lower-level modules in the light of the bigger picture to which only the higher modules have access (Chater et al., 2006; Pearl, 2000). And, it is natural to model neural computation in a Bayesian framework (Knill & Pouget, 2004; Rieke et al., 1997).

The broader meaning of "prior" is the estimate prior to the latest relevant signal for which we have a likelihood function, where all parameter estimates are understood to be probability density functions. This last understanding reflects the fundamental role that a subjective strength of belief – the Bayesian definition of a probability – plays in a practical representational system reliant on noisy and ambiguous signals from a complex world. In this conceptual framework, there is no such thing as a belief without a prior, because the property of having a strength (relative to other beliefs) is intrinsic to being a belief. The prior is by no means immutable. On the contrary, the prior is what is updated. The prior is the repository of what we have so far learned, by various means, from various sources. We need a memory mechanism to carry this distillation of our previous experience forward in time so that it may be integrated (combined with) the information we gain from our future experience.

3

Functions

The communication between the world and the brain (Figure 1.4) is a mapping from states of the world to representations of those states. Computational operations in brains and in other computing machines map their inputs to their outputs. For example, the multiplication operation maps pairs of quantities (the inputs) to their products (the outputs). From a mathematical perspective, these mappings are functions. The notion of a function is at once so simple and so abstract that it can be hard to grasp. It plays a fundamental role in our understanding of representation (Chapter 4) and computation (Chapter 7).

A function is a deterministic mapping from elements of one set of distinct entities, called the *domain*, to elements from another set of distinct entities, called the *codomain*. There is no restriction on what constitutes these entities, which is part of what makes the notion of a function so abstract. The entities in either the domain or the codomain may be physical objects such as a specific fish or house, they can be concepts such as freedom or love, or they can be numbers, whose ontological status may be debated.

Functions of One Argument

Figure 3.1 gives two examples of functions. The first, f_1, pairs a few basic kinds of animals (dogs, owls, etc.) with a few higher categories (birds, mammals, etc.). The second, f_2, pairs one set of numbers with another set of numbers. On the left side of each mapping are the domain entities (the set D); on the right side are the codomain entities (the set C). From a mathematical perspective, the functions themselves are simply the sets of pairings. Thus, f_1 is the set of pairings of the elements in D_1 with elements in C_1. The set of pairings, f_1, is, of course, distinct from the sets of the elements that enter into the pairings (sets D_1 and C_1), just as those sets are themselves distinct from the elements that they consist of.

From a practical perspective, however, functions are not simply viewed as a set of paired entities. Functions of computational interest are almost always described by *algorithms* (step-by-step processes) that will *determine* the mapping defined by a function. For example, one would like a physically realizable process that determines

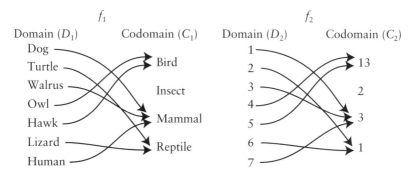

Figure 3.1   Two examples of functions. Function f_1 maps from the set D_1, which consists of some lower-order classes of animals to the set C_1, which consists of some higher order classes. Function f_2 maps from the set D_2, which consists of the numbers 1–7, to the set D_2, which consists of the numbers 1, 2, 3 and 13.

that *owl* gets mapped to *bird* (see if it has feathers, check if it lay eggs, test if it is warm blooded, etc.). An algorithm allows us to determine, given any element in the range (typically called the *input* or *argument* to the function), the corresponding member of the codomain (typically called the *output* or *value* of the function). When we are speaking from a computational perspective (which we explore in detail in Chapters 6 and 7), we will often refer to an algorithm as an *effective procedure* or just *procedure* for short. However, the terms *function*, *algorithm*, and *procedure* are often used interchangeably and understood from context. Additionally, we will refer to the effecting of a procedure as a *computation*. We say that a procedure, when effected as a computation, *determines* a function, and that the procedure, as a physical system, *implements* the function. The term *computation* usually implies that the elements of the domain and range are symbols that encode for other entities (we will discuss symbols in Chapter 5).

From the perspective of physically realized computation, a procedure is the computational machinery that specifies how several (usually, a great many) physically realized simpler functions can be put together to achieve a more complex mapping. Thus, the notion of a function gives us an abstract description of a computing machine. By means of this notion, we go from the highly abstract to concrete physical implementations.

A central question in the physical realization of a computation is whether it is in fact possible to decompose a given abstractly specified function into the structured execution of physically implemented elementary functions, and, if so, how? An important insight is that the answer to this question is sometimes "no." There are precisely and unambiguously specified functions for which it is in principle impossible to create a machine that implements them. There are other precisely and unambiguously specified functions that can in principle be implemented in a machine, but in practice, their implementation places unsatisfiable demands on physical resources.

Functions are directional mappings in which each member of the domain gets mapped to one and only one member of the codomain. This makes the mapping deterministic: specifying an element in the domain determines a unique corresponding element in the codomain. This directionality is made transparent terminologically when we refer to an element of the domain as an *input* and the element that it gets mapped to as an *output*. The converse is not true: specifying an element in the codomain does not necessarily determine a unique corresponding element in the domain, as is evident from the examples in Figure 3.1. An entity in the codomain may be paired with more than one element in the domain, or with none. The set of entities in the codomain that have specified partners in the domain is called the *range* of the function. If the range is the same as the codomain, that is, if every element in the codomain is paired with one or more elements in the domain, the mapping is said to be *onto*.

A common notation for specifying the domain and codomain for a particular function is $f: D \rightarrow C$. Either the domain, or the codomain, or both, may have infinitely many elements. For numerical functions (mappings from numbers to numbers), this is the rule rather than the exception. Consider, for example, the "zeroing" function, f_0, which maps every real number to 0: $f_0: \mathbb{R} \rightarrow \{0\}$, where $\mathbb{R}$ is the set of all real numbers. The domain of this function is infinite, whereas its codomain is the set whose only member is the number 0. Consider, for a second example, the function that maps every integer to its (perfect) square: $f_{x^2}: \mathbb{Z} \rightarrow \mathbb{Z}$, where $\mathbb{Z}$ is the set of all integers. Both its domain and its codomain are infinite sets. Note that in this example the mapping is not onto. Only the perfect squares are in the range of the function, and these are a proper subset of the integers: all perfect squares are integers, but there are infinitely many integers that are not perfect squares. Thus, the range of this function is not the same as the codomain.

The function that does the inverse mapping – from the perfect squares to their integer square roots – does not exist. This is because there are two different square roots for a perfect square (for example, 9 would have to map to both −3 and 3), and that violates the deterministic property of a function. The output of the machine for a given input would be indeterminate. There is a mapping that partially inverts the squaring function, the mapping from the perfect squares to their positive roots. But this inversion is only partial; it is not a complete reverse mapping. Thus, the squaring function has no inverse.

If f is a function and x is an input that maps to the output y, we can describe a particular input–output mapping using the functional notation: $f(x) = y$. Using the example of f_{x^2}, we would write $f_{x^2}(3) = 9$ and we say that f_{x^2} *of 3 equals 9*. It is particularly when using this notation that we refer to the input as the *argument* to the function, and the output as the *value* of the function for the argument. We may also say that f_{x^2} *when applied to the argument 3 returns (or yields) the value 9*. One way to capture the complete mapping in Figure 3.1 is to give all input–output mappings in functional form. So we would have $f_{is\_a}(Dog) = Mammal$, $f_{is\_a}(Turtle) = Reptile$, $f_{is\_a}(Walrus) = Mammal$, $f_{is\_a}(Owl) = Bird$, $f_{is\_a}(Hawk) = Bird$, $f_{is\_a}(Lizard) = Reptile$, $f_{is\_a}(Human) = Mammal$.

If distinct members of the domain get mapped to distinct members of the codomain, that is, if $f(a) = f(b)$ implies $a = b$, then we say that the function is a *one-to-one* function. If a function is both one-to-one and onto, then we say that the function is a *bijection*. This term implies that this mapping can be run either way (it is bidirectional): it defines a set of pairings in which every member of one set has a unique corresponding member of the other set. Thus, bijections are invertible: you can always go from an element in the domain to an element in the codomain *and* from an element in the codomain to an element in the domain (for example, $f(x) = x + 1$ is a bijection).

Composition and Decomposition of Functions

New functions can be constructed by taking the output (range) of one function as the input (domain) of another. Consider the f_{2x} function, which maps every real number to its double and the f_{x^2} function, which maps every real number to its square. If we feed a number to the squaring function, we gets its square, if we then feed that square to the doubling function, we get the double of that square. In this way, we have constructed a new mapping, the f_{2x^2} function. This new function pairs every number with the double of its square. Constructing new functions in this way is called the *composition of functions*. It is a major aspect of the writing of computer programs, because the commands in a computer program generally invoke functions, and the results are then often operated on by functions invoked by later commands.

Categorization schemes are functions, as f_1 in Figure 3.2 illustrates. Categorization is commonly hierarchical, and this is captured by the composition of functions, as shown in Figure 3.2.

In composing functions, it usually matters which one operates first and which second. If we feed numbers to the doubling function first and then to the squaring function, we map the number 3 to 36, but if we feed first to the squaring function and then to the doubling function, we map 3 to 18. Thus, the composition of functions is not in general commutative: it is often the case that $f_b \circ f_a \neq f_a \circ f_b$, where $\circ$ denotes composition. In alternative notation, $f_b(f_a(x)) \neq f_a(f_b(x))$. The alternative notation has the advantage of making it more apparent which function operates first (the innermost). The example of functional composition in Figure 3.2 shows that not only is the composition of functions commonly not commutative, it may well be the case that two functions can compose in one order but not in the reverse order. In Figure 3.2, one could not first apply the categorization in f_2 and then apply the categorization in f_1, because the range of f_2 is not in the domain of f_1.

The non-commutative property of the composition of functions suggests that any physically realizable system that computes such functions must be capable of sequencing in time the order of the individual functions. In turn, this implies that such computing devices must be capable of carrying the values of functions forward in time such that they can be utilized by functions that are sequenced later. Most of the functions that brains routinely compute involve the composition of functions that are determined at different points in time (numerous examples are in Chapters 11–13). In the language of computer science, one would say that a physically realized computational device, such as the brain, needs memory to carry the values forward in time, and that this memory must be capable of being written to and read from.

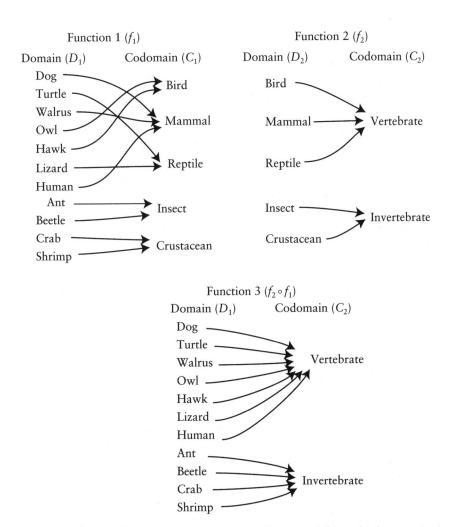

Figure 3.2   The composition of two categorization functions yields a third categorization. Its domain is that of the first function and its codomain is that of the second function.

Functions can often be decomposed into the sequential operation of other functions. Thus, the function f_{2x^2} can be decomposed into $f_{2x} \circ f_{x^2}$ and the function $f_{(2x)^2}$ can be decomposed into $f_{x^2} \circ f_{2x}$. Writing a computer program is in appreciable measure the art of decomposing a complex function into an appropriate sequence of less complex functions, which themselves are ultimately decomposed into the functions provided in the programming language being used. The functions provided by the programming language are ultimately implemented by the functions that are natively computed by the physical architecture of the computing device. This suggests that computation is inherently hierarchical in structure. This hierarchical structure allows for efficiency in determining functions. As the example above shows, if a system has the ability to compose arbitrary functions, then it would be capable of computing both f_{2x^2} and $f_{(2x)^2}$ without any additional resources to account for the sequencing. This suggests that in addition to being hierarchical, computation is also inherently modular: simple functions are often used again and again by many different, more complex functions.

A most surprising result that emerged from the work of Alan Turing, work that we will examine in detail in Chapter 7, is that all of the functions that can be physically implemented as procedures (all computable functions) can be determined through the use of composition and a very small class of primitive functions. To get a glimpse into this potential, realize that both f_{2x^2} and $f_{(2x)^2}$ can themselves by decomposed into the composition of sequential applications of the function f_{xy} that is capable of multiplying two numbers. Taking this one step further, we note that f_{xy} can itself also be decomposed into the composition of sequential applications of the function f_{x+y}. This leads naturally to our next topic.

Functions of More than One Argument

The functions we have looked at so far take one argument and return a single value. What about a function like multiplication that takes two arguments and returns a single value? We can easily generalize our definition of a function to include two or more arguments by letting there be more than one set that defines the domain. In this way, the actual domain entities become sequences (ordered lists) of elements from these sets. We write a particular such sequence using functional notation by separating the arguments by commas. For example, we can write $f_*(2, 3) = 6$. Since the domain now comes from two separate sets, the arguments to the function are themselves pairings of elements from these two sets. The set composed of all possible pairings of the elements in two other sets, A and B, is called their Cartesian product, and is written $A \times B$. The function that maps all possible pairs of numbers from the set of natural numbers $\{0, 1, 2, \dots\}$, $\mathbb{N}$, to their product is $f_* : \mathbb{N} \times \mathbb{N} \to \mathbb{N}$, as its domain is the Cartesian product of the set of natural numbers with itself.

Predicates and relations as functions

Using the Cartesian products of sets, we can express functions of an arbitrary number of arguments. Let's look at another example function that takes three arguments. Let set $P = \{$Jim, Sandy$\}$, two people. Let $A = \{$Movie, Exercise, Work$\}$, three activities that one could do. Let $D = \{$Sunday, Monday$\}$, two days of the week, and let $T = \{True, False\}$, concepts of truth and falsehood.

Our function, let's call it f_{did_they}, will map from people, activities they might have done, and days of the week to *True* or *False*, with *True* indicating that that person did that activity on the given day and *False* indicating they did not. We therefore can write: $f_{did\_they} : P \times A \times D \to T$. This function has as its domain the Cartesian product of three different sets and as its codomain the set whose only two members are *True* and *False*.

Properties and relations

Functions such as f_{did_they} in which the codomain consists of {*True, False*} are called *predicates*. They express properties and relations. A predicate that takes one argument is called a *property*. For example, if we have a domain O consisting of objects {*object₁, object₂, object₃*}, we can define a predicate f_{is_blue}: O → {*True, False*} such that $f_{is\_blue}(object_1)$ = *True* if and only if object *object₁* is blue and *False* otherwise. We can think of $f_{is\_blue}(object_1)$ as telling us whether or not *object₁* has the property of being blue.

A predicate that takes two or more arguments is called a *relation*. It expresses the existence of a relationship between the arguments. For example, take the predicate $f_{is\_touching}$: O × O → {*True, False*}. Here $f_{is\_touching}(object_1, object_2)$ = *True* expresses the relationship that *object₁* is in physical contact with *object₂*.

The Limits to Functional Decomposition

One may wonder whether functions with two (or more) arguments can be decomposed into functions with one argument. Generally speaking, they cannot. One can see why not by considering whether the $f_{is\_touching}$ can be decomposed into the composition of an $f_{touches}$ function. This function would take single objects as its argument and produce as its output an object touched by whatever object was the input. We might think that we could then replace $f_{is\_touching}(object_1, object_2)$ = *True* with $f_{touches}(object_1)$ = *object₂*. We can see this won't work because while we could have the situation $f_{is\_touching}(object_1, object_2)$ = *True* and $f_{is\_touching}(object_1, object_3)$ = *True*, we cannot have both $f_{touches}(object_1)$ = *object₂* and $f_{touches}(object_1)$ = *object₃*.

As this example illustrates, allowing only for one argument restricts the expressive power of functions. Functions of one argument cannot combine to do the work of functions with two. Take the integer multiplication function, f_*: $\mathbb{Z} \times \mathbb{Z} \to \mathbb{Z}$, which maps pairs of integers to a single integer. It is inherent in this function that the two arguments are combined into one value and cannot remain separate within two separate functions. If $f_*(x, y) = z$, there is no way that we can create two functions f_{*_part1}: $\mathbb{Z} \to \mathbb{Z}$ and f_{*_part2}: $\mathbb{Z} \to \mathbb{Z}$ that enable us to determine z without eventually using some function that can be applied to multiple arguments. Thus, we cannot realize this and many other two-argument functions by composing one-argument functions. This elementary mathematical truth is a critical part of our argument as to why the architecture of a powerful computing device such as the brain must make provision for bringing the values of variables to the machinery that implements some primitive two-argument functions. The ability to realize functions of at least two arguments is a necessary condition for realizing functions of a non-trivial nature.

Functions Can Map to Multi-Part Outputs

Above we used the Cartesian product to create functions that take multiple arguments. We can construct functions that return multiple values using the same technique. Let's look at the example of integer division. Integer division is similar to real numbered division except that it only takes integers as arguments and produces an integer instead of a real number. You can think of it as the most number of times one integer can be subtracted from the other before the result goes negative. Given $f_{int\_division}$: $\mathbb{Z} \times \mathbb{Z} \to \mathbb{Z}$, we have $f_{int\_division}(14, 3) = 4$. With integer division, there may be an integer remainder when we have done the last possible subtraction. When we divide 14 by 3, it divides 4 integral times, with a remainder of 2, that is, $14 = (3)(4) + 2$.

Therefore, we may want a function that would map from pairs of integers to two-component outputs, one component is the integer division of the two arguments and one the remainder. We could write this as $f_{int\_div\_and\_rem}$: $\mathbb{Z} \times \mathbb{Z} \to \mathbb{Z} \times \mathbb{Z}$ with $f_{int\_div\_and\_rem}(14, 3) = (4, 2)$.

Our pointing out that multi-component outputs are possible does not contradict our earlier point that a function cannot have two different outputs. There cannot be a function that maps from any perfect square to its square root, because every perfect square has two different square roots, so the mapping would be indeterminate, one would not know which square root to expect. It is possible, however, to have a function that maps from any perfect square to its square roots, because in this function its square roots are components of a single output. In such a function, the output forms an *ordered pair*. The codomain of this function is the Cartesian product $\mathbb{Z} \times \mathbb{Z}$. Note, however, that this function does not invert the mapping from integers to their squares. The domain of that function is $\mathbb{Z}$, whereas the codomain of the inverse function from the perfect squares to their roots is $\mathbb{Z} \times \mathbb{Z}$. In other words, the function that maps from perfect squares to their roots generates a different kind of entity than the entities that serve as the arguments of the function that maps from the integers to their squares. Thus, it remains true that the function mapping from integers to their squares does not have an inverse.

Mapping to Multiple-Element Outputs Does Not Increase Expressive Power

The capacity to return multi-part outputs does not buy us additional expressive power. If we have a function that takes x number of arguments and returns y number of values, we can replace that function with y functions, each taking x number of arguments and returning one value. For example, we can replace $f_{int\_div\_and\_rem}$: $\mathbb{Z} \times \mathbb{Z} \to \mathbb{Z} \times \mathbb{Z}$ with the two functions $f_{int\_division}$: $\mathbb{Z} \times \mathbb{Z} \to \mathbb{Z}$ and $f_{int\_remainder}$: $\mathbb{Z} \times \mathbb{Z} \to \mathbb{Z}$. This would result in $f_{int\_division}(14, 4) = 3$ and $f_{int\_remainder}(14, 4) = 2$. This works because each output value can be determined independently with no interactions between the outputs. Therefore, it is not logically necessary to have functions with more than one output value, whereas it is necessary to have functions with two inputs.

By combining the concept of functional composition with the fact that we only need up to two arguments and only one output value, we can use our example above regarding integer division to show how we can apply some function $f_{\wedge}$ to the integer dividend and the integer remainder of integer division. Here we would use the form: $f_{\wedge}(f_{int\_division}(x, y), f_{int\_remainder}(x, y))$.

Defining Particular Functions

Above, we were fairly informal in defining our function f_{did_they}. Somewhat more formally, we could say that f_{did_they}: $P \times A \times D \to T$ and that if $a \in P$, $b \in A$, and $c \in D$, then $f_{did\_they}(a, b, c) = True$ if person a did the activity b on day c and $f_{did\_they}(a, b, c) = False$ if they did not. Another way to define this function would be to use a *look-up table*. Look-up tables define and determine a function by giving the explicit mapping of each input to its output. Table 3.1 shows the three-dimensional look-up table for f_{did_they}. The advantage of the look-up table is that it explicitly specifies the output of the function for each possible input. Under the everyday metaphysical assumption that there are simple empirical truths, our English definition of the function establishes that it exists, because we assume that there is a simple truth as to whether a given individual did or did not do a given activity on a given day. However, our description does not tell us what those truths actually are for the people and activities and days in its domain. We may believe that there is a truth of the matter, but that truth may not be knowable. The look-up table, by contrast, specifies the truth in each case. Thus, a look-up table specification of a function is a procedure that implements that function: it gives you a means of obtaining the output for a given input. In a computational machine, that is what we want.

However, the look-up table architecture (the form of the physically instantiated procedure that implements the function) is impractical if there are a very large number of possible input combinations, for which an equally numerous set of outputs must be specified. Consider, for example, using a look-up table to implement the multiplication function over the infinite set of integers, f_*: $\mathbb{Z} \times \mathbb{Z} \to \mathbb{Z}$. To implement it with a look-up table, we would need two separate physical realizations of every possible integer symbol (one replication for the column headers and one for the row names), which is clearly impossible. As a practical matter, even if we limit our implementation to input integers between, say, minus a trillion trillion and plus a trillion trillion, we cannot possibly build a look-up table that big. It would require more physical resources than we could ever bring together in a manageable space. (We call this the *problem of the infinitude of the possible*. We will return to it repeatedly.) Moreover, in building such a look-up-table machine, we would need to precompute and put into the table the result of every possible multiplication, because look-up table machines require us to put into the machine all the possible outputs that we may ever hope to obtain back from it. (We call this the *problem of prespecification*. We also return to it repeatedly.)

Thus, if we are going to physically realize computationally important functions, such as the arithmetic functions, we are going to need architectures that permit us to make mappings from essentially infinite domains to essentially infinite ranges using modest physical resources and without having to build every possible output into the machine in advance. In effect, the machine must be able to tell us things we don't know when we have finished building it, such as: What is the product 1,234,581,247 and 7629?

As our first way of defining f_{did_they} makes clear, function definitions do not necessarily tell us how to *determine* a particular output value given the arguments to

Table 3.1   The look-up table for f_{did_they}

P	A	D	T
Jim	Movie	Sunday	False
Jim	Movie	Monday	False
Jim	Exercise	Sunday	True
Jim	Exercise	Monday	True
Jim	Work	Sunday	False
Jim	Work	Monday	True
Sandy	Movie	Sunday	False
Sandy	Movie	Monday	False
Sandy	Exercise	Sunday	True
Sandy	Exercise	Monday	False
Sandy	Work	Sunday	False
Sandy	Work	Monday	True

the function, they only establish that such a mapping exists. Indeed, we know that there are many perfectly well-defined functions that, either in principle or in practice, cannot be computed, that is, the actual mapping specified by the definition of the function cannot be fully realized by any physically realizable device.

For an example in which practical considerations arise, consider the function f_{next_prime}: $\mathbb{N} \rightarrow \mathbb{N}$, which takes a natural number (call it n), and returns the next prime number (the first prime larger than n). This is a very well-defined function with no one left in doubt that such a mapping exists. We know many parts of this mapping. For example, $f_{next\_prime}(1) = 2$, $f_{next\_prime}(8) = 11$, and $f_{next\_prime}(100) = 101$. However, our knowledge of the complete mapping is limited and probably always will be. We know that the number of primes is infinite, but at the time of this writing, we don't know any particular prime number of greater than 13 million digits. All known procedures for finding the next prime take longer and longer to execute as the arguments get bigger and bigger. Therefore, while $f_{next\_prime}(10^8) \cdot (100 \text{ million})$ certainly exists, we currently do not know what its value is. It is possible that in practice, for extremely large values n, we may never be able to determine the value of $f_{next\_prime}(n)$. Contrast this with the case of $f_{next\_integer}(n)$, where we have a procedure (the successor function, which simply adds 1) that can produce the answer in the blink of an eye for arbitrarily large n.

An example of a function that cannot be physically realized even in principle is the function that maps all rational numbers to 1 and all irrational numbers to 0. There are *uncountably* many irrational numbers within any numerical interval, no matter how small. Thus, we cannot order them in some way and begin progressing through the ordering. Moreover, most of the irrational numbers are *uncomputable*. That is, there is no machine that can generate a representation (encoding) of them out to some arbitrarily specified level of precision. In essence, uncomputable numbers are numbers that cannot be physically represented. If we cannot physically represent the inputs to the machine that is supposed to generate the corresponding outputs, we cannot construct a machine that will do the specified mapping.

On the other hand, many functions can be implemented with simple machines that are incomparably more efficient than machines with the architecture of a look-up table. These mini-machines are at the heart of a powerful computing machine. An example of such a machine is our marble machine that adds binary number symbols (see Figure 8.11).

Summary: Physical/Neurobiological Implications of Facts about Functions

Logical, mathematical facts about functions have implications for engineers contemplating building a machine that computes. They also have implications for cognitive neuroscientists, who are confronted with the brain, a machine with spectacular computing abilities, and challenged to deduce its functional architecture and to identify the neurobiological mechanisms that implement the components of that architecture. One important fact is that functions of two arguments, which include all of the basic arithmetic functions, cannot be decomposed into functions of one argument. A second important fact is that functions of n arguments, where n is arbitrarily large, can be decomposed into functions of two arguments. A third important fact is that functions with n-element outputs can be decomposed into (replaced with) n functions with one-element outputs. What these facts tell us is that a powerful computing machine must have basic components that implement both one- and two-argument functions, and it must have a means of composing functions. Moreover, these facts about functions tell us that this is all that is essential. All implementable functions can be realized by the composition of a modest number of well-chosen functions that map one or two input elements to an output element.

These logico-mathematical truths about functions tell us a great deal about the functional architecture of modern computing machines. A critical component of all such machines is a processing unit or units that implement a modest number of elementary functions (on the order of 100). Most of these functions map two input elements to one output element by means of a procedure hard wired into the component. Another critical aspect of its architecture makes it possible for the machine to compose these functions in essentially infinitely various ways. An essential component of the compositional aspect of the machine's architecture is a read/write memory. The product of one elementary function is written to this memory, where it is preserved until such time as it becomes one of the inputs to another elementary function.

Some obvious questions that these facts about functions pose for cognitive neuro-scientists are:

1   Are there a modest number of elementary functions in the brain's computational machinery, out of which the very large number of complex functions that brains implement are realized by composition?
2   If so, what are these functions?

3   How are they implemented and at what structural level? By systems-level struc-
    tures (neural circuits)? Or by cellular-level structures (e.g., synapses)? Or by molecu-
    lar structures (e.g., microRNAs)?
4   How is the composition of these functions achieved?
5   What is the memory mechanism that makes composition possible over indefinite
    time intervals? An essential fact about the composition of functions that underlies
    behavior is that there are time lags of indefinite duration between the production
    of an output from one function and its use as an input in another function.

What is the architecture that enables the machinery that implements functions
to physically interact with the symbols on which the machinery operates? These
symbols come mostly from memory (point 5). What is the structural relation between
memory, where the symbols reside, and the machinery that implements the mappings
from symbols to symbols? Are the symbols brought to the function-implementing
machinery, thereby minimizing the amount of such machinery required, while max-
imizing demands on symbol fetching? Or is the machinery in effect brought to
the symbols that are to serve as its inputs by replicating the machinery a great many
times? The necessity for implementing two-element functions makes the latter unlikely, because there would appear to be no way to structure memory so that the
elements of all possible pairs were physically adjacent. The innumerable different
pairs that may become inputs cannot in general be composed of symbols at physically adjacent locations. Therefore, the architecture must make provision for retrieving from physically non-adjacent locations in memory the two symbols that are to
serve as the input arguments and bringing them to the machinery that maps them
to an output symbol. In short, there must be a means of fetching symbols to the computational machinery that implements two-argument functions. It is not possible to
bring the machinery to the arguments, because, generally speaking, the arguments
will themselves be in two different locations.

4

Representations

In Chapter 1 we saw that if the world is to communicate information to the brain, then the brain must be capable of representing and assigning probabilities to the possible messages that it might receive. Thus, the brain is a representing system – or a collection of representing systems. The entities in the brain that represent possible messages are symbols. The aspects of the world that it represents – the possible messages for which it has symbols – constitute represented systems. There are processes – sensory processes, for example – that causally connect the brain's symbols to their referents outside the brain. There are other brain processes – the processes that control a directed reach, for example – that pick out the entity in the represented system to which a symbol in the representing system refers. The first set of processes implement functions that map from the represented system to the representing system; the second implement functions that map the other way, from the representing system to the represented system. The two systems, together with the functions that map between them, constitute a *representation*, provided three conditions are met:

1   The mapping from entities in the represented system to their symbols in the representing system is *causal* (as, for example, when light reflected off an object in the world acts on sensory receptors in an eye causing neural signals that eventuate in a percept of the object – see Figure 1.4).
2   The mapping is *structure preserving*: The mapping from entities in the represented system to their symbols is such that functions defined on the represented entities are mirrored by functions of the same mathematical form between their corresponding symbols. Structure-preserving mappings are called *homomorphisms*.
3   Symbolic operations (procedures) in the representing systems are (at least sometimes) behaviorally *efficacious*: they control and direct appropriate behavior within, or with respect to, the represented system.

The behavioral efficacy of structure-preserving mappings from the represented system to the representing system makes a functioning homomorphism, which is the two-word definition of a representation. Our task in this chapter is to explicate and illustrate this concept – the concept of a representation – because it is central to our understanding of computation and the brain. The brain's computational capacity exists primarily to enable it to compute behaviorally useful representations.

Some Simple Examples

When couched in terms at the above level of abstraction, the concept of a representation sounds forbidding. Moreover, it has long been controversial within psychology, cognitive science, neuroscience, and other disciplines concerned with understanding the mind, the brain, and the relation between them. Behaviorists argued that it should be dispensed with altogether (Skinner, 1990). Skepticism about the usefulness of the notion is also common among neuroscientists (Edelman & Tononi, 2000). Ambivalence about representation also appears in connectionist modeling circles, where the signal processing that occurs is sometimes said to be "subsymbolic" (Barnden, 1992; Brooks, 1991; P. S. Churchland & Sejnowski, 1990; Elman, 1991; Hanson & Burr, 1990; Hinton, McClelland, & Rumelhart, 1986; Rumelhart & Todd, 1993; Smolensky, 1988).

In practice, however, there need be no mystery surrounding the concept of a representation, rigorously defined; they can be extremely simple. Consider, for example, the practice of recording the height of a growing child by having him or her stand against a wall, laying a book flat on the head, butted against the wall, and making a pencil mark on the wall, using the underside of the book as the guide, and dating the mark. The graphite streak on the wall is an analog symbol. Its elevation represents the child's height as of the date the streak was made. The process of making the mark is the physical realization of a measurement function. It maps from the height of a child to the elevation of a mark on a wall. The physical realization of this function causally connects the elevation of the mark to the height of the child. The mapping is structure preserving because the ordering of the marks on the wall (their relative elevation) preserves the ordering of the heights. This ordering of the marks by their relative elevation becomes behaviorally efficacious when, for example, it is used by a parent in choosing a clothing size.

In this case, the homomorphism between the things symbolized (heights) and the symbolic system (marks on the wall) is trivially realized, because there is a natural physical homomorphism between elevation and height. In some sense, the ordering of the symbols and the ordering of the heights to which they refer are the same because the representing system (mark elevations) and the represented system (human heights) both have the same physical property (distance from a reference point). However, we must not therefore make the common mistake of confusing the symbol with what it represents. The elevation of the graphite streak on the wall is not the height of the child. Erasing it would not deprive the child of height, and remaking it lower on the wall would not reduce the child's height; it would merely misrepresent it.

The mark-on-the-wall system has it charms as an illustration of a representation, and it could hardly be simpler, but it is perhaps more instructive to consider a hi-tech version in which the encoding is not so direct. One can buy electronic scales with electronic height-slides, like the ones they put on scales in the doctor's office to measure your height while you're on the scale. The scale maps the force with which the earth's gravity acts on your body into a bit pattern, a pattern of high and low voltages in a register inside a chip. The slider-with-a-digital-transducer maps your height into another bit pattern. These bit patterns are symbols. The electronics in the scale and the slider, which implement the weight- and height-measuring functions, causally connect them to the quantities in the word that they encode. In a super hi-tech version of this, one may imagine a digital weighing and height-measuring system that would compute your body-mass index or BMI (your weight divided by the square of your height) and email the resulting bit pattern to your doctor. The doctor's computer might then email you back a report outlining an appropriate diet and exercise plan – all of this without human intervention. Thus, the representation of your height and weight and your approximately computed position on a lean–fat continuum by means of these digital symbols can be efficacious.

This somewhat fanciful hi-tech example is instructive because the homomorphism between the bit patterns in the computer and its processing of them, on the one hand, and, on the other hand, your height, weight, and BMI, is by no means trivially realized. It is created by careful engineering. There is no natural ordering of bit patterns, the symbols that represent height, weight, and BMI in the hi-tech example of a representing system. There is no physically straightforward sense in which 001111 is shorter, lighter, or "leaner" than 010010. Nor is there a straightforward sense in which the corresponding patterns of high and low voltages within the silicon chip are shorter, lighter, or "leaner" than another such voltage pattern. Height and weight and lean/fat are not properties of binary voltage patterns. If these patterns of high and low voltage are to serve as symbols of a person's location along these dimensions, we are going to have to engineer the representing system (the chip) so as to create a component that appropriately orders the symbols. We achieve this ordering by building into the operation of the machine the procedures that implement arithmetic functions with binary encoded numbers.

One of the elementary relations in arithmetic is the order relation. As noted in the previous chapter, relations are functions. Let's define this ordering relation, denoted '≥', as a mapping from all possible pairs of integers to the integers 0 and 1 ($f_\geq$: $\mathbb{Z} \times \mathbb{Z} \to \{0, 1\}$) such that $f_\geq(x, y) = 0$ when x is less than y and $f_\geq(x, y) = 1$ otherwise. Built into the chip on a digital scale is a component that implements this function on the binary encoding of integers ($f_{binary}(0) = $ '0', $f_{binary}(1) = $ '1', $f_{binary}(2) = $ '10', $f_{binary}(3) = $ '11', $f_{binary}(4) = $ '100', $f_{binary}(5) = $ '101', $f_{binary}(6) = $ '110', etc.). The transducer in the scale that translates a weight into a bit pattern is engineered so that progressively heavier loads produce bit patterns that encode progressively higher numbers. This engineering of the transducer and the ordering function creates a structure-preserving mapping from weights to bit patterns in the chip: If *weight-a* is heavier than *weight-b*, then the bit pattern to which *weight-a* maps will encode a greater integer than the bit pattern to which *weight-b* maps. Thus, when the two bit patterns are put into the component that implements the numerical order function, it will generate a 1.

The art and science of constructing measuring instruments is centered on the creation of mappings from non-numerical quantities (weight, height, length, humidity, fat : lean ratio, etc.) to numbers in ways that preserve as much structure as possible.

The more structure that is preserved – that is, the more arithmetic processing that can validly be done on the resulting numbers – the better the measurement procedure (Krantz, Luce, Suppes, & Tversky, 1971; Stevens, 1951). Bad measurement procedures or mechanisms preserve very little structure, thereby limiting the usefulness of the resulting numbers.

These days, the numbers are in a binary encoding, unless they are intended for human consumption. They are in binary form because there is readily available at very little cost machinery that can arithmetically manipulate numbers thus encoded. This machinery implements all the two-argument arithmetic functions – the functions that, together with the one-argument negation function, are the foundations of mathematics. It also implements a modest number of other elementary one- and two-argument functions. There is also readily available at very little cost devices – random access memories – that can store vast quantities of the bit patterns that serve as both the inputs to and the outputs from this machinery. This cheap and ever more compact memory machinery preserves bit patterns in a form that permits their ready retrieval. The ability of the machinery that implements the elementary one- and two-argument functions to offload the results to memory and quickly get them back again whenever needed makes it possible for that machinery to implement the composition of its elementary functions. That makes it possible to construct procedures that implement extremely complex functions.

From an information-theoretic perspective, the possible weights that a scale can measure are a set of possible messages. And the possible bit patterns to which the scale may map them, together with the symbolic operations that may validly be performed with those patterns, are the receiver's representation of the set of possible messages. The more structure that is preserved in the mapping from weights to bit patterns, the more information is thereby communicated to the chip.

The process by which the bit pattern for the body-mass index is derived from the measurements of weight and height is instructive. First the bit pattern for height is entered into both inputs of a component of the machine constructed so as to implement the mapping from the Cartesian product of binary encodings of numbers to the binary encoding of their numerical products. This component implements the $f_*: \mathbb{N}^+ \times \mathbb{N}^+ \to \mathbb{N}^+$ (multiplication of the positive integers) discussed in the previous chapter. In this case, the operation of this component gives the binary encoding of the square of your height. This symbol – newly generated by the multiplying component – is stored in memory. Then it is fetched from memory and entered into the dividend register of a component constructed to implement the division function. The bit pattern for your weight is entered into the divisor register of the dividing component, and the component cranks out the bit pattern that is their quotient. This quotient is the body-mass index. It is widely used in medicine, but also much disparaged because it is not a very good measure; there is very little arithmetic that can validly be done with it.

However, as a measure of the amount of fat relative to the amount of muscle and bone in a body, the body-mass index is clearly superior to the two numbers from which it was computed. Neither of the inputs to the dividing component was an index of a person's location along the lean–fat dimension, because a 2.7 meter-tall man who weighs 90 kilos is considered lean, while a 1.5 meter woman who weighs

86 kilos is considered overweight. Thus, the numerical ordering of either of the inputs is not an ordering on the basis of the lean/fat attribute. The ordering of the body-mass-index symbols created by means of computations on the height and weight input symbols is ordered in accord with the relative amount of body fat within a given measured individual (and, statistically, also with this quantity across individuals): As your BMI goes up, so, generally speaking, does the mass of your fat relative to the mass of your muscle and bone. That is why your physician – or even her computer – can use it to judge whether you are anorexic or morbidly obese.

The derivation of a number that crudely represents the relative amount of fat and lean illustrates the distinction between an implicit and an explicit encoding (Marr, 1982). A person's approximate position on a lean–fat dimension is implicit in symbols that specify their weight and height, but not explicit. Computation with the symbols in which the information is implicit generates a symbol in which a crude index of that position is explicit; the real-world position of a person along a lean–fat dimension is given by the position of the corresponding symbol along a symbolic dimension. And this symbolically represented information can be utilized in medical decision making with impact on one's health. Thus, it is a functioning homomorphism (albeit a weak one) constructed by computation. This is very generally the story about what goes on in the brain, the story of what it is about the brain's activity that enables animals to behave effectively in the experienced world.

In the more general and more realistic case, both brains, and computers that are coupled to the external world by devices somewhat analogous to ears and eyes (that is, microphones and cameras), constantly receive a steady stream of signals carrying vast amounts of information about the environment. As explained in the first chapter (Figure 1.4), the information that is behaviorally useful is almost entirely implicit rather than explicit in the first-order sensory signals that the brain gets from the huge array of transducers (sensory receptors) that it deploys in order to pick up information-bearing signals from its environment. The information that the brain needs must be extracted from these signals and made explicit by complex computations constructed from the composition of elementary functions.

Notation

In this section, we elaborate some notation that will prove useful in referring to the different components that together constitute a representation. For the more formally inclined, the notation may also help to make the concept of a representation clearer and more rigorous. Our concept of a representation is closely based on the mathematical concept of a homomorphism, which is important in several branches of mathematics, including algebra, group theory, and the theory of measurement. Historically, the first homomorphism to be extensively developed and recognized as such was the homomorphism between algebra and geometry, to which we will turn when we have developed the notation.[1]

---

[1] Technically, the relation between algebra and geometry is an isomorphism, which is an even stronger form of homomorphism.

A representation is a relationship that holds between two systems, a representing system and a represented system. Let $\hat{G}$ denote a representinG system and $\overleftarrow{D}$ denote the representeD system. Notationally, we distinguish the two systems both by the difference in letters (G vs. D) and by the hat (^) vs. the partial left arrow on top. We also use these latter symbolic devices (hats vs. partial left arrows) to distinguish between what is in the representing system and what is in the represented system. We put what is in the representing system under hats because the representing system we are most interested in is the brain, and also because, in statistical notation, the hat is commonly used to distinguish a symbol for an estimated value from a symbol for the true value of which it is an estimate. This seems appropriate because symbols and processes in the brain are merely approximations to the aspects of the environment that they represent. Things in the represented system have partial left arrows, because in the representations we are most interested in (brain–world representations), these are things out in the world that map to things in the head by way of the brain's many functions for establishing reference to its environment. We imagine the world to stand symbolically to the right of the brain, so processes that map from the world to the brain map leftward.

A representing system, $\hat{G}$, consists of a set $\hat{S}$ of symbols and another set $\hat{P}$ of procedures. 'Procedures' is the word with the most felicitous connotations when discussing symbolic operations, but when the discussion concerns physical "procedures" in the world or in the brain, 'processes' often seems the more appropriate word. Fortunately, it also begins with 'p', so when using words for the things designated by one or another form of our 'p' symbols, we will use 'procedure' or 'process' depending on the context. The procedures/processes – the $\hat{p}$s in the set $\hat{P}$ – are functions on subsets of $\hat{S}$. Thus, for example, if the subset of symbols in $\hat{S}$ encode numerical values, then the numerical ordering procedure is defined on them.

A represented system, $\overleftarrow{D}$, consists of a set $\overleftarrow{E}$ of "entities" – called thus because they need not be physical and the otherwise noncommittal word 'things' tends to connote physicality – and a set, $\overleftarrow{F}$, of functions defined on subsets of $\overleftarrow{E}$. Thus, for example, if the subset is people, then their pairwise ordering by height is a function defined on them. If these heights are appropriately mapped to numerical symbols (if height is appropriately measured), then the numerical ordering procedure defined on the resulting set of symbols and the ordering of the heights to which those symbols refer constitute a homomorphism.

We use the lower-case letters $\hat{s}$, $\hat{p}$, $\overleftarrow{e}$, and $\overleftarrow{f}$ to denote individual entities or functions within these sets of entities or functions.

The inter-system functions (processes) that map from the entities in the represented system to their symbols in the representing system we denote by $\overleftarrow{\Psi}$. The full left arrow reminds us of the direction of these inter-system mappings – from the represented system to the representing system.

Functions that map the other way, from symbols in the represented system to entities in the represented system, we denote by $\overrightarrow{\Psi}$. Again, the direction of the full right arrow reminds us of the direction of the inter-system mapping – from the representing system to the represented system. These functions are "onto" functions for the trivial reason that we restrict the entities in a set denoted by $\overleftarrow{E}$ to only those entities that have a representative (a symbol that refers to them) in the representing system. Thus, *a fortiori* every entity in the set is in the range of the mapping from a set of symbols to the entities they refer to.

Still other inter-system functions map from functions in the represented system to functions in the representing system. These we denote by $\overleftarrow{\Phi}$. It may help to recall at this point that the concept of a function is extremely abstract; it is a mapping from whatever you like to whatever you like. Functions are themselves entities (sets of pairings), so other functions can map from these entities (these functions) to other entities (other functions). In the homey example with which we began our discussion of representation, the ordering function on heights maps to the ordering function on mark elevations.

Finally, functions that map the other way – from functions in the representing system to functions in the represented system – we denote by $\overrightarrow{\Phi}$. Our notation is summarized in Table 4.1, whose columns remind us of the constituents of a representation, to wit, a represented system, a representing system, and the functions that map back and forth between them.

Table 4.1 Notation for representations

Representing system ($\hat{G}$)	$\hat{G} \leftrightarrow \bar{D}$ *functions*	Represented system ($\bar{D}$)
$\hat{S}$ (a set of symbols)	$\overleftarrow{\Psi}$ (the full set of processes/functions that causally connect referents to the symbols for them)	$\bar{E}$ (a set of entities referred to by symbols)
	$\overrightarrow{\Psi}$ (the full set of processes/functions that pick out the referents of symbols)	
$\hat{s}$ (a symbol in a set)	$\overleftarrow{\psi}$ a single function mapping an $\tilde{e}$ to an $\hat{s}$ (a referent to its symbol)	$\tilde{e}$ (an entity in the set of entities referred to by some set of symbols)
	$\overrightarrow{\psi}$ a single function mapping an $\hat{s}$ to an $\tilde{e}$ (a symbol to its referent)	
$\hat{P}$ (the set of procedures that map symbols to symbols)	$\overleftarrow{\Phi}$ (the full set of mappings from procedures in the represented system to corresponding functions in the representing system	$\bar{F}$ (the set of functions to which the set of symbolic processes refer)
	$\overrightarrow{\Phi}$ (the full set of mappings from procedures in the representing system to the corresponding functions in the represented system)	
$\hat{p}$ (a function defined on a set of symbols)	$\overleftarrow{\phi}$ a single function that maps an $\tilde{f}$ to a $\hat{p}$ (e.g., a relation in the represented system to a corresponding relation in the symbolic system)	$\tilde{f}$ (a function defined on the set of entities to which a set of symbols refers)
	$\overrightarrow{\phi}$ a single function that maps a $\hat{p}$ to an $\tilde{f}$	

Both of the functions that map from the representing system to the represented system, $\vec{\Psi}$ and $\vec{\Phi}$, are trivially onto functions (also called surjections or surjective functions), but, generally speaking, they are not one-to-one. They map each symbol or each function to only one entity or only one function (otherwise they wouldn't be functions!), but they can and often do map more than one symbol to the same entity in the experienced world (the represented system). An example of this, much discussed in philosophical circles, is the mapping from 'evening star' and 'morning star' to heavenly bodies.

The evening star is the first star to appear at dusk, while the morning star is the last to disappear at dawn. Of course 'evening star' and 'morning star' are typographic symbols (patterns of ink on a page or pixels on a computer screen), not something in the sky. Moreover, these patterns of ink on paper refer directly not to anything in the sky but to concepts humans have in their heads, the concepts evoked by the language 'first star to appear at night' and 'last star to disappear at dawn.' As it happens – who knew? – the physical entities to which these concepts refer are not stars; they're a *planet*, namely, Venus. Thus, we have in our heads two different symbols that map to the same referent, when we take the represented system to be the visible heavenly bodies. Because not everyone knows this, it is possible for someone to believe things about the evening star that they do not believe about the morning star. That's why this example and others like it (e.g., 'water' and 'H$_2$O') are much discussed in philosophical circles. What this shows about representations is that the validity and therefore the behavioral usefulness of the functions that map symbols to symbols *within* a representing system – the validity of the computations performed on its symbols – depends on the functions that map from the referents to the symbols and back again.

The functions $\vec{\Psi}$ and $\vec{\Phi}$ that map symbols in the representing system to entities in the represented system and procedures in the representing system to functions in the represented system must preserve structure. Let $\hat{s}_{eve}$ be the symbol for the evening star in a set of symbols, $\hat{S}_{dusk\_stars}$, for the stars that one sees come out one by one as dusk falls. Let $\hat{p}_{earlier}$ be a function that pairwise orders the symbols in this set. It is a function of the form: $\hat{p}_{earlier} : \hat{S}_{dusk\_stars} \times \hat{S}_{dusk\_stars} \rightarrow \hat{S}_{dusk\_stars}$, into which we feed pairs composed of the different symbols for different dusk stars and out of which comes one member of each pair. Let $\tilde{e}_{eve}$ be the evening star itself (Kant's "das Ding an sich"), an entity in the set of entities, $\bar{E}_{dusk\_stars}$ composed of the heavenly bodies that become visible as dusk falls. (Unlike the members of $\hat{S}_{dusk\_stars}$, the members of $\bar{E}_{dusk\_stars}$ are not symbols!) Let $\tilde{f}_{earlier}$ be a pairwise ordering of heavenly bodies on the basis of how soon they become visible as dusk falls. In contrast with the arguments of $\hat{p}_{earlier}$, the arguments of $\tilde{f}_{earlier}$ are not symbols, they are the things themselves: $\hat{p}_{earlier}$ and $\tilde{f}_{earlier}$ are distinct functions because they are defined on different domains and have different codomains. This is of course trivial, but the tendency to confuse symbols with the things they refer to is so pervasive that it must be continually cautioned against. It is a serious obstacle to the understanding of representations. Finally, let $\vec{\psi}_{dusk\_stars} : \hat{S}_{dusk\_stars} \rightarrow \bar{E}_{dusk\_stars}$ be the function that picks out the referents (the heavenly bodies) of the symbols in the set of symbols for the dusk stars, and $\vec{\phi}_{ordering} : \hat{p}_{earlier} \rightarrow \tilde{f}_{earlier}$ be the function that maps the ordering function defined on this symbol set to the order function defined on our set of heavenly bodies to which they refer. Now, finally, we can formally define homomorphism: Our two sets ($\hat{S}_{dusk\_stars}$ and $\overleftarrow{E}_{dusk\_stars}$), together with the ordering functions defined on them ($\hat{p}_{earlier}$ and $\overleftarrow{f}_{earlier}$), and the two functions that map between the things with hats and the things with partial left arrows ($\overrightarrow{\psi}_{dusk\_stars}$ and $\overrightarrow{\phi}_{ordering}$) constitute a homomorphism *iff*:

> Premise: if for every other symbol, $\hat{s}_{other}$, in $\hat{S}_{dusk\_stars}$, $\hat{p}_{earlier}$ ($\hat{s}_{eve}$, $\hat{s}_{other}$) → $\hat{s}_{eve}$ (In other words, if for every pairing of $\hat{s}_{eve}$ with any other symbol in the set, $\hat{p}_{earlier}$ gives as output $\hat{s}_{eve}$.)

> Implication: then for every other heavenly body, $\overleftarrow{e}_{other}$ in the set, $\overleftarrow{E}_{dusk\_stars}$, $\overleftarrow{f}_{earlier}(\overleftarrow{e}_{eve}, \overleftarrow{e}_{other})$ → $\overleftarrow{e}_{eve}$. (In other words, then for every pairing of $\overleftarrow{e}_{eve}$ with any other heavenly body, $\overleftarrow{e}_{eve}$ is visible before $\overleftarrow{e}_{other}$.)

This implication need not hold! In specifying the function $\hat{p}_{earlier}$, all we said was that it returns one member of the input pair; we did not say which. If it is the wrong ordering function, it will return the wrong member of each pair, the symbol that refers to a star that appears later, not earlier. (Putting "earlier" in the subscript just serves to distinguish the function from others defined on the set; it hints at but does not in fact specify the mapping.) Thus, if $\hat{p}_{earlier}$ is the wrong ordering function, the mappings from the representing system to the represented system will not preserve structure. The mapping will also not preserve structure if the function $\overrightarrow{\psi}_{dusk\_stars}$ maps $\hat{s}_{eve}$ to the wrong heavenly body, say, Mars or Polaris, instead of Venus. Thus, only when symbols pick out the appropriate referents and only when symbolic operations get mapped to the appropriate non-symbolic relations does one get a homomorphism, a structure-preserving mapping.

Notice that it is perfectly possible for the representing system to correctly represent the evening star as a planet while misrepresenting the morning star as a star, even though both symbols refer to the same entity out there in the world. The representing system may contain or be able to generate a great many correct propositions about both the evening star and the morning star, but not have any proposition that asserts the identity of the entities to which the two different symbols refer. Thus, it may entertain conflicting beliefs about one and the same thing out there in the world because: (1) the beliefs that it entertains are physically realized by symbols for that thing, not by the thing itself; (2) it may have multiple symbols for the same thing, generated by different mapping functions from and back to the thing itself; and (3) homomorphisms depend both on the functions that map from the world to the symbols and back again and on the procedures that operate on those symbols. Thus one may simultaneously believe (1) that water dissolves salt; (2) that H_2O denotes a substance whose molecules are composed of two hydrogen and one oxygen atom; (3) that NaCl denotes a substance whose molecules are composed on one sodium and one chlorine atom; (4) that liquid H_2O does not dissolve NaCl. This phenomenon gives rise to what philosophers call referential opacity: Symbols may not necessarily be substituted for other symbols even though they both refer to the same thing. In our statements about this benighted chemistry student, we cannot replace 'water' with 'liquid H_2O' and remain true to his states of belief.

The Algebraic Representation of Geometry

Pride of place among representations goes to the representation of geometry by algebra. It was the first representation to be recognized as such, and it has been without question the most productive: it has been a powerful engine of mathematical development for centuries. Moreover, it is taught in almost every secondary school, so it is a representation with which most readers are familiar. A quick review of this representation will firm up our grasp on what a representation is.

The algebraic representation of geometry is a relation between two formalized symbolic systems: geometry, which was first formalized by Euclid, and algebra, whose formal development came many centuries later. The formalization of mathematical systems may be seen in retrospect as an essential step in intellectual progress toward understanding the physical realization of computation and reasoning, a central concern of ours. Formalization is the attempt to strip the process of reasoning about some delimited domain down to simple elements and determine what can and cannot be rigorously constructed from those simple foundations. The idea, first seen in Euclid, is to begin with a modest number of definitions (setting up the things to be reasoned about), axioms, and specified rules of deduction, which are chosen to be both intuitively obvious and so simple as to have a machine-like inevitability, a mechanical relation between what goes in and what comes out, what is assumed and what is concluded. The idea is furthermore to develop a rich system that rests securely on these simple foundations. Thus, Euclid in effect gave us the concept of a formal system. Without that concept, we could not have a rigorous concept of representation, because a representation is a relation between two formally described systems.

Euclid's geometry is a symbolic system, because he worked with idealizations like points and lines that have no physical realization, although they can be usefully regarded as abstracting out some formal essence from physical things. A point in Euclid's system has, by definition, no extent, and, a line has no width and may be extended indefinitely. These attributes imply that points and lines are not things in the physical sense of thing, which requires (at least, outside rarified scientific circles) that a physical thing have mass and extension. You cannot make a "point" that has no extension. If you somehow did, you would not be able to verify that you had made it, because something with no extension cannot affect our senses. Similarly, you cannot draw a line with no width, much less extend it a trillion kilometers.

Some simple procedures and instruments (very simple machines) for implementing what we now call models of these procedures (that is, physical realizations) were an essential part of Euclid's system. The drawing of a straight line was one such procedure. The instrument for physically implementing it was an unmarked straight edge. One of Euclid's elementary building blocks (axioms) was that any two points can be joined by a straight line. A model of the line that joins them is constructed by laying a straight edge so that it contacts both points. The line joining the two points consists of all those points that also contact the straight edge. Thus, we are given a procedure for generating a line, given two points (it being tacitly assumed that the points are distinct). The drawing of a circle was another such procedure. Another of Euclid's axioms was that given any straight line segment (line joining two points), a circle can be drawn having the line segment as its radius and one of the points as its center. The instrument for implementing the procedure for constructing a circle from a line segment is the compass. The compass allows us to reproduce line segments; it guarantees that the radii of the circle (all the lines from its center to its circumference) are the same length. Euclid allowed into his system only procedures that could be accomplished with these two instruments.

Euclid built his geometric procedures (functions) by composition: first perform this procedure, then perform another procedure on the results of that procedure, and so on. For example, one of his procedures began with a line and a point not on the line and showed how to construct a line through the point that was parallel to the line. (In later versions of his system, the assertion that this was always possible and that there was only one such line was often taken as the fifth axiom in place of an axiom of Euclid's that had essentially the same role in his system.) So, at this point in the development of the system, we have a draw-a-parallel-line-through-a-point function, which takes a line and a point not on it as inputs and generates as output a line parallel to the input line that passes through the input point.

Euclid showed how to compose this function with a few other simple functions to get a ruler-marking function that took as input a line segment of arbitrary length (the ruler to be marked) and divided it into n equal segments (the units), where n could be any integer greater than one (Figure 4.1). The first procedure was to take the straight edge and lay off a line *not* parallel to the line to be ruled but passing through one of its end points. The second procedure was to take the compass, set it to some length (it does not matter what), and mark off on the just constructed second line n segments, every one of which is equal to the compass length, hence to the length of every other segment. (The compass is the instrument that implements the elementary procedure by which a line segment is made exactly as long as another.) This constructs a final point on the second line, the point at the end of the n equal segments. The third procedure (function) uses the straight edge to draw the line segment from this point to the other end of the line to be ruled. Finally, the draw-a-parallel-line-through-a-point procedure is used to draw a line parallel to this line through each of the points marked off by the compass on the second line. The points where these lines intersect the line to be ruled divide that line into n equal segments. This is an illustration of a geometric function (the ruling function), created through the composition of elementary geometric functions (drawing a line with a straight edge, marking off a segment with a compass). It is defined on the domain of line segments and positive integers greater than 1. Its output is the line segment divided into n equal subsegments.

Part of the reason the representation of geometry by algebra is so instructive is that all of the above seems far removed from algebra, which was developed out of the formalization of procedures for finding specified relations between numbers. The homomorphism between algebra and geometry is far from evident, unlike the homomorphism between height and mark elevations when the usual procedure for marking height is followed. The first to perceive the possibility of an algebraic

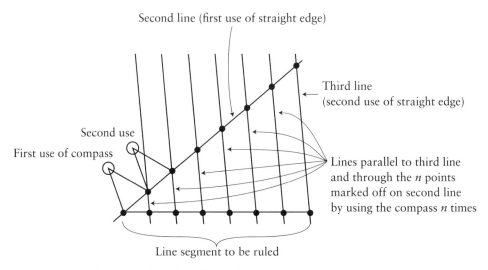

Second line (first use of straight edge)

Third line
(second use of straight edge)

Second use

First use of compass

Lines parallel to third line
and through the *n* points
marked off on second line
by using the compass *n* times

Line segment to be ruled

Figure 4.1   Euclid's procedure for ruling a line segment into *n* equal units (segments).

representation of geometry were Descartes and Fermat, who had the insight at about the same time, but quite independently, in the first half of the seventeenth century. They realized that the points in geometry could be mapped to numerical symbol structures (ordered pairs or triplets of numbers) that we now call vectors and that the lines and other curves in Euclid's geometry (the conic sections) could be mapped to equations (another basic symbolic structure in algebra) and that these mappings could be structure preserving: With the right mappings, algebraic procedures would correctly anticipate the results of the corresponding geometric procedures. The realization that it was possible to construct within algebra a structure-preserving representation of geometry was one of the most important developments in the history of mathematics.

The mapping from points to vectors is effected with the aid of what we now call a Cartesian coordinate framework (Figure 4.2). Vectors are denoted by an ordered list of real numbers enclosed in angle brackets, for example ⟨2.3, 4⟩. The ordering of the numbers within the brackets is critical: this particular vector represents the point that is 2.3 units to the right of the *y*-axis and 4 units above the *x*-axis. Reversing the order of the numbers gives a vector ⟨4, 2.3⟩ that represents a different point, the point 2.3 units above the *x*-axis and 4 units to the right of the *y*-axis.

The use of Cartesian coordinates to assign number pairs to the points in a plane is an example of a function that causally connects referents (the points) to corresponding symbols (the vectors). It is a $\bar{\psi}$ function in our notation for representations (a member of the set $\bar{\psi}$ of all such functions). The infinite set of points in the plane is its domain and the Cartesian product $\mathbb{R} \times \mathbb{R}$ is its range (all possible pairs of real numbers). The mapping is one-one and onto. Every point maps to one and only one vector, and every vector maps to one and only one point.

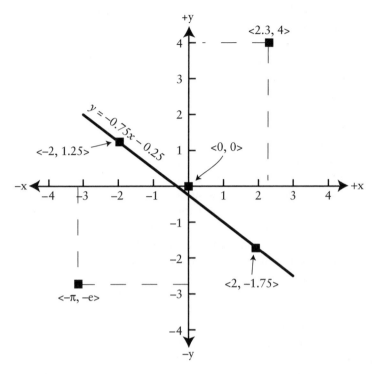

Figure 4.2 Mapping points and lines in the plane to vectors with the aid of Cartesian coordinates.

There would be little motivation for mapping points to vectors if it were not for the fact that lines and curves of geometric interest can be mapped to equations of algebraic interest. This mapping makes geometric procedures, such as the procedure for constructing a line or a circle, representable by algebraic procedures, such as the procedure for finding all the solutions to the corresponding equation. For example, the heavy line slanting downward to the right in Figure 4.2 can be mapped to the simple equation written above it, using the coordinates of any two points that define it. In this case, we use the two points whose coordinates are $\langle x_1 = -2, y_1 = 1.25 \rangle$ and $\langle x_2 = 2, y_2 = -1.75 \rangle$. From these coordinates we can obtain the coefficients, A, B, and C for the following equation, which is called the general equation of a line:

$Ax + By + C = 0$,
where $A = -(y_2 - y_1)$, $B = (x_2 - x_1)$ and $C = x_1y_2 - x_2y_1$

substituting

$-(-1.75 - 1.25)x + (2 - (-2))y + (-2)(-1.75) - (2)(1.25)$ gives
$3x + 4y + 1 = 0$ (1)

This gives us an algebraic procedure that maps from the coordinates of any two points to an equation that holds for all and only the points on the (unique) line that passes through those two points. This equation implements in the algebraic system the function implemented in the geometric system by laying a straight edge so that it contacts two points. That procedure in the geometric system picks out the unique infinite set of points that compose the straight line determined by those two points. The geometric set is composed of all those points that fall on the straight edge. In the algebraic system, solving the equation for that line – finding the unique infinite set of pairs of numbers for which the equation is valid – gives you the coordinates of all and only the points on the line.

The x and y in equation (1) are irrelevant; they are simply place holders for the inputs. What distinguishes one such equation from another are the coefficients. (The realization that it is the coefficients, not the unknowns, that really matter is basically the step required to go from algebra to linear algebra.) Thus, equation (1) maps pairs of unequal 2D vectors to ordered triplets of real numbers that represent the line passing through the two points represented by the two vectors. It is not a procedure (function) that specifies for every distinct line a unique set of coefficients, because when we use as inputs to equation (1) different pairs of 2D vectors from the same line we get different coefficients. They are, however, all scalar multiples of one another: any one is related to any other by a scale factor, a real number that when multiplied times each member of one triplet gives the members of the other triplet.

We can make the procedure (function) specified by equation (1) into one that gives a unique triplet of coefficients for each distinct line by normalizing by one of the coefficients, say B. If we divide all three coefficients by the second, we get a new set of coefficients in which the second coefficient is always 1 (because $B/B = 1$) and so can be ignored. This set of coefficients is unique. Moreover, the negation of the first coefficient of the two coefficients, $-A/B$, gives the slope, a, of the line, and the negation of the second, $-C/B$ gives its intercept, b, in the more familiar equation $y = ax + b$. This two-coefficient symbol, $\langle a, b \rangle$ for a line is useful for many computational purposes, but it cannot represent the lines that are parallel to the y-axis. All the points on any one of these infinitely many lines have the same x coordinates, so the second coefficient in the general equation, B, is zero. If it were not for this problem, we could represent all possible lines with a two-coefficient symbol. However, a two-element symbol (or *data structure*, as we will later call it) does not have enough structure to represent all the lines; for that we need three elements. We can get a unique three-coefficient symbol by dividing the coefficients given us by equation (1) by the sum of the squares of the first two coefficients, $A^2 + B^2$. The resulting coefficient triple is unique: a given line always maps to the same triplet, no matter which two points on the line we take as the inputs to the procedure.

Now, let us take stock, using the notation for representations that we developed above:

- $\bar{D}$, the represented system, is (a portion of) Euclid's system of plane geometry.
- The representing system, $\hat{G}$ is (a portion of) an algebraic system, sometimes called analytic geometry, that is used to represent plane geometry.

- Let P be the set of all points in a plane and $\mathcal{L}$ the set of all possible lines in that plane. Euclid's procedure, $\tilde{f}_{\text{straight-edge}}\colon P \times P \,|\, p \neq p \to \mathcal{L}$ maps all possible pairs of distinct points to all possible lines. It is a function in geometry, which is the represented system.

- $\tilde{\psi}_{\text{Descartes}}\colon P \to \langle \mathbb{R}, \mathbb{R} \rangle$ is Descartes' procedure for mapping points to pairs of real numbers (2D vectors), which we call the coordinates of a point. The mapping is a bijection (one-one and onto): every point maps to a vector and every vector maps to a point. This function maps from the represented system to the representing system.

- $\tilde{\psi}_{\text{Descartes2}}\colon P \times P \,|\, p \neq p \to \langle \mathbb{R}, \mathbb{R} \rangle \times \langle \mathbb{R}, \mathbb{R} \rangle \,|\, \langle r, r \rangle \neq \langle r, r \rangle$ maps all possible pairs of distinct points to all possible pairs of unequal vectors. It, too, maps from the represented system to the representing system.

- Let $\hat{p}_{\text{line}}\colon \langle \mathbb{R}, \mathbb{R} \rangle \times \langle \mathbb{R}, \mathbb{R} \rangle \,|\, \langle r, r \rangle \neq \langle r, r \rangle \to \mathbb{R}, \mathbb{R}, \mathbb{R} \,|\, {\sim}\, (r = r = r)$ be the formula in equation (1), augmented by normalization. This is a function within the representing system (algebra). It maps from all possible pairs of unequal 2D vectors, $\langle \mathbb{R}, \mathbb{R} \rangle \times \langle \mathbb{R}, \mathbb{R} \rangle \,|\, \langle r, r \rangle \neq \langle r, r \rangle$, to all the 3D coefficient vectors in which not all coefficients are equal, $\langle \mathbb{R}, \mathbb{R}, \mathbb{R} \,|\colon (r = r = r) \rangle$.

- $\tilde{\psi}_{\text{line}}\colon P \times P \to \langle \mathbb{R}, \mathbb{R}, \mathbb{R} \,|\colon (r = r = r) \rangle = \hat{p}_{\text{line}} \circ \tilde{\psi}_{\text{Descartes2}}$ is the composition of $\hat{p}_{\text{line}}$ and $\tilde{\psi}_{\text{Descartes2}}$. It maps all line-defining pairs of points to all the corresponding 3D coefficient vectors. It, too, is a bijection: every distinct 3D vector whose dimensions are not all equal represents one and only one line, and every line is represented by one and only one such vector.

- Let $\vec{\phi}_{\text{line}}\colon \tilde{f}_{\text{straight-edge}} \to \hat{p}_{\text{line}}$ be the function that associates Euclid's straight-edge procedure for picking out the line defined by two points with the algebraic procedure for finding the coefficients of the line given the coordinates of two of its points.

- Let $\tilde{\phi}_{\text{line}}\colon \hat{p}_{\text{line}} \to \tilde{f}_{\text{straight-edge}}$ be the function that associates the procedure in the algebraic system of finding solutions to the general equation of a line with the straight-edge procedure for laying off a line in Euclid's system.

- The inverse mappings from 2D vectors to points and from 3D vectors to lines and from the algebraic procedure, $\hat{p}_{\text{line}}$, to the corresponding geometric procedure, $\tilde{f}_{\text{straight-edge}}$, are $\vec{\psi}_{\text{Descartes}}$, $\vec{\psi}_{\text{line}}$ and $\vec{\phi}_{\text{line}}$.

Our algebraic system consists of two sets – the set of all pairs of real numbers and the set of all triplets of (not all equal) real numbers and a procedure for mapping pairs of 2D vectors to 3D vectors. The corresponding portion of Euclid's system also consists of two sets and a procedure – the set of all points in a plane, the set of all lines in that plane, and the procedure for mapping points to lines. These two systems together with the functions that map back and forth between them constitute homomorphisms, because the mappings are structure preserving: a point is on one of Euclid's lines *iff* its coordinates are solutions to the equation for that line (and vice versa).[2] The algebraic structure recapitulates the geometric structure.

---

[2] Because the homomorphism runs both ways, it is actually an isomorphism, which means that either system may be used to represent the other. It is this that makes graphs such a useful tool in mathematical reasoning.

Enlarging the representation

Two points also determine a circle. One serves as the center. The distance between it and the other defines the radius. There is a formula, which we won't burden the reader with, that maps from the coordinates of two points to the coefficients of the general equation of the circle that has one of the points as its center and the distance between the two points as its radius. The general equation for a circle has the form:

$$x^2 + y^2 + Ax + By + C = 0. \tag{2}$$

The solutions to this equation are all and only the coordinates of the points on a particular circle. Which circle is specified by the values of the coefficients, A, B, and C. The x and y are again irrelevant; what distinguishes one circle from another are the coefficients. Thus, the symbol for a circle is also a coefficient triplet (a 3D vector). By their intrinsic form (an ordered triplet of real numbers), these triplets cannot be distinguished from the triplets that are the symbols for lines. If they are to play their proper role in the representing system, however, they must be distinguished from the symbols for lines, because the symbols for lines are used in procedures of the kind specified in equation (1) while the symbols for circles are used in procedures of the kind specified in equation (2). The representing system must have a means of keeping track of which symbols are appropriate to which uses. We discuss the logic for accomplishing this in Chapter 5 (Symbols) and in Chapter 9 (Data Structures).

When we add to the representing system the functions that map coordinate pairs to circles, we enrich its capabilities. Now, we can answer geometric questions such as: Does this line intersect that circle? Is this line tangent to this circle, and, if so, at what point? The answer to the first geometric question translates into the algebraic question whether there are two vectors that are solutions to both the equation for the given line and to the equation of the given circle. If so, the line intersects the circle at the two points whose coordinates are those two vectors. If the line is tangent to the circle, there will be only one vector that is a solution to both equations, and that vector is the coordinates of the point at which the line is tangent to the circle. Here, again, we see that the mappings back and forth between the geometric system and the algebraic system are structure preserving. Indeed, Euclid's entire system can be algebraically represented. Table 4.2 lays out some of the foundations of this representation.

The function of a representation is to allow conclusions about the represented system to be drawn by operations within the representing system. A famous example of this use of the algebraic representation of geometry within pure mathematics concerns the geometric question whether there exists an effective geometric procedure for squaring the circle. The question was posed as early as 500 BC. It remained unsolved until 1882 – and not for lack of trying. Many top-of-the-line mathematicians had a go at it in the 24 centuries during which it remained unsolved. An effective geometric procedure is (by definition) one that can be carried out using only a compass and a straight edge (an unmarked ruler) and that gives

Table 4.2 Algebraic representation of geometry

Algebraic system ($\hat{G}$)	Geometric system ($\breve{D}$)
Algebraic symbols ($\hat{S}$)	**Geometric entities ($\breve{E}$)**
Vectors $\mathbf{r} = \langle r_1, r_2 \rangle$	Points
Pairs of vectors $\overleftrightarrow{AB} = (\mathbf{r}_1, \mathbf{r}_2)$	Line segments
Real number triples (coefficients) (r_1, r_2, r_3)	Lines
The positive real numbers, $\mathbb{R}^+$	Distances
Real number triples (coefficients) (r_1, r_2, r)	Circles
The real numbers, $\mathbb{R}$	Angles
Logical 1 and 0	Truth and falsehood
Algebraic functions ($\hat{P}$)	**Geometric functions ($\overleftarrow{F}$)**
$\langle A_1, B_1 \rangle = ?\langle A_2, B_2 \rangle$ where A and B are normalized coefficients in equation for a line	Are two lines parallel?
$\|\mathbf{r}_2 - \mathbf{r}_1\|_1 = ?\|\mathbf{r}_2 - \mathbf{r}_1\|_2$	Are two line segments equal?
$\mathbf{r} + \mathbf{r}_t$, where $\mathbf{r}_t$ is a translation vector	Translation
$\mathbf{r}\mathbf{R}$, where $\mathbf{R}$ is a rotation matrix	Rotation

an exact result. Thus, the problem in squaring the circle is to specify a geometric procedure by which one can use a compass and straight edge to construct a square whose area is exactly equal to the area of a given circle – or else to prove that there cannot be such a procedure. The representation of geometry by algebra is so tight that it was first proved that the circle could be squared if-and-only-if π is the solution to an algebraic equation. Then, in 1882, Lindeman proved that π is not the solution to any algebraic equation, thereby proving that the circle cannot be squared.

The algebraic representation of geometry is the foundation of all computer graphics, illustration software, and computer-aided design software. Every time a computer draws a line or circle or more complex curve on its screen, it makes use of the algebraic representation of geometry. There can be no doubt about the utility of this representation. If ever there was a functioning homomorphism, it is this one.

The behavioral evidence from the experimental study of insect navigation implies that there is a comparable representation even in the minute brains of ants and bees (Gallistel, 1998; 2008). The challenge for neuroscience is to identify the physical realization of the brain's symbols for points (locations) and oriented lines (courses between locations) and the neurobiological mechanisms that operate on these symbols.

5

Symbols

Symbols – at least those of interest to us – are physical entities in a physically realized representational system. The effectiveness of that system depends strongly on the properties of its symbols. Good physical symbols must be distinguishable, constructable, compact, and efficacious.

Physical Properties of Good Symbols

Distinguishability

Symbols must be distinguishable one from another because the symbol that refers to one thing must be handled differently at some point in its processing from a symbol that refers to another thing. This can only happen if the symbols are distinguishable on some basis. The properties that allow symbols to be distinguished in the course of computation – without regard to their referents (that is, their semantics) – are their syntactic properties. Syntactic properties derive from two aspects of a symbol: its intrinsic (physical) form and/or its location in space or in time. The symbol '1' differs from the symbol '0' in its form. Here and in the rest of the chapter when we enclose a symbol in single quotes, we refer to the pattern of ink on paper or the difference in electrical potential at a bit location in a bit register – the physical instantiation of the symbol – not the entity to which it refers. Thus the '1' and '0', 'V' and 'I', and the nucleotide sequences GAT (guanine, adenine, thymine) and CTG (cytosine, thymine, guanine) are distinguishable one from the other on the basis of their form, without regard to their location. On the other hand, there is no telling 'V' qua letter of the alphabet from 'V' qua Roman numeral for 5 on the basis of form alone. And there is no telling apart the triplet '2,5,2' qua symbol for a line from '2,5,2' qua symbol for a circle from '2,5,2' qua symbol for a point in a three-dimensional space. These formally identical numeral triplets are three different symbols that must be processed in different ways, but they cannot be distinguished on the basis of their intrinsic form. Similarly, there is no telling the nucleotide sequence TAT on the coding strand of DNA from the same sequence on the non-coding strand, even though the one is a symbol for the amino acid tyrosine, while the other is not. These two codons are distinguishable only by their location within the double helix, not by their form.

Because they are physical entities, symbols have a location in space and time. More often than not, there are other symbols surrounding or bracketing them in space and/or preceding and following them in time, creating a spatio-temporal context. Their context – where they are in space and time relative to other symbols – very often serves to distinguish one symbol from another, as in the following examples:

(1) 'I had to **check** my watch.'
      'I wrote a **check** to the bank.'

(2) 'Kate is **70 inches high**.'
      'Terrance is **70 inches high**.'

(3) 'MLCCXXVI'
      'MLCCXXIV'

In the first example, 'check' is a symbol for an action in the first sentence and a symbol for a thing in the second. These are different symbols but identical in their form. They are distinguished from one another by the spatial context in which they occur. If the sentences were spoken rather than written, the spoken words would again be identical in form (they are homophones, pronounced the same), but they would be distinguished one from another by their temporal context (the words that are spoken before and after). The second example is subtler, because the two formally identical symbols are different tokens for the same type. The first symbol refers to the height of Kate, while the second refers to the height of Terrance. They are not one and the same symbol because they have different referents, but their forms are identical. They are distinguished only by their spatial context (if written) or temporal context (if spoken). In the third example, whether 'I' is a symbol for a number that is to be added to the numbers represented by the other symbols in the string of Roman numerals or subtracted depends on whether it occurs before or after the symbol for the next larger symbolized number. This is an example of the positional notation principle. In Roman numerals, the principle is used sporadically, whereas in Arabic numerals, the principle that the significance of a given symbol form depends on its position in the symbol string is the foundation of the entire system for constructing symbols to represent numbers: The rightmost '9' in '99' represents 9 while the leftmost '9' represents 90. It is context not form that distinguishes these instances of the form '9'.

In the memory of a conventional computer, symbols are mostly distinguished by their spatial context, that is, by where they are, rather than by their form. The byte '01000001' represents the printed character 'A' in some memory locations, while it represents the number 65 in others, but this cannot be discerned from the byte itself; its form is the same in the different locations. The distinguishability of the symbol for 'A' from the symbol for 65 depends on location in memory, which is to say on spatial context.

This principle has long been recognized in neuroscience. It was originally called the law of specific nerve energies, but is now called place coding. Place coding means that it is the locus of activity that determines the referent of neural activity, not the form of that activity. Activity in the visual cortex is experienced as light, no matter how that activity is produced, and no matter what its spatio-temporal form (how the action potentials are distributed in space and time). It is, of course, usually produced by light falling on the retina, but it can be produced by pushing on the eyeball hard enough to excite the optic nerve mechanically. In either case, it will be experienced as light. Similarly, activity in the auditory cortex will be experienced as sound, no matter what the spatio-temporal form of that activity. Most basically, an action potential is simply an action potential. Different messages are not encoded by varying the form of the action potentials that carry them from the sense organs to the brain. They are distinguished by spatial-temporal context: which axons they travel in (spatial context) and where they fall in time relative to the action potentials that precede and follow them (temporal context).

Constructability

The number of symbols actually realized in any representation at any one time will be finite, because a physically realized system has finite resources out of which to construct its symbols. The number of atoms in a brain is a large number, but it is a finite number. It seems unlikely that a brain could use more than a fraction of its total atoms for symbols. Moreover, it seems unlikely that it could make one symbol out of a single atom. Thus, a brain may contain a large number of symbols, but nothing close to an infinite number of them. On the other hand, the number of symbols that might have to be realized in a representational system with any real power is for all practical purposes infinite; it vastly exceeds the number of elementary particles in the universe, which is roughly 10^{85} (or 2^{285}), give or take a few orders of magnitude. This is an example of the difference between the infinitude of the possible and the finitude of the actual, a distinction of enormous importance in the design of practical computing machines. A computing machine can only have a finite number of actual symbols in it, but it must be so constructed that the set of possible symbols from which those actual symbols come is *essentially infinite*. (By 'essentially infinite' we will always mean greater than the number of elementary particles in the universe; in other words, not physically realizable.) This means that the machine cannot come with all of the symbols it will ever need already formed. It must be able to construct them as it needs them – as it encounters new referents.

This principle should be kept in mind when considering the many suggestions that the brain represents different entities by means of innate neural circuitry that causes a single "gnostic" neuron (or in some schemes a population of neurons) to be activated (cf. Konorski, 1948, for the term "gnostic neuron"). The idea is that these neurons are selectively tuned to their referents by means of the specific structure of the hierarchical neural circuitry that connects them to sensory input (e.g., to the retina). These stories about the neurobiological realization of percepts are sometimes called "grandmother neuron" schemes, because they imply that the symbol for your grandmother is a neuron that is "tuned to" (selectively activated by) your grandmother. The term "grandmother neuron" is quasi-satirical. It calls attention to the problem we are here discussing, namely, that this approach to symbolization assumes an unrealistic amount of pre-specified circuit structure. Suppose your grandmothers die before you are born; will you go around your whole life with grandmother neurons that are never activated? This rhetorical question emphasizes the fact that you need a scheme that constructs symbols for your grandmothers if and when you actually have them. Whatever the internal symbol is that specifically refers to your grandmother (or your car, your couch, bicycle, girlfriend, and so on ad infinitum), it must have been constructed for that purpose when the need to refer to that entity arose. These symbols cannot have been already physically realized and assigned in advance to their referents via some prewired mapping function from sensory input indicative of that referent to the activation of the neuron specific to that referent.

When the grandmother neuron scheme is applied to the representation of quantitative variables (for example, numerosity), it assumes that there are neurons innately dedicated to the representation of specific quantities (Dehaene & Changeux, 1993; Nieder, Diester, & Tudusciuc, 2006). The brain learns to respond appropriately to a given quantity by associating neurons tuned to that quantity with neurons whose activation leads to a response (see Chapter 15). These models for how the brain symbolizes to-be-remembered quantities assume that the brain comes with a set of different symbols (different neurons) for different quantities already physically realized (pretuned to the quantity they are to refer to). This seems unlikely from a computational perspective. There are very many different possible quantities that a brain may have to represent and very many different instances of the same quantity. Consider how many different instances of the discrete quantity 2 a brain may have to deal with – how many different tokens for the type 2. Is the brain like some old lead-type print shop, which had to have on hand as many instances (tokens) of the symbol 'e' as would ever have to be set in one page? Or can it create tokens for 2 as the need arises, as in a computer? The same consideration arises with all of the quantities that a brain needs to represent. It is apt to encounter many different instances of durations of approximately 10 seconds and many different instances of distances of approximately 5 meters. It would seem that it must have a means of constructing symbols for these different instances of a given quantity as the need arises, so that it uses physical resources to store only the information it has actually gained from experience. It does not have physical memory resources pre-specified for every different piece of information it might acquire. We will return to this consideration repeatedly. As we will see in Chapters 14 and 15, it is rarely considered by neural network modelers.

Compactness

The basic form of its symbols, the elements out of which they are constructed, and the means by which one symbol is distinguished from another are considerations of great importance in the design of a computing device. Some designs make much more effective use of physical resources than do others. Suppose, for example, that we want to construct symbols to represent different durations (elapsed intervals, something we know brains routinely represent, see Chapter 12). The symbols are to be constructed by placing marbles into rows of hemispherical holes on a board. One principle that we might use to map from distinguishable durations to distinguishable symbols is to have each row be the symbol for a different duration and increment the number of marbles in a row by one for each additional second of duration symbolized by that row. We call this the *analog principle* because there is a natural ordering on the symbols (the length of the row of marbles) that corresponds to the ordering of the durations they encode: An interval that lasted 3 seconds is symbolized by a row 3 marbles long; an interval that lasted 1,004 seconds is symbolized by a row of 1,004 marbles. We are immediately struck by the discouraging size of the bag of marbles that we will need and the length of the board. The problem with this design is that the demand on these physical resources grows in proportion to the number of durations that we want to distinguish.

The same resources can be put to much better use by a symbol-construction scheme in which the number of distinguishable symbols grows exponentially with the physical resources required. (Put another way, the physical resources required grow logarithmically with the number of distinguishable symbols.) With a row of only 10 holes, and using at most 10 marbles, we can create $2^{10} = 1,024$ different symbols, if we use the binary encoding of number function. There are 1,024 different patterns of '1's and '0's that may be created in a string 10 binary digits long. We can put a marble in a given position in the row of 10 holes just in case the binary encoding of the number of seconds of duration has a 1 in that position and leave the hole unoccupied just in case the binary encoding of a duration has a 0 in that position. This scheme makes exponentially more effective use of physical resources in the creation of symbols for numerical quantity. This means that the more different symbols we need, the greater the factor by which the second design is superior to the first design. If we need a thousand distinguishable symbols for quantities, it is 100 times more efficient; if we need a million distinguishable symbols, it is more than 50,000 times more efficient.

Again, it is instructive to consider the import of this consideration in a neurobiological context. Two encoding schemes account for most of the proposals for how neural signaling distinguishes different states of the world. The first proposal is *rate coding*: different values along some dimension of experience, for example, the severity of a painful stimulus, are represented by different rates of firing in the axons that transmit pain signals to the brain. The second proposal is *place coding*: different states of the world are represented by the firing of different neurons. We touched on this above when we mentioned schemes in which different neurons are tuned to different numerosities, so that the locus (place) of neural activity varies as a function of the number of items in a set. There is abundant electrophysiological evidence in support of both of these schemes. Thus, it seems almost certain that for some purposes nervous tissue does transiently represent states of the world in both these ways. However, as a general story about symbolization in memory and communication between processing loci, both of these schemes fail the compactness test: the demand on physical resources (spikes and neurons) is proportionate to the number of different entities for which different symbols or signals are needed.

Indeed, this is quite generally true for analog symbols, symbols in which the quantity or intensity of symbol stuff grows in proportion to the size of the message set that a given quantity of symbol stuff can represent or transmit.

Consider, for example, the use of action potentials (spikes) to transmit quantitative information. The most commonly considered encoding is rate coding. In a rate code, it is only the number of spikes within some unit of time that matters; the intervals between spikes within that unit of time and/or which spikes are in which axons does not matter. Of course, the brain cannot, in general, wait very long to get the message. Thus, the unit of time over which it counts spikes cannot be large. Let us take one second as the unit, for the purpose of illustration. By a generous estimate, a neuron can fire 1,000 spikes in one second. (A more reasonable estimate would be nearer 100.) Thus, using a rate code, one neuron can transmit at most 1,000 different messages in one second. The number of spikes that will on average be transmitted within the counting interval grows in proportion to the number of messages that can be transmitted. If 1,000 messages can be transmitted and the different messages are all transmitted with equal frequency, the average number of spikes per second would be 500. (Average spiking rates that high are never in fact observed.) Suppose we use a time code instead, that is, a code in which the atomic elements are the intervals between spikes, and that the mechanism that receives the spikes can only distinguish two interspike intervals, 10 ms and 30 ms. Thus, like the binary code, this time code has only two atomic (irreducible) symbols. Different messages are represented by different sequences of these two interspike intervals within any one-second interval. If we assume that the encoding of the messages is maximally efficient, so that on average there are equal numbers of the two intervals per message, then one neuron can transmit 1,000 ms/20 ms = 50 bits per second, that is $2^{50} = 10^{15}$ different messages in one second. The average number of spikes per second will therefore be a much more realistic 50 spikes per second (rather than 500 as in the rate code). This method of using spikes to transmit messages is about 12 orders of magnitude more efficient and demands an average firing rate that is an order of magnitude less than using a rate encoding. It requires much less in the way of physical resources (energy and time expended in transmitting spikes) than does the rate code. This is a staggering difference in efficiency. It brings into strong relief the fact that we do not in fact know what the coding scheme for information transmission by means of spikes is. The rate code is an untested assumption, which has been made so often by so many different researchers that it has come to be taken as an established fact. (For a state-of-the-art analysis of this fundamental issue, and a review of the modest amount of relevant experimental research, see Rieke et al., 1997.)

We know from behavioral reaction time studies that the assumption of a one-second counting interval is too generous. Sports as we know them would be impossible if it took the nervous system that long to send one message. A commonly suggested variant of the rate code assumes that the nervous system uses many axons in parallel to send its messages. In this case, again assuming a maximal firing rate of 1,000 spikes per second, 1,000,000 messages can be sent in 30 ms if one has 30,000+ axons at one's disposal. But here, again, the physical resources required

– the number of axons – increases in proportion to the size of the set of possible messages. By using time encoding on each axon and a binary code across the axons, one could do the same job with only 20 axons.

The question of the coding scheme by which spikes transmit information has been discussed by neuroscientists for decades, albeit without resolution. By contrast, the question of the coding scheme by which the information is carried forward in time to be used to inform behavior in the indefinite future has not been discussed at all. In other words, the question of the code used by neural signals is a recognized question, but the question of the code used by neural symbols is not, probably because there is so much uncertainty about what the neurobiological realization of symbols is. If, as is widely assumed, the information gained from past experience is carried forward in time by means of changes in synaptic conductance, then one cannot avoid a number of questions. How is information encoded into those changed conductances? Is the symbolization compact? Does the number of synapses required grow in proportion to the size of the set of messages that may need to be carried forward? Or does it grow in proportion to the logarithm of the size of the message set? These questions are of fundamental importance to our understanding how the brain computes, because symbols are literally the stuff of computation. Computational mechanisms take symbols as their inputs and produce symbols as their outputs.

Efficacy

Because symbols are the stuff of computation, they must be physically efficacious within the mechanisms that implement basic functions. That is, the outputs produced by computational mechanisms (the physical realizations of functions) must be determined by their inputs. The two binary patterns of voltage levels (the low and high levels) that are entered into the two registers of a solid-state machine that implements the basic functions of arithmetic must determine the voltage pattern that appears at the output. If one neuron is the symbol for one number and another neuron is the symbol for another number, then we need to understand how these two neurons can serve as inputs to a neurobiological mechanism that will produce as its output the neuron that symbolizes the number that is the sum of those two numbers. When we put it this way – when we focus on causal efficacy – we realize that it does not make sense to say that a neuron is the symbol for something, because neurons do not combine to produce other neurons. It would make sense to say that activity in the first neuron is the symbol for one number and activity in the other neuron is the symbol for the other number (place coding of number). Then, we can readily imagine synaptic mechanisms that would combine these activities to generate activity in another neuron, the activity of which was the symbol for the sum. However, neural activity (spiking) exists in order to transmit information from place to place, from one processing locus to another. It is singularly ill suited to serve as a mechanism for preserving large amounts of information for indefinite temporal durations (we return to this issue in Chapters 10, 14, and 16). To treat spiking activity as symbols is to confuse signals with symbols.

The only mechanism that has been widely entertained as the mechanism by which information is preserved for later use in the indefinite future is a change in synaptic conductance. We just saw that there has been no consideration of how such changes might encode, for example, quantitative information (durations, distances, numerosities, and so on). There has also been no attention to the question of how such changes could determine the course of combinatorial operations, such as the arithmetic operations. If one pattern of synaptic conductances symbolizes one previously experienced interval and another pattern of conductance in a different population of synapses symbolizes a another interval experienced on a different occasion, what is the mechanism that combines those two patterns of synaptic conductances to determine a pattern of synaptic conductances that symbolizes the sum or difference of those two remembered intervals? We know that brains do compute the sums and differences of separately experienced temporal intervals (see Chapter 12). When we consider how hypothesized physical changes in neural tissue can carry forward in time an encoding of the durations of two separately experienced intervals, we must also ask how those changes could become causally effective in the mechanisms that can compute the sums and ratios of the encoded intervals? There has to be a story about how these symbols (these information-encoding changes in structure) become physically effective within computational mechanisms.

Symbol Taxonomy

Preparatory to discussing the procedures that operate on symbols in the next chapter, we develop a simple taxonomy:

- atomic data
- data strings
- nominal symbols
- encoding symbols
- data structures

Atomic data are the irreducible physical forms that can be constructed and distinguished in a representing system. These data alone or in collections can become information-bearing symbols when and if they are given a referent and constrained to play a specific role in computations. Typical examples of atomic data are the 2 bit values used in computers, the 10 digits used in numbers, the 26 letters used in words, and the 4 nucleotides used in DNA.

Data strings are the ordered forms composed of one or more of these atomic elements: a sequence of bits, a sequence of numerals, a sequence of digits, a sequence of nucleotides. The ordering allows for the compact symbols discussed above. A mechanism of concatenation for forming strings (or conceivably, structures with a more complex topology than that of a linear sequence) appears unavoidable. A machine with a very rich store of symbols must have a means of forming them out of a not too numerous store of atomic data. No language in the world has a word for the message, "After the circus, I'm going to the store to get a quart of skim milk." No system for representing discrete numbers represents 1,342,791 with a single digit or number name. Minimizing the number of atomic data is desirable in any symbol system as it reduces the complexity of the machinery required to distinguish these data. This is why computers use just two atomic data and likely why nucleotide sequences use only four.

The need for string formation and string preservation is itself a strong constraint on the physical realization of a computing machine. The ordering of the elements in the string (or more generally, the topology of the elements, how they connect one with another) must be reflected in the physical realization of the symbols in a manner that makes this topology constructable and causally effective. That is, it must be possible for the mechanisms of computation to form string structures and to be causally affected by the string structures. We see this principle at work clearly in the structure of the double helix, where the elements (nucleotides) out of which coding forms (codons) are constructed are placed in sequence, as are the codons themselves. In both cases, the sequence is (largely) determinative of the structure of the protein coded for.[1] Giving the elements a topological structure, so that their order or arrangement matters, is exactly what the analog principle does not allow for. When the atomic data are simply "placed in a bag" to form symbols, the only way to distinguish one symbol from another is to count the number of each element. As seen above, this is simply too inefficient to compose the number of symbols that a brain must represent.

Nominal symbols are data strings that map to their referents in the represented system in an arbitrary way, a mapping that is not constrained by any generative principles. The Arabic digits, for example, are nominal symbols for the numbers that they represent. There is no principle that dictates that 2 should be represented by '2.' The ink pattern '2' is not an instance of two-ness. The same is not true for the Roman numeral 'II', as it can be decoded by the principle used for constructing the Roman numerals. We call symbols such as '2' nominal symbols because their relation to their referent is arbitrary in the same way that names are arbitrarily related to their referents. There was nothing about the horse named Barbaro that dictated that his name be 'Barbaro'. If we overlook sex typing in given names, there is nothing about the men named John that dictates or even suggests that 'John' should be their name.

Encoding symbols, by contrast, are related to their referents by some organized and generative principles. For example, the binary number encoding procedure dictates that '10' is the binary symbol for 2. (The elements, '0' and '1' in this data string are, on the other hand, nominal symbols for 0 and 1.) Encoding schemes for mapping from referents to their symbols always have a purely nominal component, namely the process that distinguishes the atomic data. In the binary number system, the manner in which the numbers map to the symbols that refer to them is intimately connected to the manner in which those symbols are processed. This need not be the case, however. A retail store may keep its inventory by recording the

---

[1]   Alternative post-transcriptional splicings make it not completely determinative in some cases.

manufacturer's serial numbers for the items it has in stock. The serial numbers are usually strings composed of digits and letters. Inquiry generally reveals that the manufacturer has a system for determining the string that will be assigned to a particular item. The system may use certain letters to specify certain features of the item and the numbers may be assigned on the basis of the item's serial order of manufacture. However, the attributes of the item and its manufacturing history that determine its serial number need not be entities in the retailer's represented system. Thus, the elements within the symbol string may have no meaning so far as the retailer's representing system is concerned. In the retailer's representation, the elements of which the symbol strings are composed have no referential substructure and no syntactic roles; they serve only to differentiate one symbol (and, hence, its referent) from another symbol (with a different referent).

Data structures, which are often called expressions in the philosophical and logical literature, are symbol strings (or, possibly, structures with a more complex topology than that of a one-dimensional string) that have referents by virtue of the referents of the symbols out of which they are composed *and* the arrangement of those symbols. For example, the referent of the Cartesian vector ⟨−2.5, 3.01⟩, that is, the point to which it refers, derives from the referents for the two numbers of which the string is composed (the denoted distances from the axes of a set of Cartesian coordinates on a plane) *and* from the order of those two numbers, which comes first and which second. Similarly, the event referred to by 'John hit Mary' derives from the referents of 'John', 'hit', and 'Mary', but also from the ordering of these words; 'Mary hit John' refers to a different event. We devote an entire chapter to describing the physical realization of data structures in a conventional computer (Chapter 9).

It is difficult to distinguish sharply between encoding symbols and data structures on purely formal grounds, because an encoding symbol is a kind of minimal data structure. In both cases, there must be a body of principles (usually called a grammar) that constrains the construction of the expressions for a given referent and makes it generative. The generativity is what makes it possible for finite symbolic resources to pick out any referent from an infinitude of possible referents. The distinction between encoding symbols and data structures (symbolic expressions) generally arises from a structural feature of the system that physically implements representations. In a computer, there are only two atomic data ('0' and '1'). The rules for encoding a magnitude into strings of these data create the first higher-level unit, the word, which is the lowest level of symbol in which a programmer ordinarily works. The number of possible symbols at this level is extremely large (2^{64} in a 64-bit machine) because the number of distinguishable symbols needed at this level is extremely large. Data structures are composed of these symbolic units (these words).

One sees the same necessity for a hierarchical system of generative symbolic units at work in the structure of the DNA code. The number of possible symbols at the lowest level is only $4^3 = 64$, which is the number of possible codons, the lowest level of molecular symbols that have referents. Codons, which are triplets of neucleotides (the primitive data), refer to amino acids, but there are only 20 amino acids, so the codon code is degenerate; more than one codon may refer to the same amino acid. The number of possible symbols that may be constructed from the codons is extremely large because the number of possible referents, that is, possible proteins, is extremely large. The number of possible genetic data structures (genetic cascades) is vastly larger still.

Summary

If we take seriously the idea that the brain represents aspects of the experienced world, and if we are interested in how it does so, then we must be concerned to understand the physical properties of the brain's symbols. What properties endow them with the essential properties of good symbols: distinguishability, constructability, compactness, and efficacy?

What makes one symbol distinguishable from another? Is it the form? Or the spatio-temporal context? '1' and '0' are distinguished by their form, but '01000001' qua symbol for the letter 'A' is distinguished from '01000001' qua symbol for 65 only by its (relative) location in the memory of a computer, that is, only by spatial context. In known artificial and biological representational systems, the number of symbols distinguishable on the basis of form alone is small. The ability of the system to distinguish between symbols rests largely on the utilization of spatio-temporal context: symbols for different entities are distinguished by their location in space and time relative to other symbols. The binary representation of number is a simple instance: there are only two distinguishable forms, '0' and '1'. These two forms are used to construct symbol strings in which the power of 2 to which a '1' refers is determined by where it falls within the string. The all-or-none law for the propagation of an action potential suggests that neural signaling also rests on the principle that at the most elementary level, the distinguishable forms are the minimum possible, namely, two; there either is an action potential or there is not (within some symbolically significant interval).

The number of entities for which a powerful representational system might need a symbol is infinite (greater than the number of elementary particles in the knowable universe). But any physically realized system can only devote finite resources to the realization of its symbols. Therefore, a representational system cannot have pre-specified symbols for all the entities for which it may need symbols. That is why it is essential that there be a scheme for constructing symbols as the need for them arises. An elementary manifestation of this problem and this solution is the digital camera. The number of images for which it might need a symbol is infinite, but the number of images for which it will actually need a symbol is finite. The camera constructs a symbol for an image during the interval when the shutter is open. If it is a six-megapixel camera, the symbol consists of 6 million 24-bit binary numbers. The number of different symbols of this kind (the number of different pictures that may be taken with a 6-megapixel camera) is infinite, just as is the number of possible images. But, of course, the number of different pictures that even the most avid photographer will take is finite, because there are only 2,680,560,000 seconds in a long lifetime, and no one takes a picture every second of every day. The ratio of this number to the number of possible pictures, that is, the ratio $2{,}680{,}560{,}000/(2^{24})^{6{,}000{,}000}$ is effectively 0. (If you put this computation into

Matlab™, you get 0, because it codes $(2^{24})^{6,000,000}$ as infinite.) Thus, there is literally no comparing the number of pictures that a person could actually take with a 6-megapixel camera to the number of pictures that could in principle be taken with that camera. The camera can represent an infinite range of possibilities with finite resources, because it constructs its symbols on demand. The possibilities are infinite, but the actualities are finite.

For related reasons, symbols should be compact: the scheme for constructing symbols on demand should be such that the physical resources devoted to the realization of a symbol should increase only as the logarithm of the number of possible entities to which it could refer. This consideration makes commonly considered neurobiological coding schemes, such as rate coding and place coding, improbable as general solutions. In both of these schemes, the number of physical elements (spikes or neurons) required increases linearly with the number of messages in a set of possible messages. By contrast, the number of possible pictures that a digital camera can take grows exponentially with the number of pixels. That is why a small and cheap camera can take infinitely more pictures than any one will ever in fact take (indeed, infinitely more than all of humanity will ever take). Similarly, the number of polypeptides or proteins that a sequence of codons can code for grows exponentially with the number of codons (as the nth power of 20), which is why there is literally no limit to the number of possible proteins (or polypeptides) or humans and animals.

What the bit patterns from a camera and the codon sequences in a DNA molecule (double helix) also have in common is that they are physically efficacious within a computational system. The outcome of decoding procedures depends on their form, that is, on the arrangement of their elements. This property is absent in a number of coding schemes in the connectionist (neural network) literature. Modelers do not always distinguish between their own ability to determine different states of the world by examining the state of the network (which neurons are active and which are not) and the question of whether the information the modeler gleans from the different states of the network is physically efficacious within computational operations relevant to the supposedly represented system, and, if so, how. Whenever information about the world is implicit in the intrinsic properties of individual elements rather than explicit in their readable activity or structure, the question arises how that information can affect the course of computations, because the other parts of the system do not have access to the intrinsic properties of the elements. The sequence of codons in a DNA molecule is readable; it determines the sequence of amino acids in a polypeptide or protein. The fact that a hypothesized neuron in a timing network reaches its peak firing rate only 5 seconds after an impulse input is not readable by other neurons (see later Chapter 15). The modeler knows what the intrinsic properties of the different neurons are, but the other neurons in the system do not. When the activity of a neuron is said to code for something, one must ask how it codes for it. By what mechanism does that activity enter into computational operations in an appropriate way?

Finally, consideration of the structure of diverse symbol systems leads to a hierarchical taxonomy of symbols: At the bottom are the atomic elements, like the 4 nucleotides in the DNA code and the '1' and '0' in the codes used by computers.

These may or may not have referents. These elements are used to construct data strings, like the codons (nucleotide triplets) in DNA or the 8-, 16-, 32-, or 64-bit words in a computer. Data strings are typically the lowest level at which reference is assigned. The assignment may be essentially arbitrary, in which case the data strings become nominal symbols (literally, names). Or, there may be an encoding scheme in which a rule-governed process assigns data strings to the entities they represent. The binary encoding of number is an example of the latter. In such cases, the elements of the string may themselves have referents. In the binary scheme, the referent of an atomic symbol ('1' or '0') within the string refers to the presence or absence of a given power of 2 in a sum of powers of 2. Which power it refers to depends on its position in the string. We call symbols generated by an encoding scheme encoding symbols.

Finally, either nominal or encoding symbols (data strings to which referents have been assigned) are formed into data structures (aka expressions) that refer both by virtue of the referents of the constituent symbols and by their arrangement in time and or space.

6

Procedures

We now have a clearer understanding of the properties of physical symbols. In the represented system, $\bar{D}$, the entities can be anything, real or imagined, but in the representing system, $\hat{G}$, the symbols must be physically instantiated and distinguishable forms. We now need to understand the properties of the functions in $\hat{P}$ that play a role in physically realized representational systems.

As our understanding of symbols in $\hat{S}$ changed when we considered desirable physical properties, so must our understanding of the functions in $\hat{P}$. In this chapter we explore the properties of computable and physically realizable functions in a representational system. Computing functions is what allows functions to be put to productive use, just as distinguishing symbols and establishing referents for them is what allows symbols to be put to productive use.

Algorithms

As discussed in Chapter 3, function definitions may establish that a mapping exists from members of the domain to members of the codomain without necessarily giving a method or process to determine the output for a given input.

A clear and unambiguous method or process that allows one to determine robotically the input/output mappings of a function is called an *algorithm*. For example, the long multiplication method that grade school children are taught is an algorithm to determine the symbol for the product of two numbers. We saw some geometric algorithms in Chapter 4, such as the algorithm for determining a line segment that is $1/n$ of another line segment, where n is any integer (Figure 4.1).

To take a common example, let's say you have an endless supply of coins, denominated 25 cents, 10 cents, 5 cents, and 1 cent. Let's define a "change-giving" function that maps an amount of money 99 cents or less to the minimal group of coins that equal the given amount. Forty-three cents would map to one of the 25-cent coins, two of the 10-cent coins, one of the 5-cent coins and three of the 1-cent coins. Forty-three 1-cent coins would give the right amount of change, but not the minimal number of coins. This function is what cashiers must routinely determine (if they don't want to burden you with piles of pennies) when giving back change for a purchase. These days, the function is generally implemented by a computer in the cash register, which then dispenses the change from a coin holder. While well defined, the definition for this function does not give us a method for determining it. Here is an algorithm that determines this function for an amount owed:

1   Take the largest coin of *n* cents where *n* ≤ the amount owed.
2   Reduce the amount owed by *n* cents.
3   If the amount owed is 0 cents, return all coins taken and stop.
4   Go back to State (line) 1.

The basic operating principle is to start in State 1 (line 1), and do each state in order (unless told otherwise). *State* is a general term that refers to a discernible stage that a process (procedure) is in during which it will act in some specified way. Each numbered line above describes a state. The reader is invited to try a few examples of applying this algorithm. In general, we suggest going through the process of trying any algorithms shown to convince yourself that they determine the function they are supposed to. This will also give you a feel for the mechanical and mindless nature of the processes – what ultimately allows them to be instantiated by bio-molecular and bio-physical processes.

In this change-giving algorithm we see a number of themes that we will see again in various incarnations: There are a series of distinct states that the algorithm proceeds through. The state determines what we do at a certain moment in time. There is the composition of functions, because later steps depend on the results of earlier steps. There are a number of functions that are embedded within the larger algorithm such as subtraction (reduction) and the ≤ relation. The algorithm returns to a previously visited state (go back to State 1). The algorithm eventually stops and returns an answer. The algorithm makes "decisions" (if) based on the current situation.

The fact that this algorithm depends on other functions for which there is no algorithm presented should give us pause. How do we determine "if the amount owed is 0 cents" or "the largest coin of *n* cents where *n* ≤ amount owed?" Ultimately, if we are going to flesh out algorithms in the detail that will be needed to understand how the brain might determine such functions, we will have to flesh out all of the pieces of such algorithms with processes that leave no room for interpretation, and demand no need for understanding the English language. In the next chapter, we will show a formalism, the Turing machine, which can be used to express algorithms in a form that leaves nothing open to interpretation.

Any particular algorithm determines one function; however any particular function can be determined by many possible algorithms. Another algorithm that determines the change-giving function is a look-up table. It has 99 entries. Table 6.1 shows a few of them. To determine the function, one simply looks up the answer (output) in the table. If using this algorithm, the cashier would have a little card on which was written the coins that should be returned for each possible change amount. The cashier then simply finds the required change on the card and returns the coins associated with it.

Table 6.1 Partial look-up table for change making

Change owed (in cents)	Minimal group of coins (in cents)
3	(1, 1, 1)
26	(25, 1)
37	(25, 10, 1, 1)
66	(25, 25, 10, 5, 1)
80	(25, 25, 25, 5)

Procedures, Computation, and Symbols

The algorithms we are interested in will describe the process by which the output of a function in $\hat{P}$ is determined given the arguments to the function. All of the functions in $\hat{P}$ must have algorithms for them, as one cannot make productive use of a function unless one can determine the output for any permissible input. Since every function in $\hat{P}$ maps physical symbols to physical symbols, the algorithms will be applied to physical symbols as input and produce physical symbols for their output. Ultimately, the algorithms will be instantiated as a physical system/process that acts on the symbols and produces other symbols. We will call symbol processing algorithms *effective procedures*, or just *procedures* for short. We can think of the procedures in $\hat{P}$ as being a set of physically realized functions, and continue to use the functional terminology.

We call the process of putting into action a procedure a *computation*. We also say that the procedure *computes* the output from the given inputs and computes the function. Just as it was the case for *defining* functions, there is no universally sanctioned way to describe a procedure that can compute a function. That said, a small set of procedural primitives used compositionally appears to suffice to determine any function. We saw a glimpse of this possibility in the themes from our change-giving example.

As we saw in the last chapter, if we are to create numerous symbols in $\hat{G}$ that can be put to productive use by procedures, we will have to build them out of component pieces (data). Additionally, we saw that using concatenation with a combinatorial syntax, we could get much more bang for our buck in terms of how many symbols could be constructed per physical unit. This reasoning applies to both nominal and compact symbols. Using combinatorial syntax, one can produce d^n symbols from d atomic symbols and strings of length n.

The input symbols must be distinguished by detecting their syntax, that is, their form and their spatial or temporal context. Their referents cannot come into play, because the machinery that implements a function (procedure) only encounters the symbols themselves, not their referents. This gives symbols an important property that is not shared by the entities they represent: symbols share a common atomic structure (a common representational currency), which is used to compute functions of those symbols. This makes the description of procedures in $\hat{P}$ potentially much more uniform and capable of being formalized than are the functions for the entities that the procedures represent. Functions and entities in the represented system take a bewildering variety of physical and non-physical forms, but the machinery in the representing system that implements the corresponding functions on the symbols for those entities is most often constructed from a modest set of basic components.

An elementary neurobiological manifestation of this important principle is seen in the fact that spike trains are the universal currency by which information is transmitted from place to place within neural tissue. A spike is a spike, whether it transmits visual information or auditory information or tactile information, etc. This common signal currency enables visual signals carrying information about location to be combined with auditory signals carrying information about location. This combination determines the activity of neurons in the deep layers of the superior colliculus. We similarly imagine that there must be a common currency for carrying information forward in time, regardless of the character of that information. We return to this question in Chapter 16.

Similarly, the fact that the system of *real numbers* can be used to represent both discrete quantities, such as the number of earthquakes in Los Angeles in a given amount of time, and continuous quantities, such as the given amount of time, makes it possible to obtain a symbol that represents the rate of earthquake occurrence. The symbol is the real number obtained by dividing the integer representing the number of earthquakes by the real number representing the amount of time. If the integers were not part of the system of real numbers (the system of symbols on which the arithmetic functions are defined), this would not be possible (Leslie, Gelman, & Gallistel, 2008). Indeed, the emergence of the algebraic representation of geometry created a common-currency crisis at the foundations of mathematics, because there were simple geometric proportions, such as the proportion between the side of a square and its diagonal or the proportion between the circumference of a circle and its diameter, that could not be represented by the so-called *rational* numbers. As their name suggests, these are the numbers that suggest themselves to untutored reason. The algebraic representation of geometry, however, requires the so-called *irrational* numbers. The Greeks already knew this. It was a major reason for their drawing a strong boundary between geometry and arithmetic, a boundary that was breached when Descartes and Fermat showed how to represent geometry algebraically. In pursuit of what Descartes and Fermat started, mathematicians in the nineteenth century sought to rigorously define irrational numbers and prove that they behaved like rational numbers. They could then be added to the representational currency of arithmetic (the entities on which arithmetic functions operate), creating the so-called *real* numbers.

It is not always easy to find procedures for a given function. There exist well-defined functions for which no one has devised a procedure that computes them. Given a well-defined notion of what it means to be able to compute a function (we will discuss this is the next chapter), there are functions where it has been proven that no such procedures exist. Functions that cannot be computed under this notion are referred to as *uncomputable*. Other functions have procedures that in theory compute them, but the physical resources required render the procedures impractical. Other procedures are rendered impractical by the amount of time that it would take the procedure to compute the function. Functions for which all possible procedures that compute them have such spatial or temporal resource problems are called *intractable* functions.[1] There is a large set of computationally important functions for which the only known procedures to solve them are not practical, and yet it is not known whether these functions are intractable.[2]

The lack of efficient procedures for finding the prime factors of large numbers is the basis for many of the encryption systems that protect your information as it moves back and forth across the internet. These schemes take advantage of the fact that while it is trivial to compute the product of any two prime numbers, no matter how large they may be, the known procedures for computing the inverse function, which specifies for every non-prime number its prime factors, become unusable as the inputs become large. Given a large number that is not itself prime, we know that there exists a unique set of prime factors and we know procedures that are guaranteed to find that set if allowed to run long enough, but for very large numbers "long enough" is greater than the age of the universe, even when implemented on a super computer. Functions whose inverses cannot be efficiently computed are called trap-door functions, because they allow one to go one way but not the other.

In short, there is a disconnect between the definition of a function and the ability to determine the output when given the input. The disconnect runs both ways. We may have a system that gives us input/output pairs and yet we do not have a definition/understanding of the function. Science is often in this position. Scientists perform experiments on natural systems that can be considered inputs and the natural system reacts with what may be called the outputs. However, the scientists may not have an independent means of determining and thereby predicting the input–output relationship. Scientists say in these cases that they don't have a model of the system. We would say that we don't have a representational system for the natural system.

Coding and Procedures

As we mentioned previously, the use of concatenated symbols that share a set of data elements (e.g., '0' and '1') as their constructive base suggests that procedures in $\hat{P}$ may be able to take advantage of this common symbol-building currency. This

---

[1] Typically, the line between tractable and intractable functions is drawn when the procedures needed to implement them need an amount of spatial or temporal resources that grows exponentially in the number of bits needed to compactly encode the input.

[2] This is the class of (often quite useful) functions that are grouped together under the heading NP-Complete. If any one of these functions turns out to have a feasible procedure, then all of them do. The tantalizing nature of this makes the question of whether there is a feasible such procedure one of the most famous open questions in computer science, called the P = NP problem. The general consensus is that these functions are intractable, yet no one has been able to prove this.

does not imply, however, that the particular encoding used for the symbols is irrelevant with respect to the procedures. In fact, there is a very tight bond between the procedures in $\hat{P}$ and the encoding of the symbols in $\hat{S}$.

If the code used is nominal, the nominal symbols cannot be put to productive use by taking advantage of aspects of their form. They can only be used productively in a mapping by distinguishing the entire data string (string of atomic elements) that constitutes the symbol and then using a look-up table to return the result. This is because the string used to form a nominal symbol is arbitrary – any string can be substituted for any other without loss or gain of referential efficacy. When a large number of nominal symbols is used, it becomes impractical to distinguish them. Encoding symbols, however, can be distinguished efficiently using what we will call *compact procedures*.

To see the force of this consideration, we examine potential representational systems involving the integers, $N = \{1, 2, \ldots, 10^{30}\}$, using nominal and encoding systems, and two arithmetic functions, the parity function $f_{is\_even}: N \rightarrow \{false, true\}$, and the addition function $f_+: N \times N \rightarrow N$. Each datum (element in a symbol string) will come from the set $\{`0`, `1`\}$, and we call each datum a bit. The symbols for *true* and *false* will be `1` and `0`, respectively. Our procedures then will be of the form $f_{is\_even}: D^\otimes \rightarrow \{0, 1\}$, where $D^\otimes$, the input, is a string of bits and the output is a single bit, and $f_+: D^\otimes \times D^\otimes \rightarrow D^\otimes$, where the inputs are two strings of bits and the output is a string of bits.

Procedures using non-compact symbols

Preparatory to considering procedures for f_{is_even} and f_+ that use compact symbols, we consider briefly the possibility of using non-compact encodings. One simple way to represent integers is the hash-mark or unary code in which the number of `1` bits is equal in numerosity to the number it encodes. We can reject this out of hand, because we must be able to operate on a number as large as 10^{30} and there are only on the order of 10^{25} atoms in the human brain. Even if we devoted every atom in the brain to constructing a unary symbol for 10^{30}, we would not have the physical resources. Unary symbols are not compact.

An analog symbol would have the same problem. Analog symbols share a property with non-combinatorial digital system in that they both produce an increase in the physical mass of the symbols that is linearly proportional to their representational capacity. Like the unary symbols, the most efficient use of physical resources for analog symbols would be one whereby each symbol is distinguished by the number of atoms that compose it. We could then use weight to distinguish the symbol for one integer from the symbol for another integer (assuming that all the atoms were atoms of the same substance). The problem with using analog symbols to represent our integers is twofold. First, such symbols are not compact, so there are not enough atoms in the brain to represent what may need to be represented. Second, no weighing procedure could distinguish the weight of 10^{29} atoms from the weight of $10^{29} + 1$ atoms. In short, non-compact symbols (digital or analog) are not practical as the basis for a representational system whose symbols must each be capable of representing a large number of different possible states of

Table 6.2 The parity function f_{is_even} with a nominal binary code for the integers 0–7

Integer (base 10)	Nominal binary code	Parity
0	001	1
1	100	0
2	110	1
3	010	0
4	011	1
5	111	0
6	000	1
7	101	0

the represented system; their demand on resources for symbol realization is too high, and the symbols soon become indistinguishable one from the next.

With a combinatorial syntax for (compact) symbol formation, the form of the symbol is varied by varying the sequence of atomic data (for example, '0's and '1's), with each different sequence representing a different integer. If we form our symbols for the integers in this way, we need a symbol string consisting of only 100 bits to represent any number in our very large set of integers (because $2^{100} > 10^{30}$). The demands on the physical resources required to compose the symbol for a single number go from the preposterous to the trivial.

Procedures for f_{is_even} using compact nominal symbols

Before discussing procedures for f_{is_even}, we must consider how we will encode our large (10^{30}) set of integers, because procedures are code-specific. The decision to use compact symbols does not speak to the question of how we encode number into these symbols – how we map from the different numbers to the different bit patterns that refer to them. We consider first the procedural options when we use a nominal mapping for the integers, one in which there are no encoding principles governing which bit patterns represent which numbers. Table 6.2 shows f_{is_even} defined for one possible nominal mapping for the integers 0–7. The bit patterns shown in the second column (the input symbols), can be shuffled at will. The only constraint is that the mapping be one-to-one: each integer must map to only one bit pattern and each bit pattern must represent only one integer. The question is, what does a procedure f_{is_even} look like if we use this kind of nominal coding of the integers? Part of what gives this question force is that the codings assumed by neurobiologists are commonly nominal codings: the firing of "this" neuron represents "that" state of the world.

Whatever procedure we use for determining f_{is_even}, it will have to distinguish every one of the 100 data elements that comprise the input symbol. In addition, since there is no principled way to determine the correct output from the input, we have no choice but to use a look-up table. That is, we must directly implement Table 6.2. We first consider a procedure that distinguishes the elements sequentially, moving

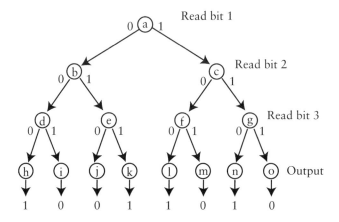

Figure 6.1   Binary search tree for determining the parity of the first eight integers using the nominal binary encoding in Table 6.2.

through the input string from right to left. As we move through the input, we will change from state to state within the procedure. Each state then will provide a memory of what we have seen so far. When we reach the last symbol, we will know what the output should be based on the state we have landed in. In effect, we will be moving through a tree of states (a binary search tree) that branches after each symbol encountered. Figure 6.1 shows the tree that corresponds to the given nominal mapping. Different input strings will direct us along different paths of the tree, in the end generating the pre-specified output for the given input (the symbol '1' or the symbol '0', depending on whether the integer coded for is even or odd).

Here is the procedure that implements the search tree shown in Figure 6.1:

1   Read bit 1. If it is a '0', go to state 2. If it is a '1', go to state 3.
2   Read bit 2. If it is a '0', go to state 4. If it is a '1', go to state 5.
3   Read bit 2. If it is a '0', go to state 6. If it is a '1', go to state 7.
4   Read bit 3. If it is a '0', output '1'. If it is a '1', output '0'. Halt.
5   Read bit 3. If it is a '0', output '0'. If it is a '1', output '1'. Halt.
6   Read bit 3. If it is a '0', output '1'. If it is a '1', output '0'. Halt.
7   Read bit 3. If it is a '0', output '1'. If it is a '1', output '0'. Halt.

We see a number of the same themes here that we saw in the change-making algorithm. There are two related properties and problems of look-up table procedures that are of great importance.

Combinatorial explosion. The search tree procedure has the unfortunate property that the size of the tree grows exponentially with the length of the binary strings to be processed, hence linearly with the number of different possible inputs. As we see graphically in Figure 6.1, each node in the tree is represented by a different state that must be physically distinct from each other state. Therefore, the number of states required grows exponentially with the length of the symbols to be processed. We used combinatorial syntax to avoid the problem of linear growth in

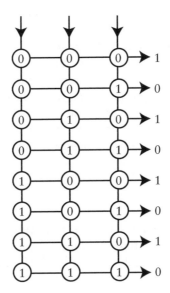

Figure 6.2 A content-addressable memory makes possible parallel search. The string to be processed is fed in at the top. All three bits go simultaneously to the three input nodes at each memory location. Each input node is activated only if the input bit it sees matches it. If all of the nodes at a given location are activated, they generate the output bit stored at that location, the bit that specifies the parity of the number represented by that location in the content-addressable memory. (The ordering of the binary numbers in this illustration plays no role in the procedure.)

required symbol size. However, because we have used a nominal encoding of the numbers, the problem has come back to haunt us in our attempts to create a procedure that operates productively on the symbols.

Pre-specification. Intimately related to, but distinct from the problem of combinatorial explosion is the problem of *pre-specification* in procedures based on a lookup table approach. What this means is that in the procedure, for every possible input (which corresponds to the number of potential symbols used for the input) it was necessary to embed in the structure of a state the corresponding output symbol that will be returned. This implies that all of the possible input/output pairs are determined *a priori* in the representing system. While one can certainly figure out whether any hundred-bit number is even, it is not reasonable to require the creator of the procedure to determine this in advance for all 2^{100} numbers. The problem with procedures based on look-up tables is that they are not productive; they only give back what has been already put in.

One may wonder whether the problem of processing a large number of nominal symbols goes away if one uses a parallel search procedure rather than a sequential procedure. We raise this question in part because, first, it is often argued that the brain is so powerful because it engages in massive parallel processing, and, second, many neural network models for implementing function are based on learned content-addressable memory nets. Content-addressable memories are look-up tables in which the different possible results are accessed through parallel search (see Figure 6.2).

As is apparent in Figure 6.2, a parallel search procedure, using a content-addressable memory table in lieu of a binary search tree, does not avoid either the combinatorial explosion problem or the problem of pre-specification. If anything, it makes the situation worse. The content-addressable memory requires a physically distinct memory location for every possible input string (leading to a combinatorial explosion). The hardware necessary to implement a comparison between an input bit and a bit stored at every location must also be replicated as many times as the length of the input. In addition, we have to store at that location the output bit specifying the parity of the integer to which that location is "tuned" (the pre-specification problem).

State memory

The sequential procedure illustrates a concept of central importance in our understanding of the possible architectures of computing machines, the concept of state memory. A state of a computing device is a hard-wired capacity to execute a particular function given a certain context. Each state essentially implements a mini look-up table of its own, and by moving from state to state, a machine can map a pre-specified set of inputs to a pre-specified set of outputs (implementing a larger look-up table). At any one time it is in one and only one of its possible states. Which state it is in at any given time depends on the input history, because different inputs lead to different state transitions. Take, for example, a typewriter (or, these days, a keyboard, which is not as favorable for our purposes, because the physical basis for its state changes are not apparent). When the Shift key has not been depressed (previous input), it is in one state. In that state it maps presses on the keys to their lower-case symbols. When the Shift key has been depressed, it maps the same inputs to their upper-case outputs, because the depressing of the Shift key has shifted the machine into a different state. In an old-fashioned typewriter, depressing the Shift key raised the entire set of striking levers so that the bottom portion of the strike end of each lever struck the paper, rather than the top portion. The fact that the machine was in a different state when the Shift key was depressed was, therefore, physically transparent.

In the tree search procedure for determining parity, the procedure travels down one branch of the tree, and then another and another. The branch it will travel down next depends on the state it has reached, that is, on where it is in the tree. The tree must be physically realized for this procedure to work because it is the tree that keeps track of where the procedure has got to. Each time the procedure advances to a new node, the state of the processing machinery changes.

The state that the procedural component of a computing machine is in reflects that history of the inputs and determines what its response to any given input will be. It is therefore tempting to use the state of the processing machinery as the memory of the machine. Indeed, an idea that has dominated learning theory for a century – and hence the attempt to understand learning and memory neurobiologically – is that all learning is in essence procedural and state based. Experience puts neural machines in enduringly different states (rewires them to implement a new look-up table), which is why they respond differently to inputs after they have had state-changing (rewiring) experiences. Most contemporary connectionist modeling is devoted to the development of this idea. A recurring problem with this approach is, like the look-up tables they result in, these nets lack productivity: in this case one only gets back what *experience* has put in. (For an extensive illustration of what this problem leads to, see Chapter 14.)

While the use of look-up tables is in many cases either preposterously inefficient or (as in the present case) physically impossible, look-up tables are nonetheless an important component of many computing procedures. As the content-addressable example (Figure 6.2) suggests, a look-up-table procedure can involve accessing memory only once, whereas a procedure implemented by composing many elementary functions, with each composition requiring reading from and writing to memory, may take much longer.

Take, for example, the use of sine and cosine tables in a video game, where speed of the procedures is a top priority. Computing the sine and cosine of an angle is time intensive. For example, one formula for $\sin(x)$ where x is in radians is given by $\sin(x) = x - \dfrac{x^3}{3!} + \dfrac{x^5}{5!} - \dfrac{x^7}{7!} + \ldots$. While one can limit the number of terms used, it may still take a fair amount of time to compute and the denominators become very large integers very quickly.

What is often done to overcome this speed problem is to make a look-up table for enough angles to give a reasonably good resolution for the game. For example, one might have a look-up table procedure that determines the sine function for each integral degree from 1 to 360. Then one only need find the closest integral angle to the input that is stored in the look-up table and use this for an approximation. One can take the two closest integral angles and then use linear interpolation to get a better and still easily computed estimate.

Procedures for f_{is_even} using compact encoding symbols

When symbols encode their referents in some systematic way, it is often possible to implement functions on those symbols using what we call a *compact procedure*. A compact procedure is one in which the number of bits required to communicate the procedure that implements a function (the bits required to encode the algorithm itself) is many orders of magnitude less than the number of bits required to communicate the look-up table for the function. And usually, the number of bits required to communicate a compact procedure is independent of the size of the usable domain and codomain, whereas in a look-up table procedure, the number of bits required grows exponentially with the size of the usable codomain and domain. We have begun our analysis of procedures with the parity function because it is a striking and simple illustration of the generally quite radical difference between the information needed to specify a compact procedure and the information needed to specify the look-up table procedure. As most readers will have long since appreciated, the parity-determining procedure for the conventional binary encoding of the integers is absurdly simple:

Read bit 1. If it is a '0', output '1'. If it is a '1', output '0'. Halt.

This function of flipping a bit (turning 0 to 1 and 1 to 0) is the function f_{not} in Boolean algebra ($f_{not}(0) = 1$, $f_{not}(1) = 0$). It is one of the primitive operations built into computers.[3] When communicating with a device that has a few basic functions built in, the procedure could be communicated as the composition $f_{output}(f_{not}(f_{first\_bit}(x)))$. This expression only has four symbols, representing the three needed functions and the input. Because these would all be high-frequency referents (in the device's representation of itself), the symbols for them would all themselves be composed of only a few bits, in a rationally constructed device. Thus, the number of bits required to communicate the procedure for computing the parity function to a (suitably equipped) device is considerably smaller than 10^2. By contrast, to communicate the parity look-up table procedure for the integers from 0 to 10^{30}, we would need to use at least 100 bits for *each* number. Thus, we would need about $(10^2)(10^{30}) = 10^{32}$ bits to communicate the corresponding look-up table.

That is more than 30 orders of magnitude greater than the number of bits needed to communicate the compact procedure. And that huge number – 30 orders of magnitude – is predicated on the completely arbitrary assumption that we limit the integers in our parity table to those less than 10^{30}. The compact procedure does not stop working when the input symbols represent integers greater than 10^{30}. Because we are using a compact encoding of the integers, the size of the symbols (the lengths of the data strings) present no problem, and it is no harder to look at the first bit of a string 1,000,000 bits long than it is to look at the first bit of a string 2 bits long. In short, there is no comparison between the number of bits required to communicate the compact procedure and the number of bits required to communicate the look-up table procedure that the compact procedure can in principle compute. The latter number can become arbitrarily large (like, say $10^{10,000,000}$) without putting any strain on the physical implementation of the compact procedure. Of course, a device equipped with this procedure never computes any substantial portion of the table. It doesn't have to. With the procedure, it can find the output for any input, which is every bit as good (indeed, much better, if you take the pun) than incorporating some realized portion of the table into its structure.

The effectiveness of a compact procedure depends on the symbol type on which it operates. When we use nominal symbols to represent integers, then there is no compact procedure that implements the parity function, or any other useful function. Nominal symbolization does not rest on an analytic decomposition of the referents. An encoding symbolization does. When the form of a symbol derives from an analytic decomposition of the encoded entity, then the decomposition is explicitly represented by the substructure of the symbol itself. The binary encoding of the integers rests on the decomposition of an integer into a sum of successively higher powers of 2 (for example, $13 = 1(2^3) + 1(2^2) + 0(2^1) + 1(2^0) = 8 + 4 + 0 + 1$). In this decomposition, the parity of an integer is explicitly represented by the rightmost

---

[3]   We conjecture that it is also a computational primitive in neural tissue, a conjecture echoed by the reflections expressed in the T-shirt slogan, "What part of *no* don't you understand?"

bit in the symbol for it. That makes possible the highly compact procedure for realizing the parity function.

Because this point is of quite fundamental importance, we illustrate it next with a biological example: If the nucleotide-sequence symbols for proteins in the DNA of a chromosome were nominal symbols, then we would not be able to deduce from those sequences the linear structures of the proteins they represent. In fact, however, the genetic code uses encoded symbols. The encoding of protein structures by nucleotide sequences rests on an analytic decomposition of the protein into a linear sequence of amino acids. Within the nucleotide sequences of the double-helical DNA molecule of a chromosome, different nucleotide triplets (codons) represent different amino acids, and the sequence of codons represents the sequence of the amino acids within the protein. The decomposition of proteins into their amino acid sequences and the explicit representation of this sequence within the genetic symbol (gene) for a protein makes possible a relatively simple molecular procedure for assembling the protein, using a transcription of the symbol for it as an input to the procedure. A small part of the genetic blueprint specifies the structure of a machine (the ribosome) that can construct an arbitrarily large number of different proteins from encoded symbols composed of only four atomic data (the A, G, T, and C nucleotides). The combinatorial syntax of these symbols – the fact that, like bits, they can be made into strings with infinitely various sequences – makes them capable of representing an arbitrarily large number of different proteins. Whatever the codon sequence, the transcription procedure can map it to an actual protein, just as the parity function and the about to be described addition function can map the binary encoding of any integer or any pair of integers to the symbol for the parity or the symbol for the sum. Biological coding mechanisms and the procedures based on them, like computer coding mechanisms and the procedures based on them, are informed by the logic of coding and compact procedures. This logic is as deep a constraint on the realization of effective molecular processes as is any chemical constraint.

Procedures for f_+

When working with symbols that refer to a quantity, the addition function is exceedingly useful because under many circumstances quantities combine additively (or linearly, as additive combination is often called). As always, the procedure depends on the encoding. If we use a unary (analog) code – symbols that have as many '1's as the integer they encode – the adding procedure is highly compact: you get the symbol for the sum simply by concatenating (stringing together) the addends (the symbols for the integers to be added). Or, if one thinks of the two numbers as being contained in two "bags," then one would get the sum by simply pouring the two bags into a new bag. The problem with this approach is not in the procedure – it could not be more compact – but rather in the symbolization (the encoding). As we have already seen, it leads to exponential growth in use of resources, so it is physically impractical. If we attempt to use a nominal coding, the symbols will be compact but we will be forced into constructing a look-up table procedure which will succumb to combinatorial explosion.

$$
\begin{array}{ll}
\textit{0110} & \textit{carry} \\
00011 & \text{addend}_1 \quad 3 \\
01011 & \text{addend}_2 \quad 11 \\
\textit{1110} & \textit{sum} \qquad 14
\end{array}
$$

Figure 6.3   The results of computing f_+ on the input 3 and 11 (represented in binary). All of the data created during the computation are shown in italics.

As we did with parity, we will pursue the use of encoding symbols by employing the binary number system for integers. So what would be a compact procedure for determining f_+? One approach is essentially the method that we learn in grade school. The numbers (as usually represented in the decimal number system) are placed one on top of the other, right justified so that the numerals line up in columns.[4] Starting from the right, each column is added using another addition procedure, f_{++}, to produce a number. This is not an infinite regress, as the sub-procedure is itself a look-up table. Since there will be carries, we may have to handle adding three numbers in each column. To make this process uniform (and thereby simplify our procedure), we place a '0' at the top of the first column, and then for every column thereafter either a '0' if there is no carry, or a '1' if there is a carry. We also add a '0' to the left end of both addends so that we can handle one last carry in a uniform fashion. To add the three numbers in each column, we use functional composition with f_{++} – $f_{++}(f_{++}(carry\_bit, addend_1\_bit), addend_2\_bit)$ – to add the first two digits and then add this result to the third digit.

Below is a procedure that computes the addition function (f_+). Figure 6.3 shows the results of this computation on the inputs '0011' (3) and '1011' (11).

1   Place a '0' at the top of the first (rightmost) column and the left end of both addend_1 and addend_2.
2   Start with the rightmost column.
3   Add the top two numbers in the current column using f_{++}.
4   Add the result from State 3 to the bottom number in the current column using f_{++}. (Here we are using functional composition of f_{++} with itself.)
5   Place the first (rightmost) bit of the result from State 4 in the bottom row of the current column.
6   Place the second bit of the result from State 4 at the top of the column to the left of the current column. If there isn't a second bit, place a '0' there.
7   Move one column to the left.
8   If there are numbers in the current column, go back to state 3.
9   Output the bottom row. Halt.

---

[4]   Note that relative spatial positioning allows one to discern the top number as the *first* addend and the bottom as the *second* addend. Addition being commutative, this distinction is not relevant; however for subtraction, for example, distinguishing between the minuend (the top number) and the subtrahend (the bottom number) is critical.

Table 6.3 Look-up table for f_{++}

a	b	$f_{++}(a, b)$
0	0	0
0	1	1
1	0	1
1	1	10
10	0	10
10	1	11

The procedure for f_{++}, which is used within f_+, can be implemented as a look-up table (Table 6.3). Note that this does *not* make f_+ non-compact. The embedded look-up table does *not grow* as a function of the input; f_{++} only needs to deal with the addition of three bits. Our addends can increase without bound without changing how we deal with each column. Here, state memory is not only useful, it is necessary. All procedures require some state memory, just as they require some structure that is not a result of experience. This is a direct reflection of the fact that if any device is to receive information, it must have an *a priori* representation of the possible messages that it might receive.

The compact procedure f_+ allows for the efficient addition of arbitrarily large integers. Like the compact procedure for f_{parity}, it does this by using compact symbols and taking advantage of the analytic decomposition of the referents. Whereas look-up-table approaches are agnostic as regards the encoding, compact procedures only function appropriately with appropriately encoded symbols. There is a tight bond between the encoding procedure that generates the symbols and the procedures that act on them.

When you get your nose down into the details of the procedures required to implement even something as simple as addition operating on compact symbols, it is somewhat surprising how complex they are. There is no question that the brain has a procedure (or possibly procedures) for adding symbols for simple quantities, like distance and duration. We review a small part of the relevant behavioral evidence in Chapters 11 through 13. Animals – even insects – can infer the distance and direction of one known location from another known location (Gallistel, 1990; 1998; Menzel et al., 2005). There is no way to do this without performing operations on vector-like symbols formally equivalent to vector subtraction (that is, addition with signed integers). Or, somewhat more cautiously, if the brain of the insect can compute the range and bearing of one known location from another known location without doing something homomorphic to vector addition, the discovery of how it does it will have profound mathematical implications.

It cannot be stressed too strongly that the procedure by which the brain of the insect does vector addition will depend on the form of the neurobiological symbols on which the procedure operates and the encoding function that maps from distances and directions to the forms of those symbols. If the form is unary – or, what is nearly the same thing, if addition is done on analog symbols – then the procedure can be very simple. However, then we must understand how the brain can represent distances ranging from millimeters to kilometers using those unary symbols. To see the problem, one has simply to ponder why no symbolization of quantity that has any appreciable power uses unary symbols (hash marks). The Roman system starts out that way (I, II, III), but gives up after only three symbols. Adding (concatenating) hash marks is extremely simple but it does not appeal when one contemplates adding the hash-mark symbol for 511 to the hash-mark symbol for 10,324. Thus, the question of how the brain symbolizes simple quantities and its procedures/mechanisms for performing arithmetic operations on those quantities is a profoundly important and deeply interesting question, to which at this time neuroscience has no answer.

Two Senses of Knowing

In tracing our way through the details of the procedures for both f_{is_even} and f_{++}, we came upon a distinction between knowing in the symbolic sense and the "knowing" that is implicit in a stage (state) of a procedure. This is in essence the distinction between straightforward, transparent symbolic knowledge, and the indirect, opaque "knowing" that is characteristic of finite-state machines, which lack a symbolic read/write memory. Symbolic knowing is transparent because the symbols carry information gleaned from experience forward in time in a manner that makes it accessible to computation. The information needed to inform behavior is either explicit in the symbols that carry it forward or may be made explicit by computations that take those symbols as inputs. Contrast this with the procedural "knowing" that occurs, for example, in the search tree implementation of f_{is_even}. State 5 "knows" that the first bit in the input was a '0' and the second bit was a '1', not because it has symbols carrying this information but instead because the procedure would never have entered that state were that not the case. We, who are gods outside the procedure, can deduce this by scrutinizing the procedure, but the procedure does not symbolize these facts. It does not make them accessible to some other procedure.

We see in our compact procedure for f_+ both forms of knowing. The look-up table sub-procedure for f_{++}, implemented as state memory, would only "know" what the first bit it received was by virtue of the fact that it was in a particular state. On the other hand, consider the knowing that takes place within the main procedure when it begins to add a new column. It knows what the carry bit is because that information is carried forward by a symbol (the bit) placed at the top of the current column earlier during the computation. f_+ can be in State 3 with a '0' in the carry position or a '1' in the carry position. This information is known explicitly.

We put the state-based form of knowing in quotation marks, because it does not correspond to what is ordinarily understood by knowing. We do not place the symbolic form of knowing in quotation marks, both because it corresponds to the ordinary sense, and because we believe that this symbolic sense of knowing is the correct sense when we say such things as "the rat knows where it is" or "the bee knows the location of the nectar source" or "the jay knows when and where it cached what" (see later chapters).

It is important to be clear about these different senses of knowing, because they are closely related to a long-standing controversy within cognitive science and related fields. The anti-representational tradition, which is seen in essentially all forms of behaviorism, whether in psychology or philosophy or linguistics or neuroscience, regards all forms of learning as the learning of procedures. For early and pure expressions of this line of thought, see Hull (1930) and Skinner (1938, 1957). At least in its strongest form (Skinner, 1990), this line of thinking about the processes underlying behavior explicitly and emphatically rejects the assumption that there are symbols in the brain that encode experienced facts about the world (such as where things are and how long it takes food of a given kind to rot). By contrast, the assumption that there are such symbols and that they are central players in the causation of behavior is central to the what might be called mainline cognitive science (Chomsky, 1975; Fodor, 1975; Fodor & Pylyshyn, 1988; Marcus, 2001; Marr, 1982; Newell, 1980).

The anti-representational behaviorism of an earlier era finds an echo in contemporary connectionist and dynamic-systems work (P. M. Churchland, 1989; Edelman & Gally, 2001; Hoeffner, McClelland, & Seidenberg, 1996; Rumelhart & McClelland, 1986; Smolensky, 1991). Roughly speaking, the more committed theorists are to building psychological theory on neurobiological foundations, the more skeptical they are about the hypothesis that there are symbols and symbol-processing operations in the brain. We will explore the reasons for this in subsequent chapters, but the basic reason is simple: the language and conceptual framework for symbolic processing is alien to contemporary neuroscience. Neuroscientists cannot clearly identify the material basis for symbols – that is, there is no consensus about what the basis might be – nor can they specify the machinery that implements any of the information-processing operations that would plausibly act on those symbols (operations such as vector addition). Thus, there is a conceptual chasm between mainline cognitive science and neuroscience. Our book is devoted to exploring that chasm and building the foundations for bridging it.

A Geometric Example

The tight connection between procedures and the encodings that generate the symbols on which they operate is a point of the utmost importance. We have illustrated it so far with purely numerical operations in which the symbols referred to integers. This may seem too abstract a referent. Do the brains of animals represent numbers? Traditionally, the answer to this question has been, no, but research on animal cognition in recent years has shown that rats, pigeons, monkeys, and apes do in fact represent number per se (Biro & Matsuzawa, 1999; Boysen & Berntson, 1989; Brannon & Terrace, 2002; Cantlon & Brannon, 2005, 2006; Gallistel, 1990; Hauser, Carey, & Hauser, 2000; Matsuzawa & Biro, 2001; Rumbaugh & Washburn, 1993). Nonetheless, a non-numerical illustration involving symbols for something arguably less abstract and something whose representation is clearly a foundation of animal behavior is desirable. In our final example, we turn to the processing of geometric symbols, symbols for locations. There is overwhelming

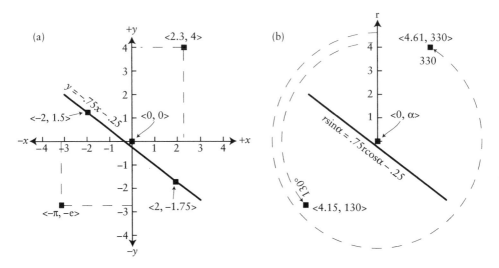

Figure 6.4 Two different ways of encoding locations and lines into vectors. (a) The Cartesian encoding. (b) Polar encoding.

behavioral evidence that animals represent locations, because the representation of locations is a *sine qua non* for effective navigation, and animals of all kinds, including most particularly insects, are gifted navigators (T. S. Collett, M. Collett, & Wehner, 2001; Gallistel, 1998; Gould, 1986; Menzel et al., 2005; Tautz et al., 2004; J. Wehner & Srinivasan, 2003; R. Wehner, Lehrer, & Harvey, 1996).

Like anything else, locations may be encoded in different ways. Whatever way they are encoded, the encoding will make some procedures simple and others complex. Which procedures are simple and which complex will depend on the encoding. The Cartesian encoding of locations (Figure 6.4a) decomposes a location into its signed (that is, directed) distances from two arbitrarily chosen orthogonal axes. An alternative is to decompose locations into a radial distance and an angular distance (Figure 6.4b). In navigation, this decomposition is called the range and bearing of a point from the origin. To effect this encoding of locations, we fix a point on the plane, called the origin or pole. The range is the distance of the location from this point. To be able to specify the bearings of locations, we draw a ray (line segment bounded at one end) from the pole running off arbitrarily far in some direction. This direction is often chosen with salient generally valid directional referents in mind, such as, for example, north, which is the point in the sky around which all of the heavenly bodies are seen to rotate, because it is the point toward which one end of the earth's axis of rotation points. This line is called the polar axis. The second coordinate in the polar encoding of location (the bearing of a location) is the angular distance through which we must rotate the polar axis in order for it to pass through that location. For the sake of familiarity, we will specify angular distances in degrees, even though radians would be preferred for computational purposes.

An awkwardness in this mapping is that there are an infinity of angular distances for any one location – thus, an infinite number of symbols that map to the same referent. First, we can rotate the polar axis either counterclockwise (as we do in Figure 6.4b) or clockwise. Either way, it will eventually pass through whatever location we are encoding, but the angular distance component of our vector symbol will have a different absolute value and a different sign, depending on which way we choose to rotate the polar axis. To forestall this, we may specify that the rotation must be, say, counterclockwise. This does not solve the problem of multiple symbols for the same referent because the polar axis will again pass through the point if we rotate it by an additional 360° or 720°, and so on. To prevent that, we must stipulate that only the smallest of the infinite set of angular distances is to be used as the second component of the symbol. Alternatively, we may use the sine and cosine of the bearing.

Another awkwardness of this encoding is that there is no specifiable angular distance for the polar point itself. Thus, the symbol for this point is different from the symbol for all other points. For some purposes, this is more than a little awkward. Nonetheless, for other purposes, this encoding is preferred because it makes the procedures for obtaining some very useful symbols extremely simple. Something that a navigator often wants to know is the distance and direction of a location (for example, the nest or the hive or the richest source of food or the nearest port when a storm threatens). Neither the distance nor the direction of a location from the origin (or from any other point) is explicit in the Cartesian encoding. They must be determined by means of a tolerably complex procedure applied to the vector that symbolizes the location. In Cartesian encoding, to determine the distance (range) of a point from the origin <0, 0> to the point <x, y>, we must compute $\sqrt{x^2 + y^2}$. To determine its direction (bearing), we must compute arcsin(y/x). By contrast, both quantities are explicit in the polar encoding of location. As in the case of determining parity from the binary encoding of an integer, we can read what we need directly from the symbol itself; the range (linear distance) of the location is represented by the first element of the vector symbol, the bearing (angular distance) by the second element. There are many other procedures that are simpler with the polar encoding than with the Cartesian encoding. On the other hand, there are many more procedures that are simpler with the Cartesian encoding than the polar encoding, which is why the Cartesian encoding is the default encoding.

The important point for our purpose is that if you change the encoding, then you must also change the procedures that are used to compute distance and everything else one wishes to compute. If one does not make suitable changes on the computational side, then the homomorphism breaks down; doing the computations no longer yields valid results. When you try to map from the computed symbols back to the entities to which they refer, it does not work. This point is of fundamental importance when considering proposed systems for establishing reference between activity in neurons or any other proposed neural symbol and the aspects of the world that the activity is supposed to represent. One must always ask, if that is the form that the symbols take, how does the computational side of the system work? What are the procedures that when applied to *those* symbols would extract behaviorally useful information?

7

Computation

In the last chapter, we saw how one could perform computations on symbols. The descriptions of the procedures had elements (themes) in common but did not put forth a common framework. They were ad-hoc and informally presented. For example, the procedure for addition involved sub-procedures that were not specified: How does one *determine* if there are two bits in a solution? How does one *find* the top column? How does one *know* which column is the "current" column? The procedures hinted at the possibility of physical instantiation, but they left doubts as to whether they could ultimately be implemented by a purely mechanical device.

And if they could be implemented, are we to believe that the brain would be composed of ever more such elaborate devices to accomplish its diversity and complexity of tasks? Put another way, is the brain a Rube Goldberg contraption where each component is a uniquely crafted physical mechanism designed to solve a particular idiosyncratic problem? Very unlikely. Wherever one finds complexity, simplicity is sure to follow.[1] It is a ubiquitous property of complex systems, both natural and engineered, that they are built upon simpler building blocks. And, this property tends to be hierarchical in nature. That is, the simpler building blocks themselves are often constructed from even simpler building blocks.

Could a single conceptual framework handle the many different computational problems that one could face? We saw that a set of primitive data, through combinatorial interaction, could serve all of our symbolic needs. Is there a similar set of computational primitives that can serve all of our computational needs? In the last chapter we gained an intuitive understanding of the nature of procedures that perform computations on symbols. Such concepts have existed for a long time; the word algorithm derives from the Persian Mathematician al-Khwarizmi who lived during the ninth century AD. Formalizing the concept of a procedure and what type of machine could implement these procedures without human aid, however, had to wait until the twentieth century.

---

[1] Credit to Perlis (1982): "Simplicity does not precede complexity, but follows it."

Formalizing Procedures

Twelve years before Shannon published his paper laying the foundations of information theory, Alan Turing published his paper (Turing, 1936) laying the foundations of the modern understanding of computation. Turing started from the intuition that we know how to compute something if we have a step-by-step recipe that, when carefully followed, will yield the answer we seek. Such a recipe is what we have called a *procedure*. The notion of a procedure was important for those working on the foundations of mathematics, because it was closely connected to an understanding of what constitutes a rigorous proof. Anyone who has scrutinized a complex and lengthy proof is aware of how difficult it is to be sure that there is not a cheat somewhere in it – a step that is taken that does not follow from the preceding steps according to a set of agreed upon rules.

Turing's enterprise, like Shannon's, was a mathematical one. He did not intend nor attempt to build an actual machine. Turing wanted to specify the elements out of which any procedure could be constructed in such an elementary and precise manner that there could be no doubt that each element (each basic step) could be executed by a mindless machine. The intuition here is that a machine cannot cheat, cannot deceive itself, whereas our minds do routinely deceive themselves about the cogency of their reasoning. Thus, he faced a twofold challenge: first, to specify some very simple operations that could obviously be implemented on a machine; and second, and by far the greater challenge, to make the case that those operations sufficed to construct any possible procedure, and were capable of performing all possible computations.

So far as we know, Turing succeeded. He created a formalization that defined a class of machines. The elements from which these machines were constructed were of such stark simplicity that it was clear that they were realizable in physical form. The machines that are members of this class are now referred to as *Turing machines*, and to date, the formalism has withstood any attempt to find a procedure that could not be identified with a Turing machine. By mathematically specifying the nature of these machines, and demonstrating their far-reaching capabilities, he laid a rigorous foundation for our understanding of what it means to say something is computable: Something is computable if it can be computed by a Turing machine. Part of the fascination of his work is that it showed that some perfectly well-defined functions were *not* computable. Thus, his formulation of what was computable had teeth; it led to the conclusion that some functions were computable and some were not. His work was closely related to and inspired by the slightly earlier work of Kurt Gödel, showing that there are (and always will be) perfectly well-formed formulas in arithmetic that cannot be proved either to be true or false using "finitistic" proof methods – despite the fact that, by inspection, the statements in question must in fact be true. Finitistic proofs do not make use of any steps that involve reasoning about the infinite, because mathematicians had come to mistrust their intuitions about what were and were not legitimate steps in reasoning about the infinite.

We say that Turing succeeded "so far as we know," because his success cannot be proven. He was trying to make our notion of what is and is not computable rigorous. Since the notion of being computable is not itself rigorous, how can one say whether a rigorous formulation fully captures it? One could, however, show that he had failed by specifying a computation that a human (or machine), yet not a Turing machine, could carry out. In this regard, Turing's formulation has stood the test of time. Almost 70 years have passed since he published his formulation. In that time, there has been a dizzying development of computing machines and intense study of computation and its foundations by engineers, logicians, and mathematicians. So far, no one has identified a computation that we – or any other known thing – can do that no Turing machine can. We have developed computations of a complexity undreamed of in Turing's day, but they can all be done by a Turing machine. In fact, they all are done on modern computers, which are examples of *universal Turing machines* – Turing machines that can emulate any other Turing machine. This does not necessarily mean that we will never discover such a computation. Brains solve a number of computational problems that we do not currently know how to program a computer to solve – face recognition for example. Perhaps brains can do computations that a Turing machine cannot do. But, if so, we have no clue as to how they do it. Nothing we currently understand about computation in the brain presents any challenge to a Turing machine. In fact, all current formally specified models of what goes on in brains *are* implemented on contemporary computers.

The thesis that a Turing machine can compute anything that is computable is now called the Church-Turing thesis, because Alonzo Church, Turing's thesis advisor, developed a closely related logical formalism, the lambda calculus, intended, like Turing's, to formalize the notion of a procedure. Church's work was done more or less simultaneously with Turing's and before Turing became his graduate student. In fact, Turing went from Cambridge to Princeton to work with Church when he discovered that they were both working on the same problem. That problem was Hilbert's *Entscheidungsproblem* (decision problem), the problem of whether there could be a procedure for deciding whether a proposition in arithmetic was provable or not – not for proving it, just for deciding whether it was provable. The conclusion of both Church and Turing's work was that there cannot be such a procedure. That is, the decision problem was uncomputable. A closely related result in Turing's work is that there cannot be a computer program (procedure) for deciding whether another computer program will eventually produce a result (right or wrong) for a given input. This is called the *halting problem*. His result does not mean that the halting problem cannot be solved for particular programs and inputs. For simple programs, it often can. (For example, if the first thing a Turing machine does is to halt, regardless of the input, then there is no question that it halts for all inputs.) What the result means is that given *any* possible pair consisting of a (description of a) Turing machine and an input to be presented to that machine, no procedure can *always* determine if the given Turing machine would halt on the given input.

Both Gödel and Church believed that Turing's machines were the most natural formalization of our intuitive notions of computation. This belief has been borne out, as Turing's machines have had by far the greatest influence on our understanding of computation. Turing's work and the vast body of subsequent work by others that rests on it focuses on *theoretical computability*. It is not concerned to specify the architecture of a practical computing machine. Nor is it concerned to distinguish between problems that are in principle computable, but in practice not.

The Turing Machine

A Turing machine has three basic functional components: a long "tape" (the symbolic memory), a read/write head (the interface to the symbolic memory), and a finite-state processor (the computational machinery) that essentially runs the show.

The tape. Each Turing machine (being itself a procedure) implements a function that maps from symbols to symbols. It receives the input symbol(s) as a data string that appears on a *tape*. Turing's tape serves as the symbolic memory, the input, and the output for each procedure. The input symbol(s) get placed on the tape, the procedure is run, and the resulting output is left on the tape. He had in mind the paper tapes found in many factories, where they controlled automated machinery – the head of the teletype machine stepping along the tape at discrete intervals. Similarly, Turing's tape is divided into discrete (digital) cells. Each cell can hold exactly one of a finite number of (digital) atomic data. Successive cells of such data can thereby create the data strings that are the foundation of complex symbols. Turing imagined the tape to be infinitely long, which is to say, however long it had to be to accommodate a computation that ended after some finite number of steps. Turing did not want computations limited by trivial practical considerations, like whether the tape was long enough. This is equivalent to assuming that the machine has as much symbolic memory as it needs for the problem at hand. He also assumed that the machine had as much time as it needed. He did not want it to be limited by essentially arbitrary (and potentially remediable) restrictions on its memory capacity, its operating speed, or the time allowed it.

The number of data (the elements from which all symbols must be constructed) used for a particular Turing machine is part of the description of that machine. While one can get by (using sub-encoding schemes) using just two atomic data (ostensibly '0' and '1'), it is often easier to design and understand Turing machines by using more atomic data. We will start by using these two atomic data along with a "blank" symbol (denoted '•') that will be the datum that appears on all cells that have never been written to. We will add more atomic data if needed to make our examples clear, keeping in mind that the machines could be redesigned to use only two atomic data. Thinking toward potential physical instantiation, one could imagine that the atomic data are realized by making the tape a magnetic medium and that each cell can contain a distinguishable magnetic pattern.

As previously noted, we enclose symbols such as '1', '0', and '•' in single quotes to emphasize that they are to be regarded as purely arbitrary symbols (really data), having no more intrinsic reference than magnetic patterns. In particular, they are not to be taken to represent the numbers 0 and 1. In fact, in the example we will give shortly, a single '1' represents the number 0, while the number 1 is represented by '11'. This, while no doubt confusing at first, is deliberate. It forces the reader over and over again to distinguish between the symbol '1' and the number 1, which may be represented by '1' or may just as well be represented by any other arbitrary symbol we may care to choose, such as '11' or '≚' or whatever else you fancy in the way of a symbol.

The symbols are simply a means of distinguishing between different messages, just as we use numbers on jerseys to distinguish between different players on an athletic team. The messages are what the symbols refer to. For many purposes, we need not consider what those messages are, because they have no effect on how a Turing machine operates. The machine does not know what messages the symbols it is reading and writing designate (refer to). This does not mean, however, that there is no relation between how the machine operates and what the symbols it operates on refer to. On the contrary, we structure the operation of different Turing machines with the reference of the symbols very much in mind, because we want what the machine does to make functional sense.

The read/write head. The Turing machine has a head that at any given time is placed in one of the cells of the tape. The head of the machine can both read the symbol written in a cell and write a symbol to it. Turing did not say the head "read" the cell, he said it "scanned" it, which is in a way a more modern and machine-like term in this age in which digital scanners are used at every check-out counter to read the bar codes that are the symbols of modern commerce. The head can also be moved either to the left or the right on the tape. This allows the machine to potentially read from and write to any cell on the tape. In effect, the read/write head can be thought of functionally as an all-in-one input transducer, output transducer, and mechanism to access and alter the symbolic memory.

The processor. What the head writes and in what direction the head moves is determined by the processor. It has a finite number of discrete processing states. A state is the operative structure of the machine; it determines the processor's response to the symbol the head reads on the tape. As a function of what state the processor is in, and what symbol is currently being read, the processor directs the head regarding what symbol to write (possibly none) and what move to make (possibly no move). The processor then also activates the next state. The finitude of the number of possible states is critical. If the number of states were infinite, it would not be a physically realizable machine. In practice, the number of states is often modest. The states are typically represented (for us!) by what is called a transition table. This table defines a particular Turing machine.

It is important to realize that allowing the tape (memory – the supply of potential symbols) to expand indefinitely is not the same as allowing the number of states of the machine to expand without limit. The tape cells are initially all "empty" (which we indicate by the '•' symbol), that is, every cell is just like every other. The tape has no pre-specified structure other than its uniform topology – it carries no information. It has only the capacity to record information and carry it forward in time in a computationally accessible manner. It records when it is written to and it gives back previously recorded information when it is read. As we explained when discussing compact symbols, a modest stretch of tape has the potential to symbolize any of an infinite set of different entities or states of the world. By contrast, each state of the machine is distinct from each other state, and its structure is specific to a specific state of affairs (pre-specified). This distinction is critical, for otherwise, as it is often claimed, one couldn't build an actual Turing machine. Such is the case only if one must deal with unbounded input, a situation that would never be presented to an actual machine. Arguments that the brain can't be a Turing machine (due to its infinite tape) but instead must be a weaker computational formalism are spurious – what requires the Turing machine architecture is not an issue of unbounded memory, it is an issue of being able to create compact procedures with compact symbols.

Our machine specifications denote one state as the *start state*, the state that the machine is in when it begins a new computation. There is also a special state called the halt state. When the machine enters this state, the computation is considered to be complete. When the machine begins to compute, it is assumed that the read/write head is reading the first datum of the first symbol that constitutes the input. Following tradition, we start our machines on the leftmost symbol. When the machine enters a halt state, the read/write head should be reading the first (leftmost) datum of the output.

The response of the machine in a given state to the read symbol has three components: what to write to the tape, which way to move (right or left or no move), and which state to then enter (transition to).

- *Writing.* The Turing machine can write any of the atomic data to a cell. We also allow the Turing machine not to write at all, in which case it simply leaves the tape as is.
- *Moving.* After it has written (or not written), the machine can move to the left one cell or it can move to right one cell. It may also choose to stay in its current position (not move).
- *Transitioning (changing state).* After writing and moving, the machine changes (transitions) from its current state to another (possibly the same) state.

That the machines thus described were constructible was obvious in Turing's original formulation. Turing also needed to show his machines could compute a wide variety of functions. Turing's general strategy was to devise transition tables that implemented the elementary arithmetic operations of addition, subtraction, multiplication, division, and ordering.[2] All of mathematics rests ultimately on the foundation provided by arithmetic. Put another way, any computation can be reduced to the elementary operations of arithmetic, as can text-processing computations, etc. – computations that do not appear to be arithmetical in nature.

---

[2] Turing's landmark paper actually achieved four major results in mathematics and theoretical computation. He formalized the notion of a procedure, he demonstrated that the decision problem was undecidable, he demonstrated the existence of universal Turing machines (universal procedures), and he discovered the class of numbers referred to as computable numbers. Our immediate concern is the formalization of the notion of a procedure.

Table 7.1   State transition table for the successor machine

State	Read	Write	Move	Next state
S_{start}	'1'	none	L	S_{start}
S_{start}	'•'	'1'	none	S_{halt}

Turing Machine for the Successor Function

Let us follow along Turing's path, by considering machines that compute the functions f_{is_even} and f_+ from the previous chapter. Before we do this, however, we will show an even more basic example – a Turing machine that simply computes the successor function on a unary encoding, that is, it adds one to an integer to generate the next integer. This machine, starting from zero, can generate each integer, one after another, by composing its previous result with itself. As usual, before creating our procedure we must settle on a code that we will use for the integers. In this case we will use the unary code, which will make for a particularly simple transition table and a good introduction to the machines. As we already indicated, we will let '1' be the symbol for the number 0 – perverse as that may seem. We will use this scheme for each unary example that we give. The symbol for the number n will be a string of $n + 1$ '1's. so '11' is the symbol for 1; '111', the symbol for 2; '1111', the symbol for 3, and so on. Each symbol for a number has one more '1' than the number it is a symbol for.

We will start our machine off with an input of zero. From this, we can repeatedly run it to generate successive integers. In the beginning, the read/write head of our Turing machine will be reading the cell containing the symbol '1'. All the other cells contain the blank symbol ('•'). Therefore the input is zero. This machine only demands two states (S_{start}, S_{halt}). Table 7.1 shows the transition table for this machine. The first column contains the state the machine may be in (in this case only S_{start} – the halt state need not be included as it reads no input and does nothing). The other columns contain the data that may be read by the head (in this case only '1' and '•'). Each entry signifies, given this combination of state and symbol read, what symbol to write ('1' or '•'), what move to make (L, R, none), and what state to transition to next.

Typically, such tables are shown pictorially in the form of a *state diagram*, which tends to be easier to follow. Table 7.1 would be transcribed into this format as shown in Figure 7.1. Here, the states are shown as circles. The transitions that occur from state to state are shown by arrows going from state to state. Each arrow coming out of a state is annotated first by the symbol that when read causes that transition, second by the symbol that is written, and third by the move of the read/write head.

When the procedure starts, the tape will look like '... • • [1] • • ...'. The box surrounding a symbol indicates the position of the read/write head. When the computation is finished, the tape looks like '... • • [1] 1 • • ...'. The machine starts in

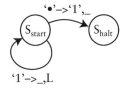

Figure 7.1 State diagram for the successor machine. The states are represented by circles, with the transitions shown by arrows. The arrows are annotated. The annotation shows what the machine read, followed by an arrow, followed by what it wrote, and, following a comma, how it moved the head (L = left one cell, R = right one cell). If it wrote nothing or did not move, there is a _.

state S_{start}. In this state, reading a '1' causes it to move the head to the left one cell, without writing anything, and remain in the S_{start} state. Now, having moved one cell to the left, it reads a '•' (a blank). Reading a blank when in the S_{start} state causes it to write a '1', and enter S_{halt}, ending the computation. The procedure implements what we might describe in English as "Put a '1' before the first symbol" – however, nothing has been left to interpretation. We don't need to invoke a homunculus that understands "put", "before," or "first symbol." One cannot help but be astonished by the simplicity of this formulation.

If we run the machine again, it will end up with '111' written on the tape, which is our symbol for 2. If we run it again, we get '1111', our symbol for 3, and so on. We have created a machine that carries out (computes) the successor function; each time it is run it gives our symbol for the number that is the successor (next number) of the number whose symbol is on the tape when we start the machine.

Turing Machines for f_{is_even}

Next we consider Turing machine formulations of the parity function (predicate) f_{is_even}: $D^{\otimes} \to \{0, 1\}$, that maps a string of bits to '1' if the input bits encode for an even number and '0' otherwise. A compact approach would use a compact procedure with compact symbols, however, the Turing machine is certainly capable of implementing a compact procedure for f_{is_even} on a non-compact representation (unary), and a non-compact procedure (look-up table) on compact nominal symbols (binary strings).

We first implement f_{is_even} using the unary encoding scheme from above (in which a single '1' encodes for 0). Figure 7.2 gives the state diagram for our procedure. Table 7.2 shows the transition table for this same procedure.

This machine steps through each '1', erasing them as it goes. It shifts back and forth between states S_{start} and S_1. The state it is in contains implicit (non-symbolic) knowledge of whether it has read an odd or even number of '1's; if it has read an odd number of '1's, it is in S_1. Given our unary encoding of the integers in which '1' refers to 0, '11' to 1, '111' to 2, and so on, this implies even parity. This is an example of an appropriate use of state memory. As it moves along the data string,

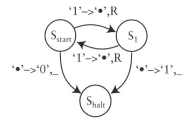

Figure 7.2   State diagram for the machine that computes the parity of integers represented by unary symbols. The machine is in S_{start} when it has read a sequence of '1's that encodes an odd integer; it is in S_1 when it has read a sequence encoding an even integer. If it reads a blank while in S_{start} (indicating that it has come to the end of the symbol string), it writes a '0' (the symbol for odd parity) and enters S_{halt}; if it reads a blank while in S_1, it writes a '1' (the symbol for even parity) and enters S_{halt}.

Table 7.2   State transition table for the parity machine on unary integers

State	Read	Write	Move	Next state
S_{start}	'1'	'•'	R	S_1
S_{start}	'•'	'0'	none	S_{halt}
S_1	'1'	'•'	R	S_{start}
S_1	'•'	'1'	none	S_{halt}

the information regarding the parity of the string – which is the only information that must be carried forward in time – only has two possibilities. This amount of information, one bit, does not grow at all as a function of the input size. The fact the machine is "reborn" each time it enters S_{start} or S_1 does not hinder its operation – the machine is compact even though the symbolic encoding is not. Once it finds the '•' (signifying that it has run out of '1's), the machine transitions to the halt state – using its implicit knowledge (the state it is in) to dictate whether it should leave a '1' or a '0'. This "knowledge" is non-symbolic. While states of the machine carry information forward in time, they do not do so in a form that is accessible to computation outside of this procedure. However, the procedure leaves behind on the tape a symbol for the parity of the number, and this is accessible to computation, because it is in memory (on the tape), where other procedures can read it.

This procedure, although implemented by a Turing machine, can be implemented on a weaker computational mechanism called a *finite state automaton*, which is a Turing machine with a multi-state processor but no read/write symbolic memory. It reads each datum in order and then produces an output. This machine for f_{is_even} never backtracks on the tape, and it never writes to it. That the problem can be solved without writing to symbolic memory means that it is solvable by such weaker

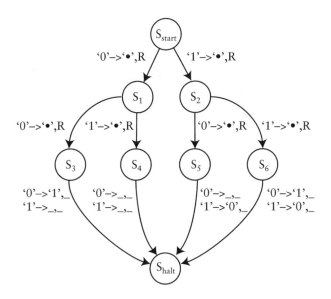

Figure 7.3 State diagram for parity-determining machine operating on nominally encoded integers. When the same state transition is caused by the reading of either bit, it is doubly annotated.

machines. Problems that may be solved without writing to symbolic memory are called *regular* problems. There are many such problems; however, there are many others that are routinely solved by animals and that *do* demand all the components of the Turing machine. They cannot be solved by a physically realizable finite-state machine, which cannot write to symbolic memory.

Next we will consider f_{is_even} as implemented on the nominal encoding from Chapter 6. Figure 7.3 shows the state diagram. It implements a look-up table, a non-compact procedure operating on a compact but nominal encoding. The procedure shown can handle an input of three bits; however, the number of states needed grows exponentially in the number of input bits supported. This Turing machine is once again emulating a weaker finite-state machine. Stepping through each datum, it uses its states to "remember" what it has seen. The structure of the Turing machine (as laid out by the transition table or by the state diagram) directly reflects the binary tree that it is implementing. Notationally, the transition arrows that go to the halt state have two labels each, indicating that these two inputs produce the same state change – but not necessarily the same actions. If comparing this tree to that in Figure 6.1, take note that here we are reading the bits from left to right.

Finally, we implement the compact procedure for f_{is_even} that operates on the compact binary encoding of the integers ('0' for 0, '1' for 1, '10' for 2, and so on). It maps them to '0' or '1' according to whether the final bit is '1' (hence, the integer is odd) or '0' (hence, the integer is even). The state diagram is shown in Figure 7.4. The procedure is easy to state in English: "Output the opposite (*not* or *inverse*) of the final bit." The Turing machine that implements this function reflects this simplicity. Its structure is similar to the procedure above that operates on the unary

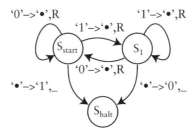

Figure 7.4 State diagram for a machine operating on binary encodings of the integers, erasing the data string as it goes. If it is in S_{start}, the last bit read was '0'; if in S_1, the last bit read was '1'. If it reads a '•' when in S_1, it writes a '0' (the symbol for odd parity) and enters S_{halt}. If it reads a '•' when in S_{start}, it writes a '1' (the symbol for even parity) and enters S_{halt}.

encoding. This machine also uses two states as memory. In this case, however, each state "knows" the *bit* it has last seen, not the *parity of the bit string* that it has seen so far. Because each bit is erased as the machine moves along, when it falls off the end of the string, it has lost its symbolic knowledge of what the last bit was. It must remember this information in non-symbolic (state memory) form.

Different procedures may be used to determine the same function, operating on the same encoding. Figure 7.5 shows the state diagram of a procedure that again uses the compact binary encoding of the integers. This machine leaves its tape (symbolic) memory intact. In S_{start}, it moves to the right along the sequence of '1's and '0's until it reads a blank ('•'), indicating that it has reached the end of the symbol string. Reading a '•' while in S_{start} causes it to move backward one step on the tape and enter S_1. In S_1 then, the read/write head is reading the last datum. It has gained access to this information in a state-independent manner. Both states S_{start} and S_1 read this last bit. The knowledge of this bit, therefore, is not tied to the state of the machine. Having carried the information forward in time in a computationally accessible form in symbolic memory, the machine (that is, the processor) is not dependent upon its own state to carry the information. Information from the past is informing the behavior of the present. By contrast, the knowledge that the machine is now reading the last bit is embodied in the processor's state; if it is in S_1, it's reading the last bit. In this state, it inverts the bit, and enters S_2. S_2 clears the tape, stepping backward when it reads a bit, through the input, erasing as it goes. Note that here we have enhanced our notation to allow for multiple symbols on the left side of the arrow. This is simply a shorthand for multiple read symbols that lead to the same actions (write, move, and state change). When it finally reads a '•', it enters S_3. In this state, it steps back to the right through the blanks left by the erasing done by the previous state, until it reads a bit. This bit is the answer to the parity question – which, again, it has remembered in symbolic form. Seeing the answer, it enters S_{halt}.

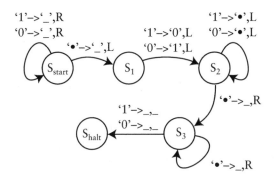

Figure 7.5 State diagram for parity-determining machine operating on binary encodings of the integers without erasing the data string.

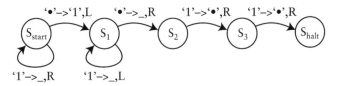

Figure 7.6 State diagram for an adding machine operating on a unary encoding of the integers ('1' for 0, '11' for 1, and so on).

Turing Machines for f_+

We now turn our attention to creating two procedures implemented on Turing machines for f_+. First, we solve the problem for a unary encoding of the integers. We again use the encoding in which the integer n is encoded by $n + 1$ '1's.

We stipulate that the symbols for the two numbers to be added will be separated by a single '•', the blank symbol. Thus, if we want to add 2 and 3, the initial state of the tape will be: . . . • • ⬚1⬚ 1 1 • 1 1 1 1 • • . . . The first string of three '1's encodes for 2, then comes the '•' that serves to separate the two symbols, and then comes the second string of (four) '1's, which encodes for 3. As usual, the reading head is at the start of the first symbol when the computation begins. Our adding machine has five states (Figure 7.6). At the end of the computation, the tape should be: . . . • • ⬚1⬚ 1 1 1 1 1 • • . . .

This machine starts by skipping over all of the '1's in the first addend while remaining in S_{start}, until it finds the '•'. It then converts this punctuation mark into '1', thereby forming one continuous data string, and then it transitions from S_{start} to S_1. At this point, we almost have the result we want. There are just two extra '1's. The first extra '1' came when we filled in the gap. The second came because of our encoding system. Each number n is encoded with $n + 1$ '1's and therefore the numbers x and y will have a total of $x + 1 + y + 1 = (x + y) + 2$ total '1's – the other extra '1'. The task remaining is to remove the two '1's. S_1 steps back through the '1's until it reads a '•', which causes it to step back once to the right and transition to S_2. S_2 reads and deletes the first '1' and transitions to S_3, which reads and deletes the second '1' and transitions to S_{halt}.

Changing the punctuation mark to a '1' may seem like a trick. The procedure takes advantage of the way the numbers are placed on the tape – the way they happened to be symbolized. This highlights the difference between reality and representation, and the importance of the encoding scheme that is chosen in representational systems. In a sense, all computation is a "trick." After all, we are representing (typically) real entities using sequences of symbols. Then, by performing manipulations on the symbols themselves, we end up with more symbols that themselves map back to entities in the real world. For these symbolic processes to yield results that reflect actual relationships in the real world may seem too much to hope for. Yet, such tricks have transformed the world. The tricks that allow the algebra to yield results that reflect accurately on geometry have been put to productive use for centuries. Such tricks allow us to determine how far away stars are. Such tricks have created the Internet. Perhaps what is most astonishing is that such tricks work for complex and indirect encoding schemes such as the binary encoding of integers. That integers can be encoded into unary (analog) form, manipulated by essentially "adding" them together, and then converted back to the integer may seem ho-hum. This coding is direct, and the procedure itself is direct. Yet, as we have stressed, this approach rapidly becomes untenable as the integers that one wants to deal with grow large. There isn't enough paper in the universe to determine the sum of $10^{56} + 10^{92}$. Yet using a compact-encoding (the decimal exponential system, or any other base for that matter) and then a compact procedure (addition as we learned as children) makes this (almost) child's play. It is no overstatement to say that the modern world would not be possible if this were not the case. Perhaps the success of such "tricks" is due to the likelihood that they are not tricks at all. Perhaps the symbolic representation of a messy reality reflects deep and simple truths about the reality that is encoded.

We come finally to consider the most complex procedure whose implementation on a Turing machine we detail – a compact procedure for f_+ operating on the binary encoding for integers. In Chapter 6 we described this procedure in what is often called *pseudo-code* – descriptions that are informal and intended for easy human consumption, but give one enough detail to go off and implement the procedure in actual computer code. Now, we use this procedure in its broadest strokes; however, we make some changes that aid us in implementing the procedure on a Turing machine.

The biggest change we make is that we augment our stock of three symbol elements ('•', '0', and '1') with two new elements, 'X' and 'Y'. We do this to minimize the number of different states in the machine. A necessary part of the addition procedure is keeping track of how far it has progressed. As always, this information can be carried forward in time in two different ways, either in symbolic memory (on the tape), or by means of state memory. If we were to do it by state memory, we would need to replicate a group of the states over and over again. Each replication would do the same thing, but to the next bits in the two strings of bits being processed. The purpose served by the replications would be keeping track of the position in the bit string to which the procedure has progressed. If we used state memory to do this, then the number of states would be proportional to the length of the strings that could be processed. By adding to our symbolic resources the two additional symbols that enable us to carry this information forward on the tape, we create a machine in which the number of states required is independent of the length of the strings to be processed.

There are other ways of achieving a procedure whose states do not scale with the length of the strings to be processed. For example, instead of enriching our set of symbol elements first with '•', and then with 'X' and 'Y', we could use only the minimal set ('0' and '1') and create a sub-procedure that functions to divide the tape into 3-cell words. The remainder of the procedure would then treat each word as an 8-symbol element ('000', '001', 010', etc.). Except for the multi-state sub-procedures that read and wrote those words, that procedure would look much like the one we here describe, because it would then be operating on 8 virtual symbol elements. Our approach serves to remind the reader that a Turing machine can have as many symbol elements as one likes (two is simply the absolute minimum), and, it keeps the state diagram (relatively) simple.

Unlike the other procedures described in Chapter 6, the procedure there described for f_+ may seem to be of a different kind. The symbols were placed in a two-dimensional arrangement and the pseudo-code procedure used phrases such as "add the two top numbers," and "at the top of the column to the left of the current column." Can we recode the symbols to be amendable to the one-dimensional world of a Turing machine? The Church-Turing hypothesis says that we can. And, indeed, it is not difficult: We put the four rows (Carry, Addend1, Addend2, and Sum) end to end, using the blank symbol as a punctuation mark to separate them. We handle the carries as they occur, essentially rippling them through the sum. That is to say, each power of two is added in its entirety as it is encountered. Rather than create the symbol string for the sum in a separate location on the tape, we transform the first addend into the sum and erase the second as we go.[3] The state diagram is in Figure 7.7.

In our example, we add the integer 6 to the integer 7 to compute the resulting integer, 13. The tape initially contains . . . • • $\boxed{1}$ 1 0 • 1 1 1 • • . . . , and it ends up containing . . . • • $\boxed{1}$ 1 0 1 • • . . .

Walking through the procedure at the conceptual level, we see the following:

. . . • • 1 1 0 •	Start with 6, the first addend (which will become the sum):
. . . • • 1 1 1 •	Add the 1 in the ones place to get 7.
. . . • 1 0 0 1 •	Add the 1 in the twos place to get 9 (the carry ripples through).
. . . • 1 1 0 1 •	Add the 1 in the fours place to get 13.

Conceptually, the machine keeps track of its progress by "marking" the bits of the first addend to keep track of which columns (powers of two) have been processed.

---

[3] Thanks to David Eck for these modifications and the associated Turing code.

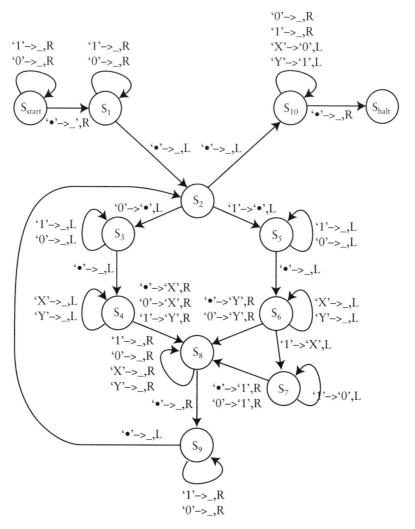

Figure 7.7 State diagram for the machine that does addition on binary encoded integers, using an augmented set of symbol elements to keep symbolic track of the progress of the procedure. S_{start} and S_1 move the head to the last bit of Addend2. The circle composed of S_2, S_3, S_4, S_5, S_6, and S_8 forms the look-up table for the sum of two binary digits $(0 + 0, 0 + 1, 1 + 0,$ and $1 + 1)$. S_7 ripples the carry through, however successive '1's lie immediately to the left in the first addend until it gets to the first '0', where it deposits the carry bit. S_{10} converts the 'X's and 'Y's back to '0's and '1's.

The marking is accomplished by temporarily replacing processed '0's with 'X's and processed '1's with a 'Y's. When the machine has finished computing the sum, it goes back and restores the 'X's to '0's and the 'Y's to '1's.

Table 7.3 shows a trace of the tape as the Turing machine computes . . . • • $\boxed{1}$ 1 0 • 1 1 1 • • (6 + 7). S_3 and S_4 operate when the bit in the first addend is '0',

Table 7.3 Trace of the procedure when adding 6 (binary 110) and 7 (binary 111) to get 13 (binary 1001)

Tape	State	Comment
· · [1] 1 0 · 1 1 1 · ·	Start	Move to the end of first Addend2
· · 1 [1] 0 · 1 1 1 · ·	Start	
· · 1 1 [0] · 1 1 1 · ·	Start	
· · 1 1 0 [·] 1 1 1 · ·	Start	
· · 1 1 0 · [1] 1 1 · ·	1	
· · 1 1 0 · 1 [1] 1 · ·	1	
· · 1 1 0 · 1 1 [1] · ·	1	
· · 1 1 0 · 1 1 1 [·] ·	1	
· · 1 1 0 · 1 1 [1] · ·	2	Working on next bit of Addend2 (ones place)
· · 1 1 0 · 1 [1] · · ·	5	Found a 1, so of to state 5 for Addend1
· · 1 1 0 · [1] 1 · · ·	5	
· · 1 1 0 [·] 1 1 · · ·	5	
· · 1 1 [0] · 1 1 · · ·	6	Addend1 has a '0', sum = 1 + 0 = 1 = (y), no carry
· · 1 1 y [·] 1 1 · · ·	8	Back to find next bit of Addend2
· · 1 1 y · [1] 1 · · ·	9	
· · 1 1 y · 1 [1] · · ·	9	
· · 1 1 y · 1 1 [·] · ·	9	Found the end, step left for next bit
· · 1 1 y · 1 [1] · · ·	2	Working on next bit of Addend2 (twos place)
· · 1 1 y · [1] · · · ·	2	Found a '1', so off to state 5 for Addend1
· · 1 1 y [·] 1 · · · ·	5	
· · 1 1 [y] · 1 · · · ·	6	Skip over y, already handled
· · 1 [1] y · 1 · · · ·	6	Addend1 has a '1', sum = 1 + 1 = 0 = (x), with carry
· · [1] x y · 1 · · · ·	7	Rippling carry, carry = 1 + 1 = 0 (x), with carry
· [·] 0 x y · 1 · · · ·	7	No more bits, placing the carry at end
· 1 [0] x y · 1 · · · ·	8	Back to find next bit of Addend2
· 1 0 [x] y · 1 · · · ·	8	Skip over x
· 1 0 x [y] · 1 · · · ·	8	Skip over y
· 1 0 x y [·] 1 · · · ·	8	
· 1 0 x y · [1] · · · ·	9	
· 1 0 x y · 1 [·] · · ·	9	Found end, left for next bit (fours place)
· 1 0 x y · [1] · · · ·	2	Found a '1', so off to state 5 for Addend1
· 1 0 x y [·] · · · · ·	5	
· 1 0 x [y] · · · · · ·	6	Skip over y
· 1 0 [x] y · · · · · ·	6	Skip over x
· 1 [0] x y · · · · · ·	6	Found a 0, sum = 1 + 0 = 1 (y), no carry
· 1 y [x] y · · · · · ·	8	Back to find next bit of Addend2
· 1 y x [y] · · · · · ·	8	Skip over y
· 1 y x y [·] · · · · ·	8	
· 1 y x y · [·] · · · ·	9	Found end, left for next bit (eights place)
· 1 y x y [·] · · · · ·	2	There is no eights place, time to clean up
· 1 y x [y] · · · · · ·	10	Change y back to 1
· 1 y [x] 1 · · · · · ·	10	Change x back to 0
· 1 [y] 0 1 · · · · · ·	10	Change y back to 1
· [1] 1 0 1 · · · · · ·	10	Found first digit, all done

while S_5 and S_6 operate when it is '1'. They discern the corresponding bit in Addend2 and write the appropriate bit over the bit that is currently in that position in Addend1. This is written either as an 'X', for '0', or a 'Y' for '1', marking the current row (corresponding to the power of two being added) as done.

One may see the near duplication of S_3, S_4 and S_5, S_6 as wasteful. Can one do better? In this case, one cannot. The look-up table approach here is necessary as the two arguments are each just one bit. Therefore, there is no useful analytic decomposition of the arguments that would allow us to form a compact procedure. This imbedded look-up table, however, does not do our procedure any harm. Regardless of how big our addends grow, the look-up table still only needs to handle two bits.

Once this bit has been handled, the procedure moves back to the right to find the next bit to be added (S_8 and S_9). The machine then returns to S_2, being reborn with respect to its state memory. After all bits are processed, the machine transitions to S_{10} where it cleans up the tape (changes all of the 'X's back to '0's and 'Y's back to '1's) and halts.

It is hard to ignore the relative complexity of the Turing machine for f_+ that uses encoded compact symbols as compared to the one that uses the unary symbols. Both procedures are compact, and yet the procedure that operates on the compact symbols requires more states. We have traded some algorithmic simplicity for a procedure that can work on an arbitrarily large number of realistically symbolizable numbers – a trade that is mandatory for any machine that needs to work with many symbols.

The reader can verify that this machine will work for any initial pair of numbers. That is, if one puts in the binary numeral for the first number, a '•', and then the binary numeral for the second number, sets the machine to the initial state, and runs it – the machine will stop when it has converted what is written on the tape to the binary numeral for the sum of the two input numbers. Thus, this machine can add any two numbers we care to give it. It is not a look-up table; it is generative. It can give us the sums for pairs of numbers whose sums we do not know (have never computed).

Turing went on to show how to create more complicated machines that generated all computable numbers (real numbers for which there is a procedure by which one can determine any digit in its decimal expansion). He also showed how to implement all five of the elementary operations of arithmetic, from which all the other operations of arithmetic may be constructed. Also, how to implement basic text processing operations such as copying and concatenating. (These can all be shown to be equivalent to arithmetic operations.) His machines were never intended to be constructed. They were preposterously inefficient. They served a purely conceptual purpose; they rendered precise the notion of an effective procedure and linked it to the notion of what could be accomplished through the operation of a deterministic machine, a machine whose next action was determined by its current state and the symbol it was currently reading.

As one might imagine, there are variants on the Turing machine, but all the ones that have been suggested have been proved to be equivalent to the machine we have described, even stochastic (non-deterministic) variants. There are other approaches to specifying what is and is not computable, notably, the theory of recursive functions, but it has been proved that the Turing-computable functions are exactly the recursive functions.

Minimal Memory Structure

In a Turing machine, the head moves step by step along the tape to bring the symbol to be read to the head, which feeds the processor, the part of the machine whose state varies from step to step within a computational procedure. If a symbol is written to memory, it is always written to the cell that is currently under the head. A critical part of each processor state is the specification of how it moves the head. Only the symbol currently being read can contribute to this determination. Moving the head brings a different symbol into play. Thus, how the head moves determines which symbol in memory (on the tape) gains causal efficacy in the next step. The movements of the head are maximally simple: either one cell to the left or one cell to the right. One might suppose that a more complexly structured memory would be needed to achieve full computational power. It turns out, that it isn't. The sequential structure imposed by placing the data on a tape is all the structure that is needed.

This amount of structure is, however, critical. Memory in a Turing machine is not a disorderly basket into which symbols are tossed and which must then somehow be rummaged through whenever a particular symbol must again enter into some computational process. Memory is sequentially structured and that structure is a critical aspect of the procedures that Turing specified. As the example of the addition procedure illustrates, the arrangement of the symbols on the tape and the sequence in which the procedure brings them into the process by moving the reading head to them are the keys to the success or failure of the procedure.

Also critical is the question of how the symbols in memory and the machinery that operates on those symbols are brought together in space and time. In Turing's conceptual machine, the processor accessed the symbols by moving the head through memory. In modern, general-purpose computers, the symbols are brought to the processing machinery by a fetch or read operation and then exported back to memory by a put or write operation. It is widely assumed in the neural network literature that it is precisely in this particular that computation in nervous tissue departs most fundamentally from computation in modern computing machines. It is thought that in neural computation the data (whether they should be thought of as symbols or not is in dispute) and the machines that operate on the data are physically intertwined in such a way that there is no need to bring the data to the machinery that operates on it. However, the developments of this conception that we are familiar with generally avoid the question of how the combinatorial operations are to be realized – operations such as the arithmetic operations in which two different symbols must be brought together in space and time with machinery capable of generating from them a third symbol. The challenge posed by the necessity of implementing combinatorial operations is that of arranging for *whichever* two symbols need combining to come together in space and time with the machinery capable of combining them. It would seem that the only way of arranging this – other than bringing them both from memory to the combinatorial machinery – is to make a great many copies of the symbols that may have to enter into a combinatorial function and distribute these copies in pairs along with replications of the machinery capable of combining each such pair. This leads to a truly profligate use of physical resources. We will see in Chapter 14 that this is what at least some neural network models in fact suppose.

General Purpose Computer

Perhaps Turing's most important result was to prove the existence of (i.e., mathematical possibility of) universal Turing machines. A universal Turing machine is a machine that, when given on its tape an encoding for the transition table for any other Turing machine, followed by the state of that machine's tape at the start of its computations (the input), leaves the output segment of its own tape in the same state as the state in which the other machine would leave its tape. In other words, the universal Turing machine can simulate or emulate any other Turing machine operating on any input appropriate to that other machine. (Remember that other Turing machines are computation-specific.) Thus, a universal Turing machine can do any Turing-computable computation, which is to say, given the current state of our understanding, any computation that can in principle be done. This is, in essence, an existence proof for a general purpose computer. The computers that most of us have on our desks are, for most practical purposes, realizations of such a machine. But their architecture is somewhat different, because these machines, unlike Turing's machines, have been designed with practical considerations very much in mind. They have been designed to make efficient use of time and memory.

The functional architecture of practical universal Turing machines reflects, however, the essentials in the functional architecture of Turing's computation-specific machines. First and foremost, they all have a read/write memory, which, like Turing's tape, carries symbolized information forward in time, making it accessible to computational operations. Turing's formalization has allowed others to investigate the consequences of removing this essential component (Hopcroft, 2000; Lewis, 1981). As we have already noted, a machine that cannot write to the tape – that cannot store the results of its computations in memory for use in subsequent computations – is called a *finite state machine*. It is provably less powerful than a Turing machine. There are things that a Turing machine can compute that a finite state machine cannot because it has no memory in which to store intermediate results. We consider the limitations this imposes in Chapter 8.

Putting the transition table in memory

The modern computer differs from the Turing machines we have so far described in a way that Turing himself foresaw. In the architecture we have so far considered, the processor with its different states are one functional component, and the tape is another. The states of the processor carry information about how to do the computation. They are a collection of suitably interconnected mini-machines. The symbols on the tape carry forward in time the information extracted by earlier stages of the computation. Turing realized that it was possible to put both kinds of information on the tape: the how-to information in the transition table could be symbolized in the same way, and by the same physical mechanisms, as the data on which the procedure operated. This is what allowed him to construct his universal Turing machine. This insight was a key step on the road to constructing the modern general purpose computer. A machine with a stored-program architecture is often called a von Neumann machine, but the basic ideas were already in Turing's seminal paper, which von Neumann knew well.

In the stored-program architecture, the processor is given some basic number of distinct states. When it is in one of those states, it performs a basic computational operation. It has proved efficient to make machines with many more elementary hard-wired actions than the three that Turing allowed – on the order of 100. Each of these actions could in principle be implemented by a sequence of his three basic actions, but it is more efficient to build them into the different states of the processing machinery.

The possible actions are themselves represented by nominal binary symbols (bit patterns, strings of '1's and '0's), which are in essence names for the various states of the machine (the equivalent of S_1, S_2, etc. in our diagrams). This allows us to store the transition table – the sequence of instructions, that is, states – in memory (on the tape). In this architecture, computations proceed as follows: the processing machinery calls an instruction from the sequence in memory. This instruction configures the processor to carry out one of its elementary hard-wired operations, that is, it puts the processor in the specified state. After placing itself in one of its possible states by calling in an instruction name from memory, the processor then loads one or two data symbols from memory. These correspond to the symbol being read or scanned by the head in Turing's bare-bones architecture. The operations particular to that state are then performed. The processor may for example add the two symbols to make a symbol for the sum of the numbers that they represent, or compare them and decide on the basis of the comparison what the next instruction to be called in must be. Finally, the resulting symbol is written to memory and/or the machine branches to a different location in the sequence of instructions. The processor then calls in from the new location in program memory the name of the next instruction in the list of instructions or the instruction decided on when it compared two values. And so on.

Storing the program in the memory to which the machine can write makes it possible for the machine to modify its own program. This gives the machine two distinct ways in which it can learn from experience. In the first way, experience supplies the data required by pre-specified programs. This is the only form of learning open to a machine whose program is not stored in memory but rather hard-wired into the machine. Machines with this structure have a read-only program memory. In the second way, experience modifies the program itself. A point that is sometimes overlooked is that this second form of learning requires that one part of the program – or, if one likes, a distinct program – treat another part of the program as data. This second, higher-level program establishes the procedure by which (and conditions under which) experience modifies the other program. An instance of this kind of learning is the back-propagation algorithm widely used in neural network simulations. It is not always made clear in such simulations that the back-propagation algorithm does not run "on" the net; it is the hand of an omniscient god that reaches into the net to make it a better net.

Using the same memory mechanism to store both the data that must be processed and the transition table for processing them has an analog in the mechanism for the transmission and utilization of genetically coded information. In most presentations of the genetic code, what is stressed is that the sequence of triplets of base pairs (codons) in a gene specifies the sequence of amino acids in the protein whose structure is coded for by that gene. Less often emphasized is that there is another part of every gene, the promoter part, which is just as critical, but which does not code for the amino acid sequence of a protein. Promoters are sequences of base-pairs to which transcription factors bind. The transcription of a gene – whether its code is being read and used to make its protein or not – is governed by the binding of transcription factors to the promoters for that gene. Just as in a computer, the result of expressing many different genes depends on the sequence and conditions in which they are expressed, in other words, on the transition table or program. The sequence and conditions in which genes are expressed is determined by the system of promoters and transcription factors. The genetic program information (the transition table) is encoded by the same mechanism that encodes protein structure, namely base-pair sequences. So the genetic memory mechanism, like the memory mechanism in a modern computer, stores both the data and the program. DNA is the inherited-memory molecule in the molecular machinery of life. Its function is to carry heritable information forward in time. Unlike computer memory, however, this memory is read-only. There is, so far as we now know, no mechanism for writing to it the lessons of experience. We know from behavior, however, that the nervous system does have a memory to which it can write. The challenge for neurobiologists is to identify that mechanism.

Summary

We have reviewed and explicated key concepts underlying our current understanding of machines that compute – in the belief that the brain is one such machine. The Church-Turing thesis, which has withstood 70 years of empirical testing, is that a Turing machine can compute anything that can be computed by any physically realizable device. The essential functional components of a Turing machine are a read/write, sequentially structured symbolic memory and a symbol processor with several states. The processor's actions are determined by its current state and the symbol it is currently reading. Its actions have two components, one with respect to the symbolic memory (metaphorically, the tape) and one with respect to its own state. The memory-focused components are writing a symbol to the location currently being read and moving the head to one of the two memory locations that adjoin the currently read location. Moving the head brings new symbols stored in memory into the process. The other component is the change in the state of the processor. The machinery that determines the sequence of states (contingent on which symbols are encountered) is the program. The program may itself be stored in memory – as a sequence of symbols representing the possible states.

The Turing machine is a mathematical abstraction rooted in a physical conception. Its importance is twofold. First, it bridges the conceptual gulf between our intuitive conceptions of the physical world and our conception of computation. Intuitively, computation is a quintessentially mental operation, in the Cartesian dualist sense of something that is intrinsically not physical. Our ability to compute is the sort of thing that led to Descartes' famous assertion, "I think therefore I am." The "I" referred to here is the (supposed) non-physical soul, the seat of thought. In the modern materialist (non-dualist) metaphysics, which is taken more or less for granted by most cognitive scientists and neuroscientists, the material brain is the seat of thought, and its operations are computational in nature. Thus, it is essential to develop a firm physical understanding of computation, how it works physically speaking, how one builds machines that compute. (In the next chapter, we get more physical.)

Second, we believe that the concepts underlying the design of computing machines arise out of a kind of conceptual necessity. We believe that if one analyzes any computing machine that is powerful, fast, and efficient, one will find these concepts realized in its functional structure. That has been our motivation for calling attention to the way in which these concepts are implemented, not only in modern computers, but also in the best understood biological machinery that clearly involves a symbolic memory, namely, the genetic machinery. This well-understood molecular machinery carries heritable information from generation to generation and directs the construction of the living things that make up each successive generation of a species. In the years immediately following the discovery of the structure of the DNA molecule, biologists discovered that the genetic code was truly symbolic: there was no chemical necessity connecting the structure of a gene to the structure of the protein that it coded for. The divorcing of the code from what it codes for is the product of a complex multi-stage molecular mechanism for reading the code (transcribing it) and translating it into a protein structure. These discoveries made a conceptual revolution at the foundations of biochemistry, giving rise to a new discipline, molecular biology (Jacob, 1993; Judson, 1980). The new discipline had coding and information processing as its conceptual foundations. It studied their chemical implementation. The biochemistry of the previous era had no notion of coding, let alone reading a code, copying it, translating it, correcting errors, and so on – notions that are among the core concepts in molecular biology.

Thus, if one believes that the brain is an organ of computation – and we take that to be the core belief of cognitive scientists – then to understand the brain one must understand computation and how it may be physically implemented. To understand computation is to understand the codes by which information is represented in physical symbols and the operations performed on those symbols, the operations that give those symbols causal efficacy.

8

Architectures

Two questions seldom considered even by cognitive neuroscientists, let alone by neuroscientists in general, are: What are the functional building blocks of complex computational systems? And how must they be configured? If the brain is a computational system, then the answers to these questions will suggest what to look for in brains when we seek to understand them as computing machines. We want to understand what kinds of building blocks are required in a computing machine and why. We also want to look at some physical realizations of these building blocks in order to more clearly distinguish between the functions themselves and the physical realizations of them. Looking at physical realizations also helps to bridge the conceptual gap between our various representations of the machines and actual machines. We will begin with the bare minimum of what might qualify as a computational machine and add functionality as needed.

We make the following initial simplifications and assumptions:

1   Our machines will take input as a *sequence* of primitive signals from two transducers sensitive to two different "states of the world." (Neurobiologically, these would be two different sensory transducers, e.g., two different omatidia in the eye of an insect.) We specify sequential input, because the focus of our interest is the role of memory in computation. The role of memory comes into sharp focus when inputs that arrive sequentially must together determine the outcome of a computation. In that case, the information about previous inputs must be remembered; it must be preserved by some physical alteration within the machine. Thus, we always have a sequence of signals. There will be no harm in thinking of these signals as the '1' signal and the '0' signal, although we will refer to them as the **a** and **b** signals and we will indicate them by the use of bold lettering. Neurobiologically, these two different inputs would plausibly be spikes in two different sensory channels, for example, two different axons coming from two different omatidia in an insect eye. In that case, we would call one axon the **a** axon, the other the **b** axon. We display the input sequence as a string of signals with the leftmost signal being the first received, and so on. Therefore, **abbab** would indicate a sequence that started with an **a** signal that was followed in time by two **b** signals, then an **a** signal, and finally a **b** signal.

2   Although our machines only take two input signals (generating signals in the two channels, **a** and **b**), they can create more signals as they make computations. These further signals will code for properties of the input sequence, such as, for example, whether the sequence contained the sub-sequence **aba**, or whether it contained as many **a**'s as **b**'s or an even number of **a**'s, and so on. Thus, a signal in one output channel indicates the presence of one particular property in the input string, while a signal in a different output channel indicates the presence of a different property.

3   One can always imagine that the signals in different channels are fed to different output transducers that convert them into distinct actions. Neurobiologically, these output signals would be spikes in motor neurons leading to muscles or secretory glands. These "effector" signals convert the computations into actions. The actions produced depend on the properties of the input, which have been recognized by the computations that our machines have performed. One can think of our machines as categorizing possible input sequences and taking actions based on which category a sequence belongs to.

4   The machines will be built out of functional components, that is, components defined by their input-output characteristics (which will be simple) and by their interaction with other components. Although the components are defined functionally, we will remain mindful that they must ultimately be physically realized. To this end, we give mechanical examples of each of the key functional components and of key patterns of interconnection. Electronic examples come most readily to mind, but they lack physical transparency: why they do what they do is a mystery, except to those with training in solid state electronics. We give mechanical examples, in the hope that they will be physically transparent. In Chapter 10, we suggest neurobiological realizations for some of these components. We do that, however, *only* to help the student make the transition from mechanical thinking to neurobiological thinking, *not* because we think the possibilities we suggest are particularly likely to be the mechanisms by which nervous systems in fact implement these functions. Those mechanisms are generally unknown. We stress the importance to neuroscience of discovering what they actually are.

5   Because they are to be embodied, our machines must obey the basic law of classical physics – no action at a distance or across time. If any signal/symbol is to have an impact on a component, the symbol/signal must be locatable at the physical location of the component at the time the component needs it. A critical point is this simple physical constraint on the realization of compositionality, that is, on the combining of symbols. Physical realizations of the symbols to be combined and of the mechanism that effects their combination must be brought to the same physical location within the machine at the same time. This is an elementary point, but its importance cannot be overstated.

To the extent that we have oversimplified things, our argument is only made stronger. Our purpose is also to make familiar different ways or levels of describing components: physical description, state diagrams, program instructions. An understanding of physically realized computation requires moving back and forth readily between these different representations of the embodied computational process.

To summarize, we seek to show that to get machines that can do computations of reasonable complexity, a specific, minimal functional architecture is demanded, an architecture that includes a read/write memory. In later chapters we explore how the behavioral evidence supports the need for such capabilities. Additionally, we will see in this chapter that the functional architecture of a Turing machine is surprisingly simple and easily embodied.

One-Dimensional Look-Up Tables (If-Then Implementation)

The great neurobiologist, Sherrington, spelled out the bare minimum of functional components needed to make a machine that can react in different ways to different states of the world (Sherrington, 1947 [1906]): receptors, effectors, and conductors. The receptors are the input transducers; they convert states of the world (e.g., the arrival of a photon from a certain direction relative to the eye) into signals. The effectors are the output transducers; they convert signals into actions. The conductors carry the signals from the receptors to the effectors. Sherrington thought that "From the point of view of its office as the integrator of the animal mechanism, the whole function of the nervous system can be summed up in one word, *conduction*" (Sherrington, 1947 [1906], p. 9). Contemporary connectionist thinking is predicated on this same assumption: it's all axonal and synaptic conduction. In computational terminology: it's all look-up tables. While we do not think that it really is all look-up tables, we do think that look-up tables are an essential part of any computing machine.

As Sherrington wrote, the first functional components that we need in constructing a look-up table responsive to the world are receptors or transducers with differential sensitivities to states of the world. In our marble machines, we realize this with the marble-releasing mechanism shown in Figure 8.1. There are two states of the world. One pushes the lever of the transducer counterclockwise (CCW); the other pushes it clockwise (CW). A counterclockwise push releases a marble into Channel **a**; a clockwise push releases a marble into Channel **b**. Our transducer mechanism enforces sequentiality in the resulting signals, because the lever can only be pushed in one direction at any one time. Thus, the transducer generates a signal in one channel or the other, but never in both simultaneously.

The mechanism shown in Figure 8.1 also shows the conduction mechanism. It is the channels that carry the falling marbles. These channels are analogous to axons in neurobiology. The marbles in them are analogous to the spikes carried by those axons.

For effectors, we use different bells, which are struck by the marbles as they fall out of the final channel in the machine. The bells, being of different sizes, ring at different frequencies when struck by a falling marble. The ringing of a bell at a particular frequency is an output.

In addition to the channels that carry the signals between the input transducers and the output effectors, we need a mechanism to mediate the convergence of signals, a mechanism analogous to synapses on a common postsynaptic neuron. In our marble machines, this mechanism is a funnel. The funnel channels marbles falling in two different channels into a common third channel (see Figure 8.2).

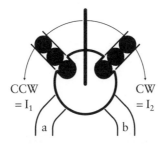

Figure 8.1   The marble machine transducer converts lever displacements in different directions into marbles released into different channels (**a** and **b**). A marble falling in a channel is a signal in a marble machine, just as an action potential (spike) propagating in an axon is a signal in a nervous system.

Table 8.1   The input–output relations for the four possible one-bit look-up tables

Inputs	*Outputs*			
I_1	O_1	O_2	O_1	O_2
I_2	O_2	O_1	O_1	O_2

There is only one class of machine that we can construct from only these components: a one-bit look-up table. It is easy to make an exhaustive list of the possible machines: For a fixed labeling of the two possible inputs (**a** and **b**) and the two possible outputs (**c** and **d**), there are only the four look-up tables shown in Table 8.1. The machines that implement these different look-up tables are shown in Figure 8.2. It is apparent in Figure 8.2 that there really are only two machines. One (top row) maps the two different inputs to the two different outputs; the other (bottom row), maps the two different inputs to one of the outputs. There would appear to be two different versions of these two machines, but the different versions arise only from the labels that we apply to the inputs and outputs, not from the structure of the machines themselves. The labels are arbitrarily pasted on, so to speak, and can be interchanged without tampering with the structure of the machine. Interchanging labels creates the two different versions of the two basic machines.

These most primitive of computational machines have only a single state. Their state diagrams are shown in Figure 8.3.

The capabilities of these machines correspond to the if-then programming construct, which allows the identification of a symbol (the function performed by the transducer in our machine) and then, based on this identification, performs a specified action. The '=' symbol checks to see if two things are equal. If they are, then the following code is executed. The ':=' symbol assigns the value on the right to the variable on the left. Each line of code here is a program corresponding to the machines above:

```
A.   IF (I=I₁) O:=O₁; IF (I=I₂) O:=O₂
B.   IF (I=I₁) O:=O₂; IF (I=I₂) O:=O₁
C.   IF (I=I₁) O:=O₁; IF (I=I₂) O:=O₁
D.   IF (I=I₁) O:=O₂; IF (I=I₂) O:=O₂
```

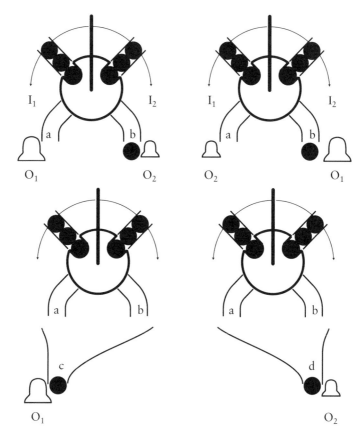

Figure 8.2   The four one-bit table-look-up machines with fixed labeling of inputs and outputs. There are really only two unique machines. Interchanging labels on either inputs or outputs converts the machines on the left to the machines on the right.

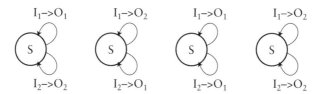

Figure 8.3   State diagrams for the 1-bit look-up tables. These machines only have one state, so all state transitions are self-transitions (the arrows loop back to the circle from which they originate). As previously explained, the input is to the left of the arrow in the text that annotates a state-transition arrow. The action taken (the output) is denoted by the symbol on the right of the arrow.

So the simplest computational machine of any interest is the one-dimensional look-up table. Its strength is it versatility: any input can be wired to any output. This machine corresponds in crude first approximation to what psychologists and behavioral neuroscientists would call an unconditioned-reflex machine.

Adding State Memory: Finite-State Machines

Let us consider now problems in which what the machine does depends not only on the present input, but also on preceding inputs. This will require memory. Suppose, for example, that we want a machine that will only do a particular action if the present input is the same as the immediately preceding input. A one-dimensional look-up table cannot solve this problem because it has no memory. It is in the same state after every input. All state-transition arrows loop back to the one state. It doesn't know what the previous input was. To respond differently to different sequences, the machine must change states and react differently in different states.

To give a machine the ability to change states, we must put in an element that can exist enduringly in two different states. The teeter-totter or rocker recommends itself (see element in center of Figure 8.4 labeled "flip-flop"). If you push one side of a teeter-totter down, it stays tilted that way. If you push the other side down, it stays tilted the other way. A machine with the functional structure of a teeter-totter, regardless of how it is physically constituted, is called a set-reset flip-flop. One state is called the Set state, the other, the Reset state. An input on the Set side puts it in the Set state if it is not already in it. If it is already in the Set state, it stays there. (Pushing down on the down side of the teeter-totter does not change its state.) Likewise on the Reset side.

The element that undergoes enduring changes of state must be able to alter the input-output characteristics of the machine. In the machine shown in Figure 8.4 we achieve this by connecting the rocker to a valve. The setting of the valve is determined by which way the rocker is tilted. For each input channel, there are two possible output channels. A marble falling in an input channel is directed into one or the other output channel, depending on the setting of the valve. Note that if the rocker is already tilted left, then a marble falling on the left does not change the rocker's state, while a marble falling on the right does. Similarly, when it is tilted right, a marble falling on that side does not change its state, while a marble falling on the other side does. Figure 8.5 shows the state diagram.

The machine in Figure 8.4, when followed by funneling that converges different combinations of output channels, implements all 16 of the functions defined on two sequential binary inputs, all possible mappings from 0 followed by 0, or 0 followed by 1, and so on, to a binary output (0 or 1). Two of these, the AND and the OR, together with a basic unary function, the NOT, constitute what computer scientists call the basic logic gates. Figure 8.6 shows the implementation of these basic gates. All of the other functions may be derived from these by composition. Moreover, any function that maps from binary vectors of arbitrary length to a binary output – any function that classifies binary vectors – can be implemented by the composition of these functions. Thus, this machinery is all that one needs

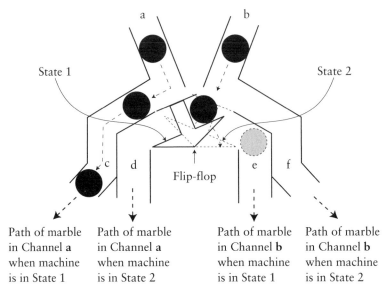

a   b

State 1   State 2

c   d   Flip-flop   e   f

Path of marble	Path of marble	Path of marble	Path of marble
in Channel **a**	in Channel **a**	in Channel **b**	in Channel **b**
when machine	when machine	when machine	when machine
is in State 1	is in State 2	is in State 1	is in State 2

Figure 8.4   Marble flip-flop with valve. This machine has two different states depending on which way the rocker (teeter-totter) at the center of the diagram has been tipped by previous input. The rocker is the mechanical implementation of the generic flip-flop. The T-shaped "gate" projecting up from the center of the rocker is a valve. It directs each of the two possible inputs into two possible outputs, depending on which state the rocker is in. Notice that a marble falling on the side to which the rocker is already tilted does not reverse its tilt, whereas a marble falling on the opposite side does.

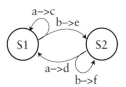

a->c
b->e
S1   S2
a->d
b->f

Figure 8.5   State diagram for the machine in Figure 8.4.

– *provided one can do unrestricted composition of functions* (!!) The machinery that implements the processor can be simple.

We have seen how to build some memory into our machine by having it change its state when it gets one signal or another. The change in state carries implicit information about what the previous input was, and it determines how the machine will react to each of the two possible input signals that follow. However, a memory only for the most recent input is not going to get us far. Can this approach be extended to make a machine with a memory for the last two inputs? It can, indeed. Figure 8.7 shows how this works in the case of the marble machine.

Our flip-flop led each of two inputs into two different channels depending on the state of the flip-flop. Thus, there are 4 channels in which an input marble may

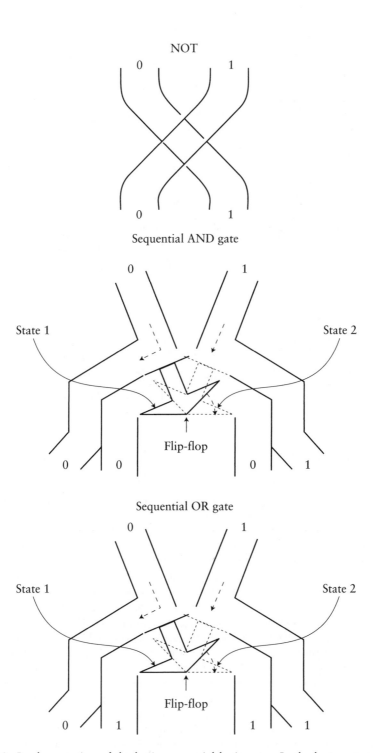

Figure 8.6 Implementation of the basic sequential logic gates. In the bottom two gates, the outputs with a common label are funneled together into a single common channel (not shown).

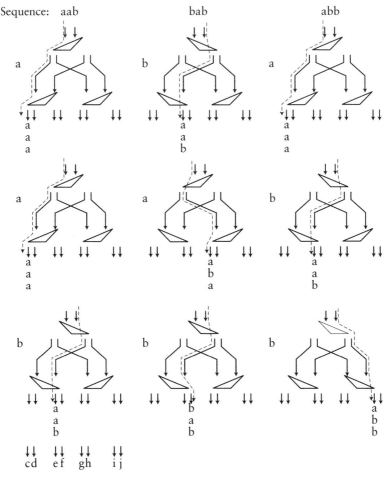

Figure 8.7 A two-back finite-state memory machine. Each vertical column gives the sequence of paths and the sequence of resulting machine states for the sequence of inputs given at the top of the column. At bottom left is the labeling of the eight output channels. In each case the machine is assumed to have had all three flip-flops tipped left at the start of the sequence. (This is the state of the machine when the last two inputs have been **a**.) The first row in a column shows the path of the first ball in the sequence and the state of the machine *after* that ball has passed through. The vertical sequence of letters at the end (bottom) of the path is the sequence that was completed by the passage of that ball. The channel in which that ball emerges is unique to that sequence. There are 8 possible sequences and 8 possible channels (**c, d, e, f, g, h, i,** and **j** – see bottom left) in which a ball may emerge, one channel for each sequence – see code table. The second row in a column shows that path of the second marble in the sequence and the state of the machine after it has passed, and likewise for the third row. The letter immediately to the left of any one diagram is the ball whose passage is indicated by the dashed line. Although this machine has 8 possible states (8 different configurations of the three flip-flops, we make use of only 4 of them, because there are only 4 possible histories when we look back only 2 steps: **aa, ab, ba,** and **bb**. Notice that sequences that have the same last two inputs leave the machine in the same state. See, for example, the state of the machine at the bottom of the first two columns. These are two different sequences, but the terminal (most recent) elements are **ab** in both cases, so they leave the machine in the same state.

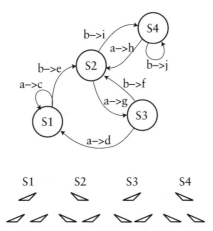

Figure 8.8 State diagram for a finite-state machine that can look 2 back. The four states of the machine are determined by the four configurations of the flip-flops that this particular 3-flip-flop machine can have. (Three-flip-flop machines with a different architecture may have as many as eight different states, because there are $2^3 = 8$ different configurations that 3 flip-flops can assume – see counter in figure below.) The configurations that define the states of the machine are shown below the state diagram.

emerge. The trick in looking two back is to cross over one member of each pair of output channels and combine it with the uncrossed member of the other pair to make two pairs of input channels to two further flip-flops (see Figure 8.7). The two further flip-flops will each have 4 output channels, so we will have 8 output channels from this second stage. That is the number we need, because there are two possible input signals (**a** & **b**) and, when we look two back, there are four possible signal histories: **aa**, **ab**, **ba**, and **bb**. Considering the two possible current inputs and the four possible histories, there are eight possibilities. We need a different output channel for each different possibility, and that is what we have – see Table 8.2. Figure 8.8 is the state diagram for this machine.

Table 8.2 Code table

Input signal sequence	Output signal
aaa	c
baa	d
aab	e
bab	f
aba	g
abb	h
bba	i
bbb	j

It is obvious that we can repeat this trick if we want to look three back. We need only add a third stage, composed of 4 flip-flops (with a total of 16 output channels), and suitably cross-connect the outputs from the second stage to this third stage. This machine will have 7 flip flops, $16 + 8 + 4 + 2 = 30$ signal channels and 28 AND gates. Moreover, it is clear that there is no reason – in principle, at least – why we cannot go on in this way indefinitely, making a machine capable of looking arbitrarily far back in determining what to do with the current input.

In practice, however, this approach should by now be setting off alarm bells in the alert reader's mind. We have been here before. We are face-to-face with an exponentially growing demand on physical resources. A look-64-back machine will need $2^{64} + 2^{63} + 2^{62} \ldots 2^2$ total signal channels, the same number of AND gates, and $2^{63} + 2^{62} \ldots 2^2$ flip-flops. These are stupefying numbers. So, this approach to looking back won't work. Yet, contemporary desktop computers can look back essentially indefinitely; looking back 64 bits is child's play. Clearly, there exist better architectures than the one we are considering, which is the architecture of a finite-state machine.

The essential failing of a finite state machine, as we have repeatedly stressed, is that it allocates hardware in advance to every *possibility*: there must be an output channel for every possible sequence – not for every sequence actually encountered, but for every sequence that might ever be encountered. In consequence, finite-state machines are rapidly blown away by the combinatorial explosions (the exponential increases in possible cases) that lurk behind every tree in the computing forest. They cannot cope with the infinitude of the possible. What is needed is an architecture that combats combinatoric explosions with combinatorics. The key to that architecture is a read/write memory. It must be possible to store sequences that actually occur in a memory capable of storing a great many extremely lengthy (but emphatically finite) sequences, drawn from the essentially infinite number of possible such sequences, and to compare those stored sequences to whatever sequences may prove to be relevant. This architecture uses memory and combinatorics to cope with the finitude of the actual.

At one time, neo-behaviorist psychologists thought that all of behavior could be explained by finite-state machines, provided we arranged it so that two marbles falling together could open or close gates and thereby change the path that subsequent marbles follow through the machine. The opening or closing of gates is a state memory. The idea was that the nervous system is basically an elaborate machine of the finite-state class. It comes endowed with a wide range of different sensory receptors, each sensitive to a different state of the world. There are, for example, millions of photoreceptors in the vertebrate retina. Each is sensitive to light coming from a slightly different direction, because the lens and cornea of the eye focus light arriving from different points in the world onto different parts of the retina. Similarly, sensory receptors along the basilar membrane of the ear are sensitive to different sound frequencies because different portions of the membrane have different resonant frequencies. Signals that start at different locations (in different sensory neurons) follow different paths through the nervous system. It was thought that certain combinations of events changed the state of the nervous system by changing its wiring diagram. This change in the wiring diagram explained why the system responded differently to inputs depending on the past history of its inputs. In other words, the idea was that the nervous system had the architecture of a finite-state machine. This is still the idea that dominates neurobiological thought. The idea is sometimes summarized by the pithy expression: Those that fire together, wire together.

Adding Register Memory

To combat combinatorics with combinatorics we need a better approach to memory. We need an approach in which combinations of state changes in memory elements (like flip-flops) can efficiently encode only what has actually happened. And, this encoding must be readable by some mechanism within the machine itself. We stress this because some of the codings that have been suggested in the neural network literature are only readable by a god outside the machine, a god who can observe the state of all the machine's components. A readable encoding is one that can be causally effective within the machine. The simplest device with a readable memory is a binary counter. It encodes and remembers in a readable form the number of inputs that have occurred. Counters are of interest because they also implement the addition operation, which is one of the key operations in the system of arithmetic on which quantitative computations of all kinds are based.

The readable binary counter and adder

A counter uses the toggle form of the flip-flop, in which there is only one input and the flip-flop changes state after each input, flipping in response to the first input, flopping back in response to the second, flipping again in response to the third (Figure 8.9), and so on. The power button on electronic devices such as computers and the remote controller for a TV are toggles: pushing the button once turns the device on; pushing it again turns it back off.

Figure 8.10 shows how to configure toggle flip-flops to make a binary counter. This configuration is also called a frequency divider, because the frequency with which each toggle in the sequence flips and flops as marble after marble is fed into the machine is one half the frequency with which the toggle preceding it in the

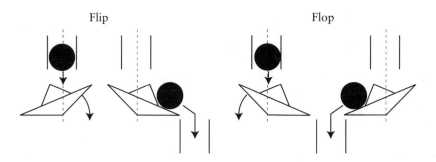

Figure 8.9 Mechanical toggle flip-flop.

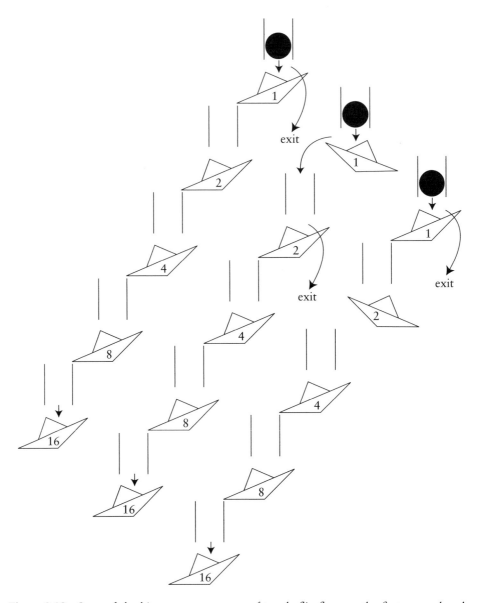

Figure 8.10 State of the binary counter array of toggle flip-flops as the first, second and third marbles enter it. For the first marble, all the toggles are in the flopped (0) position. The first marble flips the "1" toggle and then exits the array. The second marble flops the "1" toggle back to its 0 position, rolls off it onto the "2" toggle, which it flips, and then it exits. Thus, as the third marble enters, it finds the "1" in the flopped position and the "2" in the flipped position. It flips "1" and exits, leaving both "2" and "1" in the flipped position. The number of marbles that have passed through the array is given by the sum of the "number names" of the toggles that are in the flipped position. After three marbles, the "2" and the "1" are the only toggles in the flipped position, and 2 + 1 = 3. The fourth marble in will flop the "1" back to the 0 position, roll off it and onto the "2" toggle, which it will also flop back to the 0, rolling off it to flip the "4" toggle before finally exiting the array.

sequence flips and flops. The first toggle (toggle "1" in Figure 8.10) changes state with every input. However, it passes on the marble to the input to the next toggle only when it returns from the flipped state to the flopped state. Thus, it passes on only every second marble that it sees. The same is true for each successive toggle: The "2" toggle passes on to the "4" toggle only every second marble that it sees, so the "4" toggle changes state only every fourth marble. The "4" toggle passes on to the "8" toggle only every second marble it sees, so the "8" toggle changes state only every eighth marble. And so on.

Although, the array of toggle flip-flops in Figure 8.10 encodes the number of marbles that have passed through the array, as well as implementing both addition and division by successive powers of two, there is no provision for reading the facts about previous input that it encodes. We, who stand outside the machine, can see how many have passed through by noting the positions of the toggles. But how can other machinery within this machine gain access to this information?[1] We must add machinery that transcribes the configuration of the toggles into a pattern of falling marbles (a signal vector) specifying the number of marbles that have been through the array. Matthias Wandel has devised an ingeniously simple solution to this problem and built the corresponding marble machine. Figure 8.11 is a sketch of his machine.

Figure 8.11 and its caption explain how the machine functions as a readable counter. This is our first example of a machine with a read/write memory. It fights combinatorics with combinatorics. A machine built to this design can remember in readable form (that is, in a form accessible to computation) any number between 0 and $2^{64} - 1$, with only 64 toggles. Moreover, it remembers any number within that incomprehensibly vast range of numbers using at most 64 marbles, and usually (on average) many fewer.

Wandel's machine also implements some of the functionality of the processing unit in a digital computer. It demonstrates the physical realization of a compact procedure, the procedure for adding binary encoded numbers: With the release slide in the hold position, one can place marbles corresponding to the binary code for a number into the input register at the top of the machine. When the release slide is then pushed forward, these marbles all drop down the respective input channels, flip the corresponding toggle, and lodge in its input buffer. For example, if one places marbles in the "16," "4," and "1" holes, and pushes the release slide, they will flip the "16," "4," and "1" toggles and lodge in the corresponding memory buffers, storing the number 16 + 4 + 1 = 21. Now, one can place marbles in, say, the "32," "4," and "2" holes of the input register, entering the number 32 + 4 + 2 = 38. When the release slide is pushed, the marble in the "2" hole falls on the "2" toggle, flipping it and lodging in the "2" memory buffer; the marble in the "4" hole falls on the "4" toggle, which is already in the flipped position, holding a marble in the "4" memory buffer. The marble falling on it flops it back to the 0 position, releasing the marble in its buffer, which falls out of the machine. The marble that fell on the "4" toggle rolls off it to its left onto the "8" toggle, which

---

[1] It is surprising how often in the neural net literature this critical point is ignored.

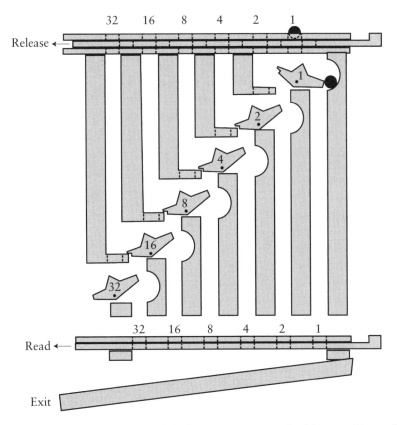

Figure 8.11 Sketch of Matthias Wandel's binary counting and adding marble machine. Input marbles are placed in the holes at the top. They are held there until the release slide is pushed forward, aligning its holes with the holes holding the marbles and with the input holes to the toggle flip-flops. If the release slide is left in the release position, then the machine simply counts the number of marbles dropped into the "1" hole. When a marble falls down the "1" input, it flips the "1" toggle and then rolls into a memory buffer (the notch to the right of the toggle), where it is retained by the flipped toggle. When a second marble is dropped through the "1" input, it flops the "1" toggle back to its 0 position, releasing the marble in the memory buffer, which then falls out of the machine by way of the exit channel at the bottom. The new marble rolls off the "1" toggle onto the "2" toggle, which it flips. This new marble lodges in the memory buffer for the "2" toggle. When a third marble comes, it flips the "1" toggle and lodges in its memory buffer. At this point there are two marbles in memory buffers, one in the "2" buffer and one in the "1" buffer. The fourth marble flops the "1" toggle back to 0, emptying its buffer, rolls off it to flop the "2" toggle back to 0, emptying its buffer, and rolls off it to flip the "4" toggle, in whose memory buffer it then lodges. The next two marbles will flip and flop the "1" toggle. The second of them will flip the "2" toggle and lodge in its buffer. Yet another marble (the seventh) will flip the "1" again and lodge in its buffer. At this point, there will be marbles lodged in the "4," "2," and "1" buffers, reflecting the fact that there have been 4 + 2 + 1 = 7 marbles. The beauty of the Wandel machine is that when the "read" slide is pushed forward, it pushes up a set of vertical rods (not shown), which tip all of the toggles into the 0 position, emptying the buffers simultaneously and creating in so doing a pattern of three falling marbles that encodes in binary the number of marbles (seven) that has passed through the array. Watch Wandel demonstrate this machine at http://woodgears.ca/marbleadd. (Reproduced by permission of the author.)

it flips. The release of the marble in the "4" buffer together with the flipping of the "8" toggle and the lodging in its memory buffer implements the "carry" operation in binary addition. Finally, the marble in the "32" hole falls on the "32" toggle, flipping it and lodging in its memory buffer. There are now marbles in the "32," "16," "8," "2," and "1" buffers. Thus, the memory buffer of this CPU now contains the number $32 + 16 + 8 + 2 + 1 = 59$, the sum of 21 and 38, the two numbers that were to be added. When the read slide is pushed, these marbles all fall out of the memory buffers together, giving the binary signal that represents the sum.

A Wandel machine with 64 toggles can add any number less than or equal to 2^{63} to any other number less than or equal to 2^{63}. Thus, it can compute 2^{126} different sums (ignoring commutativity). If we tried to do this with a look-up table, which is how neural network models commonly implement the arithmetic addition of two numerical inputs (Dehaene, 2001, see also Chapter 14), the table would have 2^{126} cells, which is to say, 2^{126} output neurons, and 2^{64} input neurons, (one for each of the 2^{63} rows and one for each of the 2^{63} columns). There are not that many atoms in the human brain, let alone neurons. It is physically impossible to implement the computation with a look-up table over a truly large range; whereas when it is implemented as a compact procedure, the demands on physical resources are trivial. However, the need for a read/write memory in the latter implementation appears to be inescapable. And, because the mechanism operates on a compact encoding of the integers, a modest degree of structural complexity in the processing machinery also appears inescapable.

The shift register

Now, we return to the problem of remembering the sequence of binary inputs going back a non-trivial number of inputs. Figure 8.12 shows how to configure flip-flops to make what is called a shift register.

As in the counter and adder, the '0' position of each flip-flop is tilted left, while the '1' position is tilted right. If a marble enters the '0' (left) side with the flip-flop in the '0' position and a marble in its '0' register memory (as in Figure 8.12), the entering marble rolls over the marble in the memory register and down to the next flip-flop, which it also enters from the '0' side. This continues until it finds a flip-flop that is either in the '1' position (flipped, in which case it will always have a marble in its '1' register) or in the '0' position (flopped) without a marble in its '0' register. In the first case, the falling marble flops the rocker back into the '0' position, releasing the marble that was in its '1' register. The released marble falls until it encounters a rocker in its '0' (flopped position). It flips that rocker into the '1' position and lodges in its '1' register. In the second case (rocker in '0' position with no marble in the register), the incoming marble lodges in the '0' register. Thus, with marbles in the '0' register of the top rocker and the '1' register of the second rocker, as shown in Figure 8.12, the occupied registers after a third marble has entered on the '0' side, will end up being <001>. The previous pattern <01> has been shifted down one rocker and the latest entry has in effect (though not in actuality) been placed at the top. (In assessing the final patterns, ignore where the incoming marble actually lodged and focus only on the resulting pattern.)

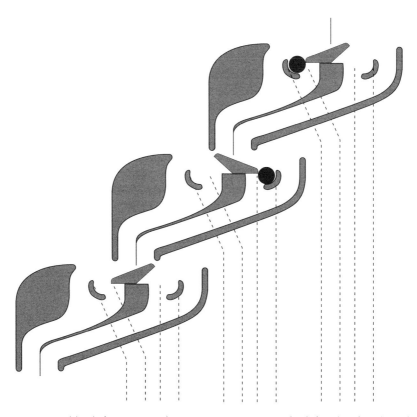

Figure 8.12   Marble shift register. The memory register on the left side of each rocker is the '0' register; the one on the right, the '1' register. In the configuration shown, there is a marble in the '0' register of the top rocker and one in the '1' register of the second rocker. There is no marble in the memory registers of the third rocker down, because there have been only two inputs. The farther back in the sequence a marble came in, the lower down in the array of rockers it lodges. Thus, the marble in the '1' register of the second rocker came first, followed by the marble in the '0' register of the top rocker. The values of previous inputs are read by a mechanism that opens panels behind the memory buffers, dropping whatever marbles are there into the channels indicated by the dashed lines, which are behind the machinery through which incoming marbles drop.

If the third marble enters instead on the '1' side, it flips the top rocker, releasing the marble from its '0' register and lodging in its '1' register. The released marble flops the second register into its '0' position, lodging in the corresponding memory register, and releasing the marble from the '1' register. The marble released from the '1' register of the second rocker flops the third rocker into its '1' position and lodges in the corresponding memory register. Thus, the final pattern is <101>. Again, this is the previous pattern shifted down one level, with the latest entry at the top.

In summary, in a shift register, the pattern in memory after each new input is the pattern before that input shifted down one level, with the new input at the top.

The memory location ('0' or '1') of the marble lodged in the topmost register indicates the side from which the most recent marble entered the machine. The occupied memory location in the next flip-flop down indicates the side from which the previous marble entered, and so on down. Thus, the sequence is preserved (remembered) by the memory locations in which marbles are lodged. Actuating a release mechanism opens doors behind the memory locations, releasing the marbles into the dashed channels. This is the read operation. It transcribes the symbol (the pattern of lodged marbles) into a signal.

We can arrange the read mechanism in three different ways. We can arrange it so that it slides in from the right, only as far as it has to in order to release the first marble. If we arrange the read operation this way, we have a last-in-first-out push down stack memory, which is the most common kind. Reading and removing the last input is called popping the stack. Alternatively, we can arrange it so that the release mechanism slides in from the left only as far as is necessary to release the lowest marble in the stack. This is a first-in-first-out memory. Finally, we can arrange it so that all the marbles are released at once, in which case what was an input sequence is converted to the same pattern but in parallel, because all the marbles fall more or less at once.

A shift register that enables the computer to look back 64 inputs requires only 64 flip-flops and $2 \times 64 = 128$ output channels and $2 \times 64 = 128$ OR gates. The material resources required grow only in proportion to the distance to be looked back, *not exponentially*. The contrast between an exponentially growing demand on material resources and a linearly (or, in the case of the counter, a logarithmically) growing demand is profoundly important. With exponentially growing demand, it rapidly becomes impossible to use state memory to look back through the input, whereas with linearly (or better yet, logarithmically) growing demand, we can record the input exactly going back a very long way indeed before putting any serious strain on material resources. A computer with a gigabyte of free RAM can look back 8,000,000,000 steps.

The essential point is that when the demand on physical resources increases exponentially, it rapidly outstrips any conceivable supply. We stress this because neurobiologists and neural network modelers are sometimes overawed by the large number of neurons in the mammalian brain and the even larger number of synaptic connections between them. They think that those impressive numbers make the brain a match for any problem. In fact, however, they do not – if the brain has the wrong architecture. If it uses a finite-state architecture to record input sequences, then it will not be able to record sequences of any appreciable length.

A shift register read/write memory architecture enables us to look after the fact for an arbitrary input sequence over very long stretches of input, without having to pre-specify a distinct chunk of hardware uniquely dedicated to each possible sequence. Our stack memory uses combinatorics to deal with the combinatorial explosion. A single stack n levels deep can record 2^n different sequences. Thus, we use exponential combinatorics in our memory mechanism to deal with the combinatorial explosion that threatens as soon as we contemplate looking back through the input sequence. We create a memory that has only a modest number of components, but can nonetheless correctly record any one from among a set of possible sequences more numerous than the set of all the elementary particles in the universe. We defeat the infinitude of the possible sequences by creating a memory that records only the actual sequence experienced.

Summary

Any computing machine (indeed, any machine), whatever its physical composition, has a functional architecture. It is put together out of components that implement distinct and simple functions. These functional building blocks are interconnected in some systematic way. To specify the functional building blocks of the machine and the arrangement of the interconnections between them is to specify the functional architecture of the system. Computer science has always been an important part of cognitive science, but, in our opinion, some basic insights from computer science about the nature of computation and its physical implementation have been largely ignored in contemporary efforts to imagine how the brain might carry out the computations that the behavioral data imply it does carry out. Computer scientists understand that there is a logic to the physical realization of computation. This logic powerfully constrains the functional architecture of successful computing machines, just as the laws of optics powerfully constrain the design of successful imaging devices. It is, thus, no accident that the functional architecture of computing machines has – in its broad outlines – changed hardly at all during the 60 years over which this development has been a central feature of modern technological progress. It would be difficult to exaggerate the importance of the role that the development of computing technology has played in the overall development of technology since World War II. At that time, almost none of the machines in routine domestic or military use depended on computing devices, whereas now it would be difficult to find a machine of any complexity that did not rely heavily on computing technology. At that time, communications technology did not depend on computing technology, whereas now computing is at the heart of it. Staggering sums of money and untold amounts of human ingenuity have gone into the development of this technology. It has been the source of vast personal and corporate fortunes. We stress these truisms to emphasize the sustained intensity of human thought and experimentation that has been focused on the question of how to make effective computing machines. The fact that their basic functional architecture has not changed suggests that this architecture is strongly constrained by the nature of computation itself.

In this and the preceding chapter we have attempted to elucidate that constraint in order to explain why computing machines have the functional architecture that they have. In the preceding chapter, we recounted Turing's insight into the basic simplicity of what was required in a machine that was in principle capable of computing anything that could be computed. Turing's analysis of the components that were necessary to implement any doable computation introduced the distinction between the two most basic functional components of a computing machine: the processor and the memory. The processor is the finite-state machine that reads symbols and creates new symbols and symbol strings. The read/write memory device carries the symbols forward in time. It makes possible the almost unlimited composition of functions. In this chapter, we spelled out some key functional elements out of which both the finite-state machine and the memory may be constructed.

Because we are concerned with the architecture of autonomous process-control computing machines, our finite machine has some functional components that did not enter into Turing's analysis. Autonomous process-control computing machines have transducers, which convert external events into internal machine signals. The signals carry symbolic information from place to place within the machine. In our marble machines, the transducer is the device that releases a marble when pushed on. The marble falling in a channel is the internal machine signal. The marbles are all the same; one signal is distinguished from another by the channel in which the marble falls. And process-control computers have effectors, which convert internal machine signals into external events within the system on which the process-control machine operates (that is, within the process that it controls). In our marble machine, placing a bell at the bottom of a channel converts the falling of the marble into the ding of the bell.

The simplest functional architecture of these three components – transducers, signal carriers, and effectors – is the look-up table. If we restrict our functional building blocks only to those three, then we can only build one-dimensional look-up tables. These are machines of such limited capabilities that one may question whether they should be considered computing machines. They have the functional structure of a typewriter that lacks a shift key. That is, they map distinct inputs (key presses) to distinct outputs (letters typed). Thus, one would consider these to be computing machines only if one considered a typewriter to be a computing machine. We are not inclined to do this ourselves, but it is of no great consequence where we draw the line between machines that have some of the functional capabilities of a computing machine and machines that are Turing machines. It is only important to be clear about the limits of lesser machines and what those limits arise from, what is missing in their functional architecture.

To make a more powerful machine, we need to add elements that perform the same function in the machine that the logical operators perform in logical propositions. The three such functions most commonly considered are the AND function, the OR function and the NOT function. We know from symbolic logic that there are other possibilities. For example, it can be shown that the three functions just mentioned can all be realized from (or analytically reduced to) the NAND (not AND) function. Thus, if one has an element that performs the NAND function, then one can construct out of it components that perform the other functions. The essential point is that a very small number of signal combining and inverting functions are essential. The AND element transmits a signal if and only if two other signals are both received. The OR element transmits a signal if and only if either one or the other of two input signals is received. The NOT element blocks or inverts the signal it receives. It transmits a '1' when it gets a '0' and a '0' when it gets a 1. (For the curious reader: the NAND element transmits a signal if and only if it does not get signals on both its inputs.)

The implementation of these functions in our marble machine was somewhat complicated by our stipulating that input signals had to occur sequentially. (We insisted on this constraint in order to put ourselves in a position to highlight the fundamental role that a read/write memory plays in computation.) Thus, our implementation of the AND and OR functions required an element that remembered what the immediately preceding signal was. Both implementations required a funnel or point of convergence, where two distinct signals (marbles falling in different channels) came together to make a single signal (a marble falling in the output channel from the gate).

The addition of these simple logical functions greatly enhances the computational capacity of our machine. Now, for example, we can construct two-dimensional and, indeed, *n*-dimensional look-up tables. To return for a moment to the typewriter analogy, we now have a typewriter in which the letter that gets typed may be made to depend on which *combination* of keys is pressed (as is the case for combinations of the Command, Control, Option, and Shift keys on a computer). Thus, we can implement many–one functions. These include the elementary operations of arithmetic: addition, subtraction, multiplication, division, and ordination, all of which map two inputs to one output. Thus, in principle at least, we now have a functional architecture that can compute in something like the ordinary sense of the term. It is not, however, a practical device for implementing even simple arithmetic because it does not implement compact procedures. While in principle we can implement the arithmetic operations in such a machine, in practice we will run afoul of the problem of pre-specification and the infinitude of the possible. If we try to use look-up tables, we will have to put into our machine distinct physical elements for each distinct combination of inputs that might ever have to be added (or subtracted, or multiplied, etc.). This will rapidly exhaust any conceivable supply of physically realized machine elements. Thus, this architecture is of limited practical use.

We take another step toward realizing full-blown computational capability by adding elements that change the state of the machine. The state of the machine determines how it will process the next input. When we depress the shift key on a typewriter, we change the state of the array of strikers so that the lower half of each striker now strikes the paper, rather than the upper half. This changes the input-output characteristics of the machine; the letter produced by pressing any given key. This was the essence of Turing's conception of the state of the "processor," the finite-state machine that is one of the two most basic components of a Turing machine. In Turing's machine, the state of the machine determines how it reacts to the symbol currently under the reading head. How it reacts is completely specified by the answers to two simple questions: (1) Will it convert the symbol (changing a '1' to a '0' or a '0' to a '1') or leave it as it is? (2) Which of its possible states will it transition to? At this stage of our elaboration of our marble machines, we had not yet introduced a memory (that is, a device for arresting the fall of a marble and retaining it in the machine for later use). However, because our machines are autonomous process-control machines, they also have an input signal. Thus, we introduced an element – the rocker or teeter-totter element – that changes the way the machine processes a marble falling in a given channel. An element capable of changing its state must have more than one state. Our rockers have two stable states, the indispensable minimum. The generic name for such a functional element is "switch" or "flip-flop."

Introducing an element with more than one stable state brings memory into the machine, because now we can set up the machine so that past inputs determine the current state of the processor. We consider how this new capability enables us to respond to different sequences of inputs in different ways. The problem we consider is how to make the channel in which a marble falls – that is, the output from our machine – depend on the sequence of past inputs. At first, the solution to this looks straightforward. We arrange the flip-flops in a cascade, such that different sequences of marbles falling through the machine leave the flip-flops in different configurations, a different configuration for each sequence. Each different configuration channels the next input marble into a different output channel. In principle, this allows us to look as far back in the sequence as we like. In practice, however, it has the same fatal flaw as the look-up table approach to the implementation of arithmetic: it leads rapidly to the exhaustion of any conceivable store of physically realized computational elements. The proof that this is so is part of the standard computer science course in finite-state automata. Thus, an architecture in which the only way that the past can affect the present process is by leaving the processor in a state unique to that past is not a viable architecture for a great many computational purposes. It succumbs to the infinitude of the possible: you do not have to look back very far before the exponentially growing number of possible sequences becomes too large to cope with.

Finally, we introduce a read/write memory element, an element that can arrest the fall of a marble and retain it for later release. The arresting and retention of a falling marble is the write operation; its subsequent release is the read operation. Now, we can fight the combinatoric explosions that bring down on us the infinitude of the possible with combinatoric codings that enable us to work only with the finite actual. When we tried to create sequence-dependent outputs that looked back as little as 64 inputs, we were already overwhelmed by the exponential increase in the possibilities, hence in the required number of rockers and output channels. Now, when the number of physical elements we need in order to remember any particular past sequence increases only in proportion to the length of that sequence, we can look back millions of steps in the input sequence. Because we can arrest a marble in its fall and release it later, together with other similarly arrested marbles, we no longer need a different output channel for every possible sequence. We can use a combinatoric code in which the number of sequences it can code grows exponentially with the number of coding elements (output channels).

Now we can also implement compact procedures, as demonstrated by the marble machine that adds binary numbers. A machine with only 64 rockers, each with a single (one-bit) memory register, can add any two binary numbers in the range from 0 to 2^{63}.

The point we wish to stress is that this logic is inescapable – the logic that makes a machine with read/write memory elements vastly more capable than a machine that can remember the past only by changing the state of the processor. This fact is a ground truth that must be faced by anyone considering how computation might be effected in any physically realized device, no matter what materials it is made of, no matter how many elements it has, and no matter how richly interconnected those elements are. In considering viable functional architectures for computing machines this ground truth is as important as are the laws of optics for anyone considering viable functional architectures for imaging devices like cameras and eyes.

9

Data Structures

We come now to consider the architectural aspect of a full-powered (Turing complete) computing device that gives the symbol processing-machinery unrestricted access to the information-carrying symbols in its memory. The key to such unrestricted access is an addressable read/write memory – memory that can be located, read from, and written to. The architecture must be capable of symbolizing its own memory locations (addresses) using encoding symbols. That is, the machine must have a representation of its memory locations, making it possible to encode the relations between symbols (forming more complex symbols) by virtue of the symbols' relation to one another within the memory. This same aspect of the architecture allows for the creation of new symbols – symbols that aren't present in the system at its inception.

Memory structures in which the relations between symbols are encoded via their topological relationships within memory are what computer scientists call data structures. As we discussed in Chapter 5, a data structure is a complex symbol. Its constituents are themselves symbols. The referent of the data structure is determined by the referents of its constituents and the syntactic (physical) relation between them.

A minimal example of a data structure is an integer encoded in binary. Each bit serves to indicate a power of two, and which power of two is indicated by the relative position of the bits. What makes this a data structure, as opposed to being simply an encoding symbol, is that it is composed of symbols (the bits) that are placed in topological relation to each other (a linear order). Which bits are where within the string determines the referent. Contrast this to an encoding where an integer is encoded using an analog property such as the number of molecules in a "bag." Here, the symbol is still an encoding symbol as the referent can be determined by a compact procedure (simply "weigh" the bag). However, as the symbol has no constituent structure, combinatorial syntax becomes impossible. Trying to form more complex symbols using this technique becomes problematic (Fodor & Pylyshyn, 1988).

Data structures composed of linearly ordered bits are so common that in modern computers, they are typically handled within the architecture of the machine as minimal packets (units) of memory. Currently, the packet size (often called the "word" size) is typically 32 or 64 bits. When these multi-bit symbols are transcribed into signals to be transported to computational machinery, they travel together on what is called a *bus*. The bus capacity is also measured in bits and indicates how many bits are transported in parallel. Even when the computational machinery that accesses a word only needs the information carried by a single bit in this sequence, the whole word is transported. Although this system is potentially wasteful with respect to memory use, it pays for itself in temporal efficiency. With a single read operation, the system gains access to one of 2^{64} possible messages. When the information carried by this signal is brought to the computational machinery, its substructure (the bits that comprise it) can be individually manipulated, allowing for operations such as addition, parity check, etc., on appropriately encoded numbers.

In a typical symbol for the binary encoding of an integer, the constituent symbols are atomic data (bits) that are physically adjacent in a strict ordering. This physical adjacency must be supported by the architecture of the machine that processes the symbols. It must be sensitive to what data is adjacent to what other data, and capable of functioning differently based on that. If there is to be any topology of the memory at all (providing for combinatorial syntax), then there is no substitute for having such a physical system for stringing together the data.[1] This places strong constraints on the architecture of memory in the brain. Neural network models of brain architecture do not provide such a topologically sensitive architecture; therefore, they do not provide a means of forming data structures.

As mentioned, the binary encoding of an integer by bits is a minimal data structure, typically not even referred to as such, as these structures are often grouped together as single units by the machine's architecture. This approach – making complex symbols simply by lengthening the string of bits – has its limits, namely the size in bits of this unit. If the word size is 64 bits, then the number of messages that can be encoded is limited to 2^{64} – probably sufficient to store integers of interest, but certainly *not* enough to form more complex symbols, such as location vectors. The encoding of a point on the plane into the symbol <4.7, 6.3> is such a data structure. The referents of the constituent symbols ('4.7' and '6.3') and their relative positions come into play in decoding this symbol.

Complex data structures encode the sorts of things that are asserted in what philosophers and logicians call propositions. Examples include: "All men are mortal," and "Socrates is a man," from which it famously follows that "Socrates is mortal." The derivation of new propositions from old ones is, roughly speaking at least, what we understand by thought. A device capable of this activity must be able to represent, access, decode, and manipulate data structures in memory.

---

[1] Technically, the data need not be physically adjacent. The architecture of the machine could realize such a *next to* operation using some arbitrary (but fixed in the architecture) topological relationship. No computer architecture uses such a technique and there is no reason to think that the brain would employ such a method. Separating the data would make the machine unnecessarily complex and would also be less efficient, as the data constituting a symbol would have to be brought together in space anyway to decode the symbol.

Finding Information in Memory

If symbols (and data structures) in memory are to be used productively, the computing machine must be able to locate them. Computer scientists refer to this process as *addressing*. An address specifies the location of the symbol in memory. In considering how the information in memory can be addressed, we need to consider the degree to which the information carried by a symbol is or is not contingent, that is, the degree to which it may change with time and circumstance.

Immediate addressing (literals)

Not all values that enter into some computations are contingent. The ratio between the circumference of a circle and its diameter does not change with time and circumstance.[2] Therefore, there is no reason to look up the *current* value of this ratio when using it in a computation. In a computation into which this value enters, the value can be built directly into the computational procedure (the mechanism). In that case, the value is not accessible outside of the procedure. Computer programmers call a built-in value a *literal* and the addressing "mode" is called *immediate addressing*, because the value is embedded into the program/procedure itself. In the Turing machine that we devised to compute the successor function, an encoding of the number that was added (1) was not on the tape (not in data memory). The use of the number 1 in this procedure was only discernible through the functioning of the machine. It was handled procedurally by the state memory. The machine's "knowledge" of this number is of the opaque implicit kind; the machine cannot gain computational access to this information outside of the state into which it is built. Immediate addressing therefore is really a degenerate case of addressing, as the value involved appears *in situ*. The machinery doesn't have to find the value. It is built into the structure that realizes the process. One could have designed the Turing machine such that the amount to be added each time was found on the tape. In this case, the number to be added could be changed by any module in the system that could gain access to this symbol. As implemented, for the machine to add a different number, say 2 instead of 1, one would have to change the states of this system – that is, rewire it.

In psychological terms, a value such as π is a plausible candidate for an innately known value. In biological terms, we might find that this ratio was implicit in the structure of genetically specified computational machinery. Whether there is any instance in which π is in fact an innately known value is not at issue here. It clearly could be. There is good evidence, for example, that the period of the earth's rotation is built into the machinery of the circadian clock; it is hard wired in the brain's biochemistry. The period of a planet's rotation is a more contingent value than is the ratio of the circumference of a circle to its diameter. The period of rotation (the duration of a day-night cycle) would be different if we lived on a different planet, whereas the value of π would be the same on any planet on which sentient

---

[2] In the locally Euclidean space of everyday experience.

life happened to evolve. From the perspective of our parochial evolutionary history, however, the period of the earth's rotation is as immutable as the value of π. You wouldn't want to wait (or prepare) for either value to change. Thus, π and the period of the earth's rotation are both plausible literals, constants whose values might be implicit in the structure of a computational device designed to represent the world in which the animals we know have evolved.

In a computer program[3] a line of code that uses a literal might look something like: 'X =: Y + 12'; indicating that the value of the variable 'X' (see below regarding variables) should be updated such that it is the sum of the value of the variable 'Y' and 12. Literals are rarely used by computer programmers, as few values can be fixed at the time the program is written. In fact, the use of literals is discouraged; they are disparagingly referred to as "magic numbers" – numbers that appear out of nowhere and without clear referents. In the example above, it may have been the case that '12' was indicating the number of months in a year; however this information is hidden from view. If it turns out that such numbers are contingent, then the program itself (the computing machinery) has to be changed – possibly in many of its parts.

Direct (absolute) addressing: Variables and their values

Most computationally important values are contingent: they vary with time and circumstance. The compass direction of the sun is an example; it changes as the day goes on. We know that this value often enters into the computations that mediate animal navigation (see Chapter 13). Even insects routinely compute the angle that they should fly with respect to the sun in order to reach a feeding site at a previously learned compass direction from the hive or nest. In doing so, the machinery of their brains takes advantage of the fact that the solar bearing of the goal (the sought-for angle) is its compass bearing (its direction relative to the north–south axis) minus the current compass direction of the sun (the sun's direction relative to that same axis – see Chapter 13). Because the sun's current compass direction varies – its value depends on the local phase of the day–night cycle (the time of day), the season, and the observer's latitude – its current value cannot be embedded in the mechanism of computation; it cannot be a literal.

Values like the sun's compass direction arise whenever experience is informative, in Shannon's sense. The possible values for the compass direction of the sun are an example of what Shannon called a set of possible messages. Sets of possible messages that may be communicated to us through our experience of the world are

---

[3] There may be some confusion regarding programs as "computational machinery." We note that a computer *qua* Turing machine has computational machinery (hardware) that implements the state changes, and then an independent memory system for holding symbols. Therefore, the "program" of a Turing machine is considered part of its fixed architecture. When we use the term "program" and show an example code fragment, we are using it to symbolize this fixed architecture. However, modern computers are examples of universal machines, machines that can read from their memory "programs" (software) that themselves symbolize procedures that are executed. The issue of whether or not the computational machinery found in animals and humans is universal is an open one. For our purposes, one can think of a computer program as the fixed architecture of the computing machine.

ubiquitous. Computer scientists use the term *variable* to refer to such sets of possible messages. A variable gives the location of a value within the representing system, its *address*. The symbol found at the address encodes the value of the variable. The address itself, which is, of course, distinct from what is found at that address, is the variable.

How then can we structure a computational device so that a symbol specifying the current value of a variable can be located and brought to the symbol-processing machinery? This is the problem of *variable binding*. Given a variable, how is its associated value located, so that it may be transported to the computational machinery that makes productive use of it? Additionally, how does one write a *new* (updated) value for this variable? The solution to both problems – an *addressable* read/write memory – is a fundamental part of the architecture of a conventional computing machine (see Figure 9.1).

The neural network architecture lacks this functional component because neuroscientists have yet to discover a plausible basis for such a mechanism. That lack makes the problem of variable binding an unsolved problem in neural network computation (Browne & Pilkington, 1994; Browne & Sun, 2001; Frasconia, Gori, Kurfessc, & Sperdutid, 2002; Gualtiero, 2007 (online); Lòpez-Moliner & Ma Sopena, 1993; Smolensky, 1990; Sougné, 1998; Sun, 1992). We believe that the only satisfactory solution to the problem is an addressable read/write memory. Therefore, we believe that there must be such a mechanism in the functional structure of neural computation. A major motivation for our book is the hope of persuading the neuroscience community to make the search for this mechanism an important part of the neuroscience agenda.

Figure 9.1 shows the structure of a memory that allows computational mechanisms to access the values of variables. The bit patterns on the left are the addresses. They are not themselves accessible to computation; they cannot be written to or read from. An address code (signal), when placed onto the address bus, selects the row with the matching bit pattern in its address field. The signal on the address bus is a probe. The memory location whose address matches the probe is activated. The bits encoding the information stored at a given address are found at the intersections of the horizontal and vertical lines to the right of the address. The vertical lines are the data lines leading to and from the data bus, the multilane highway that conveys retrieved symbols (bit patterns) to the symbol-processing machinery and from the symbol-processing machinery back to memory.

In a read operation, the computational machinery places the appropriate address signal onto the address bus, and then pulses the read/write line (which can itself be thought of as part of the address bus) in the read mode (it sends the read bit). This causes the bit pattern in the selected row to be transcribed onto the data bus. The data bus carries it back into the computation where the value was requested. In a write operation, the computational machinery puts the appropriate address signal onto the address bus, places the value to be written onto the data bus, and then pulses the read/write line in the write mode. This causes the value on the data bus to be transcribed at the intersections of the data bus and the row selected by the address bus, thereby storing the information contained in that signal into a symbol – to be carried forward in time until it is requested via another read operation.

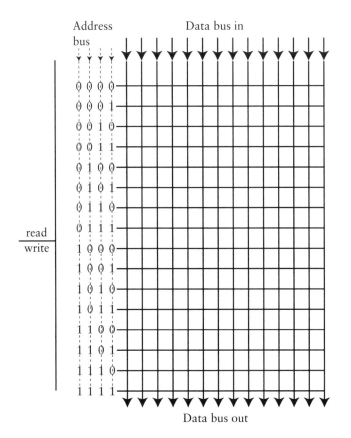

Figure 9.1   Structure of a random-access read/write memory.

A variable, then, is, physically speaking, an address; the symbol for the current value of that variable is the contents of memory at that address. The distinction between a variable (an address) and the value of that variable (the information to be found at that address) mediates the intercourse between past and present, between then and now. It is what makes it possible to bring the information gained *then* to bear on the problem one is solving *now*. It also mediates the interaction between the computational processes that extract information from experience and the computational processes that may later use that information to inform current behavior. The address of the information is the point of contact between the two processes. The information-extraction process writes the information to the address, that is, it binds the value to the variable. The utilization process reads the variable to obtain the behaviorally relevant information (the value). By using a variable to indicate the value that is needed, we need only change the value *once* at the appropriate location. That one change makes the value accessible anywhere that it is used.

Variables make it possible for different computational modules to share information – for one module to read what another has written. They make it possible to change the value that enters into a computation without changing the structure of the mechanism that performs the computation. In typical artificial neural network architectures, the system learns by rewiring the computational machinery so as to make the system behave more effectively. By contrast, in a conventional computing architecture, the system learns by changing the values of variables – and, as we will see in a moment, by creating new variables, as experience requires them. There is no rewiring in this architecture, but there is learning.

The random-access architecture allows any module to retrieve the value of any variable in constant time. Contrast this to the Turing machine architecture in which memory must be addressed sequentially. The Turing machine architecture is not a plausible model for an efficient memory, as this sequential access (searching through all of memory to find what is needed) would simply be too slow. All modern computers use the random-access model of memory.

The architecture of the random-access read/write memory is identical to the architecture of the content addressable memory that we dismissed as untenable in Chapter 6. In that case, the parallel architecture is used to implement a look-up table for a specific function. Thus, a random-access memory can function as a content-addressable memory. It could, for example, be used to determine the addition function f_+: $N \times N \rightarrow N$, for 32-bit numbers. In this use, the address bus would be partitioned into two 32-bit halves, one half for each addend. Any pair of addends would then activate a unique row (location). At that location would be stored the sum of those two addends. Activating the row would put their sum on the data bus. We would need as many addresses as we have *potential* inputs, so the scheme requires $(2^{64})(64) = 2^{70}$ bits. This is a phenomenally wasteful use of physical resources, given that it only accounts for the symbols for integers and only for the operation f_+ – and well over 99.9999% of these symbols would never be accessed, because only a small fraction of the possible sums would ever be computed by any one machine.

The same architecture used as an addressable read/write memory can be used to store 2^{64} *realized* symbols, which can be used by any function that needs them. By adding a single bus line, we gain write capabilities. This is equivalent to a computer with a trillion gigabytes of memory, the equivalent of well over 100 billion DVDs. With this (plausible) amount of storage, the brain could record over four DVDs' worth of information every millisecond over a typical lifespan (80 years). It cannot escape one's attention that the brain could potentially record everything we have ever experienced during our lifetime, without writing over or in any way reusing memory locations. The need for the brain ever to "forget," in the symbolic sense,[4] need not be an issue of physical resources. This fact itself could simplify the architecture of the brain: Its read/write memory could be *write once*. As of this writing, DVDs that use write-once-read-many (WORM) technology cost about one fourth as much, and maintain recorded symbols over 30 times longer than the equivalent unrestricted read/write technology. In the not-distant future, it may prove

---

[4] We are not making a claim here that in fact brains never forget information – that would be entirely speculative. Additionally, the use here of "forgetting" is not meant to imply that one wouldn't "forget" in the sense of losing symbol access. That this form of forgetting occurs is obvious to all of us.

to be the case that memory is so cheap and abundant that computers will never need to erase anything that has ever been stored – for better or for worse.

In computer programming, accessing values by means of addresses stored in the program (in the computational machinery) is called *direct addressing*. Directly addressed variables correspond psychologically and neurobiologically to innate variables. Note the distinction between an innate value and an innate variable. An innate *value* specifies a non-contingent quantity in the represented system (like the period of the earth's rotation), which is implicit in the structure of the representing system. (For example, the earth's period of rotation is built into the biochemistry of the circadian clock.) An innate *variable* specifies a set of possible messages whose existence is implicit in the genetically specified structure of the representing system. It specifies that set by giving the internal *location* of the symbol that represents the current value (not by giving the value itself). The value of the variable is contingent; the variable itself is not.

For example, the (presumably) innate structure of the sun–compass mechanism, which makes it possible for the nervous systems of many animals to learn the solar ephemeris function (the compass direction of the sun as a function of the time of day – see Chapter 13), has as an essential part of its structure a component that represents the sun's compass direction. What this represents is not the current value of the sun's compass direction; rather, it represents the set of possible current values. It is a variable – one of Shannon's sets of possible messages – not the current value of the variable (a member of that set). The distinction here is analogous to the distinction between a neuron that signals the value of some empirical variable, and a signal in that neuron (e.g., an interspike interval). The neuron, by virtue of the structure in which it is embedded, which renders it sensitive only to a limited set of possible messages, represents that set, the set of states of the world capable of generating a signal in that neuron. An interspike interval represents a message drawn from that set.

Indirect addressing and the creation of variables

In computer programs, direct addressing, while much more common than immediate addressing, is itself rare, because most variables are not innate. While the sun's compass direction is a candidate for an innate variable, the compass direction of a nectar source is not, because the existence of that source is itself contingent. The architecture of a representational system capable of effectively representing the reality with which animals cope must provide for the creation of symbols for the variables themselves – symbols for new sets of possible messages. The symbols for these contingent (unforeseeable) sets of possible messages cannot, generally speaking, be part of the innate structure of the computing machinery. That would require too much innate structure, most of which would never be utilized, because any given animal will in fact experience only an infinitesimal portion of the potentially important experiential variables.

In Chapter 12, we review experiments on cache retrieval in Western Scrub Jays. Birds of this species make as many as 30,000 caches (hiding-places for their food) in a six-week period in the fall. They survive over the next several months by retrieving food from those caches. They remember for each cache its location, its contents, and the date and time at which it was made.[5] Consider the variable that represents the location of the 29,567th cache – not the actual location itself, but instead the set of possible locations. In a bad autumn, when there is little food to be found, the unfortunate bird may make only 10,000 caches. Are we to imagine that there are structures in its nervous system, for example, individual neurons (so-called "grandmother neurons") or, worse yet, whole arrays of neurons (neural networks) destined by virtue of the innate structure of the system to represent the location of the 29,567th cache? If so, then those structures will not be used in a bad autumn, which may well be the only autumn the bird ever experiences. Because the bird never experiences the making of its 29,567th cache, the location of that cache never becomes a set of possible messages; there never is a value to be bound to that variable.

The need to have a memory structure capable of representing all *and only* the variables we actual encounter is strikingly evident in the phenomenon that psychologists call episodic memory, of which the jay's memory for its food caches is arguably an instance (see Chapter 12). Humans remember episodes. The episodes they remember have a rich structure, with many different variables (participants, locations, times, durations) and many different relations between them (who did what to whom). We all experience a great many episodes. For some time after experiencing an episode, we can generally retrieve considerable detail about it. While the episodes we experience are numerous, they are an infinitesimal portion of the episodes we might experience. All the episodes actually experienced by any human anywhere at any time are an infinitesimal subset of the set of all episodes that some human might have experienced somewhere some time. Thus, it is physically impossible that our brains have innate elements of their structure specific to every episode we might experience or specific to the variables of which the memory of an episode would be constituted. However, neural network models often end up assuming just that.

Contingent variables come in categories, like Nectar Sources, Caches, Episodes, Locations, Views, etc. To capture this level of representational structure, computer programmers use *arrays* and *indirect addressing*. Arrays are category-variables. Indirect addressing uses the location of an array variable to hold a symbol that gives access to other variables, that is, other addresses. In doing so it makes those variables themselves accessible to computation. Recall that only the data side of a row (a memory location) in Figure 9.1 can be transcribed onto the data bus. The only way to make the address of that row accessible to computation is to put it on the data side of another location. By placing it on the data side of another memory location, we make it a symbol. Like all symbols, it carries information forward in time in a computationally accessible form. The information that it carries specifies where the value for a variable is to be found. When placed on the data side of another location, an address becomes the symbol for the variable.

---

[5] Again, this is not to assert that they never forget one or more pieces of information about any given cache; they very likely do. The point is that the architecture of their memory must make it in principle possible for them to remember this information about an arbitrarily designated cache.

To illustrate, suppose that the value of the variable is symbolized by '10010010', and that this symbol is stored at address 00001011. Suppose that this address is itself stored at address 00010001. The computational machinery accesses the symbol for the variable ('00001011') at the latter address (00010001). It accesses the symbol for the value of the variable at the former address (00001011). The two symbols are not the same: one is '00001011', while the other is '10010010'. They are not the same because they are symbols for different things. The first is the symbol for the variable; the second is the symbol for its value. We belabor this, because we know from our pedagogical experience that it is confusing. We suspect that part of the motivation for the reiterated claim that the brain is not a computer or that it does not "really" compute is that it allows behavioral and cognitive neuroscientists to stay in their comfort zone; it allows them to avoid mastering this confusion, to avoid coming to terms with what we believe to be the ineluctable logic of physically realized computation.

An array variable specifies the first address in a sequence of addresses. Indirect addressing accesses those addresses by way of a computation performed on the symbol for that address. The computation makes use of the fact that the other addresses in the array are specified by where they are in relation to the first. Take, for example, the Source-Sweetness category, which is a record of the sweetness of the nectar at the different sources a bee has visited. Assume that the address for this category is 00000010. Stored at this address is the symbol '01000000', which encodes the address of the sweetness for the first source. This symbol encodes the fact that the sweetness for the first source may be accessed at 01000000. The sweetness of all later sources may be found at successive addresses following this address. The sweetness of the second source is at 01000001, of the third at 01000010, of the fourth at 01000011, and so on. These sweetness values may be indirectly addressed by a command that specifies the category variable, that is, the address of the category, which is 00000010, and a number, let us say, the binary number 10 (= digital 2). The indirect addressing command retrieves the symbol string ('01000000') stored at the specified address, adds to it the number (10), thereby generating a different symbol string ('01000010'), which is the symbol for the address of the sweetness at the third source. Using that symbol as an address probe, it retrieves the value at that address, which is the symbol that actually specifies the sweetness itself.

The address stored at the category address is called a pointer. Entering it into simple computations in order to obtain other addresses is called pointer arithmetic. Again, we see the power of encodings that provide for compact procedures. If the variable (address) for each of the sources whose sweetness a bee might sooner or later encode were to be embedded in the computational machinery itself, we would need to tie up a lot of physical resources implicitly representing the addresses where that information might (or might not) someday be found. If, however, the machinery uses memory arrays and indirect addressing, then it need only implicitly represent a single address, the address where the pointer to the array is to be found. This implicit representation constitutes an innate category (in our example, the Source-Sweetness category).

If the computational machinery does not use category-variables, it again confronts the problem of pre-specification. It must preallocate physical resources to implicitly represent variables it may never encounter (for example, the sweetness of the 59th source in a bee that is eaten by a bird after visiting only 11 sources). This will not do. The brain cannot predict ahead of time how many (or even which) variables will be involved in its computations.

The architectural ramifications are clear. We must have a mechanism by which a set of values (possible messages) can be accessed by referring to a variable that itself is contingent (contingent on which variable is required at a given moment in time). The value of this variable (an address) can then be made available to computation to produce an effective address (the address where the *actual* value is to be found). Note that once we have this indirection, we are unlimited in terms of being able to form hierarchies of variables. If the architecture allows for indirection (allows for encoding symbols that have internal addresses as their referent), then it need not be altered (rewired) to produce any level of indirection desired. Technically speaking, the arrays in memory may have any dimensionality, even though the structure of memory itself is linear (one-dimensional).

Addresses therefore need not just be the conduit by which computational processes gain access to the symbols on which they operate; they can themselves be symbolized. They refer to a class or category of values, the class that may legitimately reside at that address. The class is defined by the role that the values stored at that address play in one or more computational procedures.

By and large, relations are defined over variables, not over the individual values of those variables. Take for example correlation: It does not make sense to say that 1.83 meters (a value of a variable for height) is correlated with 88.45 kilograms (a value of a variable for weight), but it does make sense to say that height is correlated with weight. This correlation and many others like it inform our everyday behavior and judgments. A second example is the relation of being "the view to the north." This a class of variables ("snapshots") that play the same role in finding different locations, but, of course, each different location has associated with it a different view to the north. Any computational process that relies on remembered compass-oriented views to home on remembered locations – as we know the brains of insects do – calls up a different snapshot for each different location, but it uses them all in the same way in computing proximity to the target location. Thus, it needs to access them on the basis of what it is a class of variables has in common (e.g., the property of recording the view to the north from some location) together with what singles out one member of that class (the view to the north from a particular location). It is variables (addresses) that when symbolized may be treated as the objects of computational operations that make this possible.

The relation between the "Location" variable, whose values are vectors giving the coordinates of a location in some frame of reference, and the "View to the North" variable, whose values are snapshots, is an example of a data structure. The data structure encodes which snapshots go with which locations. A data structure is implicit in any correlation, such as the correlation between human height and human weight, because it is only through the mediation of a data structure that weight–height value pairs are created. In this case, the head variable in the structure would be the variable "Person," subordinate to which would be variables that are features of a person, variables like "Height," "Weight," "Eye Color," "Hair Color," and so on, the variables routinely recorded on identification documents, which are examples of simple data structures. Each "Person" variable has associated with it a "Weight" and "Height" variable. The values of those two variables for each person constitute the value-pairs from which the correlation is computed. The correlation is not a property of the "Person" variable, it is a property of a "Population" variable, which has subordinate to it multiple instances of the "Person" variable. Thus, there is a hierarchy of relations between variables: "Persons" are constituents of "Populations," and "Height", "Weight", etc. are subordinate to "Persons."

Data structures encode the relations (hierarchical and otherwise) between variables. The architecture of a computationally useful memory must make it possible to not only encode and recover the values of variables, it must also make it possible to encode and recover relations between them. What makes this critical operation possible is the ordering of memory locations by their (symbolizable) addresses. The elementary fact that addresses form a strictly ordered set makes it possible to specify the next address and the next after that, and so on. It is easy to miss the critical role of the strict ordering of addresses in the functioning of computing machines, because it comes for free in a random-access memory. The addresses are binary patterns, which are naturally ordered by the binary encoding of the natural numbers (the integers). In a random-access memory, locations (words) that are next to each other in the address sequence may or may not be physically adjacent. They will be if they happen to be on the same chip, but not if one location is the "last" on one chip and the other is the "first" on the next. What matters is that, whether or not memory locations are physically adjacent, they are strictly ordered by the abstract numerical properties of the bit patterns that physically implement the addressing of memory locations. The numerical ordering of the addresses makes pointers and pointer-arithmetic possible. It is by means of pointers and pointer arithmetic that data structures are physically realized.

An Illustrative Example

Let us consider how these data-addressing principles could be used to organize in computationally accessible form the hierarchical information about food caches that we know jays record (from the experiments by Clayton and her collaborators reviewed in Chapter 12). We know that they remember where they cached a morsel, what kind of morsel it was (peanut, meal worm, cricket), date and time they cached it, whether they were watched by another jay when caching it, and whether they have harvested it. We can infer from extensive experiments on animal navigation that the specification of location involves both map coordinates (the formal equivalents of latitude and longitude) and compass-oriented views of the surroundings (See Chapter 12; for a more extensive review, see Gallistel, 1990).

Table 9.1 shows how this information might be structured in the memory of a computer. Each line represents a variable and its value, a physical address and the symbol stored at that address, with a colon separating the two. If a value is under-lined, it encodes for an address, that is, it represents a variable. Symbols for non-address values with external referents are indicated by '???', because they would

Table 9.1 Illustrative data structure for encoding what jays remember about the caches they have made

Address : Content	Access	Content description
100,000 : 8	Caches[0]	Cache variables
100,001 : n	Caches[1]	Total caches
100,002 : 100,100	Caches[2]	→ Locations
100,003 : 100,200	Caches[3]	→ Bearings
100,004 : 150,000	Cashes[4]	→ Morsels
100,005 : 200,000	Caches[5]	→ Dates
100,006 : 250,000	Caches[6]	→ Times
100,007 : 300,000	Caches[7]	→ Watched
100,008 : 350,000	Cashes[8]	→ Harvested
. . .		
100,100 : 2	Caches[2][0]	Location variables
100,101 : 400,000	Caches[2][1]	→ Latitudes
100,102 : 450,000	Caches[2][2]	→ Longitudes
. . .		
100,200 : 2	Caches[3][0]	Bearings variables
100,201 : 500,000	Caches[3][1]	→ Directions
100,202 : 600,000	Caches[3][2]	→ Views
. . .		
150,000 : 100,001	Caches[4][0]	Morsels (→ Total caches)
150,001 : ???	Caches[4][1]	Morsels 1
150,002 : ???	Caches[4][2]	Morsels 2
150,000+n : ???	etc. to Caches[4][n]	Morsel[n]
. . .		
200,000 : 100,001	Caches[5][0]	Dates (→ Total caches)
. . .		
250,000 : 100,001	Caches[6][0]	Times (→ Total caches)
. . .		
300,000 : 100,001	Caches[7][0]	Watched? (→ Total caches)
. . .		
350,000 : 100,001	Caches[8][0]	Harvested? (→ Total caches)
. . .		
400,000 : 100,001	Caches[2][1][0]	Latitudes (→ Total caches)
400,001 : ???	Caches[2][1][1]	Latitude 1
400,002 : ???	Caches[2][1][2]	Latitude 2
400,000+n : ???	etc. to Caches[2][1][n]	Latitude n
. . .		
450,000 : 100,001	Caches[2][2][0]	Longitudes (→ Total caches)
. . .		
500,000 : 100,001	Caches[3][1][0]	Directions (→ Total caches)
500,001 : ???	Caches[3][1][1]	Direction 1,1
500,002 : ???	Caches[3][1][2]	Direction 1,2
500,003 : ???	Caches[3][1][3]	Direction 2,1
500,004 : ???	Caches[3][1][4]	Direction 2,2
500,000+2n : ???	etc. to Caches[3][1][2n]	Direction n,2
. . .		
600,000 : 100,100	Caches[3][2][0]	Views (→ Total caches)

be filled in from experience. n is the current number of caches stored in the data structure. To the right of each address–content pair is text that describes the nature of the information stored there. This text is, of course, for the reader's benefit only; it would not be part of the data structure. The first entry (Access) shows how the contents might be addressed in a program that used array notation. The second entry (Content description) describes the contents at that location. Arrows ($\rightarrow$) indicate the category variable (array) that begins at that address.

The first entry is (arbitrarily) at address 100,000. This address itself represents the category or concept of a cache. Its content (8) is the number of variables that are associated with (that is, subordinate to) this concept.

The next address (100,001) is the first such variable. It has a purely internal referent; it stores the current total number of caches in the data structure. This value determines the length of many of the other arrays, because those other arrays have one record for each cache. This value (the number of caches in memory), when added to the address of the first value in a subordinate array, specifies the address of the last value in that subordinate array. Making this number a variable in the data structure, that is, giving it an address, allows this value to be easily accessed as needed without having to worry about updating the value everywhere that it appears whenever another cache is added to the structure.

Addresses 100,002 through 100,008 contain the symbols for the addresses of the category variables that enter into the specification of a cache. The first of these symbols (100,100) is where the information for the Location category begins. Location on a plane is defined by two sub-categories, the names for which depend on the frame of reference. The most common frame is the geocentric frame polarized by the earth's axis of rotation. This polarization arises naturally from the universal experience of the solar and stellar ephemeredes. The solar or stellar ephemeris is the point on the horizon above which the sun or a star is seen, as a function of the time of day/night. The cyclical nature of these ephemeredes defines the time of day and entrains the circadian clock (see Chapter 12). The north–south axis is the point on the horizon half way between where the sun rises and where it sets. (It is also half way between where any star rises and sets.) It is also the point at which the sun attains its zenith (its maximum angular distance from the horizon). Thus, it is experientially salient, or at least readily obtainable from simple experience of the sun's position at salient times of day (its rising, setting, and zenith).

We know that animals, including insects, routinely use the sun for directional reference when navigating. Doing so requires knowledge of the solar ephemeris. Research has revealed a learning module dedicated to learning the solar ephemeris (see Chapter 13). The north–south axis is the direction that defines latitude, and longitude is the direction orthogonal to this. That is, the line between the point where the sun rises and the point where it sets is perpendicular to the north–south axis. Thus, it is not unreasonable to suppose that locations in the brains of terrestrial animals are specified by the values for their latitude and longitude, just as they are on most human maps.

There are, of course, other possible systems of coordinates (e.g., polar coordinates) within a geocentric frame of reference; but any such system will require (at least) two coordinates, because the surface of the earth has two dimensions. Thus, the latitude and longitude sub-categories may be taken as stand-ins for those two coordinates, whatever they may be.

The location (location of cache) variables are represented by the address 100,100. The content of the Location address (2) specifies the number of (sub-category) variables that define a Location. When this value is added to the address itself (100,100 + 2), the machine gets by pointer arithmetic the location of the last of those sub-categories. The latitude sub-category (first sub-category under Location) is represented by the address 100,101. The content of that address (400,000) is the already discussed address at which the actual number, n, of latitude variables is stored. As explained above, we have made n a variable, because we will need to access it repeatedly. The symbol for this variable is its address (100,001), the address at which the actual number itself may be found. The value of this variable, together with the address of the first latitude value, specifies the stretch of memory that is occupied by the listing of the latitudes. That listing begins at the address (400,001) immediately after the the head address + i (in this example, 400,000 + i). Similarly, the longitude of the ith location is the head address for longitude (that is, the symbol for the longitude category) + i (in this example, 450,000 + i). Again, the utility of pointer arithmetic is evident. So, also, is the utility of creating the variable n (symbolized by 100,001), by reference to which the system specifies at the head of each list of actual values where in memory that list ends.

Locations in animal navigation, as in human navigation, are defined both by geocentric coordinates (latitude and longitude) and by local bearings. Local bearings are compass-oriented views (Chapter 12 and Gallistel, 1990). They have two components. One component is a view, which is an encoding of the terrain or a terrain feature visible from a given location when looking in a given direction. These encodings are called snapshots in the animal-navigation literature, because they are analogous to the encoding of a view that is effected by a digital camera. In human navigation, views are encoded by sketches or photographs in a pilot book. The other component is the compass direction in which one must look in order to see that view (when one is at the given location).

It takes a pair of local views (called a pair of cross bearings) to uniquely specify a location by reference to local bearings, with each pair consisting of a direction and a view. Thus, the pair of local cross bearings that will enable a bird to precisely locate a cache is comprised of four values – two directional values and two snapshot values.[6] There is no computational motivation for forming categories (or concepts) out of the first and second pairs, because the designations of "first" and "second" are arbitrary. The set of all first directions have nothing in common that distinguishes them from the set of all second directions, and likewise for the set of all first views and the set of all second views. Thus, there is no motivation for arranging the "first" directions in one sequence of memory locations and the "second" directions in a different sequence, nor for arranging the "first" views in

---

[6] It may seem odd to refer to a snapshot as a value, but the binary representation of an image captured on a digital camera is simply a (very large) binary number. Thus, it is every bit as much a value as any other (pun intended).

one sequence of memory locations and the "second" views in a different sequence. Thus, in our data structure, the two directions for the local cross bearings at a cache location are found one after the other in memory, and likewise for the corresponding snapshots. By contrast, the directions (of the views) and the snapshots (the encodings of the views themselves) are very different kinds of values, subject to different kinds of computations, so the directions form one sequence in memory while the views associated with those directions form a different sequence. Notice how the organization of variables into arrays leads naturally to the formation of functional categories.

Another component of the memory for a cache is the date at which it was made. We know this is part of the record because of the experiments reviewed in Chapter 12 showing that the birds know how many days have passed since they made a given cache. The Date variable is symbolized by the address (100,005) whose content (200,000) is the address immediately after which the sequence of actual dates begins.

There is also reason to believe that the birds know how many hours have elapsed since a cache was made. To be able to compute that, they must record the time (of day) at which it was made. The Time variable is symbolized by the address (100,006) whose content (250,000) is the address immediately after which the sequence of actual times begins.

We also know that the birds note whether their caching was observed or not, because they often return selectively to the caches they were observed making, remove the contents, and cache them elsewhere (see Chapter 12). The binary variable or "flag" that records whether a cache was observed or not is represented by the address (100,007), whose content (300,000) is the address immediately after which the sequence of flags begins.

Finally, we know that the birds keep track of which caches they have harvested. The flag denoting whether a cache has been harvested or not is represented by the address (100,008) whose content (350,000) is the address immediately after which the harvest flags begin.

The structure portrayed in this example is by no means the only structure – the only arrangement of the information in memory – that could encode the relations between these variables. We have made it up without a clear specification of the computational uses to which those relations are to be put. Absent such a specification, there is no way to determine what a computationally optimal arrangement would be. There is an intimate and unbreakable relation between how information is arranged in memory and the computational routines that operate on that information, because the computational routines decode the relations that are encoded by means of the arrangement of the information in memory. As with all true codes, the encoding of the relations between variables by means of the arrangement of their locations in memory is meaningless in the absence of a structure that can correctly derive the relations from that arrangement, just as the encoding of numbers in bit patterns is meaningless in the absence of computational machinery that operates appropriately on those patterns, and the encoding of relations in a proposition is meaningless in the absence of a parser that correctly decodes the relations encoded by the arrangement of the symbols in the proposition.

Table 9.2 Illustrative data structure that orders records by sweetness

Address : Content	Access	Content description
100,000 : 4	Patches[0]	Patch variables
100,001 : n	Patches[1]	Total patches
100,002 : 200,000	Patches[2]	→ Latitudes
100,003 : 300,000	Patches[3]	→ Longitudes
100,004 : 400,000	Patches[4]	→ Densities
. . .		
200,000 : 100,001	Patches[2][0]	Latitudes (→ Total patches)
200,001 : ???	Patches[2]	[1] Latitude 1
200,000+n : ???	Patches[2]	[n] Latitude n
. . .		
300,000 : 100,001	Patches[3][0]	Longitudes (→ Total patches)
300,001 : ???	Patches[3][1]	Longitude 1
300,000+n : ???	Patches[3][n]	Longitude n
. . .		
400,000 : 100,001	Patches[4][0]	Sweetness (→ Total patches)
400,001 : ???	Patches[4][1]	Sweetness 1
400,000+n : ???	Patches[4][n]	Sweetness n

Procedures and the Coding of Data Structures

We have repeatedly stressed the interdependence of procedures and the symbols that they both operate on and produce. Compact, encoding symbols for integers (along with addressable read/write memory) make possible the realized symbolization of the finite instances of integers that one might experience in a lifetime. To operate on such symbols, it is necessary to employ sophisticated procedures, even for operations as basic as addition. As complex symbols (data structures) become progressively more complex, the potential encoding systems themselves become progressively more complex. The specific encoding used will determine the efficiency and efficacy of the various operations that one intends to perform on the data structures. Often, the choice of data structure and procedure will together determine if the operations are feasible. Choice of the appropriate data structure is so important that undergraduate computer science students typically spend one semester learning how to design data structures and another learning how to analyze the performance of various algorithms and their associated data structures.

Such increased complexities start as soon as one considers the most basic of data structures, an *ordered list*. An ordered list is exactly that, a list of symbols that are ordered by some property. To pursue this example, let's take another hypothetical data structure. There is evidence that bees record the location of different food patches they visit and can associate with each patch its sweetness (sucrose concentration – see Gallistel, 1990, for review). Following our scrub jay example, a simplified data structure for this could be as shown in Table 9.2.

Table 9.3   Illustrative linked-list data structure for ready access to sweetness

400,000 : 100,001	Sweetness ($\rightarrow$ Total patches)
400,001 : 76	Sweetness 1
400,002 : 400,003	$\rightarrow$ Sweetness 2
400,003 : 34	Sweetness 2
400,004 : 400,005	$\rightarrow$ Sweetness 3
400,005 : 12	Sweetness 3
400,006 : 400,007	$\rightarrow$ Sweetness 4, etc.

Table 9.4   Data structure in Table 9.3 after insertion of a new patch

400,000 : 100,001	Densities ($\rightarrow$ Total patches)
400,001 : 76	Sweetness 1
400,002 : 400,003	$\rightarrow$ Sweetness 2
400,003 : 34	Sweetness 2
400,004 : 400,007	$\rightarrow$ Sweetness 3
400,005 : 12	Sweetness 3
400,006 : 400,009	$\rightarrow$ Sweetness 4
400,007 : 17	Sweetness 4
400,008 : 400,005	$\rightarrow$ Sweetness 5

In the jay example, the ordering of the caches was arbitrary – we may assume that they are stored in the order that they were experienced. It would be efficacious for the bee to maintain its list of patches such that they were ordered by the sweetness of the patch (updating as needed). This would allow the bee to quickly discern which patches were the best prospects for the day. Our present data structure certainly *could* be maintained this way; however, if the bee experiences a new flower patch, it will need to insert the information for the patch into its appropriate location within the list. Each successive variable in the structure, be it Longitude, Latitude, or Sweetness, is ordered by the inherent ordering of the physical memory addresses. To insert a new patch into this structure, one has to shift all of the variables over one position in memory to create this space. A computer scientist would say that the insert operation is not well supported by this data structure.

A common solution to this problem is to use what are called *linked lists*. In a linked list, each element of the list contains two values – the symbol for the value, and then a symbol for the address of the next element. The linked list creates a virtual ordering from the fixed physical ordering of the memory. To demonstrate this scheme, we will assume that the sweetness values are represented as integers between 1 and 100 (100 being the best). Table 9.3 shows a possible linked list implementation for the densities, with made-up sweetness values entered. Now, if we had to insert a patch with Sweetness 17, we could simply insert it at the end and update our structure as in Table 9.4.

Updating the list clearly has a few issues, however nothing as demanding as shifting all of memory. Insertion of a new patch (and deletion of a patch) has been made efficient by changing our data structure.[7] While we have gained efficiency for insertion and deletion operations, we have lost efficiency if we want to be able to randomly access the *i*th patch. In our previous data structure, the *i*th patch could be easily located with simple pointer arithmetic. With the linked list structure, however, one would have to traverse through the links, keeping track of how many links have been followed. It is often possible to make hybrid data structures that solve both constraints efficiently, and such data structures can quickly become quite sophisticated.

When data structures are complex, decisions on how to encode the structure can make or break the viability of procedures that one might bring to bear on the data structure. If the structure needs to serve numerous procedures, efficient data structures again become quite complex. As we saw in Chapter 1, a similar phenomenon occurs if one employs compression and error correction codes. If sophisticated data structures are being employed by the nervous system, then it places another hurdle in the way of neuroscientists who are listening in to the signals that the brain transmits and trying to decode what they are talking about. It seems that there is no free lunch – complex problems require complex solutions. This is a point that can be easily missed, and indeed many neural network models of memory and computation do miss it.

The Structure of the Read-Only Biological Memory

The functional structure of modern computers is sometimes discussed by neuroscientists as if it were an accidental consequence of the fact that computing circuits are constructed on a silicon substrate and communicate by means of pulses of electrical current sent over wires. Brains are not computers, it is argued, because computers are made of silicon and wire, while brains are made of neurons. We argue that, on the contrary, several of the most fundamental aspects of the functional structure of a computer are dictated by the logic of computation itself and that, therefore, they will be observed in any powerful computational device, no matter what stuff it is made of. In common with most contemporary neuroscientists, we believe that brains are powerful computational devices. We argue, therefore, that those aspects of the functional structure of a modern computer that are dictated by the logic of computation must be critical parts of the functional structure of brains. One such aspect is the addressable memory architecture we have just described, which makes

---

[7] We have overly simplified the data structure here for expository purposes. To make the insertions and deletions truly efficient, we would most likely need to use a doubly linked list, one in which the links not only looked forward to the next address, but also looked back. Note, additionally, that deletions will add another issue as space will be cleared in memory that won't necessarily be reclaimed. Over time, this means that the memory will fill up with "wasted" space. When this happens in a computer program, it is called a "memory leak," and special tools are employed to find the "bugs" in the program. This leads to a whole new concern that modern computer systems typically deal with under the banner of "memory management" – a topic that we do not pursue here. In summary, making complex and efficient data structures is not for the faint of heart.

extensive use of indirect addressing to organize and make retrievable the information stored in it. Our conviction that this is part of the inescapable logic of computationally useful information storage and retrieval is strengthened by the fact that the molecular mechanism for the intergenerational transmission and retrieval of inherited information has this same functional structure.

Computers work with bit patterns, while the molecular machinery for the transmission and utilization of inherited information works with base-pair sequences. Both systems are digital. Like all workable systems we know of, they both have a very small number of primitive symbol elements. In computers, these elements number only two, the '0' state (voltage level) and the '1' state (voltage level). In the DNA of cells, there are four elements out of which information-conveying symbols are constructed, the bases adenine (A), cytosine (C), guanine (G), and thymine (T). One of these four bases is the encoding datum of a nucleotide. Nucleotides are the basic subunits in the structure of the double-helical DNA molecular. In computer memory, the encoding elements (the bits) are serially ordered in space to form a minimal combination of the elements. In the genetic mechanism, there is likewise a minimum combination, the codon, which is a linear sequence of three of the bases (e.g., AAG, TTT, CAG, etc.). Codons code for amino acids, which are the basic building blocks of proteins. They also encode punctuation symbols that tell the decoding machinery where to start and stop reading the code for a given protein (start codons and stop codons).

A word in a computer has two functionally distinct components (fields), the memory field, which contains the word itself, and the address for that memory. The word in a memory field is an information-carrying symbol; if it is transcribed to the data bus, it may enter into a computation. The address field is not a symbol; it has no access to the data bus. Insofar as it can be said to have content, that content cannot be accessed by the rest of the system (except through the device of symbolizing that content in the memory field of another address). The role of the address field is to recognize the probe on the address bus, by which the word in the associated memory field is transcribed onto the data bus for use in a computation.

A gene also has two components that are functionally distinct in the same way. There is the coding component, with the codon sequence bracketed by a start codon and a stop codon. It specifies the structure of a protein. Proteins are the principal molecular actors in the construction of a biological mechanism. They are the pieces from which the mechanism is largely constructed. They are also the principal signals that control the construction process. The second component of a gene, which may be less familiar to many readers, is the promoter. The promoter (and its negative, the repressor) are sometimes called the operon, because this component controls whether or not the other component operates, that is, whether or not it is transcribed into messenger RNA, that will carry the information to the ribosomes where it is used to direct the synthesis of the protein whose amino acid sequence it encodes. The elements of the promoter for a gene are the same elements as the elements of the coding field, the same four bases, just as the elements of an address field are the same '0's and '1's that are the elements of a word's memory field. But, like the elements in the address field of a word, they function differently. They are not transcribed. The rest of the system has no access to the information encoded by the sequence of elements in a promoter, just as the rest of a computer has no access to the information encoded in the sequence of elements in an address field.

Rather, they control the access of the rest of the system to the contents of the coding field (the analog of the memory field of a word). The role of the promoter, like the role of the address, is to respond to (recognize) a probe signal, called a transcription factor. The function of a transcription factor is to select for transcription the coding sequence associated with that promoter, just as the function of a probe signal on the address bus is to select for transcription onto the data bus the memory field associated with a given address.

The proteins synthesized when a promoter activates the transcription of a gene are often themselves transcription factors, just as the words transcribed to the bus are often address probes. Addressing the promoter of a transcription factor (synthesizing a protein that binds to its address) gives access to the addresses (promoters) of the genes to which that transcription factor binds. As that transcription factor is synthesized, it binds to those promoters, leading to the synthesis of the proteins coded by their genes, many of which may themselves be yet further transcription factors. This indirect addressing makes possible the hierarchical structure of the genome. It makes it possible to have an "eye" gene that, when activated (addressed by the transcription factor for its promoter), leads to the development of an entire eye (Halder, Callaerts, & Gehring, 1995). The eye gene codes only for one protein. That protein does not itself appear anywhere in the structure of the eye. It is a transcription factor. It gives access to the addresses (promoters) of other transcription factors and, eventually, through them, to the addresses of the proteins from which the special tissues of the eye are built and to the transcription factors whose concentration gradients govern how those tissues are arranged to make an organ.

Finally, transcription factors, like pointer variables, their computer analogs, enter into computational operations. Transcription factors combine (dimerize) to activate promoters that neither alone can activate. This is the molecular realization of the AND operation. There are also transcription factors that negate (inhibit) the activating effect of another transcription factor. This is the molecular realization of the NOT operation. All other logical operations can be realized by functional composition of these two procedures.

In short, the genome contains complex data structures, just as does the memory of a computer, and they are encoded in both cases through the use of the same architecture employed in the same way: an addressable memory in which many of the memories addressed themselves generate probes for addresses. The close parallel between the functional structure of computer memory and the functional structure of the molecular machinery that carries inherited information forward in time for use in the construction and maintenance of organic structure is, in our view, no surprise. It is indicative of the extent to which the logic of computation dictates the functional structure of the memory mechanism on which it depends.

10

Computing with Neurons

In this chapter, we give preliminary consideration to how the components of a computing machine might be implemented with neurobiological elements. We return to this question in a final chapter of a much more speculative character. We stress, however, that *all* contemporary attempts to spell out how computations are realized in the brain are speculative. Neuroscientists do not know with any confidence the answers to even the most basic questions about how computations are carried out in neural tissue. There is, for example, no consensus about what the primitive computational operations are, out of which other computations are constructed. Indeed, the question, "What are the primitive computational operations in neural tissue?" has only rarely been posed (Koch, 1999; Koch & Poggio, 1987), let alone answered to general satisfaction (Mel, 1994). Although this question strikes most engineers charged with building a machine that computes as about as elementary and basic and unavoidable a question as one could well ask, it strikes many neurobiologists as an odd question. It strikes them as odd because, broadly speaking, neurobiologists are not focused on understanding the nervous system from a computational point of view. If forced to answer, many would probably suggest that there is no set of primitive computational mechanisms. That is, of course, one possible answer to the question (cf. Koch, 1999, pp. 471ff.). It is, however, tantamount to saying that every time a different computation has appeared in the evolution of the brain's computational capacity, it has arisen *de novo*. Unlike other aspects of biological structure, more complex computational structures have not been fashioned from computational components already available. That's possible, but why should the principles that govern the evolution of computational structure be different from the principles that govern the evolution of other structures? All other biological structures are seen to arise by recombination of basic elements.

There is also no consensus about even such a basic preliminary question as how information is encoded in spike trains. It is generally supposed that spike trains serve as the inputs to the brain's computational machinery. As we have seen, the form of a mechanism that implements a computational operation is fundamentally dependent on the form in which the relevant information is encoded in the symbols on which it operates. If there is no consensus about how the values of simple variables are encoded in spike trains, there is *a fortiori* no secure knowledge about how computational mechanisms in the brain combine the information from two or more such trains. If, for example, we do not know how the durations of intervals are encoded in the input, we cannot know how the brain computes their sum, difference, or ratio.[1]

Transducers and Conductors

There are, however, elements of the problem of neural computation for which there are widely agreed upon answers. Sensory receptors are the transducers, and muscles and exocrine glands are the effectors. About that, there is no doubt. There is also no doubt that the action potential is the mechanism by which information is rapidly transmitted over "long" distances (distances greater than 10 microns). However, it is important to appreciate how slow this transmission is relative to what the builders of computational machines are accustomed to work with. It takes an action potential on the order of 10–100 microseconds to travel 100 microns, which is a more or less typical distance separating the neurons within a local circuit, such as a cortical column. The time taken for information to travel between similarly spaced electronic elements is shorter by a factor of about 100,000,000. This is a sobering difference when one reflects that minimizing the time for information to travel between computational elements is an important consideration in the design of modern computers. It makes one wonder whether it is plausible to assume that elementary computations in neural tissue are implemented by neural circuits in which the relaying of action potentials between the neurons is an essential part of the operation. This assumption is all but universal in contemporary neural network modeling (see, for example, the neural network model of dead reckoning reviewed in Chapter 14). Any such implementation will be almost unimaginably slow by the standards of contemporary electronic computing machines. The alternatives are that the elementary computational operations are implemented within single neurons, either by subcellular structures like dendritic spines (Koch, 1999, ch. 12) or at the molecular level (see Chapter 16).

On the other hand, the axonal conduction mechanism readily implements a function that it is awkward to implement within the marble machines we used to illustrate the physical realization of basic computational functions, namely, the transmission of a signal from a single source to multiple destinations. Axons branch prolifically. When an action potential arrives at a branch point, action potentials propagate down both branches. By contrast, a falling marble must fall in either one branch

---

[1] Readers interested in further pursuing the question of how information is encoded in spike trains may want to begin with the much praised text by Rieke et al. (1997) or the short treatment in Koch (1999, ch. 14). For more recent work, see Averbeck, Latham, & Pouget, 2006; Bialek & Setayeshagar, 2005; Brenner, Agam, Bialek, & de Ruyter van Steveninck (2002); Brenner, Bialek, & de Ruyter van Steveninck (2000); Brenner, Strong, Koberle, Bialek, & de Ruyter van Steveninck (2000); Deneve, Latham, & Pouget (2001); Fairhall, Lewen, Bialek, & de Ruyter van Steveninck (2001); Latham & Nirenberg (2005); Nirenberg & Latham (2003); Schneidman, Berry, Segev, & Bialek (2006); Simmons & de Ruyter van Steveninck (2005); Strong, de Ruyter van Steveninck, Bialek, & Koberle (1998).

or the other; it cannot give rise to two marbles falling in two different branches. Sherrington (1947 [1906]) emphasized the functional importance of this *divergence*, the ability to send the same signal to many different processors. Computer scientists often call this "fan out."

Sherrington also recognized the importance of the fact that action potentials *converge* at synaptic junctions. When two or more axons synapse on the same postsynaptic neuron, the effects of signals in these axons combine to determine whether the postsynaptic neuron does or does not fire. From a computational perspective, this convergence and the mechanism of signal transmission across synaptic junctions makes possible the implementation of the AND, OR, and NOT functions. Computer scientists call this property of a computing machine's architecture "fan in." The brain exhibits massive fan out and fan in relative to what is seen in contemporary computing machines, and this may be a key to understanding how it is able to make complex computations as rapidly as it does.

Synapses and the Logic Gates

Synapses are the junctions between neurons, with a presynaptic ending on one side of a very narrow cleft between two neurons and a postsynaptic membrane on the other side. Action potentials do not propagate across synapses. Rather, the arrival of an action potential at a presynaptic ending releases transmitter substance into the cleft. The binding of the transmitter substance to receptor molecules embedded in the postsynaptic membrane on the other side of the cleft alters ionic conductances in the postsynaptic neuron. The alteration is direct, in the case of ionotropic receptors. That is, the ion gate is a component of the transmembrane receptor to which the released transmitter substance binds. In the case of metabotropic receptors, the transient change in one or more ionic conductances is produced indirectly by way of an intracellular cascade of molecular reactions. In other words, it is mediated by a molecular signal transmission process within the postsynaptic neuron. The existence of this mechanism links extracellular signaling to intracellular signaling, allowing the presynaptic signals to alter the internal operations of the postsynaptic neuron. Whether directly or indirectly produced, the alteration in ion-channel conductances may either transiently depolarize the postsynaptic membrane (an Excitatory Post-Synaptic Potential, or EPSP) or transiently hyperpolarize it (an Inhibitory PostSynaptic Potential, or IPSP).

Inhibitory postsynaptic conductance changes cancel excitatory changes, thereby implementing the NOT function.

The depolarizing effects of contemporaneous EPSPs sum to produce a greater depolarization. Whether this depolarization is or is not sufficient to initiate a conducted action potential in the postsynaptic neuron depends on how large it is relative to the threshold for action potential initiation. If either of two EPSPs acting alone depolarizes the membrane beyond the threshold for initiating an action potential, the circuit comprised of those two presynaptic neurons and their common postsynaptic neuron implements the OR function.

If neither EPSP acting alone is suprathreshold but the two together are, the circuit implements the AND function.

The nonlinear thresholding that plays a critical role in implementing these indispensable logic functions need not be the threshold for the initiation of a spike at the axon hillock (where the axon originates); it may occur more locally within single dendrites (Koch, 1997). Thus single dendrites may act as logic gates. Dendrites are tree-like structures branching out from the cell bodies of neurons and covered with presynaptic endings.

The Slowness of It All

Synaptic integration processes are an order of magnitude slower than the already slow signal transmission process. From the time that an action potential arrives at the presynaptic ending until the EPSP builds to its peak is on the order of 500 microseconds (half a millisecond), while the decay from the peak response back to the resting level of polarization typically takes several milliseconds. A millisecond is an eternity in a modern computer. The computer on your desktop executes an entire floating point operation (e.g., adding two real numbers) in a thousandth of a microsecond or less. The execution of a floating point operation requires a great many ANDs, ORs and NOTs, the retrieval of symbols for both quantities from memory, and the writing of the symbol for the result back to memory.

We do not understand how computational elements operating so slowly, with such long communication delays, can execute what would seem to be extremely complex computations as fast as the brain in fact does execute them. The brain can, for example, process to the point of scene recognition and analysis ("picnic," "wedding," "baseball game," etc.) streams of disparate images coming at one image every 100 milliseconds (Potter, Staub, & O'Connor, 2004). We do not currently know any algorithm capable of recognizing and analyzing the content of these complex images anywhere near as well as the human observer does, even when given as much time as the algorithm likes to process each image. However, insofar as we currently understand this problem (image parsing, recognition, and analysis), a remotely adequate algorithm would appear to require accessing a great deal of diverse stored information and making a large number of high-level computations, each involving an even larger number of elementary computations.

How it is possible for something as slow as the brain to process 10 scenes per second is a major mystery. Contemporary neural network models are by and large models of recognition or categorization. They model a content addressable memory, in which the input of a portion of a previously experienced input vector induces the net to settle into a pattern of activity characteristic of the category to which that input belongs. The settling into a distinct pattern of activity is taken to be an implementation of the recognition or categorization computation. This settling into a stable pattern of activity (a so-called "attractor state") is an example of a computational mechanism that is fundamentally dependent on repeated (recurrent) signal transmission between thousands of neuronal elements. No one has any idea how a system based on this mechanism would be able to categorize images at the rate of 10 images per second.

The standard neurobiological answer to how it is possible for the brain to do seemingly very complex computations so fast is "massive parallelism": it breaks the problem down into innumerable very simple computations, all of which are carried out simultaneously by many different microcircuits. There may be an important element of truth in this answer. However, at this time in the development of cognitive neuroscience, this answer is mostly a cloak for ignorance. We do not know to what extent it is possible even in principle to break this and many other computational problems down into elements that may be processed simultaneously. Much less do we know how such a breakdown could be accomplished, how the elements of the problem could be directed to the appropriate microcircuits, and how the results reported from all these circuits could be collated and integrated to arrive at an answer, all with such rapidity that a throughput of 10 images per second is possible. Computer scientists have been studying massively parallel computation for decades. One thing they have learned is that it is not easy to implement, except in the case of some rather special problems. Thus, if massive parallelism is the answer, then this poses the question what the architecture of the brain tells us about how to implement massively parallel computation. To that question, there is at present no clear answer, although one suspects that the above-mentioned massive fan out and fan in are part of the answer.

There is also the following puzzle. The modern computer carries out elementary computational operations a billion to a trillion times faster than the above numbers about the speeds at which axonal and synaptic transmission mechanisms operate suggest that the brain does. Doing computations in parallel rather than in sequence trades spatial resources (the number of computational mechanisms working on different parts of a problem at any given moment) for temporal resources (the number of different parts of the problem one mechanism can process in a unit of time). Because the modern computer appears to have many orders of magnitude greater temporal resources, why can it not outperform the brain by doing the same number of operations in sequence in less time than the brain can do them all at once in parallel? Either we are seriously deceived about the rate at which neural tissue can perform elementary computational operations, or the brain has discovered much more efficient algorithms (algorithms that minimize the required number of operations), or both.

The Time-Scale Problem

Nonetheless, if we set aside puzzles about how the brain is able to execute computational operations as fast as the behavioral evidence implies that it must, then in his book, *Biophysics of computation: Information processing in single neurons*, Koch (1999) shows how experimentally demonstrated mechanisms within individual neurons are sufficient to implement a variety of computational operations. He pays particular attention to multiplication because it is an elementary instance of the nonlinear operations that are an essential aspect of computation. What he mostly avoids, however, is dealing with memory. In the opening paragraphs of his Introduction (p. 1), he writes:

> The brain computes! This is accepted as a truism by the majority of neuroscientists engaged in discovering the principles employed in the design and operation of nervous systems . . .
>
> The present book is dedicated to understanding in detail the biophysical mechanisms responsible for these computations. Its scope is the type of information processing underlying perception and motor control, occurring at the millisecond to fraction of a second time scale.

In limiting its scope to information processing on a time scale of less than a second, Koch avoids the biggest problem, the problem of relating the time scale of the known neurobiological mechanisms and processes to the time scale of behavior. The sub-second time scale is the time scale of neurobiological processes, but it is only the extreme short end of the time scale on which behavior unfolds. Most behavior is shaped by information that has been received over a time scale ranging from the most recent tenth of a second back over minutes, hours, days, months, and years. In order for behavior to be thus shaped, there must be mechanisms in nervous tissue that undergo changes of state that last minutes, hours, days, months, and years. These changes must encode information about where things are, where the animal is, how long properties last, what the surrounding scenery looks like, when in the past various events took place, and so on – all the information that demonstrably informs behavior. The function of the enduring physical changes that encode this information is to carry previously acquired information forward in time, so that it is available whenever needed in the computations that inform current behavior. Koch describes in great detail the biophysics of the spike propagation mechanism, which carries information from place to place within nervous tissue, making it available *where* it is needed. In striking contrast, he has relatively little to say about the mechanism that carries information forward in time, making it available *when* it is needed.

The time scale that Koch limits most of his discussion to is the time scale on which the changes of state in the processor component of a computing machine may be expected to endure. The processor of those computing machines whose operation we understand has only a modest number of states; it remains in any one of them only briefly; and it revisits its various states over and over again in the course of its operations. This is a reasonable first-order description of what we seem to observe in neurons. A given neuron can be in a modest number of different states. None of them typically lasts more than a fraction of a second once the stimulus or input that induced it is gone. The neuron revisits those states over and over again as new inputs come in.

Synaptic Plasticity

What is missing from the contemporary conception of neurobiological dynamics is what we see when we look at the memory elements of a computing machine. Memory elements have three essential aspects, only one of which is widely appreciated by contemporary neuroscientists: (1) they undergo *enduring* changes, changes that last indefinitely; (2) the changes encode information; (3) the changes can be read, that is, they carry information forward in time within a mechanism that makes the information accessible to future computation.

The focus of neurobiological thinking about memory has been entirely on the first aspect, that is, on finding an enduring *functional* change. (The effects of, for example, vascular accidents, endure, but they are not functional; they do not enable the brain to better direct the animal's behavior.) Finding an enduring functional change is of central importance: a change can carry information forward only so long as it endures. However, the other two aspects are equally important. If the change cannot encode information in a readable form, then it cannot fulfill the role of the memory elements in computing machines. Enduring functional changes that do not encode information in a readable form are found in the state changes of the processor. There, their inability to encode information is not a problem, because their function is to alter the processor's response to inputs, not to carry information forward in time. And that is how in fact most contemporary neuroscientists conceive of memory: they conceive of it as a change in the state of the processor, a change that makes the processor respond differently to previously experienced inputs. That is why neuroscientists prefer to talk about mechanisms of *plasticity*, rather than mechanisms of memory. The conceptual framework behind the term "plasticity" goes back at least to the British empiricist philosophers of the seventeenth century and arguably to the conception of mental function advanced by Aristotle. The idea is that experience molds the brain so that it behaves more appropriately within the experienced environment. "Conceptually, this amounts to the input changing the transition function governing how the machine switches from one state to the next. Put differently, a nervous system will act like a machine that changes its instruction set as a function of its input" (Koch, 1999, p. 470).

Contemporary neuroscience is committed to the thesis that the brain has the functional architecture of a finite-state automaton, rather than that of a Turing machine: it lacks a read/write memory. Koch (1999, p. 471) summarizes this view as follows:

> Memory is everywhere, intermixed with the computational elements, but it cannot be randomly accessed: in the concentration of free calcium in the presynaptic terminal and elsewhere, implementing various forms of short-term plasticity, in the density of particular molecules in the postsynaptic site for plasticity on a longer time scale, in the density and exact voltage dependency of the various ionic currents at the hour or day time scale, and ultimately, of course, in the genes at the cell's nucleus for lifetime memories.

A conspicuous feature of his catalog of memory mechanisms is the absence of any suggestion about how any of them could encode, for example, the duration of an event, or the direction and distance from the nest or hive, or the color and shape of a food source. All of the things that Koch lists are state variables, not memory elements, as a computer scientist understands memory.

The thesis that the brain has the architecture of a finite-state automaton rather than of a Turing machine makes it possible to ignore the coding problem as well as the problem of how the machine accesses the encoded information. The finite-state automaton does not read information from memory. Its current state simply determines its action. We illustrated this in Chapter 8 by showing how the previous sequence of marbles determines the positions of the rockers (that is, the state of the machine), and their position determines which channel an incoming marble will fall out of. The external observer, who is a god outside the machine, can determine from the position of the rockers what the preceding sequence must have been, but the machine has no need (and no mechanism) to read this from any memory; its current state determines its input–output function.

In Chapter 8, we were at pains to explain the limitations of the finite-state architecture. Our focus there was on the tendency of the finite-state architecture to be overwhelmed by the infinitude of the possible. A further difference that we did not mention is that in the Turing architecture, which stores the sequence in a read/write memory (see our marble shift register, Figure 8.12), a subsequent output can be made to depend on any part of the stored sequence. When the memory is read – when the retained marbles in our shift register are released, the machine recovers the whole sequence. It can use any part of that sequence in the next computation that it makes. By contrast, in the finite-state architecture, the action of the machine (the output channel in which the marble falls) depends entirely on the current state of the processor, which has been determined by the entire sequence. Thus, it is only possible to have differential responses to entire sequences of some necessarily pre-specified length. It is not possible, for example, to have a response that depends on whether the second half of a sequence (length not pre-specified) is the same as (or the inverse of, etc.) the first half. In other words, the absence of a readable memory radically limits computational power. The finite-state architecture requires the designer of the machine (or, in the neurobiological case, the epigenetic process) to provide in advance for every possible functionally relevant contingency. Historically, much of the inspiration behind this pervasive thesis about learning and memory has been empiricism, the belief that the brain's structure is largely determined by its experience, which has put the machine in the state it is in. There is little appreciation of the radical nativism implicit in it: the necessity of providing structurally in advance for every possible behaviorally relevant state of the world.

The plastic change that neuroscientists generally appeal to in order to explain the phenomena of memory is synaptic plasticity, an enduring functionally appropriate change in synaptic conductance produced by experience.

The idea that memory involves a change in synaptic conductance also has great appeal for psychologists, because it is the neurophysiological realization of a mechanism that has been at the center of psychological (and before that, philosophical) thinking about learning and memory for centuries, the mechanism of association (Fanselow, 1993; Gluck & Thompson, 1987; Hawkins & Kandel, 1984). Many contemporary psychologists feel strengthened in their belief that associative learning theory must be in some sense basically the correct psychological theory by what they take to be the relevant findings in neurobiology. They find in the neurobiological literature experimental evidence for a mechanism that produces enduring changes in synaptic conductance when there is a temporal coincidence of pre- and postsynaptic signals, and they take this as support for associative theories of learning and memory in psychology.

It is important to realize that the evidence for the hypothesis that a change in synaptic conductance is the neurobiological basis of memory is weaker than many psychologists appreciate. Koch (1999, p. 308) accurately sums up the current state of the neurobiological evidence when he writes:

> For over a century (Tanzi, 1893; Ramon y Cahal, 1909, 1991), the leading hypothesis among both theoreticians and experimentalists has been that *synaptic* plasticity underlies most long-term behavioral plasticity. It has nevertheless been extremely difficult to establish a direct link between behavioral plasticity and its biophysical substrate, in part because most biophysical research is conducted with *in vitro* preparations in which a slice of the brain is removed from the organism, while behavior is best studied in the intact animal. In mammalian systems the problem is particularly acute . . . Even in 'simple' invertebrate systems, such as the sea slug *Aplysia* . . . it has been difficult to trace behavioral changes to their underlying physiological and molecular mechanisms. Thus, the notion that synaptic plasticity is the primary substrate of long-term learning and memory must at present be viewed as our most plausible hypothesis. (Milner, Squire & Kandel, 1998)

The evidence that psychologists have in mind when they appeal to neurobiology to justify associative theories of learning and memory comes from the voluminous literature on long-term potentiation (LTP), which is "a rapid and sustained increase in synaptic efficacy following a brief but potent stimulus" Koch (1999, p. 317). In capsule summary of the conceptual impetus behind this complex literature, Koch (1999, p. 317) writes:

> LTP research is very popular: between 1990 and 1997, over 2000 papers on LTP were published. The excitement stems in large part from the hope that LTP is a model for learning and memory, offering the most direct link from the molecular to the computational and behavioral levels of analysis. The field of LTP is also very controversial, so that there is only a surprisingly small number of completely accepted findings.

It is the lack of agreement about basic facts and parameters that accounts in some measure for the limited attention that Koch devotes to LTP in his account of computational mechanisms in the brain. He prefers to base his conjectures about basic neural mechanisms of computation on mechanisms for which there is substantial agreement about basic facts.

One might add to Koch's characterization of the current state of LTP research that a major reason why neuroscientists think that (some form of) LTP must be the mechanism of learning and memory is that this hypothesis is consistent with what they take to be established psychological fact, namely that learning and memory are associative processes. This extrinsic support from psychology and philosophy, rather than the murky and controversial evidence from neurobiological experiment, accounts in no small measure for the fact that the synaptic plasticity hypothesis is neurobiologists' "most plausible" hypothesis about memory. In short, neuroscientists justify the study of LTP by citing associative learning as an established psychological fact, while psychologists justify associative learning models by citing "associative" LTP as an established neurobiological fact. Both groups and the progress of cognitive neuroscience would benefit from a fuller appreciation of the shakiness of the experimental foundations for the extrinsic hypotheses to which each field appeals as established fact in order to buttress weak support from the experimental evidence intrinsic to their own field. Neuroscientists would benefit from an appreciation of how weak the behavioral evidence for associative learning is (Gallistel, 1990, 1995, 1999, 2008; Gallistel & Gibbon, 2000), while psychologists would benefit from a fuller appreciation of the controversy and lack of agreement about basic facts that pervade the neurobiological literature on LTP.

Nonetheless, because long-term synaptic plasticity is the only widely accepted hypothesis when it comes to current ideas about the neurobiology of memory, it is instructive to consider how one might use this to make a neural machine that reacts to the current input in a way that depends on the sequence of previous inputs. Can we use this mechanism to make a neural machine with the same functionality as our finite-state marble machine? In considering this question, we assume that the interval that elapses between the previous inputs in a sequence and the current input may be of indefinite duration. Thus, the short-time-scale, rapidly decaying processes that Koch describes are not relevant. The relevant physical changes wrought by previous inputs must be like the changes that falling marbles produce when they change the tilt of a rocker, they must endure indefinitely. Among the many facts about which there is controversy is how long LTP in fact endures, but we will ignore this; we will assume a mechanism that produces a change in synaptic conductance that lasts indefinitely. Moreover, we will assume that this change can be bidirectional: synaptic conductance may be either increased or decreased. The latter phenomenon, an enduring decrease in synaptic conductance, is called *long-term depotentiation* (LTD).

We will, however, insist that the mechanism have one of the properties of LTP and LTD about which there is fairly general agreement (Koch, 1999, p. 318): "*induction requires (nearly) simultaneous presynaptic neurotransmitter release and postsynaptic depolarization.*" The reader may be puzzled about how changes in opposite directions may have the same causal antecedents. How can it be that transmitter release simultaneous with postsynaptic depolarization causes *both* LTP and LTD, both an increase in conductance and a decrease in conductance? There is no clear answer to this question. The usual answer is that whether one gets LTP or LTD depends on the degree to which the internal calcium ion concentration at the postsynaptic membrane is raised above its resting level by the postsynaptic depolarization. If it is only moderately elevated, LTD (a decrease in conductance) is said to result; if the elevation is greater, LTP is the result (an increase in conductance). However, there is much controversy about the specifics. All one can say with any confidence at present is that under some conditions one sees LTP, while under others one sees LTD.

The hedge about the simultaneity of pre- and postsynaptic activity conveyed by the parenthetical "nearly" is measured in tens of milliseconds: the presynaptic release of transmitter substance and strong postsynaptic depolarization must be separated in time by no more than a few tens of milliseconds. In one often-cited report, deviations from absolute synchrony between presynaptic action potentials and postsynaptic action potentials of +10 milliseconds vs. –10 milliseconds determined whether synaptic conductance was increased (LTP) or decreased (LTD, Markram, Lübke, Frotscher, & Sakmann, 1997). Moreover, there was no effect on synaptic conductance unless these small differences in the timing of pre- and postsynaptic action potentials occurred while both neurons were firing 10 times per second or faster. (This is well above typical basal firing rates, which have been estimated to be less than one action potential per second.) Nor was there any effect when the strong postsynaptic depolarization was offset from the burst of presynaptic action potentials by more than 100 milliseconds in either direction. The very complexity of this result – the complexity of the conditions for inducing either LTP or LTD in the preparation used in this experiment – suggests something about how poorly both phenomena are currently understood.

Setting these qualifications aside, we ask whether this mechanism can be used to solve simple computational problems in which memory plays a critical role. We will find that it does not get us where we need to go. It does not enable us to construct even a finite-state automaton capable of looking back one step in a sequence of inputs. Thus, it does not give us even the computing power of a finite-state machine, let alone the power of a Turing machine. What this suggests is that the most plausible neurobiological hypothesis about the mechanism of memory is seriously inadequate from a computational perspective.

The instructive power of the look-back-one computation comes from its extreme simplicity. We want to make a neural machine with the same functionality as our finite-state marble machine whose output depended not just on the current input but also on the immediately preceding input. In the marble machine, the inputs were a marble falling in one of two input channels. In the neural machine, the inputs are an action potential conducted in one of two axons. In the marble machine, the outputs were a marble falling in one of four channels, depending jointly on which channel the marble came in on and which channel the previous marble came in on. In the neural machine, the outputs are an action potential conducted in one of four outgoing axons, depending jointly on which axon the incoming action potential arrives on and on which axon the preceding input action potential arrived on. If we can create a neural circuit with this functionality, we can combine copies of it to make a machine that can look back several steps, albeit at a cost in physical resources that increases exponentially with the number of look-back steps.

The key to creating a marble machine capable of looking back one event in the input sequence was a rocker-gate element with three properties: (1) It had two thermodynamically stable (hence, enduring) states; (2) the state it was in determined which of two output channels an input marble would be directed to; (3) it did or did not transition to its other state depending on whether the input did not or did match its current state. In attempting to create a functionally equivalent neural machine, we assume for the sake of argument that Hebbian synapses exist. We assume that they have (at least) two states that endure indefinitely, a conducting state and a non-conducting state. We assume that under some conditions, presynaptic transmitter release (by an arriving action potential) together with postsynaptic

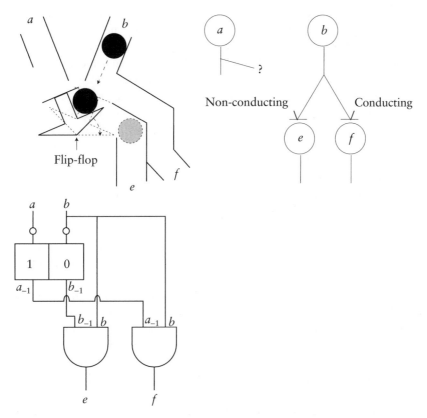

Figure 10.1 Attempting to construct a look-back element using Hebbian synapses as the memory elements. Only the right half of the symmetrical circuits are shown. On the left, as an aid to thought, we reproduce the structure of the marble machine (top) and the structure of a solid-state circuit (bottom), both having the requisite functionality. The conducting/non-conducting state of a synapse is indicated by the position of the "switch": when the switch is thrown right, the synapse is in its conducting state; when thrown left, it is in its non-conducting state. The only way to throw the switch is to have the postsynaptic neuron become depolarized at (nearly, i.e., +/− 10 ms) the same time as transmitter is released from the presynaptic neuron by the arrival of an action potential. By stipulation, action potentials cannot arrive simultaneously on *a* and *b*, because the challenge is to make an action potential arriving on *b* fire *f* if the preceding action potential also arrived on *b*, and *e* if the preceding arrived on a. Thus, one of the requirements is that an action potential on *a* reverse the states of the two synaptic switches.

depolarization (however realized) will put a synapse into its conducting state, while under slightly different conditions, the same confluence of pre- and postsynaptic events will put it into its non-conducting state.

To help us think about this problem, we make the sketch at the top right of Figure 10.1. It shows two input neurons (*a* and *b*) and two of the four output neurons (*e* and *f*), namely, the two that are to be fired by an action potential arriving on presynaptic neuron *a*. We only show two of the four output neurons, because the problem is symmetrical. If we can get the two inputs to affect those two outputs in the required way, then, by symmetry, we can achieve the same result for the other two outputs. By stipulation, synapses between presynaptic neurons *a* and *b* and output neurons *e* and *f* can be placed in either a conducting or non-conducting state. In other words, they are single-pole switches. We indicate their state (conducting or non-conducting) by a switch thrown either to the right (conducting) or the left (non-conducting).

In its initial configuration, the *bf* synapse is in the conducting state and the *be* synapse in the non-conducting state. Thus, an action potential in *b* will fire *f*, which is what we want. Suppose now that the next action potential arrives on axon *a*. It must reverse the states of the two synapses, setting the *be* synapse to its conducting state and the *bf* to its non-conducting state. How are we to make this happen? These are Hebbian synapses; they only change state when their presynaptic and postsynaptic sides are simultaneously activated. But the presynaptic sides of the *be* and *bf* synapses are not activated, because the action potential has arrived on *a* not *b*. The previous action potential arrived on *b*, but that may have been an indefinitely long while ago. We can wire our system so that an action potential in *a* depolarizes output neurons *e* and *f*, but that establishes only one of the two things that must happen simultaneously in order for the conductance to change. Thus, there does not appear to be a way to achieve the necessary changes in conducting state when the input arrives on *a*. The Hebbian induction conditions appear to be inimical to our objective.

Suppose that the conducting states of the synapses have *somehow* been reversed, indicating that the preceding action potential arrived on *a*. Suppose further that the next action potential arrives on *b*. We can assume that this fires *e*, which is what we want. It is a bit of a stretch, but we can perhaps also assume that although the postsynaptic depolarization of *e* is sufficient to fire it, this is nonetheless the intermediate level of depolarization that, when accompanied by a presynaptic action potential, causes LTD rather than LTP. In other words, we assume that the *be* synapse is switched into its non-conducting state. This is in contrast to the assumption we made earlier concerning the *bf* synapse. There, we assumed that a presynaptic input sufficient to fire the postsynaptic neuron left the synapse in its conducting state. The murky facts about just what level of depolarization is required to get LTD as opposed to LTP perhaps allows us this latitude. But how are we to get the *bf* synapse to reverse its state? We have an action potential arriving at the presynaptic ending, but there is no simultaneous depolarization of the postsynaptic membrane, because the *bf* synapse is in its non-conducting state. There is no signal in *a*, because we are considering the case where the signal arrives on *b*. Again, the induction conditions on a Hebbian synapse are inimical to our objective.

We conjecture that the problem is unsolvable within the constraints we have stipulated. Our conjecture is not a proof. If a reader finds a solution, we will be genuinely grateful to learn of it, provided that it in fact honors the constraints we have stipulated. As an additional incentive to readers who like to measure their ingenuity against that of acknowledged experts, we add that we posed this problem to a number of leading figures in the neural network modeling community. None could suggest an answer within the constraints we have stipulated.

One remarked that the problem required a "stack," that is, a read/write memory. We agree. Indeed, that comment brings us to the most popular mechanism for dealing with this problem within the neural network modeling community, which is to use reverberating activity as a read/write memory. The same expert who commented that it required a stack went on to suggest this approach.

Recurrent Loops in Which Activity Reverberates

A paper by Elman (1990) popularized the use of recurrent loops in the extraction of temporal structure. Elman is a linguist. Language unfolds in time. Any brain capable of understanding any human language must be able to extract temporal structure. Elman opened his paper by calling attention to the problem we are discussing: "[In the context of neural network theorizing] one of the most elementary facts about much of human activity – that it has temporal extent – is sometimes ignored and is often problematic" (p. 179). He then discusses solutions considered in previous modeling attempts and why they were unsatisfactory, which is basically because they begged the question by positing an input shift register that converted sequential inputs into simultaneous inputs.

Finally, he proposed the solution shown in Figure 10.2, which is taken from his paper. His model has become extremely influential. What it has that previous nets generally lacked is the "context units." As Elman explains in his caption, "activations are copied from hidden layer to context layer on a one-for-one basis, with fixed weight of 1.0." In other words, the signal values in the hidden units are written to the context units, so that the context units contain a copy of the previous signal values. The context units in turn project back to the hidden units. However, whereas one hidden unit projects to one and only one context unit, each context unit projects back to every hidden unit. Thus, the context units make the previous activity of any hidden unit available to all the other hidden units. Moreover, the back projections from the context units to the hidden units are "trainable," which is to say that the hidden unit can make of them whatever it likes (adjust the weight it gives to each different one).

Elman's recurrent loop from the hidden units to the context units and then from the context units back to the hidden units is a read/write memory. The untrainable one–one projection from the hidden units to the context units implements the write operation, while the one to all trainable projection back to the hidden units allows random access reading of any context unit by any hidden unit. As Elman writes, "The recurrent connections allow the network's hidden units to see its own previous output, so that the subsequent behavior can be shaped by previous responses. These recurrent connections are what give the network memory" (p. 182), and "the context units remember the previous internal state. Thus, the hidden units have the task of mapping both an external input and also the previous internal state to some desired output" (p. 184). This last is, of course, what we require in a machine that can look back: access to both the current input and previous input.

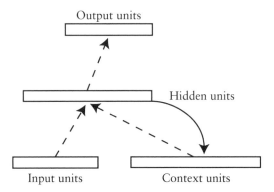

Figure 10.2   A simple recurrent network in which activations are copied from hidden layer to context layer on a one-for-one basis, with fixed weight of 1.0. Dotted lines represent trainable connections. (Reproduced by permission from Elman, 1990, p. 183.)

The essential thing to realize about Elman's solution, which has become the most common solution in the neural network literature to the problem of responding differentially to different temporal structure in the input, is that it does *not* use Hebbian synapses as memory elements. (Indeed, in Elman's model even the trainable synapses are trained by back-propagation, which is an omniscient god outside the machine.) Elman's proposal assumes instead the existence of elements to which activity can be "copied" (that is, written) and which hold that activity until the next time step, making it available to processing by the hidden units (that is, it is held in readable form). In Chapter 14, we will study in some detail the use of this same idea in a model of dead reckoning.

For the moment, we note only that this reverberating activity model of memory is implausible as a model for memory on a time scale longer than a fraction of a minute. That the model works when implemented using the noise-free read/write memory elements of a conventional computer is no surprise. On that kind of machine, the assumption that one can copy "activity" (that is, a floating point number) to memory with gain of 1 (so that the number in memory is exactly the same as the number that was copied), which memory then makes the number available to any and all other computations, is entirely reasonable. That is the essential function of memory, as a computer scientist understands it. But how should we imagine that this can be achieved in the nervous system whose biophysical reality Koch is concerned to depict? Elman does not say. But among those who have followed his lead, the assumption is that a signal somehow encoding a real number (that is, a graded quantity) is copied into a reverberating loop, where it travels around and around, neither gaining nor losing in value.

One certainly can trace loops within the connectivity of the nervous system. The hypothesis that reverberating activity in such loops can serve a critical short-term memory function goes back at least to Lorente de No (1932). It played a significant role in the earliest attempts to think about neural activity in computational terms (McCulloch & Pitts, 1943). Moreover, there is experimental evidence for it in at least one model system, the oculomotor integrator of the goldfish (Aksay, Baker, Seung, & Tank, 2000; Major et al., 2004). However, even in the goldfish oculomotor system, the activity in a loop typically declines by more than half in less than two minutes. In that loop, the rate of firing specifies the position of the eye in its socket. As the activity in that loop declines, the position of the eye drifts back to its null position. This is not a problem for the oculomotor system because it works on a time scale of seconds. In a few seconds, the drift due to the decay in the loop is negligible. If, however, activity in such a loop were to represent, say, the goldfish's distance from its nest or from its favorite hiding place, the goldfish would not – so far as its brain was concerned – need to do anything in order to get home. No matter how far it was from home, if it simply held still for a few hundred seconds, its brain would represent it as having reduced its distance to home to zero, because the circulating signal representing that distance would have decayed to the basal firing rate of the circuit. Thus, the first and perhaps foremost objection to the idea that reverberating activity can serve as a memory over indefinite intervals is that it would be difficult to prevent its becoming degraded over intervals measured in minutes at most.

The problem is that a reverberating signal must cross synapses 100 or more times per second. Synapses are thought to be inherently noisy, because the process of releasing transmitter from the presynaptic ending is stochastic (the number of quanta released by an action potential varies), and because the process of binding to postsynaptic receptor molecules is also stochastic (the fraction of transmitter released that succeeds in binding to a postsynaptic receptor varies). To preserve a reverberating signal for any length of time, there can be very little noise at the synapses that it must traverse over and over again.

A further problem is the coding: Is the magnitude of the stored value coded by the number of action potentials that pass a given point in the circuit in a given unit of time? Or in some other way? If the first way, must the action potentials be evenly spaced around the loop, so that the instantaneous firing rate (the reciprocal of the interval between any two action potentials) is constant? How could the even spacing be achieved? Or, are action potentials allowed to bunch up within the loop, so that they pass any given point in a burst? In the latter case, how does the process that reads the reverberating activity know whether it is reading within the burst or between bursts? And, if it has a way of recognizing the onset of a burst, does it know how long it must wait for the burst to come by again?

Another problem is the energetic costliness of this approach to information preservation. Signaling accounts for more than half the brain's energy demand and the adult human brain's demand for energy is 20 percent of the body's total demand (Laughlin, 2004). Storing large amounts of information for long periods in reverberating loops would tie up much of the brain's circuitry, be extravagantly wasteful of energy, and create a serious cooling problem. Neural signal transmission is not immune to the laws of thermodynamics. A substantial fraction of the energy released to do the work of signal transmission is lost as heat. Dissipating that heat would be no small problem.

These are among the many reasons why we believe that no biophysically informed neuroscientist believes that storing information in reverberatory loops can be the brain's solution to preserving large amounts of information for indefinite amounts of time. Thus, neither of the two mechanisms that have traditionally been imagined to implement memory – neither Hebbian synapses, nor reverberating activity – is suited to serve the function of carrying information forward in time in a computationally accessible form. And that brings us back to the point with which we started this chapter, the fact that at this time we do not know the answers to many of the most basic questions about how computations are implemented in neural tissue. A mechanism for carrying information forward in time is indispensable in the fabrication of an effective computing machine. Contemporary neurobiology has yet to glimpse a mechanism at all well suited to the physical realization of this function.

11

The Nature of Learning

At this time, within cognitive science and its allied disciplines, there are two quite different conceptual frameworks for thinking about learning – two different stories about what learning basically is. These stories interact strongly with our conception of the functional architecture of the brain. Part of what motivates a commitment to one story about the functional architecture of the brain is a commitment to the corresponding story about learning. Conversely, the assumption that the currently accepted story about the functional architecture of the brain is the right story biases one strongly toward one of the stories about the nature of learning. That is why we have brought together in this book a discussion of the nature of learning and the functional architecture of the brain. Although in principle, they are separate topics; in practice, they strongly influence one another.

In the first story about the nature of learning, which is by far the more popular one, particularly in neurobiologically oriented circles, learning is the rewiring by experience of a plastic brain so as to make the operation of that brain better suited to the environment in which it finds itself. In the second story, learning is the extraction from experience of information about the world that is carried forward in memory to inform subsequent behavior. In the first story, the brain has the functional architecture of a neural network. In the second story, it has the functional architecture of a Turing machine.

Learning As Rewiring

The first story about learning is plausibly exemplified by the well-known experiments by Pavlov on conditioning the salivary reflexes of dogs. Pavlov came to his experiments after a long study of the reflex secretions of stomach juices, because his original interest was in the physiology of digestion. Although he won the Nobel prize for his work on digestion, today he is much better remembered for his work on the foundations of learning. The digestive reflexes he studied can be understood in terms of the reflex pathways described by Sherrington in the classic behavioral experiments that delineated the integrative properties of the synaptic connections

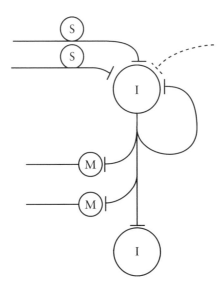

Figure 11.1 The functional architecture of a reflex arc. S = sensory neuron (selectively sensitive input element); I = interneuron (integrative element mediating convergence and divergence of signals); M = motor neuron (output element). When a path loops back to connect a neuron to itself, it is called a recurrent connection. The dashed presynaptic input represents an input created (or changed in its conductance) by experience. This is also the functional architecture of a neural network, except that in a neural network each different kind of neuron (S, I, and M) is replicated and arranged (conceptually) in layers, with the S neurons constituting the input layer, the I neurons the hidden layer, and the M neurons the output layer.

between neurons (Figure 11.1). That functional architecture remains the dominant one in contemporary attempts to understand the function of the brain.

The first element of a reflex arc is a sensory neuron. Its key function is to confer sensitivity to environmental conditions by means of differential sensitivity to stimuli. A sensory receptor responds to some stimuli and not to others. The receptors in the retina, for example, are sensitive to light but not to the chemical composition of the fluid within the eye. The receptors in the nose and tongue, by contrast, are not sensitive to light, but they are sensitive to extremely low concentrations of certain molecules absorbed into either the nasal mucosa or present in the fluid bathing the tongue.

The second functional elements are interneurons. The function of interneurons is to integrate signals from many different sensory neurons and to send signals reflecting the results of this integration to many different motor neurons and/or to interneurons, including back to themselves.

The function of motor neurons is to translate the results of the neural integration that has occurred among the interneurons into observable outputs, that is, muscular contractions and relaxations and glandular secretions (like salivation). Today, the three kinds of functional elements are commonly called the input nodes (or input layer), the hidden layer, and the output layer. The layers in question are layers of idealized neurons.

In the case of the digestive reflexes, the sensory neurons (input elements) are selectively sensitive to the chemical composition of the substances in the mouth, throat, and stomach. The motor neurons (output elements) control the secretion of different digestive juices. The integration of input signals by the interneuron elements (elements of the hidden layer) determines the pattern of secretion, the mixture of juices.

The process of signal integration in the postsynaptic neuron is at least crudely analogous to arithmetic summation. Broadly speaking, the postsynaptic neuron adds up the positive and negative inputs. If the resulting sum exceeds a threshold value, the postsynaptic neuron transmits a signal to all the neurons with which it connects. It is usually assumed that the greater the amount by which the sum exceeds the threshold, the stronger the signal transmitted. In contemporary efforts to model the computational functioning of the nervous system, the postsynaptic integration is quite literally arithmetic summation. It is not clear that this is empirically justified, because it is unlikely that the postsynaptic summation of postsynaptic potentials is linear over the range of input signals commonly received. If it is not, then it cannot be correctly modeled by arithmetic summation. In any event, it is assumed that the integration by the interneurons and the subsequent integration of interneuron input by output neurons determine the output pattern.

In the course of his digestive studies, Pavlov noticed that in dogs that had been used repeatedly, secretions were observed to occur in response to stimuli that had nothing inherently to do with digestion. He noticed that the sight or sound of the experimental preparations for delivering a digestion-relevant stimulus (e.g., food on the tongue) triggered secretions even when the digestion-relevant stimuli were not in fact delivered. He realized that this was an example of learning. There are no genetically specified connections leading from neurons in the auditory system to the motor neurons innervating the secretory glands of the digestive system, which is why sounds do not elicit secretions in the inexperienced dog. Pavlov assumed that this learning took the form of a rewiring of the nervous system. The central nervous system's assumed potential for rewiring itself is indicated by the dashed input pathway in Figure 11.1. In modern thinking, this represents an input whose synaptic conductance is initially essentially 0, but which can be increased by means of an experience-sensitive conductance-altering mechanism. To this day, there are many who do not see how it is possible to draw any other conclusion from these simple behavioral observations. The stimulus in question (for example, the sound of food being prepared) does not elicit the secretory response in the experimentally naive dog, but it does do so in the dog who has repeatedly heard those sounds and then been given food. Must not the system in some sense have rewired itself? There once was no path from the ear to the stomach and now there apparently is.

Synaptic Plasticity and the Associative Theory of Learning

Pavlov was understandably vague about exactly how this rewiring should be imagined to occur, but he set out to study the conditions under which it occurs. In doing so, he was guided by the congruence between what he seemed to have observed and one of the oldest and most popular ideas in the philosophical literature on the theory of mind, the notion of an associative connection. In the seventeenth century, the English philosopher and political theorist John Locke argued that our thoughts were governed by learned associations between "ideas." Locke understood by "ideas" both what we might now call simple sense impressions, for example, the impression of red, and what we might now call concepts, such as the concept of motherhood. He called the first simple ideas and the second complex ideas. Whereas rationalists like Leibnitz believed that ideas were connected by some kind of pre-ordained intrinsic logical system, Locke argued that the connections between our ideas were in essence accidents of experience. One idea followed the next in our mind because the stimulus (or environmental situation) that aroused the second idea had repeatedly been preceded by the stimulus (or situation) that aroused the preceding idea. The repeated occurrence of these two ideas in close temporal proximity had caused a connection to grow up between them. The connection conducted excitation from the one idea to the other. When the first idea was aroused, it aroused the second by way of the associative connection that experience had forged between the two ideas. Moreover, he argued, the associative process forged complex ideas out of simple ideas. Concepts like motherhood were clusters of simple ideas (sense impressions) that had become strongly associated with each other through repeated experience of their co-occurrence.

There is enormous intuitive appeal to this concept. It has endured for centuries. It is as popular today as it was in Locke's day, probably more popular. Some years ago, one of us gave a talk arguing that associations did not exist. Afterwards, he had a long and passionate argument with a distinguished modern proponent of the associative theory of learning and of the corresponding story about the functional architecture of the brain. Toward the conclusion of the discussion, the famous theorist asked rhetorically, "So how come when I hear 'salt' I think of pepper?" We mention this to illustrate the enduring intuitive appeal of Locke's argument and the influence it has on contemporary theories about the functional architecture of the brain and how that architecture explains behavioral phenomena. It has this appeal in part because, on first hearing, it seems that it just has to be right.

The influence on Pavlov of this well-known line of philosophical thought was straightforward. He translated the doctrine of learning by association into a physiological hypothesis. He assumed that it was the temporal proximity between the sound of food being prepared and the delivery of food that caused the rewiring of the reflex system, the formation of new connections between neurons. These new connections between neurons are the physiological embodiment of the psychological and philosophical concept of an association between ideas or, as we would now say, concepts. He set out to vary systematically the conditions of this temporal pairing – how close in time the neutral (sound) stimulus and the innately active food stimulus had to be, how often they had to co-occur, the effects of other stimuli present, and so on. In so doing, he gave birth to the study of what is now called Pavlovian conditioning. The essence of this approach to learning is the arranging of a predictive relation between two or more stimuli and the study of the behavioral changes that follow the repeated experience of this relationship. These changes are imagined to be the consequence of some kind of rewiring within a functional structure like that portrayed in Figure 11.1.

Why Associations Are Not Symbols

The functional structure portrayed in Figure 11.1 is not that of a representational system. There is no symbolic memory; hence, no mechanism for carrying forward in time the information gleaned from past experience. It is important to understand why this is so. The only thing in the functional structure in Figure 11.1 that could serve as a symbolic memory is the experience-sensitive synaptic connection represented by the dashed synaptic input. A physical mechanism that is to function as an enduring symbolic memory must be capable of adopting more than one enduring physical state. By enduring, we have in mind time scales measured in hours, days, months, and years. That is the time scale appropriate to what Pavlov studied and, more generally, to learning as a behavioral phenomenon.

If we think in discrete terms, then the mechanism must be like a switch, something that can be either in the "on" (closed) or "off" (open) state. The state of the switch must depend in some manner on the subject's experience. If we think in analog (continuous) terms, it must be like a rheostat, something whose resistance to the flow of electrical current can be adjusted to different values. Again, the setting of the rheostat must be in some manner dependent on the animal's experience. Something that is to serve as a symbol must have more than one state, because only something that has more than one state can carry information, and the function of a symbol is to carry information forward in time for use in subsequent computations. Earlier, we took note of the fact that the amount of information carried can never be more than the entropy available in the distribution of signals or symbols. Any physical element that can exist in only one state has 0 entropy, because there can be no uncertainty about what state it is in. The only element in Figure 11.1 that can be enduringly placed in more than one state is the synapse represented by the dashed input, the synapse whose conductance can be changed by experience.

Thus, in principle, synapses whose conductance can be changed by experience could be symbols. However, for them to be so, the mapping from experience to the state of the symbol must be invertible: it must be possible to deduce from the state of the synapse an aspect of the experience that produced it. In Shannon's terms, it must be possible to reconstitute the message. Put yet another way, the encoding procedure must be such as to make decoding possible. Suppose, for example, that Paul Revere's instructions to his confederate had been as follows: "If the British are coming by land and there are more than 1,000 of them, hang two lights. If they are coming by land and they are less than 1,000 strong, hang one light. If they are coming by sea and they are less than 1,000 strong, hang two lights. If they are coming by sea and they are more than 1,000 strong, hang one light." This is a bad code. It's bad because, if there is to be only one signal and it is to be generated according to these rules, then that signal is not usefully decodable. When Paul sees two lights, it could mean either that the British are coming by land and are more than 1,000 strong, or that they are coming by sea and are less than 1,000 strong. The code confounds two very different aspects of the situation. Paul's uncertainty about both aspects is as great after he sees the signal as it was before, so the signal is of no use.

The realization that Paul's uncertainty about both aspects is as great after the signal as it was before may lead one to think that when this encoding is followed, the resulting signal conveys no information. That is not true. It does convey information. In fact, if all four combined possibilities (land & > 1,000, land & < 1,000, sea & < 1,000, sea & > 1,000) are equally likely a priori, then the lantern signal conveys just as much information as in the simpler case that figures in the poem. After the signal, only two of the four combined possibilities are still possible. Therefore, the signal conveys one bit of information, just as before. However, it is not – by itself – a useful bit, because the commanders on the other side have no better idea how many men to muster nor where to position them than they had before. This reminds us again of the importance of keeping in mind the aboutness of uncertainty.

Distributed Coding

The "by itself" is an important qualification, because if we convey some more bits, then the information carried by the first bit (the first binary signal) may become useful. Suppose the instructions are to send two binary signals – the first according to the rules just specified, which leave both route and strength undecided, and the second according to the original rules (one if by land, two if by sea). Now, the values of both variables (route and troop strength) have been communicated, because the information about strength is distributed across the two signals. You have to get both signals to know how strong the British are, but you only need to get the second signal to know which way they are coming. Once you have got the second bit, you can compute from it and the first bit the troop strength. The computation involves the conditional branching that Turing realized was an essential component of any computer: If they are coming by land and the first signal was two lanterns, then the troop strength is greater than 1,000. If they are coming by land and the first signal was 1 lantern, then the troop strength is less than 1,000; and so on. This kind of if-then reasoning is mechanized by the conditional branching operation in a computer.

An even more interesting code is the fully distributed code shown in the second row of Table 11.1. In this code, we use three signals, no one of which reliably conveys the values of both variables. There are different rules for encoding each signal. The rule for the first signal is the always-ambiguous one we've been considering. The rule for the second signal is to hang one lantern in every case except the case when they are more than 1,000 strong and coming by land. The rule for the third signal is to hang one lantern in every case except when they are less than 1,000 strong and coming by land. It is left to the reader to work out exactly what uncertainty you have after seeing any single one of the three signals or any combination of two. It will be seen that you need all three signals in order to know the values of both variables.

Thus, the information about each variable is distributed across all three signals. No one signal reliably tells you the value of either variable. The latter two signals sometimes tell you the value of both variables (when the signal is 2 lanterns), but they also sometimes eliminate only one of the four possible cases (when the signal

Table 11.1 Encoding rules for multi-signal transmissions of the values of two variables: number of lanterns to be hung on each of three successive hangings (successive signals) as a function of route and number of troops

		Signal number					
		1		2		3	
	Route/Number	Land	Sea	Land	Sea	Land	Sea
Simple	< 1,000	1	2	1	1		
	> 1,000	1	2	2	2		
Distributed	< 1,000	1	2	1	1	2	1
	> 1,000	2	1	2	1	1	1

Note: The first encoding rule uses the first signal to transmit the value of the Route variable (first message) and the second to transmit the value of the Number (strength) variable (second message). The third signal is not used, although it could be used to retransmit, say, the first message – an elementary example of redundancy. The second rule distributes both messages across all three signals. It is a redundant code in that some sequences of signals are not possible, for example, the sequence 2, 2, 2. This means that if you have seen the sequence 2, 2, you know that the last signal will be 1.

is 1 lantern). If the cases occur equally often, then the less informative versions of the second and third signals will be sent on three out of every four transmissions.

Distributed codes are not necessarily bad codes. Because the transmission of each message is spread across many elements of the signal, knocking out one signal element does not leave the receiver with no information about one variable. Rather, it leaves the receiver with somewhat less information about all the variables. If these are continuous variables (like distances and durations), then the receiver gets a less precise specification of the value of each variable. If they are discrete variables, then the range of possible alternatives may not be narrowed as much as it would otherwise be. Distributed codes are used in, for example, cell phone communication, because they make the transmission much less sensitive to extraneous noise. The strengths of distributed codes account for much of the appeal of modern connectionist attempts to explain behavioral phenomena by models with the neurobiologically inspired functional architecture portrayed in Figure 11.1.

Discussions of distributed coding in the connectionist literature leave the impression that the use of distributed coding is unique to neural networks. Nothing could be further from the truth. Distributed codes are ubiquitous in modern communications and computing. In fact, the binary coding of number (like all place codes for magnitude) is a distributed code. The information about the magnitude coded for is spread across the bits (code elements) within the bit pattern symbol.

The example in Table 11.1 illustrates three important points about distributed codes. The first is that the same messages must be mapped to different signals (or symbols) in different ways. Thus, in Table 11.1, the encoding rules for each signal (each element) in the sequence are different. If the same message (e.g., that one event followed another event within some critical interval) maps to all the elements in the same way, then they all carry the same information. That is, every element but one is redundant, informationally useless. The second is that sophisticated computation is required to extract from a distributed code the values of the behaviorally useful variables. We must not lose sight of the fact that in order to act effectively – in order to judge, for example, how long to wait – the brain needs to have information about behaviorally relevant variables, not information about mixtures of variables, mixtures that themselves have no behavioral relevance. The third important point is that decoding computations must reflect in detail the complex structure of the encoding process. The more complex the encoding process is, the more complex the decoding process required to get the information into usable form.

These cautions are directly relevant to understanding why a changeable synaptic conductance – in psychological terms, an association – cannot in practice serve as a symbol – and why, therefore, models in which synaptic conductances (or associative strengths) are treated as symbols are rare. They explain, in other words, why proponents of the first story about learning – the rewiring story – often reject the idea that the brain forms enduring representations of what it has experienced. It explains why adherents of the architecture portrayed in Figure 11.1 are inclined to argue that neural processing is "sub-symbolic" (P. M. Churchland, 1989; Rumelhart & McClelland, 1986; Smolensky, 1991).

What Pavlov and those who have followed his experimental lead have discovered is that many different aspects of experience combine to determine the apparent strength of the association between two stimuli. The strength of the association – that is, the magnitude of the change in synaptic conductance – appears to depend on the delay between the sound and the food, on the strength of the sound, on the tastiness of the food, on the interval between successive pairings of sound and food, on how many pairings of sound and food there have been, and on many other aspects of the animal's experience. Thus, the strength of an association is like the single lantern signal in the above example of a "bad" encoding procedure: the value assumed by the signal depends on the values of many different variables, many different and quite unrelated aspects of the animal's experience. The values of those different variables are all confounded – run together, mixed up – in the determination of the strength of an association, just as the values of Route and Strength are confounded in the "bad" encoding rule. Thus, from the resulting strength of a single association, it is impossible to determine (even imprecisely) the value of any single one of the above list of experiential variables.

As is often the case, this critical point can be summed up succinctly in mathematical language: The function relating the strength of an association to experience is a many–one function. It maps the values of many different experiential variables to a single variable, the strength of the association. Many–one functions are not invertible. You cannot get from the value of the one back to the values of the many.

Given the many-to-one nature of the process that relates experiential variables (properties of distal stimuli) to synaptic conductance (associative strength), the only prospect for recovering from the resulting associative strengths useful facts about the experiences that produced them is to assume that distinct aspects of experience are encoded into associative strengths by a distributive encoding process. There are two problems with this assumption. First, Pavlov did his experiments in order to learn the laws governing the rewiring process – in psychological language, the association-forming process – in neurobiological language, the process relating experience to changes in synaptic conductance. His approach presupposes that the rules relating the properties of experience to the changes in synaptic conductance are quite general. If this is true, then synaptic conductance cannot serve as a distributed code, because, as we just saw, the necessary condition for its doing so is that the rules mapping a multifaceted experience to the change in one synaptic conductance (one symbol element) are different from the rules mapping the same experience (the same set of messages) to the changes in the conductance of other synapses. In fact, there have to be as many different mapping rules as there are synapses being mapped to. Thus, the assumption that the synaptic conductances themselves are symbols in a distributed encoding of behaviorally relevant aspects of the animal's experience is not consistent with the assumption that there is one or even a few rules (neurobiological processes) that relate experience to synaptic strength. There have to be as many different processes that change the strengths of synapses as there are synapses whose conductance must be changed. No one wants to assume this.

The second problem with assuming that changeable synaptic conductances encode a distributed representation of behaviorally relevant aspects of the animal's experience is that decoding a distributed representation into the values of behaviorally useful variables requires sophisticated computation with the symbols that carry the distributed code. However, the architecture in Figure 11.1 does not make the synaptic conductances accessible to computation.

The processes in the postsynaptic membrane that integrate the inputs from different synapses are computational in that they combine the inputs to yield an output. Indeed, as already noted, the combinatorial operation generally assumed in current models based on the architecture in Figure 11.1 is *arithmetic* addition of the *multiplicatively* weighted input signals, followed by a decision based on the sum. However, these computational processes do not have access to the synaptic conductances. What they have access to is the term-by-term product of the synaptic conductances and the strengths of the presynaptic inputs to those synapses. In mathematical language and notation, there are two vectors, the vector that specifies the strengths of the signals arriving at the presynaptic endings and the vector that specifies the conductances of those synapses. The first vector may be symbolized $\langle S_1, S_2, \ldots S_n \rangle$ and the second $\langle w_1, w_2, \ldots w_n \rangle$. In this symbolization, S_1 stands for the strength of the signal arriving at the first synapse, S_2 stands for the strength of the signal arriving at the second synapse, and so on, S_n standing for the strength of the signal arriving at the nth synapse. (Signal strength may be thought of as the number of spikes arriving per second.) Similarly, w_1 stands for the conductance of the first synapse, w_2 the conductance of the second synapse, and so on. If there are any enduring symbols in the architecture portrayed in Figure 11.1, then the vector of synaptic conductances, $\langle w_1, w_2, \ldots w_n \rangle$, is the equivalent of the strings of '0's and '1's in a binary symbol stored on Turing's tape. What the integrative postsynaptic process sees, however, is not this vector. What it sees is $\langle w_1 S_1, w_2 S_2, \ldots w_n S_n \rangle$. If it does not know the strengths of the presynaptic signals, $\langle S_1, S_2, \ldots S_n \rangle$, then it cannot determine $\langle w_1, w_2, \ldots w_n \rangle$ from $\langle w_1 S_1, w_2 S_2, \ldots w_n S_n \rangle$. If the postsynaptic computational processes have no way of knowing what $\langle S_1, S_2, \ldots S_n \rangle$ was – and in the architecture Figure 11.1, they do not – then there is no way that these processes can decode $\langle w_1 S_1, w_2 S_2, \ldots w_n S_n \rangle$.

In short, there are quite fundamental reasons why the architecture in Figure 11.1 is not the architecture of a representational system and why the only possible enduring symbols in Figure 11.1, the experience-dependent conductances of the synapses, are not in fact symbols. That is why those who think that learning is the rewiring of a plastic brain by experience shy away from representational theories of brain function. The anti-representational strain in this line of thought has been evident in its every manifestation during the past 100 years. Early champions of this view, like Clark Hull (1929; 1952) and B. F. Skinner (1938; 1957) went to great lengths to argue that behaviors that looked like they were informed by a representation of the subject's environment could in fact be better understood as chains of stimulus-response events involving no underlying representations. More recent versions of this view have been similarly anti-representational (Rumelhart & McClelland, 1986), arguing that neural processing is "subsymbolic" (Smolensky, 1986). An anti-representational approach to learning is also salient in the dynamical systems treatment of cognition (Port, 2002). The intuitive essence of this view is that animals act intelligently because of the rewiring effects of experience on their brains, but they do not know why what they do is intelligent because they have no enduring representation of the aspects of the world to which their action is adapted. On this view, there is only one way of knowing, and that is by modification of the state of the processor. There is no tape.

Learning As the Extraction and Preservation of Useful Information

The second story about learning is exemplified by the study of dead reckoning, which is a key component of animals' navigational systems. Dead reckoning is a simple computation, one for which effective (machine-implementable) procedures have long been known and routinely used. It illustrates the fundamental role that a symbolic memory plays in computation. And, there is strong behavioral evidence that this procedure is implemented in the brains of a wide range of animals, including many insects. In fact, the best behavioral data come from studies on ants and bees.

Figure 11.2 is a tracing of the track of a foraging ant of the species *Cataglyphis bicolor*, which inhabits the Tunisian desert. Figure 11.3 is a picture of the bleak and featureless terrain in which these ants navigate. In this example, the ant emerged from the nest, struck off to the northwest for several meters, then broke into the tortuous circling pattern characteristic of this ant when it is searching for something. At the spot marked with an X, it found the carcass of a scorpion. It bit off a chunk to carry back to the nest. The homeward journey is traced by the dashed line. Clearly, the ant knew the direction home. Experiments in which the ant is captured just as it starts for home, carried across the dessert and released in unfamiliar territory show that it also knows the distance to the nest (Wehner & Srinivasan, 1981). The released ants run the compass course from the capture point to the nest, which is, of course, not the course to the nest from the release

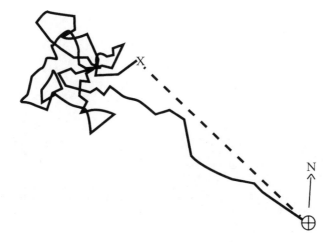

Figure 11.2   Tracing of the track of a foraging Cataglyphis bicolor. N = nest hole; X = location of food; solid line = outward journey; dashed line = homeward journey. Distance scale on the order of 10 m. (From Harkness & Maroudas, 1985, reproduced by permission.)

site. This proves that they do not require familiar landmarks to set and maintain their nest-ward course, because they are running through unfamiliar terrain on a course that does not in fact lead to the nest. When they are a meter or two past where the nest should have been encountered, they stop and begin to search for it. This proves that they do not need the familiar landmarks surrounding the nest in order to estimate that they are in the vicinity of the nest, because, in the unfamiliar terrain to which they have been experimentally transported, those landmarks are absent.

The ants obviously learn from their experience the compass direction and distance of their nest from the site at which they find food. This information cannot have been carried in their genes. The questions, then, are: What is the experience from which they learn? How do they learn from it? What does this tell us about the nature of learning? What does it tell us about the functional architecture of the brain?

The experience from which they learn is the experience of moving themselves from location to location en route to finding the food. The learning process is the continual updating of a representation of their current location by summing the successive small displacements (small changes in location) by which they have reached it. This tells us that learning is the extraction from experience of symbolic representations, which are carried forward in time by a symbolic memory mechanism, until such time as they are needed in a behavior-determining computation. This in turn tells us that the functional architecture of the brain must have as one of its basic elements a symbolic memory mechanism, a mechanism whose structure suits it to carry information forward in time in a manner that makes the information accessible to computation.

Figure 11.3   The sort of terrain in which desert ants navigate. (Photograph of the Namib desert where *Oxymyrmex* navigates; taken by Rüdiger Wehner and published with his permission.)

Updating an Estimate of One's Location

The ant is like almost all other animals whose navigational behavior has been subject to experimental study in that it keeps an ongoing estimate of its current location by updating that estimate as it moves. The mathematical term for this is *path integration*, but in English texts on the principles of navigation it is commonly called *dead reckoning*, which is thought to be a corruption from the abbreviation "ded. reckoning," for "deduced reckoning." The term "reckoning" already tells us that it is the result of a computational process. Because it is so simple, it is instructive to consider the process in some detail. Like all physically realizable computations, it is an example of an effective procedure, as defined by Turing. To drive that point home, we will consider how to implement it in a simple analog computer.

Dead reckoning requires two signals, one indicating the speed at which one is moving and the other indicating the direction relative to the earth's surface (compass direction). The signal indicating speed often comes at least in part from the propulsion system. For example, on a propeller-driven boat, it comes from the rate at which the propeller is turning. In the ant, it very likely comes in part from the neural commands that determine the rate of stepping. Such signals are called efference copy signals, because they are a copy of the outbound (efferent) signal fed to other parts of the brain to provide information about the movements that have been commanded. The efference copy is likely to be supplemented by signals from

Table 11.2   Illustrative entries in a ship's log made to "keep the reckoning" (of position)

Time	Est. speed (prev. hr)	Est. direction	Northing (knots/hr)	Easting (knots/hr)	Net change in position (nm)	
					n(+/−) N/S	e(+/−) E/W
5:00 leaving port						
6:00	4	270 (W)	0	−4	0	−4.0 W
7:00	4	270 (W)	0	−4	0	−8.0 W
8:00	4	270 (W)	0	−4	0	−12.0 W
9:00	4	270 (W)	0	−4	0	−16.0 W
10:00	6	270 (W)	0	−6	0	−22.0 W
11:00	8	(315) NW	5.7	−5.7	+5.7 N	−27.7 W
12:00	5	(0) N	5.0	0	+10.7 N	−27.7 W
13:00	5	(0) N	5.0	0	+15.7 N	−27.7 W
14:00	6	(120) ESE	−3.0	5.2	+12.7 N	−22.5 W
15:00	7	(120) ESE	−3.5	6.1	+9.2 N	−16.4 W
16:00	5	(120) ESE	−2.5	4.3	+6.7 N	−12.1 W
17:00	4	(120) ESE	−2.0	3.5	+4.7 N	−8.6 W
18:00	4	(120) ESE	−2.0	3.5	+2.7 N	−5.1 W
19:00	4	(120) ESE	−2.0	3.5	+0.7 N	−1.7 W

proprioceptors in the legs indicating leg movements and also perhaps by signals from hair cells on the body that bend in response to the movement of the air. The compass-direction signal can come from many different sources, but the preferred source, the one that dominates all other sources when it is available, is the direction of the sun. In Chapter 13, we discuss the learning mechanism that makes it possible to use this source for a compass-direction signal.

The computations required to extract from these two signals the information about one's current location are indicated in Table 11.2, which is an example of the record (ship's log) that navigators are taught to keep. (See also Figure 11.4.) In this somewhat simplified example, we assume that the navigator sets sail from the port of Thinadhoo in the southern Maldives, in the Indian Ocean, almost on the Equator. Its Equatorial location recommends it for this example, because, on the Equator, both a degree of latitude and a degree of longitude are equal to 60 nautical miles, which simplifies the keeping track of latitude and longitude in the final column of the log.

The navigator notes the speed and direction of sail at regular intervals, usually no longer than an hour, and whenever there is a noticeable change in either speed or direction. Speed is in nautical miles per hour (knots). For purposes of numerical calculation, direction is given in its most common numerical form, which is in degrees clockwise from north. As a check against numerical error, it is usually also recorded in "points of the compass notation," that is, as N, NE, E, SE, and so on. (ESE is east-southeast, which is half way between E and SE.)

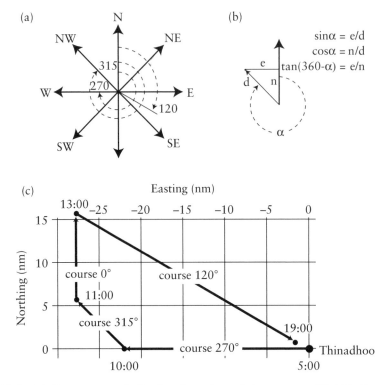

Figure 11.4   (a) Compass rose indicating the points of the compass (N, NE, E, etc.) and the numerical system for representing compass direction. (b) Trigonometric relations. (c) The navigator's track: 1 = position at 10:00; 2 = position at 11:00; 3 = position at 13:00; tip of last arrow is her position at 17:00. Notice that, as planned, she is arriving well upwind of her destination.

The course is due west for the first four hours and the speed holds steady at 4 knots (entries in second column). In calculating how far she has progressed, the navigator multiplies her speed by the duration of the interval over which that speed has been maintained. (This is done in the "Northing" and "Easting" columns.) Thus, at the end of four hours, she notes in the log that she is 4 hrs × 4 nm/hr = 16 nm miles west of Thindadhoo. (See the "−16" entry in the e(+/−) column of the Net Change columns.) Ordinarily, she must first decompose her speed into her northing (how fast she is progressing to the north or south) and her easting (how fast she is progressing to the east or west). On this first leg, this step in her calculations is trivial, because she is only moving along the east–west axis. Thus, her northing is 0 nm/hr and her easting is −4 nm/hr (by convention, east is positive and west negative). At 9:00, her speed increases to 6 knots, but this does not appear in the log until the 10:00 entry, because the speed estimates are for the interval just ended. Thus, between 9:00 and 10:00, her easting decreases by another 6 nm, so that her net easting from Thindahoo at 10:00 is −22 nm (22 nm west – see entry in e(+/−) column).

At 10:00, she turns northwest (a compass course of 315°) and her speed picks up to 8 knots. Now, she must decompose her speed into its N/S and E/W components. This is the Etch-A-Sketch™ procedure in reverse. An Etch-A-Sketch™ tablet has two knobs, one of which makes the pen move along the horizontal axis and one along the vertical axis. In playing with it, one soon learns that one can draw angled lines by turning both knobs at once. The angle of the line drawn is determined by the relative rates at which they are turned: the faster the vertical knob is turned relative to the horizontal knob, the steeper the slope of the line drawn. Metaphorically, the navigator's vessel is drawing a line on the earth's surface. If the navigator draws her course on a chart (map) of the surface, then she literally draws a line that represents her track. To compute her northing and easting, she must calculate the speeds at which the two knobs would have to be turned in order to generate her speed along her track. In other words, she must figure out how far she must progress along an east–west axis and simultaneously how far along a north–south axis in order to progress 1 nm along a line that bisects the angle between these two perpendicular axes.

To figure this out, she must know the proportions between the sides of a right triangle, with her track as the hypotenuse and the two other angles equal. The determination of these proportions is trigonometry (literally, the measuring of triangles). The proportions we want for this calculation are the sine and cosine of the angle that the track forms with line pointing due north. The sine is the proportion between the side opposite the angle (that is to say, the east–west side) and the hypotenuse, while the cosine is the proportion between the side adjacent to the angle (that is to say, the north–south side) and the hypotenuse. The angle is 315° when the rotation is clockwise (positive), which is equivalent to a counterclockwise rotation of 45° in what by convention we call the negative direction of rotation. The $\sin(315)$ = $\sin(-45) = -0.707$, while the $\cos(315) = \cos(-45) = 0.707$. In other words, on this course, the progress along each of the perpendicular axes is a bit more than 7/10ths of the progress along the course itself (the track she is tracing). The negative sign of the sine tells us that her track is left of the north–south axis, and the positive sign of the cosine tells us that it is above the east–west axis. Thus, together the two signs tell us what quadrant the track lies in (the quadrants being NE, SE, SW, and NW, when taken in their clockwise order).

In the old days, the required trigonometric proportions were obtained from trigonometric tables. It has long been known how to calculate the proportions using the elementary operations of arithmetic, but the calculation is a bit tedious and therefore prone to error. These days, the navigator would use a pocket calculator, which has built into it procedures for calculating trigonometric proportions. Thus, she gets her northing and easting by punching in her compass course, then hitting the requisite button (the "sin" or "cos" button), which calls the procedure that translates that number into a number specifying the proportion, then she punches in her speed and hits the "times" button, which gives her speed along one or the other axis, that is, her northing or her easting. Now all she has to do is multiply these by the number of hours during which she has been making those speeds, which in the present case is one hour. She adds the result of this calculation, the calculation of her most recent north–south and east–west displacements, to the previous totals (in the Net change columns) to get her net displacement, that is, the net change in her location since the start of her trip. The last two numbers in the Net change columns tell her location relative to Thinadhoo as of her most recent reckoning. Put another way, they tell her where she is on a chart (map) that has Thinadhoo at its origin (at the intersection of the north–south and east–west axes, so that Thinadhoo's coordinates are <0, 0>). The above sequence is another illustration of the fundamental role that the composition of functions plays in computation.

It is easy to translate this into a location on any other chart on which Thinadhoo itself has a known location. For the last two hundred years or so, most marine charts have been drawn in a coordinate framework in which the Equator is the east–west axis and the longitude of Greenwich England is the north–south axis. In that framework, Thinadhoo's coordinates are 72.9333° east longitude and 0.5333° north latitude (this latter coordinate is what recommended it to us as a starting point in this example). Because in this part of the world map degrees of latitude and longitude are equal to each other and to 1/60th of a nautical mile, the navigator can compute her latitude and longitude in the standard coordinates simply by dividing the numbers in the Net change columns by 60 and adding the results to the latitude and longitude coordinates for Thinadhoo. This is an example of a coordinate transformation. Most of navigation is a coordinate transformation of one kind or another.

This simple computation updates her estimate of her location as she goes along, which is extremely useful if she is using a chart to tell her where there are, for example, reefs that need to be avoided. However, the representation of her location on a chart with Thinadhoo at its origin does not give her the variables she needs for the most obvious behavior, namely, heading back to where she started, which she decides to do at 13:00. To set the course for home, she needs the range (distance) and bearing (direction) of Thinadhoo. She has the information implicitly because her position and Thinadhoo's position are being carried forward by the symbols in her log (see the entries in the Net change columns for 13:00), but she does not have the information explicitly, in the form in which she needs it to set her course back to Thinadhoo.[1] In this regard, she is like Paul Revere after he has seen the signal but before he has consulted his code book, which enables him to translate the signal into militarily relevant variables. In this case, she can translate the numerical symbols for her position into numerical symbols for the distance and direction to Thinadhoo as follows: To get the bearing, she needs the proportion (ratio) between her N/S displacement and her E/W displacement, which is $-27.7/15.7 = -1.76$.

---

[1]   Using polar coordinates, it is possible to do the calculation in such a way that the range and bearing of home are directly given by the position coordinates. It is, however, a bad idea to do the calculation in that way, because at each computation of your most recent displacement, you make use of your computation of the net prior displacement. Thus, the errors that went into that earlier computation (due, for example, to errors in the speed and direction signals) enter in repeatedly, making the computation inherently less accurate (Gallistel, 1990, p. 75). This is another example of the intimate correspondence between the mapping from referents to their symbolic representatives and the processing of those symbols. Changing one requires changing the other. Sometimes the required change may be for the worse.

Knowing this proportion (the tangent), she can use the atan function on her pocket calculator to find the bearing of her position from Thinadhoo. This is atan(−1.76) = −60° from north. The opposite direction (180 − 60 = 120°), is the bearing of Thinadhoo from her position. That is the course she must make good to get back to port.

The numerical symbols that represent her distance (range, r) from Thindahoo are obtained from the symbols specifying her position by the Pythagorean formula for the hypotenuse of a right triangle: $r = \sqrt{n^2 + e^2}$. By 19:00, she calculates that Thindahoo is less than a mile south of her current position and less than 2 miles east. It's time to start looking for the entrance lights.

Her track out and back is indicated in Figure 11.4. It is much simpler than the ant's, which means that the ant did much more computing, but the computations it did are just those spelled out here, repeated over and over again.

The role of symbolic memory

The most important thing to appreciate from this example is the fundamental role that symbolic memory plays in making it possible. The principles behind the computation are extremely simple: Use your compass direction to decompose your speed into perpendicular components and keep the running sum of those components. The symbolic memory is the key to keeping the running sum. In this case, as in most other cases, the experiences from which the subject extracts the information that it needs to behave effectively do not happen all at once; they are spread out in time. At each moment the subject gets sensory and efference copy information from which it can estimate the displacement it is undergoing at that moment. To get its net displacement, it must be able to add up its successive displacements. To do that, it must carry forward the information from earlier displacements in a form that enables the system to add the current displacement to the earlier displacements. The functional architecture required for this is the functional architecture of a Turing machine.

Physical realization

The physical implementation of this computation can be simple and direct. The computation has only three stages: (1) Obtaining the sine-cosine representation of the direction of movement; (2) multiplying that representation by a representation of the speed; (3) keeping a running sum of the results. The hydraulic system in Figure 11.5 implements the computation. To measure the boat's speed, we couple the drive shaft leading to the propeller to a pump ("speed pump" in Figure 11.5a) driving water into a common reservoir: the faster the shaft turns, the higher the water pressure in the reservoir. The pressure in the reservoir represents (is the symbol for) speed. Water passes out of the reservoir through four small pipes. The flows in these pipes (amount of water passing through per unit of time) are regulated by piston-valves in two plates that are moved back and forth along orthogonal axes by means of pins fixed to the periphery of a magnetic compass disk (Figure 11.5b).

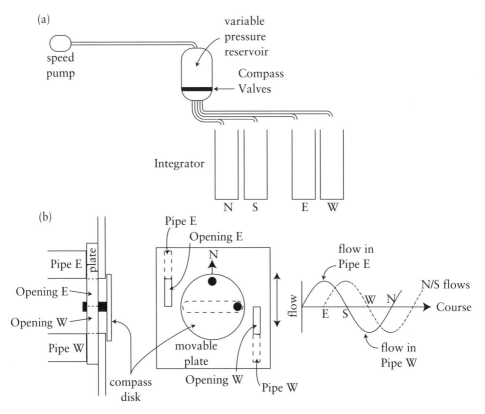

Figure 11.5   Functional architecture of an hydraulic dead-reckoning machine. (a) shows the overall structure; (b) shows details of the compass-driven valves that control the flows to the E–W buckets (integrators).

The detail at the left of Figure 11.5b shows only one of these two plates, the plate with the E–W valves. These two valves control the flows in the E–W pair of pipes. The flow in the E pipe represents the (positive) easting, while the flow in the W pipe represents the negative easting (that is, "westing"). In the diagram, the boat happens to be headed due north, and so both the E valve and the W valve are closed; there is no flow in either pipe. The E–W plate rotates with the boat, while the compass disk, of course, always points toward north. The E–W movable plate is constrained so that it can only move up and down (on the page, fore and aft relative to the boat). As the compass disk rotates, the pin through the slot in the movable E–W plate forces the plate to move either up or down. Suppose, for example, that the boat turned and headed northwest ($\alpha = 315°$). The compass disk would rotate clockwise with respect to the movable plate. As it did so, the pin would push the movable plate down, opening the W valve to a bit more than 7/10ths (= $\sin\alpha$ = 0.707) of its maximum. Thus, whenever the boat's heading lies anywhere in the west (anywhere in the half circle from 180°–360°), there will be a flow in the W pipe, the magnitude of which (the amount of water per unit time) will represent how fast the boat is progressing to the west. Whenever the boat's heading lies anywhere in the east, there will be a flow in the E pipe proportional to the rate at which the boat is progressing eastward. And similarly for the N and S pipes, whose flows are regulated by the two valves in the other movable plate (not shown), which is driven by the other pin, back and forth along the axis perpendicular to the E–W plate's movement.

Next, we need to integrate these flows. "Integration" sounds like a fancy and scary mathematical procedure. The mere mention of the word is enough to shut down cortical activity in more than half of a large introductory course in psychology. Physically speaking, however, it is preposterously simple to implement. We simply direct the flows into tall buckets, tall enough so that there is no danger of a bucket filling up within the span of the kinds of trips on which we plan to use this machine. We empty all four buckets at the start of each trip. At any time during our trips, the height of the water in the E bucket represents the total distance that we have progressed to the east, ignoring progress to the west, that is, negative progress, progress in the opposite direction. Likewise, the height of the water in the W bucket represents our total progress to the west, ignoring all eastward progress. The difference in these two heights, hence difference in hydraulic pressure between the two buckets, represents how far east or west we are of where we started. And similarly for the N–S pair of buckets. These two differences in hydraulic pressures (the E–W pressure difference and the N–S pressure difference) are the analog symbols for our position in a coordinate framework with our starting point at the origin and the traditional directions (N–S/E–W) as its axes. We could, if we wish, use those hydraulic pressures as the inputs to another analog mechanism that would compute for us the range and bearing of home. (This is left as an exercise for the mechanically inclined reader.)

The idea of a plate moved back and forth by the turning of a compass disk may give the reader a suggestion about how to generate bit patterns representing the sine and cosine of the boat's heading. Suppose we use a 4-bit code. This will allow us to break the magnitudes of the sine and cosine into $2^4 = 16$ equal intervals, which means that we can represent these quantities to an *average* accuracy of roughly ±5%. For a 4-bit code, we need four switches. When all four switches are open, we have the bit pattern 0000, which represents, in digital notation, sine magnitudes from between 0 and 1/16 = 0.0625. When only the first switch is closed, we have the bit pattern 0001, which represents, in digital notation, sine magnitudes between 0.0625 and 0.125; when only the second switch is closed we have 0010, representing 0.125–0.1875; when the first and second switches are both closed, we have 0011, representing 0.1875–0.25; and so on. Imagine that the switch levers are spring loaded and pressing down on the movable plate, so that when the tip of the lever comes to a depression or hole in the plate, it drops into the hole, closing the switch. When the plate moves further, the edge of the hole pushes the lever back up, opening the switch. Now, it is just a matter of cutting the right hole pattern in the movable plate. The mechanism just sketched is an example of an analog-to-digital converter. If we put a float on top of the water in a tank in which the height of the water is proportional to speed, then a similar mechanism will give us a bit pattern to represent speed. We can proceed from there using the machinery for adding and multiplying bit patterns.

As always in this book, we describe ways of physically implementing these computations in order to demystify computation, in order to strengthen the reader's sense of computational processes as physical processes, with symbols as physical variables within a machine that are operated on by the machinery. In this case, part of our purpose is to demystify both integration and the encoding. There are many ways of physically achieving both.

12

Learning Time and Space

When neurologists begin an exam of an elderly patient or a patient who has suffered a brain injury, the first thing they check for is orientation in space and time: Does the patient know where he or she is? At home? In a hospital? What city? What state? What country? Do they know the approximate time of day (morning, afternoon), day of the week, month, year? Can they remember the name of a president? Is he president now? If not, about how long ago was he president?

We mention this to make two points: First, the ability to locate oneself in space and time is the foundation for the ability to act appropriately. If you do not know where you are nor that it has been many a year since George Washington was president, your mind is truly failing. You probably cannot take care of yourself.

Computational Accessibility

The second point is that maintaining a spatio-temporal location requires us to carry forward in time an enormous amount of acquired information in a computationally accessible form: You must know not only roughly where Beijing, Paris, Moscow, Cairo, Buenos Aires, New York, and Boston are, you must also be able to exploit this knowledge to compute approximate ranges and bearings between any two of them. Is the distance between Cairo and Beijing greater or less than the distance between Boston and New York? Is Moscow north or south of Cairo? How about Cairo and Buenos Aires? In going from Paris to Moscow is it shorter to go east or to go west? We query our fund of spatio-temporal knowledge in innumerable ways. Readers who know at least roughly where these cities are will be able to answer these questions, even though they did not foresee these questions when they learned where the cities are.

The just posed questions about distances and directions between world cities are stand-ins for similar questions that we ask ourselves day-in and day-out about our local environment. Is the dry cleaner closer than the drugstore? Would I go near the soccer field on my way to the dentist? Does Seth live near Mohammed? At this moment, am I closer to Hospital X or Hospital Y? Can I walk there in an hour? Can I drive there in an hour? Do I have time to pick up Jeffrey before my appointment with Tabisha? Could one woman load a tractor trailer with books in one hour? Could she load a cardboard box with pillows in a day? The first important thing to recognize about these examples is that they require us to use acquired information about locations and durations and rates and sizes. This information has been carried forward in time from the different periods at which it was acquired. The second thing to note is that the number of different questions that we can answer by reference to the information thus acquired is for all practical purposes infinite.

It is this latter point – the infinitude of possibly desirable computations – that shifts the architectural focus to the critical importance of computational accessibility. The architecture of a brain must enable it to bring together for computational purposes distinct pieces of information (temporal, spatial, volumetric, weight, etc.) whose computational conjunction was not foreseen at the time the information was acquired. Acquired information is not simply pumped back out again to inform the same behavior that was appropriate when the information was acquired.[1] It is combined with other information – often quite disparate information, acquired at other times and other places – to inform behaviors that were often inappropriate, irrelevant, or impossible at the time the information was acquired. Crucially for our argument, there are infinitely many such combinations that a brain may be called on to make. That is why brains cannot have an architecture that requires that every computational combination one might need to make be foreseen in advance and hardwired into them. No matter how big we imagine the brain to be, there are simply too many possible combinations to make this architecture workable.

The ability to combine temporal, spatial, and other information in a variety of computations is present in many non-human animals. In this chapter, we review some of the relevant behavioral evidence. In a later chapter (Chapter 15), we consider attempts to explain timing phenomena within the confines of the currently presumed functional architecture of the brain. We will see that the essential problem with all such proposals is the problem of computational accessibility: information is not carried forward in such a way as to make it generally accessible to computation.

Learning the Time of Day

Like almost all organisms, including plants and bacteria, most animals have a built-in clock, called the circadian (approximately daily) clock, which enables them to adapt their behavior to the ubiquitous 24-hour day–night cycle. In mammals, the master clock is an endogenous biochemical oscillation in the neurons that compose a small area called the suprachiasmatic nucleus, which is part of the hypothalamus (Earnest, Liang, Ratcliff, & Cassone, 1999; Hastings, 2002; Sujino et al., 2003). The hypothalamus is the brain's executive center; it establishes the animal's behavioral and physiological goals and coordinates the behavior with the physiology (Adams,

---

[1] Although that was how the behaviorists conceived the process of learning, a conception that continues in neural net modeling.

2006; Gallistel, 1980; Kelley, Baldo, Pratt, & Will, 2005; King, 2006). This master clock synchronizes clocks within many other body tissues (for example, the kidney and the liver) and in other parts of the brain.

Gallistel (1990) reviewed the literature showing that animals, including insects, routinely record the time of day at which events occur and use this record to inform their subsequent behavior. The two most studied phenomena that involve remembering the time of day corresponding to some event or observation are feeding-anticipatory activity and the sun-compass. When rats are kept in an environment with continuous access to a running wheel and access to food that is restricted to one or two feeding periods each day, they run more vigorously in the wheel in the hours preceding the onsets of the feeding periods (Bolles & de Lorge, 1962; Bolles & Moot, 1973; Bolles & Stokes, 1965; Richter, 1922).

The subjects' estimate of how close the current time of day is to the time at which food has previously become available is determined by the phase of their circadian clock. When the day–night cycle that ordinarily entrains this clock (synchronizes it with the earth's daily rotation) is eliminated, the clock runs free, that is, it runs at its endogenous period. This period is never exactly 24 hours and it is never exactly the same in two different subjects. Thus, the free-running circadian clocks in different subjects gradually drift out of phase with the earth's rotation cycle and with one another (Scapini, Rossano, Marchetti, & Morgan, 2005). Like cheap mechanical watches that are not reset each day, so that after some number of days the watches do not agree with one another and every watch tells the wrong time, so it is with circadian clocks. As a result, when food deprivation is reinstated – after a month or more in which there was unrestricted access to food, hence no running in the wheel in anticipation of the onset of food access – each subject shows anticipatory running activity according to his own clock (Edmonds & Adler, 1977a, 1977b; Rosenwasser, Pelchat, & Adler, 1984). The anticipatory activity of a given subject occurs at the right times on that subject's clock, which are not the right times by the clock on the wall (which is synchronized to "true time," that is, to the earth's rotation), nor by the clocks of other subjects. This proves that the time of day that is stored in memory is the time on the subject's internal endogenously active clock. More technically, it is the phase of the circadian clock at the time of food onset.

Very similar phenomena were observed in foraging bees as early as 1910 (Buttel-Reepen, 1915; Forel, 1910) and systematically investigated by students of von Frisch (Beling, 1929; Stein-Beling, 1935; Wahl, 1932). This work showed that foraging bees remember the time of day together with the shape, color, and odor of the food sources they encounter. When trained to get sugar water from sources at different locations and/or with different odors, colors and shapes at different times of day, then offered a choice between those different sources, bees' preference depends on the time of day at which they are offered the choice: they prefer the location, odor, color, or shape from which they previously got food at that time of day. (See Gallistel, 1990, for detailed review.) Bees make ideal experimental subjects because the foraging bee does not consume the nectar that it harvests on each visit; it transports it to the hive and gives it up there. Thus, the same forager visits a source over and over again in the course of the day, without satiating.

One result bears particular mention. It demonstrates first that remembered experiences are stamped with the time of day of the experience, even in bees. It also demonstrates that the remembered time of day of a previous experience can be compared to the current time of day to inform current behavior. Koltermann (1971) worked with 285 individually trained and tested bees. Each bee regularly visited his feeding source about every 5 minutes from early in the morning till late in the afternoon during one training day and then again during one test day. On the quarter hour, for 9 successive hours, from 9:00 to 17:15 of the training day, Kolterman placed filter paper impregnated with essence of geranium under his sugar-water beaker for three visits. Thus, on this one training day, the bee smelled geranium when it visited the source between 9:15 and 9:30, but not from 8:30 to 9:15, nor from 9:30 to 10:15. It smelled geranium again from 10:15 to 10:30, but not from then until 11:15, and so on throughout the day, with the last smell of geranium from 17:15 to 17:30.

On the test day, which immediately followed the training day, the beaker was again full of sugar water and had no odor – except for 5-minute (one-visit) test intervals that recurred at half-hour intervals: 8:50, 9:20, 9:50, 10:20, and so on to 17:20 and 17:50. During these short one-visit test intervals, the bee was confronted with two beakers. Both were empty, but the only way that the bee could ascertain that a beaker was empty was by landing on it and entering it. One empty beaker smelled of geranium, the other of thyme. Previous work had shown that bees have no innate preference between geranium and thyme odors and that they associate either with nectar and with the time of day equally readily. Notice that the test intervals coincided alternately with intervals during which the bees either had not or had smelled geranium. Thus, at the 8:50 test, the bee was choosing between a beaker that smelled of an odor (thyme) it had not associated with nectar and a beaker that smelled of an odor (geranium) it had experienced together with nectar, but not at that time of day. On the next test, a half hour later, it was confronted with the same choice, but now at a time of day when it had smelled geranium as it harvested the nectar. The third test occurred at a time of day when geranium had not been smelled, the fourth at a time of day when it had, and so on.

Regardless of the time of testing, the bee preferred the geranium beaker to the almost complete exclusion of the thyme beaker. Thus, they remembered which odor was associated with nectar regardless of the time of day. This is theoretically important. It shows that the memory may be accessed independently of the time of day at which it was laid down. It is not the case that the phase of the circadian clock determines which memories are accessible. Rather, the phase of the circadian clock at the time of the experience is part of what is accessed, as is shown by the fact that the intensity with which the trained bees sought nectar in the geranium-smelling beaker depended strongly on the time of testing. During intervals when – given the previous day's experience – they had reason to expect nectar in a source smelling of geranium, they repeatedly landed on and re-entered the empty geranium-smelling beaker. (If a little anthropomorphic license is allowed, this is "I just can't believe it's not there" behavior.) By contrast, during intervals (at times of day) when they had no reason to expect nectar from a source smelling of geranium (but rather from an odorless source), they landed and entered much less frequently. Kolterman's bees strongly differentiated alternate half hours from 8:50 to 17:50, 19 in all! That is, they gave evidence of having registered the presence or absence of geranium at 19 different times of day in a single day's training.

The fact that animals learn multiple times of day is the second point of major theoretical import. It rules out the most common attempts to explain time-of-day learning in non-representational terms. These explanations try to understand the phenomenon as an instance of entrainment, the entrainment by food of circadian oscillations (Mistlberger, 1994). Such an explanation for Kolterman's data would require 19 different geranium-entrainable oscillators, each entrained by a different one of the geranium events that the bee experienced. The very suggestion makes a mockery of the concept of entrainment.

The learning of the circadian time, place, smell, shape, color, and odor of food sources is well documented in insects, whose brains are, of course, small, containing on the order of a million neurons. This reminds us of the problem of combinatorial explosion (the infinitude of the possible), which hovers around attempts to explain learning within the confines of contemporary neurobiological thinking. Bees and ants can distinguish dozens of locations. Those locations are defined with respect to their geometric relations to many surrounding and encompassing landmarks and landscapes (M. Collett, Harland, & Collett, 2002; T. S. Collett, Dillmann, Giger, & Wehner, 1992; Fukushi & Wehner, 2004; Mather, 1991; Menzel et al., 2005; Roche & Timberlake, 1998). Bees can distinguish many odors and many shapes and many colors. Thus, the combinatorial possibilities, the combinations of location, time of day, color, shape, odor, and surrounding scene that a bee *might* have to encode are enormous in number. As previously noted, this is a fundamental problem for a functional architecture in which all the *possible* combinations must be represented in the genetically prespecified wiring of the system. Because the number of combinations *actually* experienced by any one subject is many orders of magnitude less than the combinations that *could be* experienced, an architecture that only invests memory capacity in the combinations that actually occur is greatly favored.

The second much-studied phenomenon in which remembering the time of day at which observations are made plays a fundamental role (circadian phase) is the sun-compass mechanism (see Wiltschko & Wiltschko, 2003, for recent review). We review this phenomenon in the next chapter (Chapter 13).

Learning Durations

In the experimental paradigms that psychologists have devised for the experimental study of associative learning, the durations of the intervals between simple events are varied so as to vary the amount of information that one event provides about the timing of another event (Gallistel, 2003). The events that occur, their durations, and the durations of the intervals between the events constitute what is called an experimental protocol. In one common protocol, there is a tone whose onset predicts a weak electric shock to the skin surrounding the eye of a rabbit. The shock is experienced as a tap threatening the eye. It elicits a blink. It is called an unconditioned stimulus (US for short), because it elicits a blink even in the inexperienced rabbit. The tone is called a conditioned stimulus (CS for short), because it does not elicit a blink except in a rabbit that has been conditioned by the repeated experience of a predictive relation between tone and shock. This protocol is an instance of a Pavlovian conditioning protocol.

The standard associative analysis of this simple example of learning, which is presented in any textbook on learning, focuses on the fact that the eye blinks in response to the tone; it does not focus on the fact that the blink is appropriately timed. That is, the latency between tone onset and the learned blink approximately equals the latency between the tone onset and the shock (Kehoe, Graham-Clarke, & Schreurs, 1989; Weidemann, Georgilas, & Kehoe, 1999; White, Kehoe, Choi, & Moore, 2000). Nor does it focus on the fact that the ratio between two intervals, the interval from tone onset to the shock (called the CS–US interval) and the interval between successive shocks (called the US–US interval) is a major determinant of how rapidly the rabbit learns to blink (Gallistel & Gibbon, 2000).

The fact that the rabbit blinks in response to a CS that predicts a threat to the eye is readily understood in terms of a functional architecture in which learning consists of the modification of synaptic conductances. The presumed modification of one or more synaptic conductances is almost universally assumed to be the neurobiological realization of the psychologist's concept of an association, which is why this experimental paradigm is common in the study of associative learning. The fact that the rabbit blinks at the right time is less readily explained in associative terms. It implies that the rabbit's nervous system carries forward in time information about the interval between tone onset and shock delivery. As we have explained, it is unclear how this information could be carried by modifications in synaptic conductance. Thus, the fact that the rabbit blinks at the right time is a theoretically awkward fact. Theoretically awkward facts abound in any science, but they are rarely discussed at the introductory level, because there is a premium on telling a coherent story.

There is even less attention given to the fundamental role played in the acquisition of conditioned behavior by the ratio between the CS–US interval and the US–US interval (see Chapter 13). The behavioral importance of this ratio implies that the brain carries forward in time information about both of these intervals in a computationally accessible form, a form that permits it to compute their ratio. Associative accounts of learning presume that the brain has the functional architecture of a neural network. This architecture makes it particularly difficult to envisage how the information about experienced temporal intervals can be carried forward in a computationally accessible form, as we will explain in Chapter 15.

That the rabbits learn the durations of the experimenter-chosen intervals in this protocol is peculiar neither to this paradigm nor to rabbits. There is extensive evidence that the animal subjects in standard laboratory learning paradigms learn the intervals in the protocols. In another common protocol, for example, a pigeon pecks an illuminated key on the wall, which sometimes causes a hopper full of grain to appear for a few seconds, allowing the bird to eat a few grains. In one version of this, there is a fixed interval between the last appearance of the hopper (the US) and the next possible appearance. Pecking will not make it reappear until this fixed interval has elapsed. The first peck after the interval has elapsed makes the hopper appear again. Under these circumstances, the birds do not peck immediately after the last appearance. They wait approximately half the fixed interval and then abruptly begin to peck. This is true for fixed intervals ranging from tens of seconds to almost an hour (Dews, 1970). Again, this implies that the pigeons learn the experimenter-chosen US–US interval.

Episodic Memory

Episodic memory refers to our ability to remember the time, place, and other properties of an episode. The recollection of episodes is the stuff of everyday life for humans. The stories we tell each other are generally about episodes we have experienced. However, it was only rather recently that psychologists interested in memory distinguished this use of memory from our ability to remember facts not connected with an episode, such as, for example, the meaning of a word or the location of our home (Tulving, 1972). For years after the distinction became widely recognized, it was widely supposed that non-human animals did not remember episodes. Indeed, episodic memory is sometimes operationally defined in such a way as to preclude the possibility that a non-verbal animal could have episodic memory (Tulving, 1989). It has been argued that the ability to verbalize the when and where of the episode is a sine qua non, a criterion that would exclude non-verbal animals by fiat. Recently, however, ingenious experiments by Nicholas Clayton and Anthony Dickinson and their collaborators have clearly demonstrated detailed memories for specific episodes in scrub jays.

The relevance of the experiments on episodic memory in the present context is, first, that these experiments with birds show that the architecture of animal memory supports the retrieval of an infinitude of different possible conjunctions of disparate facts. This point first emerged with the experiments on time, locale, odor, color, and shape memory in bees, reviewed above. Each of these conjunctions occurs only once; information about a given conjunction is not slowly impressed on a plastic nervous system by its repeated occurrence. Second, they show the computational use that animals make of the information about time of occurrence that they carry forward in memory. Birds do not simply remember the times of hiding and retrieving episodes, they compute temporal relations between those times.

In times of plenty, many birds gather food and store it in caches. Some species make more than ten thousand caches, each cache in a different location, with the locations spread over square miles of the landscape (Vander Wall, 1990). Weeks and months later, during the winter when food is scarce, they retrieve food from these caches. This tells us that these birds have a memory that can carry forward over long periods of time the coordinates of more than ten thousand different locations. Clayton and Dickinson have made this phenomenon the basis of an extensive series of experiments demonstrating that scrub jays remember not only where they cached food, but also what kind of food they cached, when they cached it, whether they have subsequently emptied the cache, and who was watching when they made it.

The caching spots in these experiments were the sand-filled pockets in ice cube trays. The foods used in the initial experiments were peanuts and bits of dog chow; in later experiments, peanuts, crickets, and wax worms. Caching was generally done in multiple caching phases, followed by one or more recovery phases in which the birds retrieved food from some of the cached locations. The locations available for making caches and the locations from which recoveries could be made were restricted in various ways from phase to phase. The birds' preferences between the foods they were recovering was manipulated in various ways, as was relevant auxiliary information available to them, such as how long it takes different kinds of food to go bad. In this way, Clayton and her collaborators were able to demonstrate the jay's ability to integrate information of diverse kinds, acquired at diverse times. The integrations required that information about when something happened be accessible to computation in what the authors call a flexible manner. The essence of flexibility is that the information gained from an experience be carried forward in memory in such a way that it is accessible to computation. As they point out, preserving the information in the form of changes in associations (synaptic connections) does not confer the requisite flexibility. Only a read/write memory does that.

In the first experiment (Clayton & Dickinson, 1999), jays first cached peanuts in one tray, then they cached chow in another. Either 4 hours later or 1 week later, the experimenters induced a transient preference for peanuts or chow by satiating the jays on the other. If you have just eaten a lot of peanut butter, you prefer ice cream, and vice versa. The same is true of other omnivores like rats and jays: when they have just eaten a lot of one food, they prefer another food. When the jays were sated on peanuts, they visited preferentially the caches in the tray where they had hidden dog chow; when sated on chow, they visited preferentially the caches in the tray where they had hidden peanuts. They did this whether the food remained where they had put it or had been pilfered by the experimenter, leaving all caches empty. This proves that they remember what they hid where, that is, which kind of food they hid in which tray. They remembered it equally as well whether tested 4 hours or 1 week after making their caches. They combined the information about their preference at the time of recovery – information that did not exist and could not have been foreseen when the caches were made – with information about where they had cached what in order to decide on where to search.

In the second experiment (Clayton & Dickinson, 1999), the jays cached peanuts on the left halves of two different trays in two successive caching phases. In two further caching phases, they cached chow on the right halves of the same trays. In an initial recovery phase, 3 hours after the last of the caching phases, the jays were allowed to recover (that is, empty of their contents) the caches they had made on the right side of one tray and the left side of the other. Before this first recovery phase, both trays had both peanuts and chow. After it, one tray had peanuts in its left half and nothing in its right half, while the other tray had chow on its right half and nothing on its left half. The jays were then sated on one or the other food and allowed to recover caches again in trays that were now, for the first time, fully accessible. The contents of the caches that the jays had not emptied in the first recovery phase had, however, now been pilfered by the experimenter. All the caches were empty. Nonetheless, the jays searched preferentially the caches that "ought" to have contained the food they now desired. In making the decision about where to search, they integrated information from the caching phases (where they cached what), from the first recovery phase (which caches they had emptied), and information about their current preference state.

The third experiment tested whether the jays could also take account of what they had learned about the time it takes different foods to decay to inedibility. Hand-reared jays, with no experience of decaying food, were given repeated trials of caching and recovery. As in the preceding experiment, they cached two different foods in two different caching episodes before being allowed to recover their caches. As before, their caching was restricted to halves of the trays: in the first of each pair of caching episodes, they were allowed to cache peanuts on one side of a tray; in the second episode of each pair, they were allowed to cache either mealworms or crickets on the other side. Thus, on some trials, they hid peanuts and mealworms (peanuts-and-mealworms trials), while on other trials, they hid peanuts and crickets (peanuts-and-crickets trials). Either 4 hours, 28 hours, or 100 hours (4 days) after each pair of caching episodes, they were allowed to recover food from both sides (both kinds of caches). The experimenters knew that the jays preferred mealworms and crickets to peanuts. On trials with only a 4-hour delay, both the mealworms and the crickets were fresh (not decayed). At that elapsed interval, the jays preferred to retrieve from the caches where they had hidden either mealworms or crickets (depending on whether it was a peanuts-and-mealworms or a peanuts-and-crickets trial).

On trials where a 28-hour delay was imposed between caching and recovery, the cached mealworms were replaced by mealworms that had been artificially rotted by the experimenters (soaked in liquid soap and dried in the sun until black). The crickets and peanuts, on the other hand, both remained fresh over that delay. Thus, on the first few peanuts-and-mealworms trials with a 28-hour delay, the jays found inedible "rotten" mealworms where they had cached delectable fresh mealworms, while on peanuts-and-crickets trials, they found crickets that were still fresh. On trials with a 100-hour (4-day) delay before recovery, by contrast, both the meal-worms and the crickets had rotted; only the peanuts remained fresh.

As might be expected, the caches to which the jays directed their searches changed over repeated trials of different kinds – in a manner that took account of both what had been hidden where, how long it had been since it was hidden, and what the birds had learned about the rates of rotting. Control birds that never encountered rotted caches preferred the caches where mealworms and crickets had been hidden no matter how long the delay between caching and recovery. The experimental birds preferred those caches when only 4 hours had elapsed. When 28 hours had elapsed, their preference after a few trials of each type depended on whether it was mealworms or crickets that they had hidden on the "better" side of the tray. If it was mealworms, they preferred the peanut caches, but if it was crickets, they preferred the cricket caches. When 4 days had passed, their preference after a few trials was for the peanut caches, whether it was mealworms or crickets that they had hidden on the "better" side of the tray. These preferences were seen even on trials where the caches were all empty.

In a follow-on test, the jays that had learned the different rates of rotting of meal-worms and crickets on separate trials involving either mealworms and peanuts or crickets and peanuts were allowed to cache mealworms on one side and crickets on the other side, then tested for recovery preference at delays of 4 and 28 hours (with all caches empty). After a 4-hour delay, there was a slight preference for the caches where mealworms had been hidden, while after 28 hours, there was a pro-nounced preference for the caches where crickets had been hidden.

In another variation designed to show that it was not simply some decaying sense of "familiarity" that determined search preference at recovery time, the same expe-rienced subjects were allowed to cache peanuts and mealworms on one day and peanuts and crickets on another – in a different tray. They were allowed to recover their caches from both trays 4 hours after the second pair of caching episodes. There were two trials of this nature in the experiment. On one of them, the peanuts-and-mealworms caching occurred on Day 1 and the peanuts-and-crickets caching on Day 2. On this trial, it was 28 hours since the mealworms had been hidden in the peanuts-and-mealworms tray. On the other trial, this order was reversed. Thus, on that trial, it was only 4 hours since the mealworms had been hidden in the peanuts-and-mealworms tray. (In fact, all the caches were empty during the tests.) The jays with experience of the different rates at which mealworms and crickets rot pre-ferred the mealworm caches when they were only 4 hours old, but they preferred cricket caches when the mealworms were 28 hours old.

In the final experiment in this series, Clayton et al. (2001) had the jays cache peanuts and mealworms in Tray 1 on Day 1 and the same combination in Tray 2 on Day 2. For hours after the caching on Day 2, they were allowed to recover from either Tray 1 or Tray 2. When presented with Tray 2, they preferred to search the (empty) caches where they had hidden mealworms; when presented with Tray 1, they preferred to search the caches where they had hidden peanuts.

In an extension of these experiments, Clayton, Yu and Dickinson (2003) first gave the jays experience with cricket caches that remained fresh after 1 day but were rotten at 4 days. When their recovery preference was tested at intermediate delays of 2 and 3 days (with empty caches), jays thus trained preferred the caches in which crickets had been hidden to the caches in which peanuts had been hid-den at these intermediate delays; their preference switched to the peanut caches only after a delay of 4 days. Thus, they seem to have concluded that crickets remain fresh for 3 days before rotting. Next, they were allowed to cache peanuts and crick-ets on three successive days, each day with a different tray – Tray 1 on Day 1, Tray 2 on Day 2, and Tray 3 on Day 3. On Day 4 they were allowed to recover caches from Tray 1, and on Day 5 from Tray 2. The crickets recovered on those two days had been in storage for 3 days (not 4), but they were rotten! Thus, on those two recovery days, the jays had opportunity to learn that, contrary to what they had previously supposed, crickets go bad after only 3 days. The essential point of this experiment was that they acquired this information only on Days 4 and 5, that is, in the two days that followed their making caches in Tray 3 on Day 3. Thus, at the time they made the caches in Tray 3, they were under the mistaken belief that the crickets in those caches would remain fresh for 3 days. The ques-tion was whether what they subsequently learned about how long it really takes a cricket to decay would affect their cache preference on Day 6, when they recovered the caches from Tray 3 that they made on Day 3. Indeed, it did. Now, only 3 days after caching peanuts and crickets in the same tray, the birds preferred to recover from the (empty) caches in which they had hidden peanuts.

As we will see in Chapter 15, current theorizing about the neurobiological mechanisms of timing attempts only to explain how it is that an animal can make a response at the appropriate time. All of these theories make the assumption that some neuron or set of neurons becomes active (or simultaneously active) only within a certain time window after a time marker has occurred, and that only the active neurons become associated with the response. In other words, these theories all avoid the assumption that the time of occurrence and duration of an interval can be written to memory and retrieved when needed in subsequent computations. They do so because these theories are constrained by our current understanding of what is and is not neurobiologically plausible, and a write/read memory mechanism is not among the mechanisms currently regarded as neurobiologically plausible. Thus, none of these theories attempts to deal with the behavioral evidence demonstrating computation with remembered times of occurrence and remembered temporal intervals. What this brilliant series of experiments with food-caching jays demonstrates is that information about times of occurrence and the durations of intervals is in fact stored in a manner that makes it accessible to computation. The time at which something happens is stored in a memory whose structure permits the brain to retrieve that information in order to compute the duration of the interval that has elapsed between that time (e.g., the time when the cache was made) and an arbitrary later moment in time (the moment at which recovery is contemplated). Similarly, the information about the duration of the interval within which a given type of food decays is stored in a manner that permits the remembered decay interval to be compared to the interval elapsed since a cache was made. The interval information can be acquired before the time-of-occurrence information or after. In either case, the two kinds of information – as well as information about the contents of the cache, how long it takes that kind of content to decay – can be combined in ways that could not have been foreseen when the information was acquired. Once again, the infinitude of the possible looms. There are many possible locations, many possible kinds of food, many possible rates of decay, many possible delays between caching and recovery – and no restrictions on the possible combinations of these possibilities. No architecture with finite resources can cope with this infinitude by allocating resources in advance to every possible combination.

13

The Modularity of Learning

Most contemporary theories of learning assume a basic learning mechanism, or, in any event, a modest number of learning mechanisms. They are distinguished by their properties – for example, whether or not they depend on temporal pairing – not by the particular kind of problem their special structure enables them to solve. Indeed, people doing neural network modeling, which is currently the most widespread form of associative theorizing, are sometimes at pains to point out that the network has solved a problem in the absence of an initial structure tailored to the solution of that problem (e.g., Becker & Hinton, 1992). Historically, the general process tradition is rooted in the empiricist philosophy of mind.

An alternative conceptualization, rooted in zoology and evolutionary biology, takes it for granted that biological mechanisms are hierarchically nested adaptive specializations. Each such mechanism constitutes a particular solution to a particular problem. The foliated structure of the lung reflects its role as the organ of gas exchange, and so does the specialized structure of the tissue that lines it. The structure of the hemoglobin molecule reflects its function as an oxygen carrier. The structure of the rhodopsin molecule reflects its function as a photon-activated enzyme. One cannot use a hemoglobin molecule as the first stage in light transduction and one cannot use a rhodopsin molecule as an oxygen carrier, any more than one can see with an ear or hear with an eye. Adaptive specialization of mechanism is so ubiquitous and so obvious in biology, at every level of analysis, and for every kind of function, that no one thinks it necessary to call attention to it as a general principle about biological mechanisms.

From this perspective, it is odd that most past and contemporary theorizing about learning does not assume that learning mechanisms are adaptively specialized for the solution of particular problems. Most theorizing about learning assumes that there is a general-purpose learning process in the brain (see, for example, Domjan, 1998, pp. 17ff.), a process adapted, if at all, then only to solving the problem of learning. What is missing in this tradition is an analysis of what the problem of learning is. What are the features of the material that is to be learned that constrain the form of the learning mechanism? From a biological perspective, the assumption of a general-purpose learning mechanism is equivalent to assuming that there is a general-purpose sensory organ, which solves the problem of sensing.

A computational/representational approach to learning, which assumes that learning is the extraction and preservation of useful information from experience, leads to a more modular, hence more biological conception of learning. For computational reasons, learning mechanisms must have a problem-specific structure, because the structure of a learning mechanism must reflect the computational aspects of the problem of extracting a given kind of representation from a given kind of data. Learning mechanisms are problem-specific modules – organs of learning (Chomsky, 1975) – because it takes different computations to extract different representations from different data.

Example 1: Path Integration

We have already seen an illustration of this principle in the case of dead reckoning, one of the modules by which the animal learns where it is. This mechanism integrates velocity with respect to time to obtain position. The computation that it performs reflects an analytic fact about the world: position is the integral of velocity with respect to time. This analytic fact has the same status as the laws of refraction have in our understanding of the lens of an eye. To understand why and how a lens works, you have to understand the laws of refraction. To understand why and how dead reckoning works, you have to understand the mathematical relation between velocity and position. With this understanding comes an understanding of why dead reckoning is not a general-purpose learning mechanism. It solves only one problem, because the computation that it carries out is specific to that problem. No one supposes that humans learn language by dead reckoning. We are far from being entirely clear about the computations by which natural languages may be understood and produced, let alone learned; but, whatever they are, we can be confident that integrating velocity with respect to time is not one of them. This learning mechanism is self-evidently specific to the problem of extracting a representation of one's position from velocity data. From our perspective, dead reckoning is a paradigmatic example of a learning mechanism, because it specifies the computation by which a behaviorally useful representation is extracted from sensory and efference copy data.

Why then do many people find the idea of path integration as a paradigmatic and notably simple instance of learning perverse? The reasons offered are revelatory. First, it is argued that it is a special-purpose innate mechanism designed to do this and only this. In short, it's an adaptive specialization. This is equivalent to arguing that the eye is not a representative example of a sensory organ because it is designed specifically for vision. It presupposes that there is such a thing as a general-purpose learning mechanism. This is the presupposition that both the biological approach and the computational/representational approach to learning call into question.

Another reason offered for regarding path integration as unusual is that the ant does not have to experience its outward journey repeatedly before it knows the way. A variant of this argument is that the ant does not get better at running home with repeated practice. These objections reify another assumption of associative theory, which is that learning involves the gradual strengthening of something. To be sure, the conditioned response in classical conditioning does not usually appear until there have been several co-occurrences of the conditioned and unconditioned stimuli, but the only apparent justification for making strengthening through repetition part of the definition of learning is the conviction that there is a general-purpose learning mechanism and that the classical conditioning paradigm captures its essence. If we think that path integration captures the only essence of learning that is there to be captured, then we are not going to make strengthening by repetition part of the definition of learning.

There is a problem-specific reason why the learning seen in the traditional paradigms requires repetition of the critical experience. The traditional "associative" learning paradigms all involve prediction over time. The animal learns that one stimulus (the CS) may be used to anticipate the occurrence of another (the US). Inherent in *this* problem is the problem of coincidence. Just because one event precedes another on one or two occasions is no guarantee that there is a reliable predictive relation between them. Intuitively, the existence of a reliable predictive relation can only be estimated from the repeated experience of that relation. However, as we will see later in this chapter, it is not really the repetition per se that matters, but rather the amount of mutual information between the predicting and the predicted event. The problem of distinguishing coincidences from true and persistent predictive relations is inherent in the problem of learning predictive temporal relations, but it is not an aspect of the problem of estimating your position from real-time processing of your velocity. Conversely, the mathematical relation between position and velocity plays no role in the problem of extracting from experience which events can be used to predict which other events. Thus, the learning of predictive relations depends to some extent on repetition, while learning your location by dead reckoning does not.

Example 2: Learning the Solar Ephemeris

The path integration computation requires a signal that indicates the compass direction in which the animal is progressing. Compass direction is direction relative to the axis of the earth's rotation, the north–south axis. Many animals use the sun's position for this purpose, which is remarkable because the sun does not have a fixed compass direction. Its compass direction varies continuously during the day. Moreover, the manner in which it does so depends on the season of the year and how far the observer is to the north or south of the Equator. In short, the compass direction of the sun at a given time of day is a contingent fact about the world. If, however, the observer can overcome this problem, then the sun has advantages as a directional referent. It can be seen from almost any vantage point, and, most importantly, it is so far away that earth-bound movements of an extent realizable by an animal in one day have very little effect on its direction. This is not true of earthly landmarks. The landmarks one can see are rarely farther away than the distance one can traverse in a small fraction of a day, which means that they change their compass direction as one moves. That makes them poor indicators of compass direction.

Human navigators also routinely use the sun as a compass referent; they have understood how to do so explicitly for centuries, and implicitly probably for eons. The trick is to know the time of day and to learn the compass direction of the sun as a function of the time of day, that is, to learn the solar ephemeris.

Animals, including humans, have a built-in clock, which solves the first part of the problem, knowing the time of day. The circadian clock mechanism is another example of the innumerable ways in which the enduring structure of the world they inhabit is reflected in the innate structure and functioning of the animal mechanism. The period of the clock is innate; it is fixed by the genes at approximately 24 hours, because that has been the period of the earth's rotation for as long as there has been life on earth. The duration of this period is not a mathematical truth, like the relation between position and velocity, but it is a universal truth within the framework within which life on earth has evolved. What is contingent upon one's longitude (east–west position on the globe) is the phase of this cycle. When you fly from London to Hawaii or Beijing, that phase changes dramatically, which is the principal reason why you experience jet lag and a disrupted pattern of waking and sleeping. There is a learning mechanism, called the entrainment mechanism, that is specialized for adjusting the phase of the brain's circadian clock to the local phase of the solar cycle.

We see here in a maximally simple example what we would argue is a very general truth about learning mechanisms: they do not learn universal truths. The relevant universal truths are built into the structure of a learning mechanism. Indeed, absent some built-in relevant universal truths and the strong constraints they place on the form of the representation that can be extracted from a given experience, learning would not be possible. If general process theorists could be induced to contemplate the question posed earlier, "What is the formal characterization of the problem that would be solved by a general purpose learning mechanism, assuming that such a mechanism were possible?", they would realize that without much narrower specification, the problem of learning is an ill-posed problem. It is computationally insoluble, because there is no way of determining what would constitute a solution. It will not do to say that the problem of learning is the problem of forming associations, because that "answer" reifies an assumed solution to an ill-posed problem.

The second part of the problem of knowing the sun's direction is to know the compass direction of the sun for any given time of day. Bees and ants and birds (and probably many other animals as well) have an organ that learns this. Remarkably, bees, at least, learn the complete function from only a few observations, that is, without having seen the sun at most times of day. The learning of the solar ephemeris in bees illustrates the force and broad application of Chomsky's poverty-of-the-stimulus argument. Chomsky (1988) observed that the conclusions that humans draw about the grammatical and phonological structure of the languages they learn go beyond what is justified by the limited samples from which they learn. Similarly, as we shall see, the conclusions that bees draw from limited observations of the sun's trajectory go beyond what is justified by their limited observations. Indeed, experimental work on bees' learning of the solar ephemeris provides the most unequivocal example of the poverty-of-the-stimulus argument that we know of, because the bees' prior experience can be rigorously controlled, which is never possible with human infants learning a language.

The structure of the organ that learns the solar ephemeris also illustrates a key idea in contemporary theories of language learning – the idea of parameter setting (Chomsky & Lasnik, 1993). In the language learning literature, this is the idea that there is a universal grammar with a modest number of settable binary parameters. Languages differ grammatically in their settings of these parameters. Learning to speak and understand a language is a matter of learning the settings for that particular language. (See Baker, 2001, for an exceptionally clear exposition and illustration of this approach to language.) The concept of a genetically specified function with experience-settable parameters explains the ability of a learning organ to know more than it has observed, that is, to overcome the poverty of the stimulus. As already noted, the circadian clock is the simplest example of such a mechanism: its period is genetically specified, because it is an environmental universal; its phase is experientially determined, because it is a contingent fact about the animal's environment.

The key experiment here was done by Dyer and Dickinson (1994), following earlier work of a similar nature by Lindauer (1957; 1959). Dyer and Dickinson used the dance of the returning bee forager (von Frisch, 1967). The just-returned forager dances on the vertical surface of the honeycomb, inside the hive, out of sight of the sun. The dance is in the form of a figure 8. The bee circles first one way, then the other. In the middle stretch, where the loops of the 8 converge, the dancing bee waggles as it runs (flicks its abdomen from side to side). The direction of the waggle run relative to the vertical indicates the direction of the food source relative to the sun. If the bee runs straight up while waggling, it indicates that one must fly toward the sun; if it runs horizontally to the right, it indicates that one must fly with the sun on one's left; if it runs straight down, it indicates that one must fly away from the sun; and so on. The number of waggles during each waggle run indicates the distance: the more waggles, the farther the food.

The compass direction of the source from the hive (α in Figure 13.1), equals the compass direction of the sun (σ in Figure 13.1) plus the solar bearing of the source (δ in Figure 13.1). Thus, when the experimenter, who observes the dance through a window on the hive constructed for that purpose, observes the direction of the waggle run, he can infer from it and from the compass direction of the source, the direction in which the dancer believes the sun to be.

In Dyer and Dickinson's experiment, they raised bees in an incubator without a view of the sun. Then, they allowed them to forage around their artificial hive, but only in the late afternoon, when the sun was sinking in the west. The bees learned to fly back and forth between the hive and a feeding station, which was located some tens of meters away to (for concrete example) the west of the hive. When these foragers arrived back in the hive, they did a dance in which the waggle run was directed more or less straight up, indicating that, to get to the food, one should fly toward the sun.

Dyer and Dickinson allowed their bees to forage only in the late afternoon, until a morning came when the sun was completely hidden by a heavy overcast. Then, for the first time, Dyer and Dickinson allowed their bees to forage in the morning.

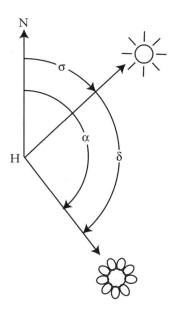

Figure 13.1 Diagram of the angular (directional) relations. H = hive; N = north; σ = the compass direction of the sun. This direction is locally constant; it is the same regardless of where the bee is within its foraging range. α = the compass direction of the flower from the hive; δ = the solar bearing of the flower from the hive, which is the direction that the bee must fly relative to the sun in order to get from the hive to the flower.

One might suppose that bees do not do their dance when overcast prevents their seeing the sun. How can you tell another bee how to fly relative to the sun if neither you nor the other bee can see the sun? But bees do dance when they cannot see the sun; other bees do attend to the dance; and they do fly in the direction indicated by the dance, even when they cannot see the sun as they fly? How can this be?

The key thing to realize is that once you have formed a compass-oriented map of the terrain within which you are navigating, you do not need to see the sun in order to set a course by the sun, provided you know the time of day and the sun's solar ephemeris, its compass direction at different times of day. If I tell you to fly away from the sun at 9:00 in the morning, a time at which you know the sun lies more or less due east, then I am in effect telling you to fly west. If you have a map of the terrain and you know the direction at which the sun must be relative to that terrain at that time of day, then you can fly in the indicated direction by reference to appropriate terrain features. You fly toward the landmarks that lie to the west of your hive on your map, that is landmarks that lie in the direction opposite the direction in which you know the sun must currently be.

The key to this scheme is the mechanism that learns the solar ephemeris. Learning the solar ephemeris – learning where the sun is at different times of day in relation to the terrain around the hive – is what makes the bee's map of that terrain compass oriented.

Returning now to the Dyer and Dickinson experiment: They allowed the bees to forage in the morning only when the sky was overcast, so that they could not see the sun. These bees, who had only seen the sun above the terrain lying to the west of the hive, flew to the food, and when they returned, they did the waggle dance, telling the other bees how to fly relative to the (unseen) sun. The astonishing thing is that the waggle run was now directed straight down rather than straight up. They were telling the other bees to fly away from the sun. This implies that they believed that the sun in the morning was positioned above the terrain in the direction opposite the food (Figure 13.2), even though, in their experience, it had always been positioned above the terrain in the direction of the food. Their experience of the sun, which was confined to the late afternoon, gave no grounds for a belief about where it is in the early morning (the poverty of the stimulus). Nonetheless, these inexperienced bees had an approximately correct belief. They believed it to lie over the terrain to the east of the hive. For those who are uncomfortable with the attribution of beliefs to bees, the above can be reworded in terms of the compass direction of the sun specified by nerve signals in the brains of the dancers. These signals specified an eastward solar direction in the morning, even though the experienced sun had always been westward.

These fascinating results suggest the following model for the mechanism that learns the solar ephemeris (cf. Dickinson & Dyer, 1996): Built into the nervous system of the bee is a genetically specified neural circuit. It takes as input signals from the bee's circadian clock. It gives as output a signal specifying the compass direction of the sun. If we imagine this signal to be the firing rates of two pairs of compass neurons in the brain, a N/S pair and an E/W pair, and if we imagine that different firing rates correspond to different compass directions, then the function in question is the one that determines the firing rates of the compass neurons at different phases of the bee's circadian clock.

In the model, the general form of the function relating the output of the bee's circadian clock to the firing rates of its compass neurons is genetically specified. The specification is such that the firing rates for phases of the circadian clock 12 hours apart indicate opposing compass directions. One can imagine a genetically specified dynamic biochemical process in the brain, closely analogous to the one that implements the bee's circadian clock. The genetically specified learning mechanism leaves two things to be specified by the bee's experience: (1) the terrain views associated with a given set of firing rates, which are required to anchor the compass signal to the local terrain; (2) the kinetics of the change in the firing rates, how they change as the circadian clock mechanisms runs through its cycle. The terrain views are analogous to the words in a lexicon. The kinetics of the ephemeris function are analogous to the grammar of a language. Observing the sun at a few different times of day suffices to determine the values of the experience-settable parameters in the innately specified ephemeris function. Fixing the values of those parameters adapts the universal function to the locally appropriate variant. It transforms the step function that one sees in the data from the inexperienced bees in Figure 13.2 into the continuous function traced by the solid line that indicates the true solar ephemeris for the locale and the season of the experiment. The dance of bees with a fuller experience of the sun's movements at that locale tracks this solid line,

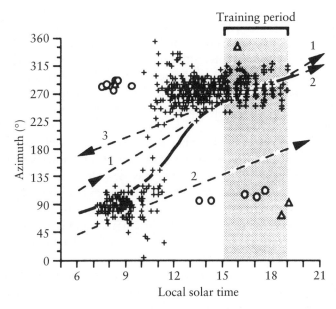

Figure 13.2 The compass direction (Azimuth) of the sun indicated by individual bee dances, as a function of the time of day, in bees with prior experience only with the afternoon sun (Training period). The food source was to the west of the hive (azimuth 270°). The solid line indicates the true solar compass direction for the latitude and season of the experiment. The bee's dance indicates what these minimally experienced bees believe the solar ephemeris to be. Note that the bees believe that the sun shifts from due east to due west abruptly around noon, which is what it would do in equatorial regions, where bees are believed to have evolved. Note also that the bees seem uncertain whether the sun is in the south or the north at noon. (It would be in the south if they were in the northern hemisphere and in the north if they were in the southern hemisphere.) As the solid line shows, north of the tropics, the sun moves continuously into the south during the morning, then continuously from the south into the west during the afternoon. The closer one is to the tropics, the more discontinuous this movement becomes: the sun lingers longer almost due east during the morning and moves more rapidly into an almost due west direction soon after noon. Around noon, it is so nearly directly overhead that its azimuth is hard to estimate. The dashed, numbered curves are for various models of how the bee might extrapolate the sun's angular velocity (all of them refuted by these data). The circles and triangles are outlier dances from two different individuals. (From Dyer & Dickinson, 1994, reproduced by permission of the authors and publisher.)

because they have learned from their experience the parameter values appropriate for the local solar ephemeris.

The interest of this model for present purposes is that it is an example of learning by parameter setting. The genes specify the general form that the relation between compass direction and time of day must take. In mathematical terms, they specify the function that is to be fitted to the data provided by experience. What is left for experience to specify are the values of a few parameters in the function. Materially speaking, experience specifies the levels of a few physical variables in the mechanism that specifies where the sun is at different stages of the circadian cycle. What this learning mechanism does is allow the bee to get quickly and with limited data to an approximately correct representation of the local solar ephemeris. It solves the poverty of the stimulus problem. It enables the bee to estimate where the sun will be at times when it has never seen the sun, just as knowing the grammar of French enables one to speak and understand French sentences one has neither heard nor spoken before.

Modern theories of language learning in the Chomsky tradition are similar in spirit. The basic, high-level form of the grammar of any conceivable human language is assumed to be given by genetically specified language learning machinery. This genetically specified general structure for any human language is what linguists call the universal grammar. Much research in linguistics is devoted to specifying what that general form is. The general form has in it a number of parameters whose value must be specified by experience. These are generally thought to be binary parameters (the language must either do it this way, or it must to it that way). Learning the language reduces to learning the parameter settings. When the child has got all the parameters set, it knows the language. It can produce and understand sentences it has never heard for the same reason that the bee can judge where the sun is at times of day when the bee has never seen the sun. As in the bee, the universal truths relevant to the problem at hand are built into the structure of the learning organ. It is only this built-in structure that constrains the problem sufficiently to make it a well-posed computational problem. Without this structure, learning would not be possible in the first place. A consequence of this structure is that the inferences the learner draws from limited experience go beyond what is justified by that experience. What is extracted from experience is jointly determined by what the experience reveals and what is known a priori. This, of course, brings us back to the Bayesian view of knowledge acquisition elaborated in Chapter 2.

Example 3: "Associative" Learning

The Pavlovian and operant experimental paradigms that psychologists use to study the laws of learning were created to study the principles of association formation. Their creators shared with contemporary connectionist modelers the assumption that the general nature of learning was already known; it was associative. The problem was to determine the details of the associative process and how it could explain whatever was observed. The Pavlovian paradigm expresses this ambition in its purest form because it involves simply pairing two stimulus events, as we explained in the previous chapter when describing the protocol for conditioning a rabbit to blink in response to a stimulus that predicts an imminent threat to its eye. The so-called instrumental or operant paradigm (the terms are interchangeable) involves presenting the animal with a reward or punishment immediately after it has made a particular response. In both cases, however, it is assumed that what mediates the change in behavior observed as the animal's exposure to the training protocol is prolonged is the strengthening of associative connections. In both cases, close temporal pairing is taken to be an essential feature of the protocols. Close temporal pairing has been taken to be *the*, or at least *a* sine qua non for the strengthening of associative connections for as long as there have been associative theories of learning.

The Pavlovian and operant paradigms were not intended to be laboratory analogs of particular learning problems that animals had been observed to solve in the field. This does not mean that the paradigms do not in fact instantiate problems of a particular kind. In fact they do. They are problems in multivariate, non-stationary time series analysis. That is, like the dead reckoning problem, they have a particular mathematical form. Any mechanism suited to solving them must reflect that form in its structure.

They are *time series* problems because what the animals are learning is the temporal relations between events; hence, the extent to which the occurrence of one event predicts the occurrence of another. They are *multivariate* time series problems, because there are many different events or time-varying conditions that may or may not predict the time or rate of US occurrence. An important challenge the animal faces is the problem of figuring out what predicts what. (In the operant literature, this is often called the assignment of credit problem.) Finally, the protocols are often instances of *non-stationary* time series, because the contingencies commonly change from one phase of the experiment to another. In extinction experiments, for example, the rate of reinforcement (US delivery) is higher when the CS is present, but only during the training phase of the experiment. During the extinction phase, the rate of reinforcement is zero when the CS is present. This is an example of a non-stationary temporal dependency, a temporal contingency that itself changes over time. It has been known since the early days of the study of both classical and operant conditioning that the subjects detect these changes in the contingency, and alter their behavior appropriately. The ability to recognize and respond appropriately to non-stationary contingencies requires a particularly sophisticated kind of time series analysis.

Contingency, not pairing

One of the most important discoveries to emerge from the modern study of conditioning is that temporal pairing is neither necessary nor sufficient for conditioning. What subjects respond to is the contingency between the CS and US, not the temporal pairing. There is a contingency between the CS and the US just in case there is mutual information between their occurrences. Temporal contingency cannot be reduced to temporal pairing. There is contingency between a conditioned stimulus (CS) and an unconditioned stimulus (US) either when the US occurs only in the presence of the CS (Figure 13.3b) or when the US occurs only when the CS is absent (the explicitly unpaired protocol, Figure 13.3c). Both the positive and the negative contingencies induce conditioned responses to the CS (Colwill, 1991; LoLordo & Fairless, 1985; Rescorla, 1969). In the first case (Figure 13.3b), the conditioned response that emerges as exposure to the protocol is prolonged indicates that the animal anticipates the occurrence of the US when the CS comes on. In the second

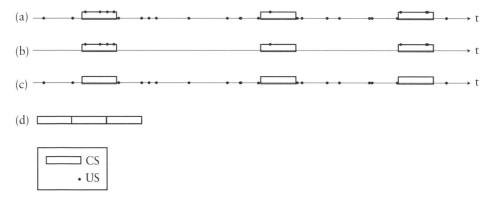

Figure 13.3 Contingency cannot be reduced to temporal pairing, and temporal pairing does not imply contingency. (a) There is temporal pairing between CSs (rectangles) and US (dots), but no contingency, because both are independently programmed random events. (b) There is temporal pairing between CS and US and a positive contingency, because the USs occur only in the presence of the CSs. (c) There is no temporal pairing between CS and US, but there is contingency, because the USs occur only in the absence of the CSs. (d) When the CS intervals are strung together, it is apparent that a substantial number of USs would have occurred in the presence of the CSs if they did not suppress US occurrence, that is, if there were no negative contingency. t = time.

case (Figure 13.3c), the response that emerges indicates that the animal anticipates the non-occurrence of the US. In the first, the CS and US are paired, while in the second, they are never paired. Thus, temporal pairing is not necessary.

The modern era in the study of conditioning began with the almost simultaneous discovery by three different laboratories of the fact that the learning mechanism responsible for the emergence of a conditioned response to the CS in conditioning experiments solves the multivariate problem in ingenious and sophisticated ways (Kamin, 1969; Rescorla, 1968; Wagner, Logan, Haberlandt, & Price, 1968). All of the experiments also showed that temporal pairing is not sufficient for the emergence of a conditioned response to the CS, completing the demonstration that temporal pairing is neither necessary nor sufficient in "associative" learning.

The most basic of these experiments was Rescorla's "truly random control" experiment, which contrasted the effects of the protocol in Figure 13.3b (the usual "temporal pairing" protocol) with the effects of the protocol in Figure 13.3a (the truly random control). The temporal pairings between CS and US are the same in both protocols, but in the protocol in Figure 13.3b, there is a contingency between the CS and the US, while in the protocol in Figure 13.3a, there is not. In Rescorla's experiment, the USs (the dots in Figure 13.3) were brief, mildly painful shocks to the feet, while the CSs (the rectangles) were two-minute long tones. The co-occurrences (temporal pairings) of tones and shock were the same in the two protocols, but the rats exposed to the contingent protocol developed a fear response to the CS (anticipating the shock that it predicted), while the rats exposed to the non-contingent protocol never developed such a response to the tones. They did, however, develop a fear response to the experimental chamber. This indicates that they had solved the multivariate problem: they had figured out that it was being in the box that predicted shock, not hearing a tone. For present purposes, however, what is important about this experimental result is the fact that the rats in the truly random control condition (Figure 13.3a) did not develop a conditioned response to the tone, despite its pairing with the shocks. This demonstrates that temporal pairing is not sufficient for the emergence of a conditioned response.

In the blocking paradigm (Kamin, 1969), a short tone or light (the CS) is presented by itself, with a shock or food delivery (the US) coincident with CS termination. When the subject has developed a conditioned response to this first CS, the second CS is introduced. It has the same duration as the first CS and is always delivered at the same time. Shock or food continue to be delivered at the offset of the two CSs. Thus, the second CS is perfectly redundant. It gives the subject no information over and above the information the subject obtains from the CS whose predictive power it first experienced. The subject fails to develop a conditioned response to the second CS no matter how often it is paired with the US. This is another demonstration that the temporal pairing of CS and US is not sufficient to produce a conditioned response.

In the relative validity protocol (Wagner et al., 1968), there are three CSs, denoted A, B, and X. The CS denoted X is presented on every trial. On half the trials, it is presented together with the CS denoted A, while on the other half, it is presented together with the CS denoted B. In one group of subjects, USs are delivered only on the AX trials, never on the BX trials. In another group of subjects, USs are delivered on a random half of the AX trials and a random half of the BX trials. Thus, for both groups, X is paired with the US on half the trials. However, the group for which the US occurs only on AX trials develops a conditioned response only to the CS denoted A, while the other group develops a conditioned response only to the CS denoted X (despite the fact that the CSs denoted A and B are paired with the US on half of all the trials on which they occur, just as is X). A statistician accustomed to "partialing out the variance" in a multiple regression problem would understand both results: in the first group, only the CS denoted A accounts for all the variance that can be accounted for; in the second group, only the CS denoted X does. In other words, the subjects (rats and pigeons) solve this rather complex multivariate problem. The results are a further demonstration that temporal pairing is not sufficient.

The delta rule These results caused a crisis in associative learning theory. In pre-1970 versions of the theory, associations developed independently of one another. These experiments demonstrated that they did not. They implied that whether an association developed between a CS and a US depended not simply on whether they were temporally paired, but also on the strengths of the associations between other CSs (other predictors) and that US. In 1972, Rescorla and Wagner published their famous paper in which they developed a "competitive" version of associative learning theory. In this version, the associative process was such that different associations to the same US (different possible predictors of its occurrence) competed for a limited total associative strength. There was an upper limit on the sum across all the associations to a given US. On any given trial, the size of a possible increment in associative strength was limited by the difference between the current value of that sum and the maximum possible (asymptotic) value of that sum. In one way or another, this assumption appears in a great many contemporary connectionist models. It is called the delta rule.

The assumption of an upper limit on total associative strength and the assumption that the sum across all current associations is subtracted from it have, so far as we know, never been seen as responding to a constraint inherent in the mathematical character of the problem of temporal prediction. As we have already mentioned, there is no tradition within associative learning theory of first analyzing the structure of the problem that is being solved and then considering how that structure is reflected in the properties of the mechanism that solves it. Such analyses are antithetical to the general process assumption, the assumption that a single learning mechanism solves every kind of learning problem.

An information-theoretic analysis of the temporal prediction problem shows, however, what it is about the problem that necessitates the assumption that Rescorla and Wagner introduced: The source entropy constitutes an upper limit on the amount of information that can be communicated to a receiver about that source. In this case, the source entropy is determined by the stochasticity of the US, the uncertainty about when it will occur. A CS reduces that uncertainty only insofar as it communicates information to the subject. The subject's uncertainty about when the US will occur limits the amount of information the subject can obtain from a CS: the less that uncertainty is, that is, the more it has already been reduced, the less the information that can be obtained from an additional CS, an additional source of information about the US. It is inherent in the problem of temporal prediction that potential predictors drain a finite pool of communicable information. When the subject's uncertainty about the time of occurrence of the next US has been reduced to the limits imposed by the uncertainty inherent in the processes that determine US occurrence, together with the inescapable limit on the precision with which the subject can represent time, then no more information can be communicated to the subject. Thus, Rescorla and Wagner's landmark paper can be seen as introducing into the assumed structure of the associative process something that reflects a key aspect of the problem of temporal prediction.

Although associative learning theory has been the conceptual framework within which neuroscientists searched for the neurobiological mechanisms underlying learning and memory, the delta rule has never had an impact on neurobiological thinking about the mechanism by which experience changes synaptic conductance. Unlike the older associative theory, which is what continues to guide neurobiological thinking, contemporary associative theory lacks neurobiological transparency. If synaptic conductances are identified with associative strengths, then the Rescorla-Wagner model and all models that make similar assumptions in order to explain experimentally documented cue competition – which is to say all contemporary models – require that synaptic conductances be treated like the values of readable variables in a computational process. The learning mechanism must compute the sum across a set of synaptic conductances and subtract that sum from another value (representing the asymptotic limit on the possible value of the sum) to obtain the

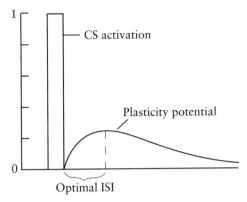

Figure 13.4 The window of associability as portrayed schematically by Gluck and Thompson (1987). The function gives the assumed sensitivity of the association-forming process to the interval between the offset of the CS and the onset of the US. Hawkins and Kandel (1984) assume a similar function. A function something like this is implicit in an approach to learning that assumes that the temporal pairing of events is a sine qua non for the formation of an association. ISI = interstimulus interval. (Figure and caption reproduced from Gallistel, 1990, p. 566.)

quantity that determines the size and sign of the changes in those same conductances. No one has any idea what this mechanism might look like, neurobiologically speaking. Thus, contemporary neuroscientific research on the neurobiology of association formation proceeds as if contemporary associative theory, in which cue competition plays a central role, did not exist.

The window of associability The Rescorla-Wagner theory maintained the temporal pairing assumption, which has been central to associative theory for centuries. It did not, however, define what constituted temporal pairing. How close in time do two events have to occur in order to be temporally paired from the standpoint of the association-forming mechanism? This is an obvious and unavoidable question for anyone interested in the neurobiological identity of the underlying mechanism. The concept of temporal pairing presumes the existence of a window of associability (Gluck & Thompson, 1987; Hawkins & Kandel, 1984; Sutton & Barto, 1981, 1990) – see Figure 13.4. Two events are associable if and only if they are separated by less than the width of this window. Absent a quantitative specification of the window, temporal pairing is not empirically defined. Given the obvious centrality of a quantitatively specified window of associability to a physically realizable associative mechanism, most non-specialists are surprised to learn that the width of the window has never been experimentally established for any learning paradigm. Rescorla (1972) surveyed the experimental literature attempting to specify the width of the window. He concluded that the literature did not give even an approximate answer. Nothing has changed in the 35 years since his review appeared. Despite this, the conviction that temporal pairing is the basis of association formation continues undiminished (Miller & Escobar, 2002). Its persistence is a testimony to the extent to which concepts that are regarded as analytic necessities are maintained, not only in the absence of empirical support, but even in the face of experimental results that are irreconcilable with them.

The tenacity with which students of learning have maintained their belief in the central importance of temporal pairing suggests that they intuit an aspect of the problem that makes this belief compelling. Again, information theory brings out an aspect of temporal prediction that is inherent in the problem itself: the closer in time a warning signal comes to the event of which it warns, the more information it provides about the timing of that event. As Balsam and Gallistel (submitted) show, the mathematical development of this intuitively obvious point gives an account of the best quantitative data on the effects of varying the temporal parameters of a Pavlovian protocol. These data are deeply resistant to explanation by the traditional notion of temporal pairing. Moreover, they challenge another bedrock assumption, namely, that the repetition of "trials" (instances of temporal pairing) slowly strengthens associative connections. What the data on "temporal pairing" imply – and what recent direct experimental tests confirm (Gottlieb, 2008) – is that the number of trials is not per se a learning-relevant parameter of the Pavlovian conditioning protocol.

The quantitative result to be explained is the tradeoff between the delay of reinforcement (that is, the interval separating the US from the onset of the CS, T in Figure 13.5) and the average interval between USs ($\bar{I}_c$, in Figure 13.5). Figure 13.5 plots data from many different laboratories using the pigeon autoshaping paradigm, a commonly used version of the Pavlovian protocol in contemporary research on associative learning. In this protocol, the illumination of a round key set into one wall of the test chamber is the CS. The raising of a hopper, giving the pigeon brief access to the grain, is the US. Brief access to the grain hopper coincides with the termination of key illumination. It does so whether the pigeon pecks the key or not. The observation of the contingency between key illumination and food presentation induces the pigeon to peck the key in anticipation of the soon-to-come opportunity to peck the grain, just as the observation of the contingency between the ringing of a bell and the presentation of food induced Pavlov's dogs to salivate in anticipation of the food.

The irrelevance of the number of trials

Figure 13.5 plots the median number of reinforced trials prior to acquisition as a function of the proportion between the base interval and the warning interval. The base interval is the expected interval between successive USs. The warning interval is the delay between key illumination and the appearance of the food hopper. The data in Figure 13.5 are consistent with the hypothesis that the slope of the linear relation (on log-log coordinates) is -1. In other words, they are consistent with the hypothesis that each doubling of the $\bar{I}_c/T$ proportion halves the number of reinforced trials (N_r) required to induce a conditioned response to the illuminated key. Put another way, moving the warning closer by a factor of 2 reduces by a factor of 2 the number of warnings that must be experienced before the bird begins to respond to them by pecking at the warning stimulus (the illuminated key).

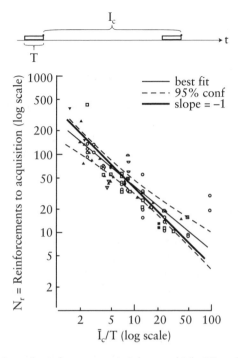

Figure 13.5 The number of reinforcements (trials on which CS and US were paired) required for the appearance of a conditioned response, as a function of the ratio (proportion) between the average US–US interval ($\bar{I}_c$) and the delay of reinforcement (T), on double logarithmic coordinates. Based on data first presented in Gibbon & Balsam (1981). The schematic at the top shows the intervals to which these symbols refer. Rectangles represent the CSs, dots the USs.

If −1 is the true slope of the regression of log N_r on log ($\bar{I}_c/T$), then the number of reinforced trials is not a learning-relevant parameter of these protocols, because, as shown schematically in Figure 13.6, deleting a given proportion of the trials in a protocol (by a factor of, say, 8), *while keeping the duration of training fixed*, increases the $\bar{I}_c/T$ proportion by the same factor, which reduces the number of trials required by that same factor. That is, reducing the number of trials in a protocol by any factor (up to and including $1/n$, where n is the initial number) should not affect the intensity or frequency of the resulting conditioned response, provided that the duration of the protocol is held constant by increasing the spacing between trials in proportion as the number of trials is reduced.

Information-theoretic deductions

The discovery of contingency effects, blocking, and related cue-competition phenomena initially led students of traditional learning paradigms to describe the laws or principles of learning in informational terms (e.g., Rescorla, 1972). Learning did

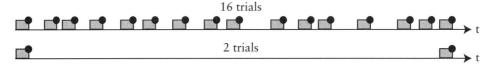

Figure 13.6   These protocols will be equi-effective if the true slope of the regression in Figure 13.5 is −1. The Gottlieb experiments tested this prediction by reducing the number of trials by a factor of 8 while holding the duration of the protocol constant, as here illustrated. In several experiments, he found that the reduction had no effect on the efficacy of the protocol. Reducing the number of trials by a factor of 8 increases the $\bar{I}_c/T$ ratio by the same factor.

not occur unless the CS conveyed new information, in which case the US "surprised" the subject (Kamin, 1967), because it was "unexpected." There has also been some theorizing that the rewarding property of conditioned stimuli was related to the extent to which they reduced uncertainty about the delivery of primary reward (Bloomfield, 1972; Egger & Miller, 1963). These formulations have intuitive appeal, but they have been treated gingerly for fear that they might not describe mechanizable processes (Clayton, Emery, & Dickinson, 2006). This fear rests on the assumption that learning is not a computational process. As we now show, the only assumption required to make these intuitions rigorous is that the brain can compute the mutual information between CS and US. The computation reduces to the computation of the rates of US occurrence under different conditions.

As we learned in the first chapter, the information that a signal (for example, a CS) communicates to a receiver (the subject in a conditioning experiment) is measured by the reduction in the receiver's uncertainty regarding the state of some stochastic aspect of the world. The amount of information that can be communicated is limited first by the available information (source entropy, how much variation there is in that aspect of the world), and second by the mutual information between the signal the subject gets and the variable state of the world (roughly, the correlation between the signal received and the state of the world). The foundation of an information-theoretic analysis is the specification and quantification of the relevant uncertainties: What is the behaviorally relevant aspect of the world about which the subject is uncertain, how can we quantify the subject's uncertainty, and by how much can a CS reduce that uncertainty?

Many aspects of the world might be manipulated in learning experiments, but what is usually manipulated in Pavlovian conditioning experiments is the timing of the US relative to the CSs. Effective Pavlovian CSs change the subject's uncertainty about when the next US will occur. Thus, the answer to the first question is that the subject is uncertain about when the next US will occur.

In simple cases, the source entropy (available information) can readily be calculated, at least to first order. We begin by distinguishing between paradigms in which the CS signals a change in the rate parameter (as in Figure 13.3), and more conventional "delay" paradigms, in which the onset of the CS occurs at a fixed interval prior to the US.

In Rescorla's truly-random-control experiments, the US was generated by a random rate (Poisson) process, which is entirely characterized by the rate λ (the average number of USs per unit time). Random rate processes are of special interest in analyzing temporal uncertainty because they maximize the source entropy. When the scheduling of USs is controlled by any other stochastic process, there is less objective uncertainty about when the next event will occur (less source entropy).

Rescorla held constant the US rate in the presence of the CS and varied its rate in the periods when the CS was absent. Subjects developed a conditioned response to the CS, except in the critical condition, when the US rate was the same in the absence of the CS as in its presence. We show now that this result is predicted by considering the uncertainty about US timing in the presence and absence of the CS.

As we learned in the first chapter, the quantity of uncertainty, H, is called the entropy. The differences in the amount of uncertainty about the timing of the next US in the presence and absence of the CS quantifies the information that the CS conveys about the timing of the US. The entropy rate (uncertainty per unit time) in a random-rate process is (see Rieke et al., 1997, p. 116 & appendix A10 for derivation):

$$\dot{H} = \lambda \log_2\left(\frac{e}{\lambda\Delta\tau}\right), \tag{1}$$

where $\Delta\tau$ is the minimum difference in time that the subject can resolve, which is assumed to be much smaller than the average interval between events. The average interval between the events is $\bar{I} = 1/\lambda$, so the average entropy per event is

$$\bar{H} = \frac{1}{\lambda}\lambda \log_2\left(\frac{e}{\lambda\Delta\tau}\right) = k - \log_2 \lambda \tag{2}$$

where $k = \log_2\left(\frac{e}{\Delta\tau}\right)$. The difference in the per-event entropies is:

$$\bar{H}_C - \bar{H}_{CS} = (k - \log_2 \lambda_C) - (k - \log_2 \lambda_{CS}) = \log_2 \lambda_{CS} - \log_2 \lambda_C = \log_2 (\lambda_{CS}/\lambda_C)$$
$$= \log_2 (\bar{I}_c/\bar{I}_{cs})$$

where λ_C is the overall or contextual US rate (the number of USs per unit of time in the test chamber), λ_{CS} is the US rate in the presence of the transient CS, and $\bar{I}_c$ and $\bar{I}_{cs}$ are the reciprocals of these rates, that is, the expected intervals between USs. The critical condition is the one where $\lambda_{CS} = \lambda_C$, in which case $\bar{I}_{CS}/\bar{I}_C = 1$ and $\bar{H}_C - \bar{H}_{CS} = \log_2 (1) = 0$. In words, the presence of the CS conveys no information about the timing of the next US. This analysis renders ordinary intuitions about this experimental result mathematically rigorous by resting the analysis on a conventional information-theoretic foundation.

The Rescorla result has often been analyzed in terms of the conditional probabilities of the US in the presence and absence of the CS. Such an analysis is incomplete. Differences in rates cannot be straightforwardly reduced to differences in conditional probabilities, because there may be more than one occurrence of the US during a single occurrence of the CS. In that case, the conditional probability of US occurrence is undefined. More importantly, an analysis in terms of differences in conditional probabilities does not reveal the critical role of the relative temporal intervals on the strength of the CR, nor does it clarify the meaning of temporal contiguity.

In the Rescorla experiment, unlike in most Pavlovian conditioning experiments, the temporal interval between CS onset and the US was not fixed; USs could and did occur at any time after CS onset – near the onset, in the middle of the CS, or near its end. And, more than one US could occur within a single CS, as shown in Figure 13.3a. This highlights unanswered questions of where in time to position a window of associability relative to CS onset, how wide to make it, and what to do when there is more than one US within a single such window. This conceptual difficulty is brought into strong relief by the fact that in the truly random control, the subject develops a conditioned response to the test chamber, the so-called background or context. This phenomenon, background or context conditioning, is an important aspect of contemporary associative theorizing. It is seen even in *Aplysia* (Colwill, Absher, & Roberts, 1988), a sea slug with a relatively simple nervous system that has been much used in attempts to determine the neurobiological mechanism of association formation.

The background conditioning phenomenon raises a conceptual difficulty with the notion of a trial, a notion that is intimately connected to the concept of temporal pairing. Experimentalists generally assume that each occurrence of a potentially predictive (informative) stimulus constitutes a trial. They arrange their experiments so that the predicted event occurs at most once during any one occurrence of the predicting stimulus. In connectionist theorizing, input to the net is invariably structured by discrete trials. In Rescorla's (1968) experiment, each "occurrence" of the chamber stimulus – that is, each experimental session – lasted two hours, during which the rat experience several shocks at unpredictable times. Subjects developed a conditioned response (fear) to the test chamber. The question is, How many "background" trials were there?

One could naively assume that each session constituted one trial, hence one pairing of the chamber and shock. This ignores the fact that there were many shocks during that one "trial." Worse yet, that assumption does not yield the result that Rescorla and Wagner were after in applying their revised cue-competition model of the associative process, the well-known Rescorla-Wagner model. On that assumption, trials involving noise and shock occur much more often than trials involving the chamber alone and shock. If there are many tone-shock trials for every one chamber-shock trial, then in the model, the tone-shock association crowds out the chamber-shock association. That is the opposite of what is observed. In the truly-random-control condition, the association between chamber and shock (the context conditioning) crowds out the association between the tone and the shock.

To make their account go through, the chamber-shock trials have to be more frequent than the tone-shock trials. Rescorla and Wagner (1972) achieved this by what they acknowledged was an ultimately indefensible ad hoc assumption, namely, that when a rat was in the chamber, the rat had an internal trial timer that, *mirabili dictu*, parsed its experience of the box into a sequence of two-minute long trials. Because there were on average 10 minutes when the tone was not present for every 2 minutes when it was, there were six times as many "trials" with only the chamber and the shock (background-alone "trials") as there were "compound trials," during which the tone (together with the omnipresent chamber) was paired with the shock.

When conditioning is seen as driven by the change that a CS produces in a subject's uncertainty about the timing of the next US, there is no longer a theoretical problem. We have already seen that a simple formal development applies to the case in which the rate of US occurrence is conditioned on the presence or absence of the CS. The same analysis explains background conditioning, because placement in the experimental chamber changes the expected rate of US occurrence, hence, the subject's uncertainty about when the next US will occur (Balsam, 1985). More formally, the per-event entropy, conditioned on the subject's being in the chamber, is less than the unconditioned per-event entropy (over the course of days or longer). We would expect the strength of anticipatory responding controlled by a context to be a function of the overall US rate in the chamber context, and the empirical data are consistent with this expectation (Mustaca, Gabelli, Papine, & Balsam, 1991). Thus, the information-theoretic analysis readily applies to paradigms in which the US occurs repeatedly within a single occurrence of the CS and/or there is no fixed interval between CS onset and US onset. In both cases, temporal pairing, as traditionally understood, is undefined.

We consider next the application of an information-theoretic analysis to the traditional temporal pairing case, in which the US occurs a fixed time after CS onset. We assume a random rate of US occurrence while the subject is in the apparatus, with an expected (average) interval between USs in that context of $\bar{I}_C = 1/\lambda_C$.

In the traditional delay paradigm, the presence of a CS does not change the US rate (the reciprocal of the expected interval between USs). A subject that could not perceive the CS would detect no changes in US rate. Rather than signaling a change in rate, the CS signals when the US will occur, because there is a warning interval of fixed duration between the onset of the CS and the occurrence of the US. Given the empirically well-established scalar uncertainty in subjects' representation of temporal intervals (Gibbon, 1977; Killeen & Weiss, 1987), we assume that after CS onset a subject's probability distribution for the time at which the US will occur is Gaussian with $\sigma = wT$, where w is the Weber fraction (coefficient of variation) and T is the duration of the CS–US interval (aka, the delay of reinforcement). The experimental value for w, based on the coefficient of variation in the stop times in the peak procedure, is about 0.16. It is surprisingly constant for widely differing values of T and subject species (Gallistel, King, & McDonald, 2004). The entropy of a Gaussian distribution is:

$$H = \frac{1}{2} \log_2 \left[2\pi e \frac{\sigma^2}{(\Delta\tau)^2} \right]$$

Substituting wT for σ and expanding, we obtain an expression for the subject's uncertainty about the timing of the next US after CS onset. (The subject's uncertainty will diminish somewhat as time elapses during the CS, because the time elapsed is itself a source of information. We neglect this.)

$$H = \frac{1}{2}\log_2\left[2\pi e \frac{(wT)^2}{(\Delta\tau)^2}\right] = \frac{1}{2}\log_2 2\pi e + \frac{1}{2}\log_2 w^2 + \frac{1}{2}\log_2 T^2 + \frac{1}{2}\log_2\left(\frac{1}{\Delta\tau}\right)^2$$

$$= \frac{1}{2}\log_2 2\pi e + \log_2 T + \log_2 w + \log_2\left(\frac{1}{\Delta\tau}\right)$$

$$= \frac{1}{2}\log_2 2\pi e + \log_2 T + \log_2 w - \log_2(\Delta\tau)$$

Equation (2), for the entropy in the context of the test chamber, when written in terms of the US–US interval, $\bar{I}_C$, rather than λ_C, is:

$$\bar{H}_C = \log_2\left(\frac{e}{\Delta\tau}\right) + \log_2 \bar{I}_C = \log_2 e + \log_2 \bar{I}_C - \log(\Delta\tau)$$

The difference between this context-conditional uncertainty and the uncertainty conditioned on the presence of the transient CS is:

$$\bar{H}_C - \bar{H}_{CS} = (\log_2 e + \log_2 \bar{I}_C - \log_2(\Delta\tau)) - (\frac{1}{2}\log_2 2\pi e + \log_2 T + \log_2 w - \log_2 \Delta\tau)$$

$$= \log_2 e + \log_2 \bar{I}_C - \log_2(\Delta\tau) - \frac{1}{2}\log_2 2\pi - \frac{1}{2}\log_2 e - \log_2 T - \log_2 w + \log_2 \Delta\tau$$

$$= \frac{1}{2}(\log_2 e - \log_2 2\pi) + \log_2 \bar{I}_C - \log_2 T - \log_2 w,$$

whence:

$$\bar{H}_C - \bar{H}_{CS} = \log_2\left(\frac{\bar{I}_C}{T}\right) + k, \tag{3}$$

where $k = \frac{1}{2}\log_2\left(\frac{e}{2\pi}\right) - \log w.$

Equation (3) gives the intuitively obvious result that the closer CS onset is to the US (that is, the shorter the warning interval), the more CS onset reduces the subject's uncertainty about when the US will occur. We suggest that it is this intuition that underlies the widespread but erroneous conviction that temporal pairing is an essential feature of conditioning. Importantly, equation (3) shows that closeness is relative. What matters is not the absolute duration of T, the warning interval, but rather $\bar{I}_C/T$, its duration relative to the average interval between USs in that context. This explains why it is not possible to define an empirically defensible window of associability – the elusive critical CS–US interval, falling within which a CS and US will become associated. There is no such interval. The relevant quantity is a unitless proportion specifying relative proximity, not an interval. Moreover, there is no critical value for this proportion. Rather, the empirically determined "associability" of the CS and US is strictly proportional to this ratio, as we now explain. In what follows, we define and use associability in a purely operational sense. We are skeptical that the concept of an associative connection has a future in the theory of learning. But we suspect that the use of associability to define the readiness with which a predictor event comes to elicit the behavioral or cognitive anticipation of the predicted event is too deeply embedded in the language ever to be replaced.

Equation (3) gives a quantitative explanation for Figure 13.5, the plot of the number of reinforced trials required for the appearance of an anticipatory response to the CS, as a function of $\bar{I}_C/T$, on double logarithmic coordinates. It is commonly assumed that the less associable the CS and the US, the more CS–US pairings will be required to produce an anticipatory response. We make this assumption quantitative by assuming $A = 1/N_r$, where A = the associability of a CS and US in a given protocol and N_r = the number of "reinforcements" (CS–US pairings) required before we observe an anticipatory response to that US. Equation (3) says that the unitless ratio $\bar{I}_C/T$ is the protocol parameter that determines the amount of information that CS onset conveys about US timing. (The other relevant parameter is w, the measure of the precision with which a subject can represent a temporal interval.) This is essentially the same quantity as the unitless quantity $\bar{I}_C/\bar{I}_{CS}$ that proved to be critical in analyzing the information content of the CS in the Rescorla paradigm. There, it was the ratio of the expected intervals between USs in the presence and absence of the CS. In standard temporal pairing paradigms, it is the ratio between the expected CS–US interval (the warning interval) and the expected US–US interval (the base interval). We call this ratio the *informativeness* of the CS–US relation. It is the factor by which CS onset reduces the expected interval to the next US.

Figure 13.5 is a plot of $\log N_r$ against $\log (\bar{I}_C/T)$. As already noted, its slope is approximately −1. Thus, empirically −$\log N_r = \log (\bar{I}_C/\bar{I}_{CS}) = \log (\bar{I}_C/T)$. Taking antilogs, $1/N_r = A \propto \bar{I}_c/\bar{I}_{cs} - 1$. In words, associability is proportional to informativeness (minus 1, so that it goes to 0 when the ratio goes to 1). This derivation explains why the number of trials is not a directly relevant parameter of a conditioning protocol (Gottlieb, 2008, see Figure 13.6). Reducing the number of trials by a given factor increases the informativeness of the remaining trials by the same factor.

Our approach to the operational definition of associability parallels the strategy common in psychophysics, in which the sensitivity of a mechanism is defined to be the reciprocal of the stimulus intensity required to produce a response. Our analog to the required stimulus intensity is the required number of reinforcements; our operational definition of associability as the reciprocal of the required number of pairings (minus 1) is the analog of sensitivity (the reciprocal of required intensity). In an associative conceptual framework, the associability is the rate of learning. In our framework it is the speed with which a behavioral response to a predictive relation emerges: the stronger the predictive relation between cue and consequence, the fewer the repetitions of the experience required before the subject begins to respond to the cue.

Consider next what happens to uncertainty when the time between events is fixed rather than randomly distributed. First, consider the case in which we let the US function as its own CS by fixing the US–US interval. Now, it is the preceding US that enables the subject to anticipate when the next US will occur. Now, $T = I_C$. The informativeness (their ratio) is now 1, so log $(I_C/T) = 0$, and equation (3) says that the information conveyed by the preceding US is

$$k = \frac{1}{2}\log_2\left(\frac{e}{2\pi}\right) - \log w = 0.22 - \log w. \quad \text{(Note: For } w < 1, -\log w > 0.)$$

The smaller w is, that is, the more precisely a subject can time and remember a fixed interval, the more information one US gives about the timing of the next US. For $w = 0.16$, $k \cong 2$, so fixing the US–US interval gives as much information about the timing of the next US as a fourfold change of rate in the Rescorla paradigm. We know that subjects are sensitive to the information in a fixed US–US interval because there is an increase in anticipatory responding as the fixed interval between USs elapses (Ferster & Skinner, 1957; Kirkpatrick & Church, 2000; Staddon & Higa, 1993). Indeed, the principal motivation for varying the intertrial interval in the traditional temporal pairing paradigm is to forestall confounding an anticipatory response to the elapsing intertrial interval with an anticipatory response to the CS. Interestingly, the information provided simply by fixing the CS–US interval does not appear to determine the speed with which subjects decide to respond to a predictive cue other than the preceding US (Gallistel & Gibbon, 2000). Associability appears to depend only on informativeness, which we have defined as the factor by which the onset of the CS reduces the expected time of the next US. Thus, fixing the time between CS onset and the US occurrence does not affect associability (defined as the inverse of the amount of training required to produce a conditioned response to a CS), but it does affect response timing.

We return finally to the blocking, overshadowing, and relative validity experiments, which originally inspired intuitions about the importance of the informativeness of the CS–US relation. In their classic form, these experiments use the delay paradigm, and the competing CSs have the same onsets. Consequently, the entropy of the (subjective) US timing distribution conditioned on knowledge of the time of one or the other CS onset is the same as the entropy conditioned on knowledge of both onsets. Thus, processing both CSs does not yield any greater reduction in the uncertainty about the timing of the US than can be achieved by processing only one of them. We assume that there is a processing cost in extracting the information a CS carries about the timing of the next US. We further assume that subjects choose not to incur this cost unless it purchases a reduction in their uncertainty. These assumptions explain the blocking, overshadowing, and relative validity effects, the principal effects in the extensive literature on "cue competition."

Summary

Learning processes are modular because the structure of an information-extracting process must reflect the formal structure of the information that is to be extracted and the structure of the data from which it is to be extracted. This simple point has been illustrated with three examples of learning processes with radically different structures. The first two, learning by path integration and learning by fitting an innately specified function to observational data, lie outside the range of phenomena ordinarily considered in textbooks on learning. It is hard to conceptualize them in associative terms, and contemporary textbooks on learning take it for granted that learning is basically associative in nature. The third example, the Pavlovian conditioning paradigm, comes, however, from the heart of the animal-learning tradition, the foundation on which all contemporary approaches to the neurobiology of learning build.

By considering first the formal properties of the problem that the learning mechanism engaged by the classic experimental paradigms appears to be solving, we have solved a core problem that has remained unsolved for centuries, namely, the problem of defining temporal pairing in an empirically defensible way. In so doing, we have derived from first principles a profoundly counterintuitive recent experimental result: the "number-of-trials-doesn't-matter" result (Gottlieb, 2008). And, we have integrated the derivation of the role of temporal pairing with the derivation of the cue-competition results that revolutionized associative theorizing in the early 1970s. No previous effort to understand these phenomena has integrated the understanding of cue competition with the understanding of the role of temporal pairing. What is perhaps particularly remarkable in a field where free parameters are used with profligacy is that the derivations follow from a simple principle, with no dependence on free parameters.

All of this was achieved by assuming that the computations that mediate the appearance of conditioned behavior in the standard conditioning paradigms are every bit as much structured by the exigencies of the problem to be solved as are the computations carried out in deriving position from velocity, and the solar ephemeris from a few observations of the sun's azimuthal position. The analytic relation between velocity and position is built into the brain mechanism that mediates dead reckoning. The universal characteristics of the solar ephemeris are built into the mechanism that learns the local ephemeris. That a random rate is the maximum entropy distribution of events in time and that independent random rates are additive (see Gallistel, 1990, ch. 12) are built into the computational mechanism that solves the problem of temporal prediction. The modularity of learning mechanisms is a corollary of the assumption that these mechanisms are computational in nature. If the computational character of learning mechanisms is granted, then the fact that it takes different computations to extract different representations from different data implies the modularity of learning.

14
Dead Reckoning in a Neural Network

Implementing the dead reckoning computation in a machine with a symbolic memory is easy (see Chapter 11). Now, we consider now how to implement it in a machine with the architecture of a neural network, an architecture that does not have a symbolic memory. In the past decade, several models have been suggested (Blair & Sharp, 1996; Droulez & Berthoz, 1991; Redish & Touretzky, 1997). All of them are based on the idea of a self-sustaining bump of neural activity whose location within a network is taken to represent either the subject's orientation (direction of motion) or its location within an experimental environment that establishes a frame of reference. In all the models, provision is made to move the activity bump about in a suitable way as the animal moves through its environment. We consider at some length the most extensively developed model of this kind (Samsonovich & McNaughton, 1997). It has features that one encounters often in contemporary efforts to model the computations implied by the behavioral data while remaining at least notionally faithful to known neurobiological mechanisms.

Samsonovich and McNaughton do not adhere to the sub-symbolic school of connectionist thought. It is hard to see how anyone interested in modeling dead reckoning could adhere to that view; it would seem to imply that a system could set a course for home without having any representation of where it was. Early on in their paper, they write:

> The planar path integration concept involves (1) selecting a physical reference frame ... (2) performing integration of the velocity vector over time in this reference frame to update the currently represented, or "perceived," coordinates. This implies two necessary building blocks: an internal representation of the planar coordinates, maintained independently of immediate exteroreceptive stimuli, and a mechanism of updating based on idiothetic information. (Samsonovich & McNaughton, 1997, p. 5902)

The first of the two building blocks (functional components) that they recognize as necessary in any scheme is a component that carries the information about the subject's current location forward in time. In a Turing architecture, the symbolic memory does this. The second building block is the computational component, which adds the newly gained information about the current displacement to the accumulated previous information from earlier displacements. The accumulated prior information must be accessible to computation in that there must be a means of combining the currently arriving information with the previously accumulated information in order to update the representation of location. In a Turing architecture, this is accomplished by reading from memory a symbol carrying the accumulated information, entering it into the processor's addition registers along with the symbol carrying the current information, adding the two symbols to get a symbol that can carry forward the information about the latest position, and storing the result back in the symbolic memory.

The question is, how do we accomplish the same thing in a machine with a functional architecture that lacks a read/write memory? The answer is: it is complicated. We urge readers to consult the original paper to see just how complicated. (It is accessible online through, among others, the PsychInfo bibliographic database, which most university libraries give free access to.) We consider the paper at some length here, but we do not begin to do justice to its full complexity. In particular, we leave out most of the mathematics. The mathematics we leave out do not arise from the inherent complexity of the dead-reckoning computation. As we have seen, the computation is a simple one, easily implemented in both an analog machine and a digital machine. The mathematics that we pass over arise from the complexities one encounters in trying to implement the computation in a machine whose architecture is ill suited to the implementation of simple computations like this.

The architecture of their model is shown in Figure 14.1. It is composed of seven arrays – seven networks of neurons, each with its own distinct pattern of intrinsic connections. One of the seven arrays, I, is itself composed of many separate layers, only one of which is active at any one time. The locus of activity within each of these arrays represents the value of one variable. Thus, this architecture uses an array of neurons to represent one variable and it uses the location of the active neurons within the array to specify the value of the variable.

We focus our attention first on the H array, because the locus of activity of the neurons in this array already represents the outcome of a directional dead-reckoning process – the integration of angular velocity (turning rate) to obtain current heading. The ideas underlying the achievement of that outcome direct the achievement of a similar outcome for locational dead reckoning.

Angular dead reckoning depends on sensory (and perhaps also motor, that is, efference copy) signals carrying information about the rate at which one is turning. The underlying principle is the same as the principle we saw at work in the log book by which the navigator in Chapter 11 kept track of her location. It is the idea at the foundation of the calculus. Like most basic mathematical ideas, it is very simple: if we know the rate at which a variable is changing its value, that is, if we know the small changes that occur in small units of time, then we can obtain the current value of that variable by integration, that is, by adding up all the small changes. If we start out facing a target on a wall, and we begin to turn right (clockwise) at 30° per second (that is, making a change of 30° in each second), and we continue turning at this rate for 12 seconds, we will have turned at total of $12 \times 30° = 360°$, and we will again be facing the target on the wall. In the language of the calculus, our angular velocity was constant at 30°/s, and the integral

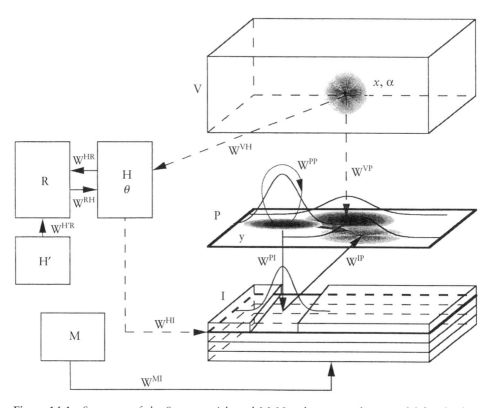

Figure 14.1 Structure of the Samsonovich and McNaughton neural-net model for dead reckoning. V = array of cells sensitive to different views of the environment; the locus of activity (represented by the cloud) within this array varies as the animal's view of the environment changes. R = an array of neurons whose firing depends jointly on the compass-orientation of the head and the rate at which this orientation is changing (α and α'). H = an array of neurons whose firing depends only on head orientation ("compass neurons"). H' = an array of neurons whose firing depends only on the rate at which the head orientation is changing (angular velocity neurons). P = an array of neurons whose firing depends on where the subject is within the environment ("place neurons"). M = an array of neurons whose firing depends on the speed at which the animal is moving. I = an array of neurons sensitive both to the animal's location and its direction of movement. This array combines the effects of inputs from the H, M, and P arrays to produce an activity pattern that, when projected back to the P array, appropriately shifts the locus of activity in the P array. The locus activity in the P array represents the animal's current location within the environment. (Reproduced from Samsonovich & McNaughton, 1997, Figure 2, p. 5002, by permission of the publisher and authors.)

of this velocity over an interval of 12 seconds is 360°. Thus, if we are provided with a signal that specifies the rate at which we are turning, we can obtain our current direction by integrating that signal over time. The key to integration over time is memory, the capacity to carry forward in time the previously computed sum of all the previously specified small changes.

Reverberating Circuits as Read/Write Memory Mechanisms

But how can we do this in a machine that has no memory, no element whose function is to carry information forward in time? We must somehow endow the machine with a memory. The key to doing this is to notice that if the network has recurrent connections, connections that allow a signal to return to its point of origin, then those loops can be exploited to give the system a memory, albeit, realistically, only a short one. In the very early years of computing (late 1940s), this is how online symbolic memory (memory that will be used soon and repeatedly, cache or register memory in current technical language) was implemented. Signals carrying the information that would be required in the near future were sent on round-trip journeys in a transmission medium in which signals traveled relatively slowly (Hodges, 1983, ch. 6). The idea of creating short-term memory in the nervous system by reverberating circuits goes back to roughly the same period (Lorente de No, 1932). And it is the same idea: store information by having it circulate within a circuit. That is why we have stressed the similarity of function between signals and symbols. Signals carry information from place to place; symbols carry information forward in time. Because it takes time to carry information from one place to another, you can in principle carry information forward in time by having it circulate in a signal loop.

In Figure 11.1, the axon of one of the interneurons has a branch that synapses (ends) back on the interneuron itself. This is the simplest kind of recurrent connection, a monosynaptic recurrent connection. Figure 14.2 shows a multisynaptic recurrent pathway in which two interneurons make excitatory connections with one another. Now, when one interneuron transmits a spike to the other, that spike may excite the other sufficiently that it in turn transmits a spike – indeed, conceivably even several spikes – back to the first interneuron. In either case, it would appear that when we have either monosynaptic or multisynaptic recurrent connections in a neural network, spikes could in principle circulate indefinitely within those loops. Thus, the existence of recurrent connection loops within the nervous system makes it possible for neural activity to persist in the absence of the transient incoming signal (or external stimulus) that initiated the activity.

Self-sustaining activity in a reverberatory neural circuit can serve as a memory. It will be particularly effective as a memory if we make the gain in the loop greater than 1. Suppose that the synaptic connection that a neuron makes with itself is so strong that a single presynaptic spike triggers two postsynaptic spikes. Suppose that the neuron is, to begin with, inactive, and, by means of some other inputs, we trigger a single spike in it. That spike will soon arrive back by way of the recurrent connection, and it will trigger two spikes; they will soon arrive back and trigger four; they will soon arrive back and trigger eight; and so on. In short order, the neuron will be firing spikes as fast as it can, and it will continue to do so indefinitely, assuming that it does not exhaust itself in so doing (an unlikely assumption). In other words, a neuron with a strong enough recurrent connection will behave as a switch. Activating it changes its state from inactive to active, and it stays in the active state. We can put it back into the inactive state – open the switch – by an inhibitory input strong enough to overcome the self-excitation. And, of course, if the neuron's axon branches terminate on other neurons, those other neurons in effect read the state of the switch. Thus, we could use self-exciting neurons to implement a digital symbolic memory. The neurons in this scheme would have only two states – active and inactive. Thus, the activity state of each neuron could carry one bit of information.

As we saw in Chapter 10, it is not hard to use synaptic integration processes to make basic logic gates (AND and OR). The gates allow one to decode memory symbols and perform computations with them. Samsonovich and McNaughton (1997) make essential use of neurons as AND gates in the look-up tables that implement the computational operations in their model (see below). Thus, in principle, nothing prevents our making a conceptual model of the brain using the schematics for a modern computer as our guide. Nothing prevents us from creating models in which we use neurons to build a Turing machine with its program in its memory.

The only thing that prevents contemporary neural modelers from following this lead and imagining that the brain is a conventional computer built out of neurons is a widely shared conviction that this would be in some sense cheating, that this is not the way the brain is in fact built. Thus, modelers find themselves in the following position: they do not want to assume that the brain has the functional architecture of a Turing machine, and, in particular, that it has a read/write symbol memory, because there is no basis in current neurobiology for this assumption. However, there are simple computations – dead reckoning being one of them – that cannot be done without a read/write symbolic memory, and there is strong behavioral evidence that the brain does them. In making models of how it does them, theorists must therefore create something within the constraints of a neural network architecture that behaves something like a read/write symbol memory that preserves over time the information carried by transient incoming neural signals. For more than half a century, the only option that has suggested itself is the use of reverberatory circuits. This is the assumption that the brain preserves information in computationally usable form by having neural signals (spike trains) travel in circles.

However, because of the widespread belief that the nervous system does not have a read/write memory, theorists seldom make it clear that when they make essential use of reverberating circuits, they are bringing one in unannounced through the back door. For the same reason, they are reluctant to exploit the full power of the idea. Also at work here is the issue we take up later about whether it is plausible to assume that neural circuits could in fact reverberate in the delicately poised way assumed in these models – for the lengths of time they would have to do so if these models were realistic portrayals of what is really going on in the nervous system of a dead-reckoning ant journeying over the desert floor for tens of minutes or a homing pigeon navigating by dead reckoning for tens of hours.

The reverberating circuitry at the heart of the Samsonovich and McNaughton model is shown in Figure 14.2. The idea is that there is a line or circle or sheet of neurons in which each neuron makes strong excitatory connections with its close neighbors and weaker inhibitory connections with all of the neurons that are not its close neighbors. In Figure 14.2, we only show the connections that a single neuron makes, because it gets too messy when we try to show the repetition of this

Inhibitory synapse

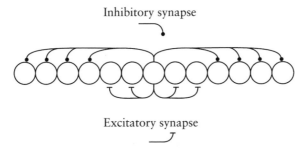

Excitatory synapse

Figure 14.2 The basic connectivity pattern in moving-activity-bump models (aka continuous attractor models). Each neuron makes strong excitatory connections with some other neurons that also make strong excitatory connections with it, thereby creating local reverberatory circuits. In addition each neuron makes weaker inhibitory connections with the many neurons not in its immediate neighborhood. The pattern is shown for only one neuron, but all the other neurons are assumed to have the same connectivity pattern. The notion of neighborhood is actually defined by the pattern of connectivity rather than by anatomical location. The local neurons are by definition the ones with which a given neuron exchanges excitatory connections, regardless of where those neurons may actually be anatomically located. Similarly, the remote neurons are by definition the ones with which it exchanges inhibitory connections, regardless of where they really are.

pattern for each neuron. However, the pattern is repeated for each neuron in the line. Each neuron forms an excitatory reverberatory circuit with its close neighbors. The spikes it sends to them excite them and the spikes they transmit back excite the source still further, sending a still stronger signal out again to the neighbors, whence again it will come back, and so on. This is called positive feedback for obvious reasons: the consequences of an increase in firing rate come back to push the firing rate higher still, just as they would if the neuron made an excitatory connection with itself. As the firing rates build up in one neighborhood, the inhibitory effects of activity in that neighborhood on the activity of neurons remote from it get stronger. Thus, when one neighborhood gets ahead of the others, a bump of self-sustaining activity builds there.

Whether an activity bump builds or not and how stable it is depend critically on the quantitative details, which are numerous. In the jargon of the craft, these models are "parameter sensitive"; they work only for an often narrow range of values for several critical parameters. One can see already that they have a lot of parameters. One must specify how many other neurons a neuron makes excitatory connections with, how strong each of those connections is, how strong the inhibitory connections are, how long it takes spikes to travel along the various connections, the mathematical form of the postsynaptic effect of each spike, and so on. The available experimental data rarely constrain the values of these parameters to within less than one or two orders of magnitude. These models get very complicated, and their behavior depends critically on a great many quantitative details. This is an obstacle to making a realistic assessment of their plausibility. That they can be made to work at all is generally demonstrated by means of a numerical computer

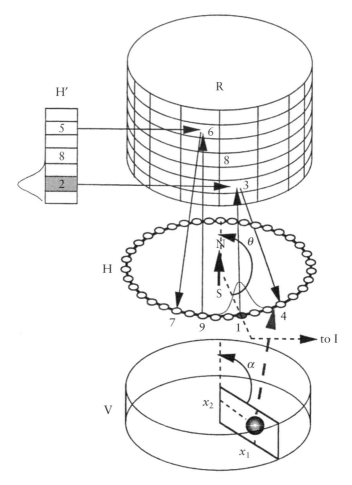

Figure 14.3 The model for directional dead reckoning proposed by Skaggs et al. (1995) and assumed by Samsonovich et al. (1997) in their model of locational dead reckoning. H′ = linear array of cells selectively tuned to the rate of turning; R = cylindrical array of cells sensitive both to current orientation and rate of turning (rate of change in orientation). H = circular array of cells selectively sensitive to current orientation; V = array of cells selectively sensitive to different views of the environment; the locus of activity (represented by the cloud) within this array varies as the animal's angle of view changes. The arrow from a locus within V to a point on the H circle indicates the writing to memory of the heading indicated by a transient view of the environment. The arrows back and forth between the H circle and the R cylinder indicate the process by which the information in memory about the current heading is combined with transient signals indicating the rate at which the heading is changing in order to appropriately shift the locus of activity in the H circle, thereby updating the representation of the current heading. (Reproduced from Figure 3 in Samsonovich & McNaughton, 1997, p. 5904, by permission of the publisher and authors.)

simulation. The simulation program divides time up into very small increments and recalculates increment by increment the values of a large number (in this model, tens of thousands) of variables in accord with complex equations provided by the modeler. In mathematical terminology, the behavior of the system is determined by an extensive set of simultaneous nonlinear differential equations for which no analytic solution exists. As any mathematical physicist will tell you, this means that it is hard to determine with confidence what such a system will in fact do. Writing a computer program to evaluate such a system of equations is a complex, tedious, and error-prone undertaking, whose outcome often depends strongly on debatable assumptions about the initial conditions – the values of the variables when the program starts to run – and the boundary conditions – the limits beyond which the values of variables cannot go for logical or physical reasons. For this reason, claims about what such a system will do and how well it will do it must be regarded with caution. It is important to ask: (1) Have simplifying assumptions been made whose implausibility and criticality call into question the simulation? (2) Has the behavior that the computer program says the model shows been shown to occur in an actual neural network? (3) If so, has the behavior of that network been shown to be the consequence of the posited reverberatory connections. There is not much evidence of this last kind, because the second requirement is hard to satisfy (see for recent review Major et al., 2004). We consider later some of the simplifying assumptions in the Samsonovich and McNaughton model and their bearing on its workability and plausibility.

Setting aside doubts about how realistic this kind of circuitry is, we see that it constitutes a read/write memory. In their model, Samsonovich and McNaughton assume that the animal's heading is represented by just the kind of circuitry shown in Figure 14.2, but in circular form (see H in Figure 14.3). The location of the activity bump, that is, the subset of neurons that are active and suppressing the activity of the rest, represents the subject's current heading (place coding). Although an activity bump will form somewhere in the circle even in the absence of external input, an external input specifying a heading can write to this memory circle by selectively boosting activity at one point in the circle. This will cause the bump to move to that point. That is what the inputs from the view-sensitive array, V, in Figure 14.3 are assumed to do. Different headings produce different views of the environment, and these different views are assumed to activate different locations within the V array. Thus, the location of activity within the V array is assumed to represent the subject's heading, as determined from its view of its environment. Locations within V that represent a heading are assumed to project to a particular location on the H circle. Locations in V representing neighboring headings project to neighboring neurons within the H circle. When a brief view of its environment informs the rat of its compass heading, the transient activity in V excites the corresponding locus in the H circle, moving the activity bump to that locus. In the absence of further input, it will stay there, thereby carrying forward in time the information carried by the transient input signal that caused the bump to move there. This representative of a behaviorally useful fact is in the form of neural activity, which means that it is accessible to computation. It can serve as an input to combinatorial operations in the nervous system. Unlike a synaptic conductance, it can be read.

Implementing Combinatorial Operations by Table-Look-Up

Updating, H, the representation of current heading, requires adding the representation of the current change in heading (in mathematical notation, ΔH or H')[1] to the current value of H. The current value of H' is represented by the locus of activity in the H' array. So now the question becomes, when we represent the values of two variables by the locus of activity in two different arrays, how do we implement addition? We need to find a way of combining the locus of activity in one array with the locus of activity in another array so as to generate a locus of activity in a third (not necessarily a different) array, and the combinatorial process must be governed by the rules that define arithmetic addition. More specifically, we want to combine the locus of activity in the H array with the locus of activity in the H' array so as to generate a new locus of activity in the H array, but the combinatorial process must be so constructed that it mimics the way present angular velocity combines with present position to determine future angular position. If our combinatorial process in the nervous system does not mimic this real-world process, it will be useless. (It won't be a functioning homomorphism.)

The cylindrical R array is their solution to this problem. The arrows leading from the H array and the H' array to the R array indicate that this is where the combination (arithmetic addition) occurs. The R array is a look-up table. The H input specifies the column in which the answer is to be found; the H' input specifies the row. The cells at the intersection of the specified column and the specified row are activated by these two inputs. In other words, the cells in the R array are logical AND gates. They become active only when both their inputs are active. The only cells with both inputs active will be the cells at the intersection of the specified column and row. One sees why the R array must take the form of a cylinder, that is, a stack of circles. Each of these circles is in effect a copy of the H circle. A given cell, H_{g+}, in the H circle projects to (sends excitatory connections to) the corresponding cell in each level of the R stack. Each of those R cells sends a projection back to a nearby locus on the H circle. How near and in which direction depends on the level of the circle in which the R cell is located. Levels near the bottom send projections back to points relatively distant in the counterclockwise direction (arrow from cell 3 in the R cylinder to cell 4 in the H circle). Levels near the top send projections back to points relatively distant in the clockwise direction (arrow from cell 6 in the R cylinder to cell 7 in the H circle).

The closer the R cell is to the vertical middle of the cylinder, the closer its back projection is to H_g. Why? Because angular velocity is represented by the locus of activity in the H' array, with maximally rapid counterclockwise turning exciting cells at the bottom of H' and maximally rapid clockwise turning exciting cells at the top, and slow turning exciting cells toward the middle. The faster the subject is turning, the farther the activity bump in H must move from H_g. The arc distance from H_g of a back-projection from a given row of the cylinder R is equal to r arcsin

---

[1] We are deliberately equating the differential with the derivative, because in numerical integration, it is always the differential that actually enters into the computation.

H', where H' is the value of the angular velocity for the row in question and r is the implicit diameter of the circle H and the cylinder R (with all "distances" measured in neuron units). In short, the trigonometry, the multiplication, and the addition are mirrored in the structure of the neural circuit that carries out the combinatorial operation. We see again that a representational system, a functioning homomorphism, must have processes whose formal characteristics are the same as the formal characteristics of the represented system. This is true regardless of the computational architecture.

The Full Model

Now we are in a position to understand the architecture of the larger system (Figure 14.1), because it recapitulates the main ideas behind the architecture in Figure 14.3. The P array plays the role of the H circle. It has the same intrinsic system of near excitatory connections and far inhibitory connections, but now these connections extend along two dimensions, so we need many more neurons and many more connections. (In their simulation, Samsonovich and McNaughton assume that the P array has 45,000 neurons. If we assume that every neuron sends either an excitatory or an inhibitory connection to every other neuron in the array, that gives $45,000^2 = 2,025,000,000$ connections – and the I array is much bigger still.) The locus of the self-sustaining activity bump in this array represents the subject's two-dimensional position within the environment. (P is for "place"; the model was in part inspired by the experimental evidence that there are place cells in the hippocampus, cells that fire only when the animal is in a particular place.) As in the model of angular dead reckoning, the representation of place is anchored to views of the environment by means of the input from the V array. The animal's speed is represented by the locus of activity in the linear M array. The M array is one-dimensional (linear) and the P array two-dimensional (rectangular) because speed is a one-dimensional variable (it can be represented by a single number), while location (on a plane) is two-dimensional (it is represented by a pair of numbers, that is, by a two-dimensional vector). The H array is one-dimensional but circular rather than linear, because activity in that array represents the value of a circular variable (direction).

As before, the computational problem is to combine the symbols for current location, speed, and direction in the mathematically necessary way to yield a new value for the current location. As before, this is done by means of a look-up table, the I array in Figure 14.1. (I stands for "integrator" in the neurobiologists' sense of term, the mechanism that combines the values of variables, whether or not the combinatorial operation is what mathematicians understand by "integration"). The look-up table now has three dimensions. The third dimension is the layers of the I array (Figure 14.1). The projections from the active cells in P activate a column within the I array (arrow from one of the activity bumps in P down to the activity bump in I). Again the cells in the I array function as AND gates, three-legged AND gates. The projection down from the P array is one leg (one input). The projection from a single cell ("place") in the P array is to a small circle of cells within each layer of the I array. The cells in this circle all have one leg activated by the same place in the P array. The cells in the H array, which, we recall, represents direction, project to these circles in such a way that the locus of activity in the H array determines which cell within the circle within a given layer has its second leg activated. Put another way, the projections from a given locus in the H array spread vertically across layers, going to the same point within each of the stack of circles, and this is repeated for every stack of circles. The third leg (input) of a cell (AND gate) is provided by the projections from the M array. The locus of activity in the M array determines the layer of the activated cell; different layers corresponding to different speeds. The upshot is that the locus of activity in the I array is jointly determined by the inputs from the H (heading), M (speed), and P (place) arrays in such a way that it represents both the velocity vector (the direction and distance in which the position activity bump must move) and the current position. The symbolic role of each I cell – what activity at that locus represents – determines its pattern of projection back to the P array. If $P_{r,c}$ represents the locus within the P array from which a cell in the I array receives its input, then its projection back to the P array is in the direction from $P_{r,c}$ determined by where the I cell is within its circle and at a distance determined by which layer the I cell is in. As before, the mathematics have been built into the connectivity patterns. Even neural networks become modular when they are made to deal with a computationally well-defined problem, like dead reckoning.

The Ontogeny of the Connections?

So what, one may ask, establishes these complex connectivity patterns? Samsonovich and McNaughton (1997) do raise and forthrightly answer this question in a couple of places:

> Briefly, for present purpose, the prewiring of the multichart attractor map [the P array] is assumed without consideration of how this occurs. (p. 5904)

and

> Connections between H and I cells are also preconfigured and fixed. In other words, each chart has a built in compass. (p. 5905)

We mention this not as any sort of criticism, but as an indication of what we believe to be the ineluctable nativism inherent in any representational machinery. It is difficult, for us at least, to imagine a pattern of experience and a set of induction rules – or experience-driven rewiring principles – that would enable the representational machinery itself to assume the requisite form within any reasonable span of experience (within, say, one lifetime's experience, which for the ant is a week or so). The issue of the nativist vs. empiricist origin (ontogeny) of the requisite machinery comes up because the neural network tradition is by and large an empiricist one. It assumes that the brain is relatively formless to begin with (randomly connected) and that the experiences it has together with a few learning principles that change connections on the basis of that experience suffice to endow it in time with the wiring pattern it needs to cope with the world in which it finds itself.

The issue of the ontogeny of the representational machinery is of some importance, because it is our sense that one of the things that make empiricists uncomfortable with the assumption that the brain symbolically represents aspects of the world revealed to it by its experience and uses those representations to control behavior is that when one spells out what is required to implement this idea, one necessarily makes some elaborate and very specific assumptions about the structure of the machinery in the brain. The empiricist feels that these accounts assume too much prior structure. The champions of a representational approach believe that if we do not assume quite a bit of prior representational structure, there is no prospect of explaining the behavior that we observe.

This is an echo of the debate between philosophical nativists, like Kant and Leibnitz, and philosophical empiricists, like Locke, Hume, and Berkeley. In our terms, Kant can be understood to have argued that a certain amount of representational structure was a precondition for having any experience whatsoever. Therefore, that representational structure could not derive from experience because experience itself was made possible only by virtue of the prior existence of that representational structure.

Today, thanks to the power of modern computers, we are in a position to adopt a quasi-experimental approach to this ancient question. Because the behavioral evidence for dead reckoning is strong, and because the computation that must somehow be accomplished is so clear, we think this is an excellent area in which to explore the extent to which currently assumed rewiring rules and some to-be-specified assumptions about the structure of experience could produce the representational structure necessary for a neural network to compute its position function from its velocity function – online in real time.

Neural network modelers still use much the same rewiring rules that Locke suggested – at least when it comes to so-called unsupervised learning. The rewiring rules commonly applied in cases of supervised learning are roughly those suggested in their qualitative form by Thorndike and Hull more than half a century ago and in something like their contemporary quantitative form by Bush, Mosteller, and Estes about half a century ago and Rescorla and Wagner more than 30 years ago. We now have the computational power to determine what these durable rewiring principles can achieve when applied to a well-defined problem for which fully satisfactory computational solutions have long been known. The question is whether, if we start with a randomly connected net, and assume one of the currently popular unsupervised learning algorithms or the very widely used back-propagation algorithm, and we stipulate some, one hopes, half-way plausible experiences, will we end up with a net structured like the one in Figure 14.1? Or will we end up with a net with no discernible representational machinery, but which nonetheless computes its position from signals specifying its velocity (online!)?

The insistence that the computation be carried out online is critical, because it concerns a pivotal issue, the issue of the necessity for a symbolic memory that carries information forward in time. We could eliminate the temporal aspect of the problem by recasting the problem as simply one of mapping an input vector to an output vector. There is a tendency in the neural network literature to do this to a variety of problems, that is, to give information that determines the output to the net all at once, in one big input vector, even though, in the behavior being modeled, the information arrives in dribs and drabs spread out over long intervals. If a digitized representation of the animal's entire velocity function is given as the input vector, we do not doubt that the net can be trained to give out a digitized representation of the entire position function. But that finesses the issue of carrying information forward in time, which is the central issue. In the real world, the animal never sees the velocity function (the record of velocity as a function of time); it sees only tiny pieces of it, one piece after the next. It must integrate these pieces over time on line, as the data come in. For that, we believe that a read/write symbolic memory capable of carrying information forward in time is indispensable. That is why we are not surprised to find that the Samsonovich and McNaughton model has such a mechanism prewired into it. Because we think mechanisms that implement the basic operations of arithmetic are equally indispensable, we are not surprised to find that they, too, have been prewired into the Samsonovich and McNaughton model in the form of elaborately structured look-up tables.

How Realistic Is the Model?

As we mention above, there is a question how much credence one should give to the reported success of simulations like this, because of the enormous complexity of the models and the resulting complexity of the computer programs that numerically simulate them. (Recall that there are more than two billion connections within the P array alone, which is but one of seven intricately interconnected large arrays.) Simplifying assumptions and shortcuts are almost always required, but their impact on the validity of the results seldom receives extensive analysis and discussion. To illustrate this point, which applies broadly to almost all neural network simulations, we discuss three of the simplifying assumptions and shortcuts in the Samsonovich and McNaughton model.

Converting the Euclidian plane into the surface of a torus

In the section on the numerical implementation of their model, a cryptic clause is appended to the sentence specifying the size of the P array:

> In the simulations of Figure 9 . . . each layer of the P-I system was composed of $n = 256 \times 192 \approx 45,000$ model neuronal units, *distributed in a square lattice on a torus (i.e., a rectangle with periodic boundary conditions)*. (p. 5905, italics added)

We call the clause we have italicized cryptic because we doubt that most readers would notice it and that few of those who did would know what it meant, or why it was done, or what untoward effects it might have.

In generalizing the model from the directional dead reckoning to dead reckoning on the Euclidean plane, the problem arises that, whereas a circle has finitely many neurons and no boundaries (end points), a segment of a plane with finitely many neurons necessarily has boundaries (edges). The problem this presents is that the basic repetitive pattern of intrinsic connections shown in Figure 14.2 cannot continue as the edges of the rectangle are approached. Neurons at and near the edges cannot have the same connection pattern as neurons in the center, because there are no neurons beyond the edges. This is awkward. Moreover, the problem cannot be ignored, because the changing pattern of connectivity near the edges causes the self-sustaining activity bump to behave badly. To solve this problem, the modelers in effect curled the rectangle first into a tube, connecting its two long edges together, and then curled the tube into the shape of a doughnut (in technical language, a *torus*), connecting the two ends of the tube together. When a rectangle is thus converted into the surface of a donut, it no longer has edges, so the edge problem goes away.

In technical language, this is called a *kluge* – a quick-and-dirty solution to a problem, carrying with it the risk that it may give rise to problems of its own. This particular kluge is common, despite the fact that it does not take much thought to see that it does indeed give rise to problems of its own. In making the rectangle into a torus, we made the four points at the corners into a single point. There is now one single neuron whose activity symbolizes *the* corner location. We italicize 'the' because in the representation of a rectangle used in this simulation, there is only one corner location, and it has as its near neighbors (the neighbors with which it made excitatory local connections) the points lying in the vicinity of all four of the corners of the original rectangle. In other words, points in the represented world that are maximally distant from each other are in this symbolic world maximally close. Put another way, the torus is not a homomorphism for the plane, which means that the representing system has functionally relevant properties that the represented system does not and vice versa.

Clearly, this kluge limits the computational operations that could validly be performed with this representation. But does it otherwise matter? That depends on whether one thinks that the problem that the kluge solved could be solved in other more plausible, but presumably more complex, ways.

Clamping the total number of active units

The intrinsic long-range inhibitory connections play a critical role in this model. Without them, the activity bump is not localized; the local positive feedback spreads activity throughout the net until every neuron is firing as fast as it can all the time. However, when we recall that the model has more than two billion connections just within the P array – most of them inhibitory – it will be appreciated that it is difficult to compute these effects in a realistic way in a realistic amount of time. The computation would have to track each impulse as it propagated from each neuron to all the neurons inhibited by that neuron. Because these neurons lie at different distances from the source neuron, the spikes will arrive at them at different times. And then one must compute the time course of the inhibitory postsynaptic action of each arriving impulse. The time courses for inhibitory postsynaptic potentials are thought to be quite rapid, which means that one would have to use very short time increments, and so on. The amount of computation that must be done rapidly gets out of hand. To make the computation tractable, Samsonovich and McNaughton (1997) did not try to model the inhibition:

> ... the amount of inhibition (uniformly distributed among all units) [was] adjusted at every discrete time bin, so that the total number M of firing units was preserved near the given level ... (p. 5904)

and later

> All synaptic connections ... are excitatory; the role of interneurons implicitly present in the model consists of adjustment of the global thresholds *h* at each iteration, according to Equation 4. Thus, in the terminology of Amit (1989), the model contains a *hard constraint* for the total activity in each array. (p. 5906)

This is an understandable shortcut, but it leaves one wondering whether the model would behave itself if the inhibitory connections were realistically simulated. The relative timing of excitatory and inhibitory effects can have a big impact on the dynamic stability of a net. This shortcut takes that complication out of the picture. At each small time step, every neuron is fully cognizant of the inhibitory effect on it of the activity of every other neuron in the net during the preceding time step. There is a god outside the machine, mediating communication between its elements in a manner that frees communication from the ordinary constraints of time and space and the messiness that those constraints can produce in a complex signaling system.

Parameter sensitivity and noise

Another concern that one may have is the parameter-sensitivity issue, which we raised previously, and the related issue of noise. It is hard to judge the extent to which these issues are important in assessing the success of the Samsonovich and McNaughton simulation, because they do not discuss the effects of manipulating parameter values or noise. (In at least some of their simulations, they set at least some of the noise sources to 0.) The absence of such a discussion is not at all uncommon in the neural network literature, but practitioners of the art are generally well aware of the issue, because they are the ones that set the parameters, including the noise parameters, and observe the results. Moreover, it is known that introducing even modest amounts of noise into a net can destroy its functionality (Maas & Sontag, 1999).

To illustrate the potential importance of the particular values used for the many different parameters and the levels of noise assumed, consider how we might make more effective use of the information-preserving characteristics inherent in a reverberatory circuit. We might think to use a single neuron as an integrator. (We know of cases in which modelers have done this.) Suppose that we connect a neuron to itself with a synaptic conductance of 1, so that a spike arriving at the presynaptic ending triggers one and only one postsynaptic spike, which spike will itself make its way round the loop and arrive in time at the presynaptic ending. Now, however many spikes we put into the recurrently connected neuron from an external source, that number will circulate perpetually within that one neuron.

You do not have to know much about real neurons to realize that there are problems with this idea. How fast can a real neuron fire spikes? Does not the postsynaptic effect of one spike depend on the residual effects of the spikes that preceded it? How long do those residual effects last? What is the dependence (the synaptic interaction between successive spikes)? Is the interaction linear or nonlinear? (If there is a firing threshold, and there always is, then it will be nonlinear.) Is it reasonable to assume that there is no relevant random variability (noise) in the process of synaptic transmission, involving as it does inherently stochastic processes such as the release of packets of transmitter substance? All these questions come quickly to mind, or should do so.

They come readily to mind in the present context, because Samsonovich and McNaughton tried to build a model using an approximation to actual neurons, a model with so-called *integrate-and fire-neurons*. That they tried to do so is a measure of their ambition. Very few neural network models of this degree of complexity use integrate-and-fire neurons. Most connectionist models ignore the fact that neural signals come in the form of spikes and that the effects of a presynaptic spike on postsynaptic potential have a complex time course. Trying to take all that into account makes the models too complex and computationally intractable. Therefore, most models make the radically simplifying assumption that the signal a neuron transmits can be treated as single continuously variable quantity (technically a real number, or more realistically, given that the models are evaluated by computer simulation, a floating point number). And most models assume that the effects of synaptic transmission can be represented by simply scaling the transmitted quantity (making it bigger or smaller and/or changing its sign).[2] And most models assume that there are no nonlinear interactions between the quantities transmitted in successive time bins.

In making simplifying assumptions as radical as this, a neural network model forfeits any claim to being neurobiologically realistic. When one is this far removed from the reality that initially inspired the effort, it seems less unrealistic to posit that the quantity transmitted is 1 (or 3.1416 . . . or 2.718 . . . or −0.3333 . . . or whatever quantity one wants) and the synaptic conductance is 1, and therefore the gain in the loop is 1, and therefore the quantity transmitted (say, pi to 1,000 digits) will circulate in the loop from time step to time step, undiminished and unaugmented, for as long as we need it to. In other words, we can store the quantity in the reverberating loop and add to or subtract from it whenever we like. That is just what we need to be able to do in dead reckoning. Because a model with this mechanism as its integrator will be implemented on a conventional computer, with a noise-free symbolic memory, running the simulation does not immediately alert us to the fatal lack of realism in our assumptions regarding the integrator mechanism.

---

[2]   The thresholding occurs after the postsynaptic effects at all the different synapses have combined into one local effect at the axon hillock; it does not occur at the individual synapses.

The roboticist, Rodney Brooks, once remarked that "The trouble with simulations is that they are doomed to succeed." What he meant was that, because simulations more or less unavoidably leave out much of the messiness of the physical reality they are intended to represent, the simulation of the operation of a complex machine (he had in mind robots) succeeds even though, when we actually build a machine in accord with the simulated principles, it fails utterly. In the present case, if we actually built our machine out of real neurons, we would discover that we could not realize a neural loop with a noise-free gain of exactly 1, and that any departure from the value 1, no matter how small, was eventually disastrous. Suppose, for example, that the gain was 0.99 or 1.01 instead of 1.00. . . . Each time the circulating quantity goes around the loop it is diminished or augmented by the gain in the loop. With neural loops, the quantities circulate rapidly, let us say, 10 cycles per second. Thus at the end of 10 seconds, the circulating quantity is 0.99^{100} = 0.37 or 1.0001^{100} = 2.7, depending on whether the gain was slightly less or slightly more than 1. So our integrator is unrealistically parameter sensitive. The gain in its loop has to be *exactly* 1.

It is also unrealistically noise sensitive. Even if we assume that the average gain is very precisely 1, there are bound to be small random departures from this value on any one round, and those small random departures accumulate. The accumulation of small errors – in so-called random walk processes – is much studied in the statistical literature. As one suspects intuitively, the longer the walk goes on, the greater the average deviation from a straight line. How rapidly the walk moves away from the straight line (how rapidly the quantity in our loop drifts away from its original value) depends on how much noise there is. When you integrate by reverberation, you are integrating the noise, which means that a one-time deviation contributes over and over again to the cumulative error. Thus, to judge how realistic a simulation is, we need to have some idea of the noise to be expected in actual synaptic transmission and the sensitivity of our model to noise.

In short, absent a lengthy and highly technical analysis of parameter and noise sensitivity – and, we regret to say, even perhaps after such an analysis – it is difficult to say how realistic a model actually is. The fact that the simulation worked is at best weak evidence that such a mechanism exists and actually works in any real brain.

Lessons to Be Drawn

To focus, as we did in the preceding section, on the question of how realistic the model is, is to miss the spirit of the undertaking. Although the model was inspired by a mixture of behavioral and neurobiological data, and although various arrays in it were tentatively identified with specific structures in the mammalian brain, it was not in the end put forward as a hypothesis about the structure and function of identified brain areas. It was put forward in the spirit of, "The mechanism could be something like this." It was put forward as a working out of the very widespread belief within the neuroscience community that the complex computations that the brain appears to perform are realized by the connectivity patterns within the brain, by how it is wired.

In some sense, this belief cannot be false. No one believes that how the brain is wired is irrelevant to how it functions (although, in another era, both Karl Lashley (1950) and Paul Weiss (1941) could be read as arguing something like that). Nonetheless, one wants to dispel some of the mystery surrounding this conviction by showing how assumptions about patterns of connectivity could explain interesting computational capacity. Exactly how can patterns of neuronal connection be used to implement a simple computation? Considered in that spirit, the Samsonovich and McNaughton model is highly instructive. Most of its most salient features are found in most of the models we know of. Let us summarize those features.

How are variables represented? Variables are represented by arrays of neurons. The value of the variable is represented by the locus of activity within the array (place coding). Thus, for each variable, there is an innate structural mechanism that binds those values to that variable. Activity in a given neuron represents the value of a given variable just in case that neuron falls within the array that represents that variable. This is an extravagant use of neurons, but there is electrophysiological evidence for it (see Gallistel, 1990, ch. 14, for a review of that evidence).

How is information carried forward in time? The information carried by ephemeral sensory and motor signals is carried forward in time by reverberatory loops, just as in very early computing machines.

How is the information carried forward in time made computationally accessible? The information carried by the signals that travel in circles around reverberatory loops is computationally accessible because the neurons within the loop send branches to other neural networks. Thus, the activity circulating in the loop appears (with a period depending on its circulation time) as inputs to those other nets.

How are the combinatorial computational operations implemented? Combinatorial operations are implemented by look-up tables. Signals representing operand values appear as inputs to the rows, columns, and layers of these tables. The value of one operand is represented by which row is activated; the value of a second operand by which column is activated; the value of a third operand, if there is one, is represented by which layer is activated. The neurons within the table are configured as AND gates. Only the cell(s) whose row, column, and layer input are all activated becomes active itself. The locus of the active cell(s) represents the value of the variable that results from the combinatorial operation.

When looked at from the perspective of what is currently known or assumed about the structure and functional principles of the nervous system, these features are eminently reasonable, which is why they appear often in neural network models. When looked at from the perspective of what computer scientists think they understand about what it takes to make an effective computing machine, they are profoundly puzzling.

From the beginning, computer scientists have appreciated that the key features of a powerful computing machine were speed, efficiency, and reliability. Turing himself was obsessed with this. The first machines were slow and unreliable and the program code inefficient. The path to the powerful machines we use today has been made by relentless improvements in the speed and reliability of the hardware and the efficiency of the coding schemes and computational algorithms.

The generally supposed speed and reliability of neural hardware is many orders of magnitude less than the speed and reliability of the roughly equivalent solid-state elements in modern computers. Moreover, the inefficiencies of the coding schemes supposed in neural networks and in the structures required to implement computational operations are stupefying. Yet, this supposedly slow, supposedly inefficient, supposedly unreliable, and supposedly very badly designed device routinely solves computational problems that defeat our most powerful current computers; it solves them rapidly; and it does so in very small physical spaces. (The brain of an ant is the size of a pinhead and has on the order of only 1 million neurons.) Something must be wrong. Not all of these suppositions can be true. Or, there is something profoundly wrong with our current understanding of the physics of computation, how computation can and must be efficiently realized in machines working at ordinary pressures and temperatures.

The Samsonovich and McNaughton model uses on the order of 50,000 neurons to represent locations within one experimental space. With their information-coding scheme, processed by their symbol-processing machinery, their model represents at most 50,000 different locations. In fact, because there is a great deal of spread of activity from one neuron to another in their model, i.e., a great deal of redundancy, which reduces coding efficiency, the actual number of distinct places that their 50,000 neurons can encode is one or two orders of magnitude less – more like 5,000 or 500 than 50,000. But let us assume 50,000. This is less than 2^{16}. It is less representational capacity than is found in a single word of an old-fashioned computer with 16-bit words. Contemporary desktop and laptop machines have 64-bit words. A word is the amount of information that can be stored in a single addressable location. It is, in a sense, the minimum amount of information that a contemporary computer scientist thinks is worth bothering with. That the nervous system should be supposed to use 50,000 neurons to represent 16 bits' worth of information boggles the mind of an ordinary computer scientist, who looks forward to the day in the not distant future when a conventional computer will represent that much information with fewer than 50,000 molecules. (A molecule occupies roughly 12 orders of magnitude less volume than a neuron.)

If we used a binary scheme to encode locations, we could do it with only 16 neurons. The state of activity (on or off, 1 or 0) of the first 8 would encode the row position (y-axis coordinate in the rectangular environment) and the state of activity of the second 8, the column position (x-axis coordinate). In this scheme, the firing pattern <00000011, 01000000> would represent the same location represented by the firing of a cell 3 rows down and 128 rows over in the Samsonovich and McNaughton scheme. We saw above that when we have recurrent connections, it is easy to have neurons behave in an all or nothing manner, either inactive or active (like switches, or like the flip-flops in an electronic computer). Indeed, when there are recurrent excitatory connections, it is difficult to get neurons to behave in a graded manner. Thus, there can be no objections to binary activity coding on grounds of neural plausibility. Moreover, this scheme does not require us to roll the plane up and curl the resulting tube into a loop, making a segment of a Euclidean plane into the surface of a torus. It does not lead us to make a representation in which one cannot tell from the representation which corner of a rectangle the subject is in.

It might be thought that it would be difficult to construct a reading mechanism if we used a much more efficient binary code to represent current location. But we know that this is not so. The mechanisms that encode and decode into and out of binary code in a conventional computer are made of AND gates and inverters. That neurons can be configured to behave as AND gates is an essential assumption underlying the use of look-up tables to implement combinatorial operations in the Samsonovich and McNaughton model and the many other neural network models that employ look-up tables for this purpose. In fact, here, too, there is room for orders of magnitude reduction in the numbers of neurons used, because implementing the computation with binary machinery is orders of magnitude more efficient than the Samsonovich and McNaughton table-look-up scheme: it will be recalled that the I array, the look-up table, which implements symbol combination, uses many times more neurons than are used in the P array – on the order of 500,000 neurons. Here again, a modest number of AND gates and inverters is all that is needed to implement hard-wired arithmetic with binary numbers.

In thinking about these issues, it is important to bear in mind that the 500,000 neurons in the I array implement the arithmetic combination of the values of the M, H, and P variables and only those variables. The array is hard wired to operate on only those three networks, and those three networks are hard wired to represent only those variables. If we have any other variables that we want to combine in the same way, we need to have other arrays to represent them and another combinatorial array to operate on them. Computation in a neural network is not implemented by compact procedures, as it is in a device with a Turing machine architecture. Therefore, computation lacks what is called productivity (Fodor & Pylyshyn, 1988; Pylyshyn, 1986). It cannot apply the same computation to variables whose existence is not provided for in the hard wiring of the system. Put another way, it cannot produce as an output an answer that the maker of the system did not hard wire into one of its look-up tables. When you create a compact procedure for extracting square roots, it will extract for you the square roots of numbers you never specifically considered in constructing the procedure. When you build a look-up table to extract square roots, it will extract only those roots you put into the table in the first place.

The numbers of neurons used has to matter. First of all, when you add up the neurons in all seven arrays in the Samsonovich and McNaughton model, it comes to something like one million. There are only about that many neurons in the brain of an ant, and an ant is a very good dead reckoner, probably better than the rat. It does not make sense to assume that it uses every neuron in its brain to carry out dead reckoning. It solves many other, much harder computational problems than this. For example, it recognizes landmarks.

Second, and more importantly, the more neurons you use, the more time the computation must take – if we assume the architecture in Figure 14.1. The more neurons in an array, the farther away the average neuron in an array must be from the average neuron in the other arrays that communicate with it in the carrying out of computations. The farther away the communicating neurons are from one another on average, the longer on average it takes for signals to travel between them, and the more energy is expended in transmitting those signals. In the architecture portrayed in Figure 14.1, the computation is implemented by signals traveling back and forth between the different arrays. Thus, the bigger these arrays, the more slowly the computation advances.

In short, a striking thing about the architecture in Figure 14.1 is its prodigal waste of physical resources. Even if we assume that computation at this elementary level is in fact made possible by the manner in which neurons are connected to one another, the architecture in Figure 14.2 uses several orders of magnitude more neurons than other equally feasible architectures. Moreover, it must repeat the waste for every different computation that needs to be accomplished. In a conventional computer, there is only one bit of machinery for combining symbols; it is used over and over again to combine whatever symbols need combining. In the architecture proposed in Figure 14.1, each different simple computation that must be accomplished, each different combination of symbols, requires a different chunk of machinery to do the combining. And each such chunk is composed of tens or hundreds of thousands of neurons. If simple computations like those required for dead reckoning could be carried out within single neurons, then it might make sense to assume that the same computational machinery was replicated thousands of times in order to accomplish the same computation with thousands of different variables. But if every addition and multiplication of a different set of variables requires the dedicated use of another 10,000–100,000 neurons, even brains as large as the mammalian brain will rapidly exhaust their supply of neurons. And they will waste precious time sending signals back and forth between widely separated signal-processing elements. If the goal of cognitive neuroscience is to understand how the computations underlying effective behavior are physically implemented in brains, the architecture in Figure 14.1 is profoundly unsatisfactory. It does not appear to be physically realistic.

Memory again

Another profoundly unsatisfactory aspect of the architecture in Figure 14.1 is the manner in which it solves the read/write memory problem. First, there is a very serious question whether it is physically plausible to assume that information can be carried forward in time within reverberating circuits when time is measured on a scale of minutes to hours, let alone days to years. Samsonovich and McNaughton report that the activity bump in their model could remain stable for at least 6 seconds. Ant foraging journeys can last a half hour and more (1,800 seconds or more) and rat journeys tenfold longer still. We do not believe that anyone believes that it is physically realistic to imagine that information can be reliably preserved in a reverberating circuit over these durations.

Second, and more important, is the extremely limited access to computation provided by the memory architecture in Figure 14.1. The only computational machinery that has access to the information about current location stored in the P array is the I array, and the only computation the I array can perform is the updating of location. Of course, one may readily imagine that neurons in the P array project to other computational arrays as well. But in the architecture of Figure 14.1, the only computations that have access to the information stored in P are the ones that have been foreseen in advance and hard wired into the brain. Note, for example, that the roughly one million neurons whose interconnections are indicated in Figure 14.1 do not enable the brain to compute the home vector, the direction in which the ant must turn and the distance it must run in order to get home. For that computation, we will need to send a projection from the P array to yet another array, an array dedicated to computing the home vector.

Worse yet, there is no provision for remembering the location where the rat now is. When the foraging ant whose track is shown in Figure 11.2 re-emerges from the nest, it does not repeat the random search that led to its discovery of a food location. It goes straight back to the food location. When the foraging bee returns from a food location, it does a dance in which it transmits to other foragers the location of the source from which it has just returned. In other words, even insects remember locations.

By remembering the coordinates of many different locations and the views encountered at those locations, they create a map of their environment, which enables them to navigate from an arbitrary location to another arbitrary location within it. In a machine with a dead-reckoning mechanism (or effective procedure) and a *general-purpose* read/write memory (Turing's tape), a mechanism that enables it to read whatever it has written, there is no mystery about the creation and use of a map.

In terms of the architecture portrayed in Figure 14.1, when the animal encounters a location of interest, it need only record the locus of activity in the P array and the locus of activity in the V array. (The locus of activity in the V array is an encoding of the view.) If it does this for each different location of interest that it encounters, it builds itself a map. But the architecture in Figure 14.1 makes no provision for this. Firstly, because we are now contemplating the preservation of information over a time scale measured in days or longer, a time scale for which reverberating circuit memories are surely inadequate. And secondly, because the memory architecture in Figure 14.1 does not make the stored information generally available. It makes it available only to the particular combinatorial operations with the particular variables that were foreseen at the time when the system was originally wired. This is a critical point, so we spell it out in some detail.

Suppose that we create another V network and another P network – V_2 and P_2 – for the purpose of storing the locus of activity in V and P when the rat finds an interesting location. Those networks can only have one locus of activity at any one time, so they can only store one location and one view. When the rat encounters a second location of interest, there must be a third replication of the V and P networks if it is to remember the coordinates and view and that location. When it encounters a third location, there must be a fourth replication, and so on. Thus, on this architecture, when it remembers 10 different locations and 10 different views, it has 10 different arrays for remembering the coordinates of a location and 10 different view-memory arrays for remembering the encoding of the view at each of those locations. Now suppose it needs to compute the range and bearing of Location 5 from Location 2. On this architecture, it needs an array dedicated in advance (hard wired for) this particular computation. If it needs to compute the range and bearing of Location 7 from Location 2, it needs a different array, likewise dedicated to that particular computation. Indeed, even if it wishes to compute the range and bearing of Location 2 from Location 5 (same trip as in the first computation but in the return direction), it needs a separate array for that. Thus, a memory limited to only 10 locations requires $2\binom{10}{2} = 180$ different prewired arrays to compute the different courses that an animal using that limited map may need to compute. This rapid proliferation of multi-neuron computational chunks occurs because, in the architecture of Figure 14.1, only the machinery hard wired to do a preordained particular computation with a particular set of variables has access to the information stored in a memory array. Unlike Turing's tape, this memory architecture does not make stored information generally accessible. In computer terminology, this architecture requires a different CPU for each different combination of symbols that may need to be carried out. In which case, of course, "central processing unit" is a misnomer. It is called that because in a conventional computing architecture a single (central) processing unit does whatever symbol combining is required.

In considering how implausible it is to use a different neural array composed of thousands of neurons for each different case in which the same two-argument function is to be computed, we must recall that scrub jays remember more than 10,000 different cache locations. A plausible computation that a bird might wish to make is the range and bearing of one remembered cache from another. This is the computation it would make in determining the course to take from a cache it has just emptied to the cache it plans to empty next. Actually, two computations are required, one to extract the bearing (direction in which to fly), and the other the range (how far to fly). In a memory that contains 10,000 locations, there are 20 billion different ordered pairs of locations, that is, 20 billion different range and bearing computations that a bird *might* need to make. If we imagine that there are two distinct nets specific to each possible ordered pair, then we are imagining 40 billion different nets. If each such array contained on the order of 500,000 neurons, the number of neurons that would have to be innately dedicated just to computing how to get from one cache to another would be on the order of $4 \times 10^{10} \times 5 \times 10^5 = 2 \times 10^{16}$, which is to say 20 quadrillion neurons. That is several orders of magnitude more neurons than there are in the human brain, and the brain of a bird has orders of magnitude fewer neurons than the human brain. Moreover, most of those nets would never be used, because in any one lifetime, any one bird will actually compute only a negligible fraction of the ranges and bearings it must be able to compute.

In discussions of why brains make such effective computers despite the supposedly noisy and unreliable hardware, the slow speed of signal propagation, the lack of a read/write memory, and the lack of compact procedures in their functional architecture, appeal is often made to the vast numbers of neurons to be found in brains, the even vaster numbers of synaptic connections between those neurons, and the presumed advantages of having memory somehow reside in modifiable connections between those neurons. Koch and Hepp (2006), for example, write: "The reason for the unprecedented computational power of nervous systems is their high degree of parallelism . . . Furthermore, unlike the von Neumann architecture of the programmable digital computer, the brain intermixes memory elements in the form of modifiable interconnections within the computational substrate, the neuronal membrane. Thus no separate 'fetch' and 'store' cycles are necessary."

In the minds of theorists, large numbers of neurons and the even larger numbers of connections acquire magical powers. Just mentioning these numbers makes profound computational problems dwindle to insignificance. But what a "high degree of parallelism" means, physically speaking, is what we are now discussing: the use of replications of the same computational hardware so that repetitions of the same computation with different variables are carried on by physically distinct parts of the computational machinery. The advantage of parallel computation is that computations do not have to wait their turn; they can all happen at once, precisely because each one is effected by a different part of the machine. The disadvantage is that the amount of hardware required can easily get out of hand. The numbers of neurons in brains, while impressively large, are no match for the numbers of permutations that arise in even very modest problems, like the problem of computing in an instant the range and bearing between an ordered pair chosen at random from 10,000 locations stored in memory, a problem that poses no challenge to a $10 pocket calculator. There are not enough neurons in any brain to allow an architecture in which each such computation is effected by a different neuron, let alone by a different network of neurons.

Making do without a read/write memory, that is, without "fetch" and "store," gets more challenging still when we add temporal information to the location information in memory (when an item was hidden), and information about what was hidden at each location, and information about whether what was hidden has subsequently been retrieved, and information specifying how the state of decay of a hidden item depends on the time elapsed since it was hidden. And then, we require that all of this preserved information be accessible to computations that could not have been foreseen at the time it was stored. The Clayton and Dickinson experiments on episodic memory in the scrub jay bring this challenge to the center of attention, which is why we reviewed them at such length in Chapter 12.

Summary

Dead reckoning is an important behavioral phenomenon because it is experimentally well documented and computationally well understood and it seems to require a mechanism for carrying information about position forward in time in a computationally accessible form. In a computational machine that has a symbolic read/write memory, this computation poses no problems. In a computational machine with the functional architecture of a neural network, it poses a severe challenge. It makes us confront the difficulty we face in trying to understand the computational capacity of brains – even insect brains – within the constraints imposed by our current understanding of the functional architecture of the nervous system. From one perspective, the Samsonovich and McNaughton neural network model – discussed here because it is representative of a large class of models – may be seen as demonstrating that the challenge can be met. From another perspective – our perspective – it may be seen as demonstrating in detail how severe the challenge is and how implausible are the proffered solutions to it.

15

Neural Models of Interval Timing

Gibbon's (1977) Scalar Expectancy Theory (SET), which is the dominant psychological model of interval timing, assumes a read/write memory. The output from a startable and resettable timer, representing the duration of a timed interval, is written to memory at the conclusion of the interval, when the timer is reset. When the event that started the timer recurs, the interval timer starts timing again from zero, generating a ramp signal. The height of the ramp at any moment represents the duration of the interval elapsed up to that moment. The duration previously written to memory is read from memory to form the denominator of a comparison ratio, with the ramp as its numerator. The momentary value of the ratio represents the increasing proportion between the currently elapsing interval and the reference interval retrieved from memory. When the proportion exceeds a decision criterion, the animal begins to respond.

Timing an Interval on First Encounter

The initial identification of the intervals to be timed poses conceptual and practical problems for this model. The model in effect assumes that the subject already knows that a given stimulus predicts a given event at some fixed interval. But how does the animal come to know this? How does it deploy its interval timers when it does not yet know what follows what? The infinitude of the possible lurks here. At any moment, there are a potentially infinite number of "interesting" intervals elapsing (intervals of potential behavioral importance), but the system cannot have an infinite number of timers running. Suppose a subject finding itself in a novel environment observes a light come on, followed somewhat later by tone, then by food delivery, and finally by shock. There are reasons to believe that the subject learns all of the intervals: the interval from light onset to light offset, the interval from light onset to tone onset, the interval from light offset to tone onset, the interval from light onset to food onset, and so on (see Figure 15.1).

In this catalog of intervals, there are six that begin with the light onset (Figure 15.1). Are we to assume that when the light onset was first observed, the brain started six timers running, resetting one to zero when the light went off (and writing its

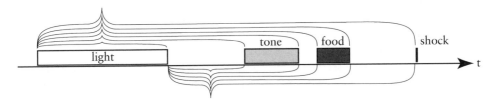

Figure 15.1   A modest number of events define a great many intervals. In this figure, there are 4 events. Only the 11 intervals that begin with either light onset or light offset are indicated. If predictable (repeated) intervals are recognized by means of resettable interval timers, the problem is to know how many such timers should be set running at the first occurrence of a light onset.

final reading to memory), resetting the second when the tone came on, resetting the third when the tone went off, and so on? How did it know that only six would be needed? In pondering this question, it is important to bear in mind that subjects routinely learn the intervals between motivationally neutral stimuli, like tone onsets and light onsets, intervals that may never become behaviorally relevant (e.g., Barnet, Cole, & Miller, 1997). This is important because it implies that at any time there are many different intervals elapsing that may or may not prove behaviorally important. Using interval timers that are started, stopped, and reset in order to identify the temporal structure of experience – what predicts what at what intervals – would seem to require the animal to have an arbitrarily large number of timers running at any one moment. The problem is not that the number of intervals defined grows as the square of the number of events (onsets and offsets) that define them (although this does suggest that the range of events whose temporal relations can be computed is in some way restricted). The problem is the infinitude of the possible. The brain would have to set timers running to measure all the intervals that might occur but in fact do not, that is, all the potential intervals, as opposed only to the intervals actually experienced. As we will see, this is also a problem with neurobiologically inspired models that try to explain timing by changes in the strengths of connections between neurons with prespecified post-stimulation dynamics.

An alternative approach to the computational problem of identifying predictable temporal relations between numerous possible events, which avoids the computational explosion inherent in the infinitude of possible intervals, is to record times of occurrence and extract repeated fixed intervals from these records by post-hoc computation (see Gallistel, 1990, pp. 311ff.). In this approach, the interval from Event 1 to Event 2 is obtained not from an interval timer, but rather by subtracting the time of occurrence of Event 1 from the time of occurrence of Event 2.

The clock from which times of occurrence are obtained in this model runs continuously; it is never reset. This model assumes that the brain has the functional equivalent of the internal clock in a conventional computer, an internal representation of the time elapsed between a reference moment in the distant past and the current moment. Gallistel (1990, ch. 9) suggested that a plausible way to time-stamp the records of events is to record the momentary phases of a number of oscillators whose periods range from very short (a second or less) to very long (on the order of twice the expected lifetime of the subject). Since then, behavioral evidence suggestive of such a scheme has been found (Crystal, 2001).

The assumption that the brain has an internal time-keeping system that can provide times-of-occurrence seems far-fetched, but there is extensive experimental evidence that animals ranging from insects to birds routinely do encode the times of occurrence of events (Gallistel, 1990, ch. 9). The results from the food-caching experiments reviewed in Chapter 12 imply that the birds in those experiments in effect recorded the date and time at which they made a cache. How else could they know how long it had been since they made that cache?

Dworkin's Paradox

There is another line of evidence from a very different and more physiological source. Dworkin (1993) reviews the behavioral and physiological literature on homeostatic regulation, emphasizing the fundamental role that learning plays in homeostasis, that is, in the preservation of the internal environment, the environment of the cells of which the body is composed. Dworkin is an authority on the properties of interoreceptors, the sensory neurons that monitor the internal variables that are held constant by homeostatic mechanisms (Dworkin, 2007). He calls attention to the following paradox: homeostatic behavior depends on knowledge of the current values of physiological variables that change slowly or infrequently. However, interoreceptors, like sensory neurons in general, signal the changes in the variables they monitor, not their steady state; hence, not their current value (Figure 15.2). How, Dworkin asks, does the brain know the current values of the variables it is regulating, given that it receives no signals indicative of those values? He does not offer an answer, but he stresses the fundamental importance of the question.

A communications engineer would appreciate the logic. The information necessary to compute the current value of a variable is contained in a record of the changes in that value, just as the information necessary to specify where one is relative to a starting point is contained in and computable from the record of one's step-by-displacements (the principle underlying dead reckoning). The current value is the initial value plus the sum of all the changes. Therefore, signaling the steady-state values of variables is a waste of signal energy and signal-processing resources. It is more efficient to signal only the changes. However, this works only if the receiver has a read/write memory, which it can use to keep a computationally accessible record of those changes. If all that is needed is the current value, then the only thing that need be kept in the read/write memory is the current value of the sum.

If all that the brain requires for regulatory purposes is the current values of the variables, the integrals (running sums) can be computed as the system advances in time; records of past changes need not be kept. If, however, the system is to anticipate predictable challenges to its steady state, based on its past experience, then it will need to keep a time-stamped record of the changes. Dworkin (1993) reviews the extensive evidence that animals do learn to anticipate predictable challenges to

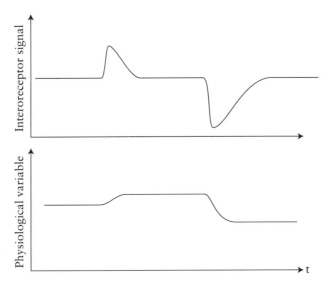

Figure 15.2 The Dworkin paradox. Interoreceptor signals specify changes in the values of the variables that they monitor, not the steady state, but regulatory responses depend on the steady-state values. How does the brain know the steady-state values? A possible answer comes from the observation that the lower curve (current value versus time) is the integral of the upper curve (sensory signal versus time).

the internal environment. For similar evidence that they learn to anticipate predictable pharmacologically induced changes, see Siegel (1999; Siegel & Allan, 1998).

Neurally Inspired Models

Both SET and the Gallistel model (computed differences in time of occurrence) assume a read/write memory. In SET, timer readings are written to memory at interval offset and read from it when a reference value for a currently elapsing interval is required. In the computed difference model, times of occurrence are written to memory and read from memory during the computation of the observed differences in event times, that is, the intervals between events. As Hopson (2003), in a useful review of timing models, points out, "whereas the oscillators [that figure in these models] are very neural, the learning and memory systems . . . are not. The state of the array [of oscillators] is stored, retrieved and acted upon in a representational rather than associational manner" (p. 30). Again, we see in this quotation the equation of associative theories of learning and memory with neurobiologically plausible models. Hopson takes it for granted that a neurobiologically plausible model must treat the memory mechanism not as a read/write mechanism, a mechanism whose function is to carry information forward in time, but rather as a change in state, a rewiring, of the mechanism that generates actions. Hopson is concerned to elaborate a model

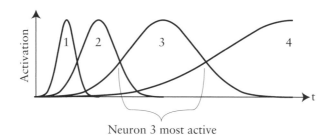

Figure 15.3   Illustrative firing dynamics of the first four neurons in the kind of spectral timing array assumed by Grossberg and Schmajuk (1989). The origin is at stimulus onset. The neurons exhibit a spectrum of dynamic, with the firing rate of each different neuron in the array peaking at a different time. When a response to the start stimulus that activated the array is reinforced, the most active neuron in the array becomes associated with that response. The braces indicate the post-stimulus interval over which Neuron 3 is the most active. At the conclusion of the interval, the stop stimulus increments the associative connection between each neuron in the array and the output neuron in proportion to each neuron's level of activity; the more active a neuron is at that moment, the greater the increment in its connection to the output neuron.

of timed behavior that depends only on a general-purpose associative learning mechanism, a mechanism that changes the conductive connections between notional neurons in a network that transmits signals from inputs to outputs. In this chapter, we review some of the more prominent models of this kind. What emerges is that these models have the same computational implausibilities that are evident in attempts to model dead reckoning without recourse to a read/write memory mechanism. In particular, they require the allocation in advance of prespecified physical resources (multi-neuron timing networks) for all possible intervals between all possible pairs of events. Thus, they do not scale; they are crushed by the infinitude of the possible. Secondly, information about previously experienced intervals, insofar as it can be said to be preserved by the enduring physical changes those experiences produced (the associations), is not readable; it is not accessible to computation.

An influential neurally oriented associative theory of timing is Grossberg and Schmajuk's (1989) spectral timing model (STM). It assumes that any stimulus whose temporal relation to a reinforcing event can be learned activates an array of neurons, whose activity (firing rate) rises and falls over some interval. The interval spanned by this rise and fall varies from neuron to neuron within the array. Thus, the neurons within the timing array for a specific stimulus exhibit a spectrum of dynamics (Figure 15.3).

The model assumes that when a response (for example pecking a key) produces reinforcement (the appearance of food), the increment in associative strength between any neuron in the array and the motor neurons whose firing mediates the production of the reinforced response increases as a monotonic function of that neuron's activity. The braces in Figure 15.3 indicate the interval after stimulus onset during which Neuron 3 is the most active neuron. Reinforcement (e.g., the opening of a food hopper) during this interval increments the associative connection between Neuron 3 and the pecking response more than it increments the associative connection between the less active neurons and that response. When the stimulus that (by prespecification) activates this array recurs, the activities again rise and fall according to their innate dynamics. Early on in conditioning, after relatively few trials, the neurons whose firing peaks close to the time at which reinforcement has previously been given have formed correspondingly stronger associations. Therefore, the postsynaptic signal in the population of output neurons peaks at the interval at which reinforcement has been given. Appropriate thresholding of this signal gives a response at approximately the appropriate time.

In this model, the strengths of the associations to the more active neurons grow more rapidly during training, which is why timed responding is seen early in training. However, the strengths of the associations to the less active neurons also grow – and to the same asymptote. Thus, asymptotically – after many trials – all the neurons in the array become equally strongly connected to the output neurons, and the model no longer gives a timed response. This is strongly at variance with well-established experimental fact: Response timing does not get worse with increased training. Indeed, it is common in timing experiments to run thousands of trials. Grossberg and Schmajuk suggest that this defect can be remedied by adding a slow passive temporal decay term to the delta-rule differential equation that describes the connection-strengthening. This, however, would make the model forget what it has learned about the timing simply as a function of the passage of time. Again, this is at variance with experimental fact. Subjects in timing experiments remember the intervals more or less indefinitely.

One could fix the problem by changing the assumed association-forming mechanism. One might postulate a winner-take-all mechanism in which the only the most active neuron's output synapses get strengthened. Or, one might postulate a competitive Rescorla-Wagner type strengthening mechanism. In the Rescorla-Wagner model of the association-forming process, the strengths (synaptic weights) of all the competing associations are summed and their sum is subtracted from an innately specified quantity that represents the asymptotic value of this sum, the value to which it must eventually converge (from either below or above). In a competitive association-forming process, the associations that rise rapidly crowd out the more slowly rising associations. In the limit, at asymptote, the strength of the single strongest association becomes equal to the asymptotic net associative strength. When the strength of this one association is subtracted from the asymptotic quantity, the difference is zero, and so the other associations are not incremented.

The commitment to some kind of neural plausibility is an obstacle to the adoption of either of these solutions. In the winner-take-all model, the mechanism that strengthens the conductance (synaptic weight) at one output synapse must receive information about the activity levels at all the other synapses. How does it get this critical information? How does it determine whether any one of the other activity levels exceeds the local activity level? And how does that determination block the change in synaptic conductance when the activity level somewhere else exceeds the local activity level? In postulating the competitive model, one must ask how the local mechanism "knows" the strengths of the other synapses? Other elements of the brain do not have access to the strength of a synapse. The postsynaptic elements do not know the strength of the synapse through which a signal has been received, because the strength of the signal received confounds the strength of the synapse with the strength of the presynaptic signal. What is it in the local mechanism that represents the maximum possible asymptotic value of that sum? How is the sum of the other strengths determined and how is it subtracted from its maximum possible asymptotic value to get the difference that determines the magnitude of the local increment or decrement in synaptic conductance? None of these questions is easy. In posing them one calls attention to the formidable obstacles that stand in the way of reconciling the behavioral evidence for ubiquitous interval timing with the contemporary understanding of neurobiology (cf. Miall, 1996).

The commitment to neural plausibility among modelers for whom this is an important consideration is, however, elastic. For example, Hopson (2003) gives a short and thoughtful review of previous models, in which neurobiological plausibility is a significant consideration (see above quote). He then advances a model of his own, in which the synaptic weights are adjusted by back propagation. Back propagation is notable for both its psychological and its neurobiological implausibility. It is psychologically implausible in that it assumes an omniscient tutor that knows what the output of the neural network ought to have been. (Of course, this makes it neurobiologically implausible as well.) It is neurobiologically implausible in that the adjustment of the weights is done by a god outside the system. The weight-adjusting algorithm computes the contribution of each connection to the observed error, that is, to the discrepancy between the output pattern that ought to have occurred and the one that in fact did occur. (To do that, it also needs to know what those weights are.) It adjusts each weight in the light of its computed contribution to that error. The back-propagation algorithm is not itself implemented within the constraints of the neural plausibility that is otherwise insisted on. Moreover, it makes full and frank use of the computational machinery of a conventional computer, including most particularly its read/write memory.

Miall (1989, 1992) has advanced a "beat" model in which the interval elapsed since a synchronizing start signal is represented by the subset of oscillators that are momentarily in phase (Figure 15.4). A similar model has been suggested by Mattell and Meck (2000). In this model, the event that starts the timer synchronizes the oscillations of an array of oscillators. The period of each oscillator within the array is somewhat different from that of each other oscillator. Therefore, the oscillators soon go out of phase, that is, their outputs no longer coincide in time. As they continue to oscillate, different combinations "beat" (come back into momentary phase agreement) at different intervals.

The beat principle is used by piano tuners. The tuner sounds a tuning fork whose frequency of oscillation is known to be correct and simultaneously sounds the corresponding note on the piano. If the note sounded has a slightly different frequency (an incorrect frequency), one hears beats as the sound waves created by the vibrating tuning fork and by the vibrating piano string come into and out of phase. When waves from the two sources are in phase, they reinforce each other ("constructive interference"), making a louder sound; when they are out of phase, they cancel each other ("destructive interference"), making a weaker sound. The period of the beats

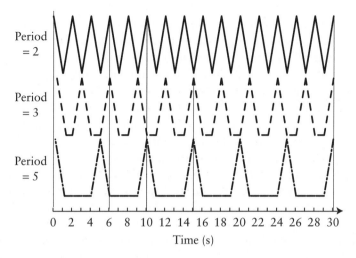

Figure 15.4 The principle underlying beat-frequency models of the interval timer. When three oscillators (pacemaker neurons), with periods of 2, 3, and 5 seconds, are synchronized at 0 seconds (interval onset), different subsets come into phase again at different intervals thereafter (see thin vertical lines linking the peaks of in-phase oscillators).

is the common denominator of the two periods, the shortest interval into which both periods go an integer number of times.

In Figure 15.4, the oscillators have periods of 2, 3, and 5 seconds. The first two oscillators come back into phase at $2 \times 3 = 6$ seconds; the first and third at $2 \times 5 = 10$ seconds; the second and third at $3 \times 5 = 15$ seconds; and all three at $2 \times 3 \times 5 = 30$ seconds. Miall supposes that the entire array synapses on a common postsynaptic neuron, which gets a signal from the reinforcing event that terminates the interval being timed. The temporal coincidence between the firing of the postsynaptic neuron by this reinforcing signal and the firing of a subset of pacemaker neurons strengthens the synaptic connection between that subset and the postsynaptic neuron. This strengthening is somehow normalized and thresholded so that the postsynaptic effect of spikes in the array is superthreshold (fires the output neuron) only when spikes from the entire subset coincide. Thus, on subsequent occasions, when the start event resynchronizes the array of pacemaker neurons, the output neuron will fire at the end of the previously experienced interval. The normalization of efficacy across the subpopulation of pacemakers whose connection to the output was strengthened is essential to the model. It is necessary to prevent the in-phase firing of a subset from firing the output prematurely. The mechanism by which this normalization is achieved is not specified.

Miall (1996) calls attention to two advantages of this model: First, it can time intervals much longer than the period of any of the pacemaker neurons in the array. This may be seen in the illustrative example in Figure 15.4, which can time an interval of 30 seconds even though the longest pacemaker period is only 5 seconds.

Secondly, the coding efficiency in the generation of the time signal is much greater than in the spectral model, where there is a different neuron for each small difference in duration. Grossberg and Schmajuk assume 80 different dynamic spectra (thus 80 different neurons) to cover a range from a few milliseconds up to 1.8 seconds. Using 80 pacemakers in the beat scheme one could in principle encode a much greater range of possible intervals with comparable precision. This is a consideration of some importance, because, as Miall (1996) points out, one of the problems facing any attempt to understand animals' interval-timing capability within the constraints imposed by our current understanding of neurobiology is the radical difference in time scales. The time scale of neurobiological events, including the periods between impulses in pacemaker neurons, is small fractions of a second to a few seconds, but the time scale for the interval timing capacity manifest in behavior ranges from a fraction of a second to hours, days and even, in all likelihood, years. The time scale assumed in Grossberg and Schmajuk's (1989) simulation of their spectral model is neurobiologically realistic in having an upper limit of 1.8 seconds. However, it excludes most of the range over which interval timing has been behaviorally demonstrated.

Miall (1996) suggests that an additional advantage of this model is that the same array can encode (remember) many different intervals. Here, however, it runs afoul of what is called the assignment of credit problem. In order for the same array to encode multiple interevent intervals, the different starting events for these different intervals must all be able to synchronize that array, and the different interval-terminating events must all provide a synapse-strengthening stop signal to the postsynaptic neuron. The problem then is that the representation of the interval's duration is decoupled from the representation of the events that mark its onset and offset. The synchronization of the array no longer implies the occurrence of any particular starting event and the firing of the array when one of the previously associated subsets comes back into synchrony no longer coincides with the occurrence of any particular interval-terminating event. Thus, an essential feature of any data structure, a means of representing what relates to what, is lost.

Miall (1996) points out that a problem with this model is its hypersensitivity to small changes in the periods of the pacemakers within the array. For example, adding just 0.1 second to the periods of the two most rapid oscillations, changing their values by 5% or less, from 2 and 3 to 2.1 and 3.1, changes their beat period by an order of magnitude from 6 seconds to 65.1 seconds. Thus, the model only works if one assumes that there is essentially no variability in the periods of its pacemakers. That is not a reasonable assumption, as Miall acknowledges.

Another problem is that the model does not capture an essential characteristic of timed behavior: it is anticipatory; the animal begins to respond well before the end of the interval being timed. Generally speaking, it responds when some more or less fixed proportion of the interval has elapsed. To illustrate this, Figure 15.5 plots the probability that pigeons pecking on a fixed-interval schedule of reinforcement have resumed pecking as a proportion of the interval that has elapsed since the previous reinforcement. In a fixed-interval schedule, there is a fixed interval following each reinforcement (each brief period of access to the grain hopper) during which pecking the illuminated key on the wall of the test chamber will not produce

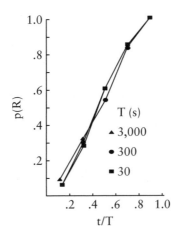

Figure 15.5 The probability that pecking has resumed as a function of the proportion of the fixed interval that has elapsed in pigeons pecking for food reinforcement on fixed-interval schedules of reinforcement. T = the fixed interval; t = the time elapsed since the last reinforcement (last brief access to the grain hopper); p(R) = probability that pecking has resumed (the rate of pecking, once it has resumed, is nearly constant). (Data are from Dews, 1970; the plot is based on a plot of Dews' data in Gibbon, 1977, reproduced by permission.)

renewed access to the food. The first peck following the termination of this fixed interval produces renewed access to the food. Pigeons learn not to peck in the period immediately following the last access, when pecking is futile. They resume pecking after some proportion of the fixed interval has elapsed. Exactly when they resume pecking varies from one inter-reinforcement interval to the next. Thus, when one averages over many such repetitions of the inter-reinforcement interval, one gets a plot in which the probability of pecking increases as the proportion of the interval elapsed increases. In the experiments by Dews (1970), the data from which are plotted in Figure 15.5, the fixed interval for one small group of pigeons was 30 seconds (half a minute); for another, it was 300 seconds (5 minutes); and for the third 3,000 seconds (50 minutes). The striking thing about this plot is that the function relating the probability of resumed pecking to the proportion of the fixed interval that has elapsed is invariant over a 2 order of magnitude change in the fixed interval, from half a minute to 50 minutes. Regardless of the duration of the fixed interval, the probability that a pigeon had resumed pecking exceeded 0.5 when about half the interval had elapsed.

The results in Figure 15.5 are unintelligible on Miall's model of the timing process, because his timing array gives no indication of how much of the interval being timed has elapsed. These results are in principle intelligible on the spectral timing model, because the interval of suprathreshold activity for the most strongly associated neuron may (under some parametric assumptions) span a range from well before the end of the target interval (T in Figure 15.5) to well after. However, the intervals involved are all 2 or 3 orders of magnitude longer than those modeled by

Grossberg and Schmajuk (1989), which is to say that they lie well outside the range of plausible firing rate dynamics. They require neurons whose response to a transient event does not peak until almost an hour after the event. This is the timescale problem that Miall (1996) calls attention to. It should also be recalled that the spectral model only works early in training before the more slowly growing associative strengths catch up with those that grow more rapidly.

The Deeper Problems

Despite their neurobiological orientation, one may question the neurobiological plausibility of these models. And their psychological adequacy – their ability to explain the results of the large literature on interval timing, as it is manifest in animal behavior – leaves much to be desired. What we now emphasize, however, are the deeper problems in these models, the problems that stem directly from their avoiding recourse to a read/write memory. We call these the deeper problems because we believe they are inescapable; they grow directly out of the assumption that brains do not have a read/write memory. The commitment to neurobiological plausibility among those attempting to build neurally "inspired" models of many behavioral phenomena is not so much a positive commitment to using only neurobiologically plausible mechanisms. If it were, then back propagation would not be the learning mechanism assumed in the great majority of such efforts. Rather, it is a negative commitment, a commitment to not using a read/write (symbolic) memory. The problems we now highlight are the problems that flow directly from that negative commitment. They are by now familiar problems: the inability to cope with the infinitude of the possible and the lack of computational accessibility.

Like neurally inspired models of dead reckoning, neurally inspired models of interval timing allot in advance different physical resources (arrays of neurons) to every different interval that the animal may ever need to time, that is, to all possible intervals of demonstrated behavioral relevance (all the intervals that we know that some animal somewhere may time). The problem is that the resources available to be allocated are finite while the set of possible intervals is for all practical purposes infinite. In the spectral-timing model, for each different event that may mark the onset of an interval to be timed and for each different event that may mark its offset and for each different interval that may elapse between each such pair[1] – thus for all possible triplets of onset marker, offset marker, and interval – there has to be a different array of neurons. The dynamics of the neurons in each different array must duplicate the dynamics of the neurons in every other such array. Each such array must contain a neuron whose firing rises and falls in a few milliseconds, another whose firing rate rises and falls in a few tens of milliseconds, and so on up to – abandoning altogether a commitment to neural plausibility – a neuron whose firing rate rises and falls over a span of a year. These allocations must be made in advance, even though the vast majority of the arrays thus allocated will never in fact be used,

---

[1] Animals readily learn more than one interval between the same two marker events.

because the triplet of onset event, offset event, and interval for which they provide, while certainly possible, will never occur in the lifetime of that particular animal. In the jargon of computer science, these models do not scale. The demands they make on physical resources in order to cope with even a modest fraction of the reality with which they must in fact cope are unsatisfiable. There just are not enough neurons. The number of neurons in a brain, however large it may be, is no match for the infinitude of the possible. Moreover, the neurons in a brain are needed for other tasks. The whole brain cannot be given over to interval timing any more than the whole brain can be given over to dead reckoning.

The second problem is that they do not carry information about the intervals between events forward in time in a computationally accessible form. The associations that form in interval-timing models do not themselves encode either the durations of the intervals or the events that mark their onsets and offsets. Longer intervals do not give rise to stronger (or weaker associations) in a manner that would enable an associative decoder to recover the interval simply from the pattern of associative strengths that it produced. The information about interval duration resides not in the strength of the association that a given neuron in the array has made with the output neuron, but rather in the dynamics of that neuron. In order to recover the interval represented by the associative strengths in the spectral model, the decoder would need to know the dynamics of each neuron, but other neurons do not have access to this. Thus, there is no way in which the interval between events A and B may be added or subtracted from the interval between events B and C to get the interval between A C. But we know that brains do just this; they compute with intervals (Barnet, Arnold, & Miller, 1991; Barnet & Miller, 1996; Cole, Barnet, & Miller, 1995).

Another manifestation of the computational character of interval timing is the fact that food-caching jays can estimate how long it has been since they made a particular cache. They can compare this estimate to the rotting interval that they have learned for the kind of food they put in that cache (Clayton et al., 2006; see Chapter 12). These models provide no insight into how this might be possible. In this regard, they stand in marked contrast to SET, the dominant information-processing model of interval timing. Like other information-processing models, it takes the existence of a symbolic read/write memory for granted. It also assumes that the time signal is in a readable accumulator. Thus, it routinely assumes that the values of elapsing intervals are compared to values retrieved from memory.

As we noted at the outset, SET itself falls victim to the infinitude of the possible when considered as a model for how animals discover predictable intervals between events. It does so because of its reliance on resettable interval timers. However, a model in which predictable intervals are discovered by retrospective computations on recorded event times conquers the infinitude of the possible because it only has to have memory resources adequate to record the events it actually does observe and to record the predictable intervals that it actually does experience. As always, the set of events and predictable intervals between events that any one animal will ever experience, while large, is emphatically finite and incomparably less numerous than the essentially infinite set of events and predictable intervals between events that any animal might experience.

16

The Molecular Basis of Memory

The question of the physical basis of memory is one of the great questions in the life sciences. It has been recognized as such for more than a century. In Chapter 10, we quoted Christopher Koch to the effect that for over a century the leading hypothesis of both theoreticians and experimentalists has been that the physical realization of memory in the brain was an enduring change of some kind wrought by experience in the conductance of a synapse. This is the synaptic plasticity hypothesis. However, as Koch notes, it has proved extremely difficult to establish a convincing link between the behavioral manifestations of memory and its biophysical substrate. The upshot is that ". . . the notion that synaptic plasticity is the primary substrate of long-term learning and memory must at present be viewed as our most plausible hypothesis" (Koch, 1999, p. 308).

We could go farther and say that it is not only the most plausible hypothesis, it is the only hypothesis that has ever been seriously entertained by the community of researchers interested in the physical basis of memory. By our lights, that is the problem. The reason that after a century of determined effort by armies of investigators we still do not have a convincing story about the physical basis of memory is the plasticity hypothesis itself. It fundamentally misrepresents the nature of what it is we should be looking for.

The Need to Separate Theory of Memory from Theory of Learning

We argued in Chapter 11 that this misrepresentation of the nature of memory derives from a longstanding misrepresentation of the nature of learning within psychology. Because of its historical roots in the empiricist philosophy of mind, psychology has conceptualized learning as the remolding of a plastic brain by experience. On this view, learning and memory are one and the same process. Learning is the remolding process; and the remolded brain embodies memory in the altered connections that experience has produced. That explains why Koch takes synaptic plasticity to be an hypothesis that explains *both* learning and memory.

On the view that we have argued for, learning is the extraction from experience of behaviorally useful information, while memory is the mechanism by which information is carried forward in time in a computationally accessible form. On this view, it is hard to see how one could have a single hypothesis about the physical basis of both learning and memory. The physical basis for one could not be the physical basis for the other. One could know with certainty what the mechanism was that carried information forward in time in a computationally accessible form, but have no idea what the mechanism was that extracted a particular piece of information from some class of experience. Computer scientists know the mechanisms that carry information forward in time within a computer, but this knowledge does not tell them how to compute a parsing of video input useful to a robot trying to recognize objects of a given kind. Conversely, one might believe with some certainty that one had correctly identified the neurobiological machinery that extracted a particular kind of information from a particular kind of experience, but have no idea how the nervous system was able to carry that information forward in time in such a way that it was accessible whenever it was needed in some later computation. This is pretty much the situation in which researchers who study mechanisms of sensory processing find themselves. Their focus is on the mechanisms by which the brain computes properties of distal stimuli from the sensory signals generated by proximal stimuli. They do not concern themselves with the question how the information thus extracted may be preserved for later use.

The Coding Question

The importance of correctly characterizing the nature of memory lies in the fact that this characterization determines what properties a proposed mechanism of memory must possess. If a memory mechanism is understood to be a mechanism that carries information forward in time in a computationally accessible form, then the first and most basic property that a proposed mechanism must possess is the ability to carry information. The synaptic plasticity hypothesis in any of its historically recognizable forms fails this first test. There is no way to use this mechanism in order to encode the values of variables in a computationally accessible form. That is why whenever the need arises in neural network modeling to carry values forward in time – and the need arises almost everywhere – recourse is had to reverberating activity loops. That is also why one can search in vain through the vast literature on the neurobiological mechanisms of memory for any discussion of the coding question. The question "How could one encode a number using changes in synaptic conductances?" has, so far as we know, never even been posed. And yet, if our characterization of the nature of memory is correct, then this is the very first question that should arise whenever suggestions are entertained about the physical identity of memory in the brain.

It is important to realize that this is a well-posed question to which unequivocal answers can readily be suggested. Suppose, for example, that one were to suggest that the memory mechanism co-opted some of the molecular machinery by which phylogenetically acquired information is transmitted from generation to generation. If alterations in nucleotide sequences in either DNA or RNA were a proposed mechanism of memory, then the answer to the coding question would be immediately apparent: How to encode a number in a nucleotide sequence is no mystery. The mystery is how to construct machinery that could effect the encoding. We have no idea what the machinery might look like that would transcribe information from a spike train into a nucleotide sequence. How to gain access to the encoded number is also a mystery. We have no idea what the machinery might look like that would transcribe a nucleotide sequences into a spike train. But how it is that a nucleotide sequence could in principle encode a number is no mystery at all. Thus, such a proposal, wild as it is, passes the test that the synaptic plasticity hypothesis fails. And that is progress. Because there is no point in pondering how to transcribe information from spike trains into some enduring physical change if there does not appear to be any way for that enduring physical change to carry information. You cannot transcribe information into a medium that cannot hold information.

A second example of a possible memory mechanism that again answers the first question is a molecule like rhodopsin. Rhodopsin is a photon-activated molecular switch. It has two different configurations (isomeres). The absorption of a photon flips the switch from what might be regarded as its "open" (inactive) state to its "closed" (active) state. Both states are thermodynamically stable; no matter which state the switch is in, the system does not have to expend energy maintaining it in that state. This is highly desirable in a basic memory element from which one is to imagine constructing a memory system capable of storing large amounts of information. It stands in marked contrast to suggestions that memories are maintained in reverberating activity loops. One would have thought that the extravagant waste of energy in any such system would have been enough to have long ago taken such suggestions off the table, but, as we saw in Chapter 14, this is far from the case.

When we have settable molecular switches at our disposal, there is again no mystery about how to use them to encode a number. So this suggested mechanism passes the first test. It is not so hard to imagine transcription mechanisms from spike trains to settings of these switches and from those settings back to spike trains. The transcription from these switch settings to spike trains is what the first two stages of neural processing in the retina effect. We understand a lot about the mechanisms by which information about the number of photons captured by the molecular elements of the photosensitive array inside a rod are converted to the spike trains in ganglion cells that carry that information to the brain for further processing. It is also not hard to imagine how a spike train releasing transmitter onto a metabotropic receptor could set in motion an intracellular molecular cascade that changed the settings of intracellular molecular switches. Metabotropic receptors give external signals access to the cell's internal signal system, which is much richer and more complex than one would realize from most standard texts in neuroscience.

So, are we suggesting that the memory mechanism is a change in nucleotide sequences or some other ingenious adaptation of the molecular machinery that is already known to have an information-carrying function? Or are we suggesting the mechanism is a bistable molecular switch like rhodopsin? No. We refuse to make any specific hypotheses about the molecular basis of memory, because we have no faith in our ability to guess the answer to this profound mystery. We do think that both suggestions should be given some consideration, if for no other reason than that such consideration may lead to more promising or plausible alternative suggestions. At the very least, considering these suggestions brings the coding question into the center of attention, which is where it belongs in any discussion of the physical basis of memory.

A Cautionary Tale

In our reluctance to speculate about the molecular mechanism of memory we are greatly influenced by the history of molecular genetics. Before Watson and Crick (1953) deduced the structure of DNA, the gene was such a profound biochemical puzzle that a substantial minority of biochemists doubted its physical reality (Judson, 1980). They thought genetic theory was a physically unrealizable fantasy founded on a biochemically unrealizable entity, the gene. A gene was assumed to have two utterly mysterious properties: it could make a copy of itself and it could direct (not catalyze, but actually direct) the synthesis of other molecules. Because the properties of a gene assumed by geneticists made no biochemical sense, some biochemists simply refused to believe in its physical reality, despite what I think almost anyone in retrospect would argue was a very large body of evidence and theory arguing that there had to be such a thing. Even some geneticists were content to regard genes as just a convenient way of talking about the huge body of experimental facts that had grown up around the study of patterns of inheritance.

Other biochemists were persuaded by the geneticists' data and theory that there must in fact be genes, that they were the sort of thing for which one could hope to have a biochemical account. They speculated about the biochemical nature of the gene. What impresses us is that, so far as we know, none of these speculations got close to the mark. The solution was beyond the power of pre-1953 biochemists to imagine. And yet, it was dazzlingly simple. When one looked at the structure suggested by Watson and Crick (1953), the scales fell from one's eyes. It was apparent that here in principle was the solution to both mysteries. The two strands, with their complementary sequences of nucleotides, immediately suggested how *this* molecule might make a copy of itself, as Watson and Crick noted in their famously coy one-sentence penultimate paragraph. It was also clear that this structure was in principle capable of encoding any information one liked, including, a fortiori, information about the sequence of amino acids in a protein. In fact, the structure immediately put the coding question at the center of the discussion for those alert to the profound importance of what Watson and Crick had achieved (Judson, 1980). As in the contemporary neuroscience of memory, the coding question can be said to have hardly existed prior to the revelation of the structure of DNA. Coding questions and answers thereto are now, of course, embedded in the foundations of molecular biology.

Why Not Synaptic Conductance?

In our experience, it is easier to persuade people that memory is a mechanism that carries information forward in time in a computationally accessible form – and that the coding question is indeed a question that must be answered – than it is to persuade them that it is, *therefore*, unlikely that changes in synaptic conductance are the mechanism of memory. The synaptic plasticity hypothesis has a truly formidable grip on people's imagination. They have great difficulty imagining that it could not be true. They always want to know, at this point in the discussion, why could the mechanism not be changes in synaptic conductance? The short answer is that, of course, it could be. But we think that it is not a likely possibility. Here is why.

First, if we go there, we have to give up the underlying idea that we can identify a change in synaptic conductance with the traditional notion of an associative bond. Associative bonds clearly cannot encode information. No associative theory ever propounded specifies encoding and decoding rules for associations, rules that would enable a reader who knew the encoding rule to deduce from the vector of association strengths the states of the world that created those association strengths. It is no accident that associative theories have always been anti-representational. They have always been so because associations were never conceived of in such a way that would enable them to function as symbols, that is, as entities that carry information forward in time by virtue of their enduring physical form.

Second, and closely related to the first point, we would have to change fundamentally the traditional conception of the architecture in which these putative memory elements (changeable synaptic conductances) are assumed to be embedded. If our story is going to be that there exists a mechanism that transcribes the information in a spike train into changes in synaptic conductances in such a way as to preserve that information, then the traditional considerations about the role of temporal pairing become irrelevant. The information in spike trains may very well reside in the intervals between the spikes (Rieke et al., 1997); indeed, we think it does reside there. But assuming that does not give us a story about how that information is transcribed into an enduring physical change that preserves the information in a computationally accessible form. There is no reason to assume that the process would bear any resemblance to the processes traditionally assumed to mediate changes in synaptic conductance. We would also have to assume that in order to access the information encoded in the synaptic conductances, the system probes the synaptic conductances with a read signal. We *can* assume all these things; indeed, if we are going to make plastic synapses the memory elements, we must. In our experience, one's enthusiasm for the idea diminishes when one contemplates the assumptions that must be made to make it work.

In the final analysis, however, our skepticism rests most strongly on the fact that the synapse is a circuit-level structure, a structure that it takes two different neurons and a great many molecules to realize. It seems to us likely for a variety of reasons that the elementary unit in the memory mechanism will prove to be a molecular or sub-molecular structural unit. Our rhodopsin-like switch molecule suggestion is a mechanism in which the basic memory element (a switch-like molecule) is a molecular-level unit, while our nucleotide-sequence suggestion is an example in which the element is a sub-molecular unit.

A Molecular or Sub-Molecular Mechanism?

The first relevant consideration is that it is clearly possible to implement this function at the sub-molecular level, given how much of the requisite machinery is already realized at the sub-molecular level in DNA and RNA. A large share of the very successful effort that has driven the ever-increasing power of computers has been the relentless reduction in the physical resources required to store a bit. This reflects the fundamental role that storing and accessing information plays in computation – the central theme of this book. For something as basic as memory, the simpler, more compact and less energetically costly the realization of this basic function is, the better it is. To our mind, it would be more than a little curious if a basic function that could be better implemented at the lowest possible level of structure (the sub-molecular) were found to be implemented instead at the circuit level, an implementation requiring orders of magnitude more physical resources.

The second, closely related consideration is the evident and profoundly puzzling speed of neural computation. How it is possible for the nervous system to compute the complex functions that it does compute as fast as it does, given that signals travel eight orders of magnitude more slowly in the nervous system than they do in a conventional computer? In computation, most of the signal flow is to and fro between memory, where the symbols reside when not entering into computations, and the processing machinery that implements the primitive two-argument functions. We believe that this aspect of the structure of a conventional computer is dictated by the ineluctable logic of physically realized computation. Given that signals travel slowly in neural tissue, the only way to minimize the time consumed in transferring information from memory to the processing machinery and back again is to place both the memory machinery and the processing machinery as close together as is physically possible. This is where Feynman's (1959) famous argument that "There is plenty of room at the bottom" comes into play. When interpreted in a neurobiological context, we take the force of his argument to be that sub-molecular and atomic structures are many orders of magnitude smaller than the cellular or circuit structures. Insofar as functions and structures that are imagined to be implemented at the level of cellular or circuit structure can in fact be implemented at the level of molecular structure, there is a gain in functional capacity of many orders of magnitude. One can accomplish much more in much less space – and in much less time, because much less time is wasted transmitting signals over needlessly long distances.

Bringing the Data to the Computational Machinery

Here, we remind the reader why we think the architecture of any powerful computing machine must be such as to bring the data to the computational machinery.

Complex functions can be realized by the composition of functions of two variables, but they cannot be realized by the composition of functions of a single variable. Thus, a computing machine must physically realize some two-argument functions. To physically implement a two-argument function, that is, to make a machine that gives the requisite output for each pair of input values, the values of the two input variables must converge in space and time on the processing machinery that generates the output for those two particular inputs. In order that two numbers be added, they must converge on machinery that can generate their sum.[1] In a powerful computing device, the number of different variables whose values might have to be summed is essentially infinite. Values cannot practically be stored in memory in such a way that they are all physically adjacent, each with every other, *and* with processing machinery capable of generating a sum. Because the two values that may need to be summed cannot generally be physically adjacent in memory, the computing machinery cannot be brought to where they are. They are not in one place; they are in two different places. Therefore, the architecture of the computing machine must make provision for values to be retrieved from physically different locations in memory and brought to the processing machinery that implements the primitive two-argument functions.

The question arises whether a distributed representation of the values stored in memory does not invalidate the above argument. The idea behind a distributed representation is that the same set of memory elements (e.g., plastic synapses) is used to represent all of the values stored in a memory, with the state of every element contributing to the representation of every value. In such a representation, the different values are not located at different places within the memory. It is not the case that some memory elements are used to represent some values, while other memory elements are used to represent other values. The representation of every value is distributed across all the memory elements. So, contrary to what we said above, the values are stored in such a way that every value is physically at the same location as every other value. They are all of them everywhere.

Such representations are possible. Encryption procedures generate them. An encryption procedure treats the bit patterns in successive words of memory as one huge bit pattern and performs on that pattern a hard-to-invert arithmetic operation (e.g., multiplication by a large prime) that generates a new bit pattern that is unintelligible. Only if one knows the prime by which the set of values was multiplied is it possible to recover the original set of values (decrypt the encrypted memories). The essential point for present purposes is that the recovery of any single one of the values in the original set of bit patterns depends on knowing every bit in the bit pattern generated by the encryption. Thus, there is a clear sense in which every bit (hence, every memory element) in the encrypted representation participates in the representation of every value in the encrypted set of values.

The problem is the unintelligibility of the distributed representation. The values thus represented are not accessible to computation. Indeed, the goal of the encryp-

---

[1]   In what follows, we continue to use the sum function as a stand-in for the set of primitive two-argument functions implemented by the computational hardware.

tion is to render them inaccessible to computation. We believe (but we cannot prove) that there is no way to realize primitive two-argument functions within a distributed representation of their arguments. The question is this: Does there exist a physically realizable distributed representation of a large number of distinct values such that one can send into that representation two probe signals to activate an arbitrarily chosen pair of the values therein represented, and another signal that specifies a two-argument function of those values, and get out the value of the specified function for the specified input values? We believe that this is impossible, because, for one thing, we do not see how it can be possible to simultaneously activate two and only two of the values represented in the distributed representation.

We can imagine that the distributed representation is such that when we send in one probe signal (input vector) we get one signal out from the memory (one output vector) and when we send in a different probe (a different input vector), we get out a different output vector. That, however, is not what is required. If that is the only capability we have, then in order to realize a function of two values stored in that distributed memory, we need to first extract one value, hold it in a memory register while we extract the second value, then bring the two sequentially extracted values to the machinery that can realize the specified two-argument function, and then put the value thus obtained back into the distributed representation, changing in the process the value of every memory element(!). Thus, even though values in a distributed memory are "all in the same place," this scheme nonetheless requires that they be separately extracted and brought to the machinery that realizes a two-argument function.

It is difficult (for us at least) to imagine how two and only two different values in a distributed representation could be simultaneously activated. Presumably, their activation would require the activation of the memory elements that encode them. But in a distributed representation, every memory element participates in the representation of every value. Thus, a probe for any value must activate every memory element. How can the activation states of one and the same set of memory elements *simultaneously* represent *two and only two* different values arbitrarily chosen from among the large number of values whose representation is distributed across that entire set of memory elements?

This last question brings us back to a point we stressed in Chapter 10 and again in Chapters 14 and 15, namely that in schemes in which plastic synapses within neural networks are thought to be the memory elements, the values of the synapses themselves do not (and, except under highly constrained circumstances) cannot encode the values of variables. What they encode are not the values themselves, but rather a procedure that will generate different values *given different input vectors*. In such schemes, the memory elements do not themselves represent values. All that the connection weights represent are procedures for generating different values (output vectors) given different input probes. This is another manifestation of the idea that learning is a rewiring that alters behavior but does not represent the experienced world. That's why these schemes have a finite-state architecture. As we have just noted, their architecture does not realize a system in which there is no need to bring the arguments to the machinery that implements the functions of those arguments. Indeed, the look-up tables that generally implement two-argument functions in neural network computations (see, for example, Chapter 14) do get signals from memory (the moving bumps of activity) and send signals back to those moving bumps.

As has been pointed out by others (Fodor & Pylyshyn, 1988), the great weakness of neural network models is their inability to offer a generally effective solution to the problem of compositionality. In our terms, the problem is their inability to provide compact procedures that implement functions of two arguments without pre-specification of the possible arguments. As we have attempted to show, this problem appears over and over again when one contemplates contemporary neural network models for things like dead reckoning and spatial and temporal maps, data structures for which there is strong behavioral evidence in insects and in vertebrates far removed from humans. Why try to use such an architecture to implement a complex computation like parsing, when it cannot plausibly be used to carry out even extremely simple computations like dead reckoning or vector addition and subtraction?

In sum, we do not know what the physical mechanism of memory is. Moreover, we refuse to conjecture, except by way of illustration, what it might be. We refuse because we believe that we are unlikely to conjecture the correct answer in the face of our present level of ignorance. We are mindful that biochemists were to unable to conjecture the answer to the molecular structure of the gene in the face of much more abundant and relevant evidence, such as, for example, the Chargaff ratios (see Judson, 1980). What we do know is some of the properties that the mechanism must possess. It must be capable of encoding the values of variables. That is, it must be possible to see how, at least in principle, the proposed physical change could carry forward in time a number. We focus on the carrying of a number, because any system that can carry a number can carry any kind of information. It must achieve very high information density (bits per cubic micron). It must have low volatility; hence, a low use of energy to maintain the physical changes that carry the information forward in time. It must be capable of entering either directly or via transcription into physically realized compact procedures for implementing two-argument functions. That is a more detailed set of specifications than has heretofore guided the search for the physical basis of memory. It much more strongly constrains viable hypotheses.

Is It Universal?

Finally, bringing our book full circle, we consider an assumption implicit in our discussion so far, which is that it is reasonable to suppose that the mechanism of memory is universal. Our reasons for supposing that it is rest squarely on a point of Shannon's that we discussed in the opening pages. The function of memory in a computing device is to enable the present to communicate with the past. By carrying information forward in time in a computationally accessible form, memory makes possible the composition of functions, which is at the heart of computation. It makes the results of functions executed earlier accessible as arguments of current functions. Shannon began by pointing out that in considering the communication of information, one need only consider the probability distribution on the set of possible messages. One need not consider the semantics of those messages, what they are about. Put simply, information is information: in the end, it is all bits.

The modern communication and information technology industry bears witness to the truth of this insight. In designing a storage medium, such as a video disk, engineers are concerned only with how many bits it can hold, not whether those bits will encode text messages or images or sound streams. Similarly, in auctioning off or purchasing a segment of the electromagnetic spectrum, the government and industry are concerned only with how many bits can be sent per unit of time, not with the content of those bit streams.

The insight also finds striking confirmation in the fact that nucleotide sequences encode for both the amino acid sequences of proteins and promoters, the sites where transcription factors bind to DNA so as to initiate the transcription of one or more genes. The distinction between promoter encoding and amino-acid sequence encoding is roughly the distinction between encoding the data on which a program operates and the program itself. Conceptually these are very different. As we have explained at length, program code and data code play very different roles in the operation of a computing device. And, promoter sequences and so-called coding sequences play very different roles in the machinery by which inherited information finds expression in organismic structure. But, in both cases, the essence of the matter is the carrying of information. For that purpose, it is a logico-mathematical truth that if you can carry any kind of information, you can carry every kind of information.

The universality of the action potential as the medium for carrying information from one place to another within nervous systems is a further illustration of Shannon's insight. The action-potential mechanism is not domain- or modality-specific. Whenever information must be carried from one place to another, the same mechanism is used. Because the function of memory is to carry information from one place in time to a later place in time, we see no more reason to suppose that different mechanisms are required for different kinds of messages here than to suppose that different kinds of action potentials are required or different kinds of DNA.

In stressing this, we stress a central message of our book: Memory is a simple function. Simple as it is, however, it is absolutely indispensable in a computing device. If the computational theory of mind, the core assumption of cognitive science, is correct, then brains must possess a mechanism for carrying information forward in time in a computationally accessible form. This elementary insight will someday transform neuroscience, because, as of this writing, neuroscience knows of no plausible mechanism for carrying a large amount of information forward over indefinitely long intervals in a form that makes it accessible to the mechanisms that effect the primitive two-argument functions that are at the heart of computation.

Until the day comes when neuroscientists are able to specify the neurobiological machinery that performs this key function, all talk about *how* brains compute is premature. It is premature in the same way that talk of how genes govern epigenesis was premature prior to an understanding of what it was about the structure of a gene that enabled it to carry inherited information forward in time, making it both copyable and available to direct the creation of organic structures. Symbolic memory is as central to computation as DNA is to life.

References

Adams, D. B. (2006). Brain mechanisms of aggressive behavior: An updated review. *Neuroscience and Biobehavioral Reviews*, 30, 304–18.

Aksay, E., Baker, R., Seung, H. S., & Tank, D. W. (2000). Anatomy and discharge properties of pre-motor neurons in the goldfish medulla that have eye-position signals during fixations. *Journal of Neurophysiology*, 84, 1035–49.

Amit, D. J. (1989). *Modeling brain function: The world of attractor neural networks*. New York: Cambridge University Press.

Averbeck, B. B., Latham, P. E., & Pouget, A. (2006). Neural correlations, population coding and computation. *Nature Reviews Neuroscience*, 7(5), 358–66.

Baker, M. C. (2001). *The atoms of language*. New York: Basic Books.

Balsam, P. (1985). The functions of context in learning and performance. In P. Balsam & A. Tomie (eds.), *Context and learning* (pp. 1–21). Hillsdale, NJ: Lawrence Erlbaum.

Barnden, J. A. (1992). On using analogy to reconcile connections and symbols. In D. S. L. M. Aparicio (ed.), *Neural networks for knowledge representation and inference*, (pp. 27–64). Hillsdale, NJ: Lawrence Erlbaum.

Barnet, R. C., Arnold, H. M., & Miller, R. R. (1991). Simultaneous conditioning demonstrated in second-order conditioning: Evidence for similar associative structure in forward and simultaneous conditioning. *Learning and Motivation*, 22, 253–68.

Barnet, R. C., Cole, R. P., & Miller, R. R. (1997). Temporal integration in second-order conditioning and sensory preconditioning. *Animal Learning and Behavior*, 25(2), 221–33.

Barnet, R. C. & Miller, R. R. (1996). Second order excitation mediated by a backward conditioned inhibitor. *Journal of Experimental Psychology: Animal Behavior Processes*, 22(3), 279–96.

Becker, S. & Hinton, G. E. (1992). Self-organizing neural network that discovers surfaces in random-dot stereograms. *Nature*, 355(9 January), 161–3.

Beling, I. (1929). Über das Zeitgedächtnis der Bienen. *Zeitschrift für vergleichende Physiologie*, 9, 259–338.

Bialek, W. & Setayeshagar, S. (2005). Physical limits to biochemical signaling. *Proceedings of the National Academy of Sciences*, 102(29), 140–6.

Biro, D. & Matsuzawa, T. (1999). Numerical ordering in a chimpanzee (*Pan troglodytes*): Planning, executing, and monitoring. *Journal of Comparative Psychology*, 113(2), 178–85.

Blair, H. T. & Sharp, P. E. (1996). Visual and vestibular influences on head-direction cells in the anterior thalamus of the rat. *Behavioral Neuroscience*, 110, 643–60.

Bloomfield, T. M. (1972). Reinforcement schedules: Contingency or contiguity? In R. M. Gilbert & J. R. Milleinson (eds.), *Reinforcement: Behavioral analysis* (pp. 165–208). New York: Academic Press.

Bolles, R. C. & de Lorge, J. (1962). The rat's adjustment to a-diurnal feeding cycles. *Journal of Comparative Physiology and Psychology, 55*, 760–2.

Bolles, R. C. & Moot, S. A. (1973). The rat's anticipation of two meals a day. *Journal of Comparative Physiology and Psychology, 83*, 510–14.

Bolles, R. C. & Stokes, L. W. (1965). Rat's anticipation of diurnal and a-diurnal feeding. *Journal of Comparative Physiology and Psychology, 60*(2), 290–4.

Boysen, S. T. & Berntson, G. G. (1989). Numerical competence in a chimpanzee (*Pan troglodytes*). *Journal of Comparative Psychology, 103*, 23–31.

Brannon, E. M. & Terrace, H. S. (2002). The evolution and ontogeny of ordinal numerical ability. In Marc Bekoff, Colin Allen, & Gordon Burkhardt (eds.), *The cognitive animal: Empirical and theoretical perspectives on animal cognition* (pp. 197–204). Cambridge, MA: MIT Press.

Brenner, N., Agam, O., Bialek, W., & de Ruyter van Steveninck, R. (2002). Statistical properties of spike trains: Universal and stimulus-dependent aspects. *Physical review. E, Statistical, nonlinear, and soft matter physics, 66*(3, pt 1), 031907.

Brenner, N., Bialek, W., & de Ruyter van Steveninck, R. (2000). Adaptive rescaling maximizes information transmission. *Neuron, 26*(3), 695–702.

Brenner, N., Strong, S. P., Koberle, R., Bialek, W., & de Ruyter van Steveninck, R. (2000). Synergy in a neural code. *Neural Computation, 12*(7), 1531–52.

Brooks, R. A. (1991). Intelligence without representation. *Artificial Intelligence, 47*, 139–59.

Browne, A. & Pilkington, J. (1994). Variable binding in a neural network using a distributed representation. Paper presented at the IEE Colloquium on Symbolic and Neural Cognitive Engineering, February 14.

Browne, A. & Sun, R. (2001). Connectionist inference models. *Neural Networks, 14*(10), 1331–55.

Buttel-Reepen, H. B. v. (1915). *Leben und Wesen der Bienen*. Braunschweig: Vieweg.

Cantlon, J. F. & Brannon, E. M. (2005). Semantic congruity affects numerical judgments similarly in monkeys and humans. *Proceedings of the National Academy of Sciences, 102*(45), 16507–12.

Cantlon, J. F. & Brannon, E. M. (2006). Shared system for ordering small and large numbers in monkeys and humans. *Psychological Science, 17*(5), 401–6.

Chater, N., Tenenbaum, J. B., & Yuille, A. (2006). Probabilistic models of cognition: Conceptual foundations. *Trends in Cognitive Sciences, 10*(7), 287–91.

Chomsky, N. (1975). *Reflections on language*. New York: Pantheon.

Chomsky, N. (1988). *Language and problems of knowledge*. Cambridge, MA: MIT Press.

Chomsky, N. & Lasnik, H. (eds.). (1993). *Principles and parameters theory, in syntax: An international handbook of contemporary research*. Berlin: de Gruyter.

Churchland, P. M. (1989). *A neurocomputational perspective: The nature of mind and the structure of science*. Cambridge, MA: MIT Press.

Churchland, P. S. & Sejnowski, T. J. (1990). Neural representation and neural computation. In W. Lycan (ed.), *Mind and cognition: A reader* (pp. 224–51). Oxford: Blackwell.

Clayton, N., Emery, N., & Dickinson, A. (2006). The rationality of animal memory: Complex caching strategies of western scrub jays. In M. Nuuds & S. Hurley (eds.), *Rational Animals?* (pp. 197–216). Oxford: Oxford University Press.

Clayton, N., Yu, K., & Dickinson, A. (2001). Scrub jays (*Aphelocoma coerulescens*) can form integrated memory for multiple features of caching episodes. *Journal of Experimental Psychology: Animal Behavior Processes, 27*, 17–29.

Clayton, N. S., Bussey, T. J., & Dickinson, A. (2003). Can animals recall the past and plan for the future? *Nature Reviews Neurosciences, 4,* 685–91.

Clayton, N. S. & Dickinson, A. (1999). Memory for the content of caches by scrub jays (*Aphelocoma coerulescens*). *Journal of Experimental Psychology: Animal Behavior Processes, 25*(1), 82–91.

Clayton, N. S., Yu, K. S., & Dickinson, A. (2003). Interacting cache memories: Evidence for flexible memory use by Western Scrub-Jays (*Aphelocoma californica*). *Journal of Experimental Psychology: Animal Behavior Processes, 29,* 14–22.

Cole, R. P., Barnet, R. C., & Miller, R. R. (1995). Temporal encoding in trace conditioning. *Animal Learning and Behavior, 23*(2), 144–53.

Collett, M., Harland, D., & Collett, T. S. (2002). The use of landmarks and panoramic context in the performance of local vectors by navigating bees. *Journal of Experimental Biology, 205,* 807–14.

Collett, T. S., Collett, M., & Wehner, R. (2001). The guidance of desert ants by extended landmarks. *Journal of Experimental Biology, 204*(9), 1635–9.

Collett, T. S., Dillmann, E., Giger, A., & Wehner, R. (1992). Visual landmarks and route following in desert ants. *Journal of Comparative Physiology. Series A 170,* 435–42.

Colwill, R. M. (1991). Negative discriminative stimuli provide information about the identity of omitted response-contingent outcomes. *Animal Learning and Behavior, 19,* 326–36.

Colwill, R. M., Absher, R. A., & Roberts, M. L. (1988). Context-US learning in *Aplysia californica. Journal of Neuroscience, 8*(12), 4434–9.

Cox, R. T. (1961). *The algebra of probable inference.* Baltimore, MD: Johns Hopkins University Press.

Crystal, J. D. (2001). Nonlinear time perception. *Behavioral Processes, 55,* 35–49.

Dehaene, S. (2001). Subtracting pigeons: Logarithmic or linear? *Psychological Science, 12*(3), 244–6.

Dehaene, S. & Changeux, J. P. (1993). Development of elementary numerical abilities: A neuronal model. *Journal of Cognitive Neuroscience, 5,* 390–407.

Deneve, S., Latham, P. E., & Pouget, A. (2001). Efficient computation and cue integration with noisy population codes. *Nature Neuroscience, 4*(8), 826–31.

Dews, P. B. (1970). The theory of fixed-interval responding. In W. N. Schoenfeld (ed.), *The theory of reinforcement schedules* (pp. 43–61). New York: Appleton-Century-Crofts.

Dickinson, J. & Dyer, F. (1996). How insects learn about the sun's course: Alternative modeling approaches. In P. Maes, M. Mataric, J.-A. Meyer, J. Pollack, & S. Wilson (eds.), *From animals to animats* (vol. 4, pp. 193–203). Cambridge, MA: MIT Press.

Domjan, M. (1998). *The principles of learning and behavior.* Pacific Grove, CA: Brooks/Cole.

Droulez, J. & Berthoz, A. (1991). A neural network model of sensoritopic maps with predictive short-term memory properties. *Proceedings of the National Academy of Sciences, USA, 88,* 9653–7.

Dworkin, B. R. (1993). *Learning and physiological regulation.* Chicago: University of Chicago Press.

Dworkin, B. R. (2007). Interoception. In J. T. Cacioppo, L. G. Tassinary, & G. G. Berntson (eds.), *The handbook of psychophysiology* (pp. 482–506). New York: Cambridge University Press.

Dyer, F. C. & Dickinson, J. A. (1994). Development of sun compensation by honeybees: How partially experienced bees estimate the sun's course. *Proceedings of the National Academy of Sciences, USA, 91,* 4471–4.

Earnest, D. J., Liang, F. Q., Ratcliff, M., & Cassone, V. M. (1999). Immortal time: Circadian clock properties of rat suprachiasmatic cell lines. *Science, 283*(5402), 693–5.

Edelman, G. M. & Gally, J. A. (2001). Degeneracy and complexity in biological systems. *Proceedings of the National Academy of Sciences (USA)*, 98, 13763–8.

Edelman, G. M. & Tononi, G. (2000). *A universe of consciousness: How matter becomes imagination.* New York: Basic Books/Allan Lane.

Edmonds, S. C. & Adler, N. T. (1977a). Food and light as entrainers of circadian running activity in the rat. *Physiology and Behavior*, 18, 915–19.

Edmonds, S. C., & Adler, N. T. (1977b). The multiplicity of biological oscillators in the control of circadian running activity in the rat. *Physiology and Behavior*, 18, 921–30.

Egger, M. D. & Miller, N. E. (1963). When is a reward reinforcing? An experimental study of the information hypothesis. *Journal of Comparative and Physiological Psychology*, 56, 122–37.

Elman, J. L. (1990). Finding structure in time. *Cognitive Science*, 14, 179–211.

Elman, J. L. (1991). Distributed representations, simple recurrent networks, and grammatical structure. *Machine Learning*, 7, 195–224.

Fairhall, A. L., Lewen, G. D., Bialek, W., & de Ruyter Van Steveninck, R. R. (2001). Efficiency and ambiguity in an adaptive neural code. *Nature*, 412(6849), 787–92.

Fanselow, M. S. (1993). Associations and memories: The role of NMDA receptors and long-term potentiation. *Current Directions in Psychological Science*, 2(5), 152–6.

Ferster, C. B. & Skinner, B. F. (1957). *Schedules of reinforcement.* New York: Appleton-Century-Crofts.

Feynman, R. (1959). There is plenty of room at the bottom. Speech to the American Physical Society Meeting at Caltech, December 29; published in February 1960 in Caltech's *Engineering and Science* magazine.

Fodor, J. A. (1975). *The language of thought*: New York: T. Y. Crowell.

Fodor, J. A. & Pylyshyn, Z. (1988). Connectionism and cognitive architecture: A critical analysis. *Cognition*, 28, 3–71.

Forel, A. (1910). *Das Sinnesleben der Insekten.* Munich: E. Reinhardt.

Frasconia, P., Gori, M., Kurfessc, F., & Sperdutid, A. (2002). Special issue on integration of symbolic and connectionist systems. *Cognitive Systems Research*, 3(2), 121–3.

Fukushi, T. & Wehner, R. (2004). Navigation in wood ants *Formica japonica*: Context dependent use of landmarks. *Journal of Experimental Biology*, 207, 3431–9.

Gallistel, C. R. (1980). *The organization of action: A new synthesis.* Hillsdale, NJ: Lawrence Erlbaum.

Gallistel, C. R. (1990). *The organization of learning.* Cambridge, MA: Bradford Books/MIT Press.

Gallistel, C. R. (1995). Is LTP a plausible basis for memory? In J. L. McGaugh, N. M. Weinberger, & G. Lynch (eds.), *Brain and memory: Modulation and mediation of neuroplasticity* (pp. 328–37). New York: Oxford University Press.

Gallistel, C. R. (1998). Symbolic processes in the brain: The case of insect navigation. In D. Scarborough & S. Sternberg (eds.), *An Invitation to cognitive science*, vol. 4: *Methods, models and conceptual issues* (2nd edn., pp. 1–51). Cambridge, MA: MIT Press.

Gallistel, C. R. (1999). The replacement of general-purpose learning models with adaptively specialized learning modules. In M. S. Gazzaniga (ed.), *The cognitive neurosciences* (2nd edn., pp. 1179–91). Cambridge, MA: MIT Press.

Gallistel, C. R. (2003). Conditioning from an information processing perspective. *Behavioural Processes*, 62, 89–101.

Gallistel, C. R. (2008). Learning and representation. In R. Menzel (ed.), *Learning and memory*. Vol. 1 of *Learning and memory: A comprehensive reference* (ed. J. Byrne). Oxford: Elsevier.

Gallistel, C. R. & Gibbon, J. (2000). Time, rate, and conditioning. *Psychological Review*, 107, 289–344.

Gallistel, C. R. & Gibbon, J. (2002). *The symbolic foundations of conditioned behavior.* Mahwah, NJ: Lawrence Erlbaum.

Gallistel, C. R., King, A., & McDonald, R. (2004). Sources of variability and systematic error in mouse timing behavior. *Journal of Experimental Psychology: Animal Behavior Processes*, *30*(1), 3–16.

Gibbon, J. (1977). Scalar expectancy theory and Weber's law in animal timing. *Psychological Review*, *84*, 279–335.

Gibbon, J. & Balsam, P. (1981). Spreading associations in time. In C. M. Locurto, H. S. Terrace, & J. Gibbon (eds.), *Autoshaping and conditioning theory* (pp. 219–53). New York: Academic Press.

Gibbon, J., Church, R. M., & Meck, W. H. (1984). Scalar timing in memory. In J. Gibbon & L. Allan (eds.), *Timing and time perception* (vol. 423, pp. 52–77). New York: New York Academy of Sciences.

Gluck, M. A. & Thompson, R. F. (1987). Modeling the neural substrates of associative learning and memory: a computational approach. *Psychological Review*, *94*, 176–91.

Gottlieb, D. A. (2008). Is the number of trials a primary determinant of conditioned responding? *Journal of Experimental Psychology: Animal Behavior Processes*, *34*, 185–201.

Gould, J. L. (1986). The locale map of honey bees: Do insects have cognitive maps? *Science*, *232*, 861–3.

Grossberg, S. & Schmajuk, N. A. (1989). Neural dynamics of adaptive timing and temporal discrimination during associative learning. *Neural Networks*, *2*, 79–102.

Gualtiero, P. (2008). Some neural networks compute, others don't. *Neural Networks*. doi: 10.1016/j.neunet.2007.12.010.

Halder, G., Callaerts, P., & Gehring, W. J. (1995). Induction of ectopic eyes by target expression of the *eyeless* gene in *Drosophila*. *Science*, *267*, 1788–92.

Hanson, S. J. & Burr, D. J. (1990). What connectionist models learn: Learning and representation in connectionist networks. *13*, 471–89.

Harkness, R. D. & Maroudas, N. G. (1985). Central place foraging by an ant (*Cataglyphis bicolor Fab.*): A model of searching. *Animal Behaviour*, *33*, 916–28.

Hasher, L. & Zacks, R. T. (1984). Automatic processing of fundamental information: The case of frequency of occurrence. *American Psychologist*, *39*, 1372–88.

Hastings, M. H. (2002). A gut feeling for time. *Nature*, *417*, 391–2.

Hauser, M., Carey, S., & Hauser, L. (2000). Spontaneous number representation in semi-free-ranging rhesus monkeys. *Proceedings: Biological Sciences*, *267*, 829–33.

Hawkins, R. D. & Kandel, E. R. (1984). Is there a cell-biological alphabet for simple forms of learning? *Psychological Review*, *91*, 375–91.

Hinton, G. E., McClelland, J. L., & Rumelhart, D. E. (1986). Distributed representations. In D. E. Rumelhart & J. L. McClelland (eds.), *Parallel distributed processing* (vol. 1, pp. 77–109). Cambridge, MA: MIT Press.

Hodges, A. (1983). *Alan Turing*. New York: Simon & Schuster.

Hoeffner, J. H., McClelland, J. L., & Seidenberg, M. S. (1996). Discovering inflectional morphology: A connectionist account. Paper presented at the 1996 Meeting of the Psychonomics Society, Chicago, IL.

Hopcroft, J. E., Motwani, R., & Ullman, J. D. (2000). *Introduction to automata theory, languages and computability* (2nd edn.). Boston: Addison-Wesley Longman.

Hopson, J. W. (2003). General learning models: Timing without a clock. In W. H. Meck (ed.), *Functional and neural mechanisms of interval timing* (pp. 23–60). New York: CRC.

Hudson, T. E., Maloney, L. T., & Landy, M. S. (2008). Optimal compensation for temporal uncertainty in movement planning. *PLoS Computational Biology*, *4*(7), e100130, 100131–9.

Huffman, D. A. (1952). A method for the construction of minimum-redundancy codes, *Proceedings of the Institute of Radio Engineers*, 4, 1098–101.

Hull, C. L. (1929). A functional interpretation of the conditioned reflex. *Psychological Review*, 36, 498–511.

Hull, C. L. (1930). Knowledge and purpose as habit mechanisms. *Psychological Review*, 37, 511–25.

Hull, C. L. (1952). *A behavior system*. New Haven, CT: Yale University Press.

Hulme, C., Roodenrys, S., Schweickert, R., Brown, G. D. A., Martin, S., & Stuart, G. (1997). Word-frequency effects on short-term memory tasks: Evidence for a redintegration process in immediate serial recall. *Journal of Experimental Psychology: Learning, Memory and Cognition*, 23, 1217–32.

Jacob, F. (1993). *The logic of life* (trans. B. E. Spillmann). Princeton, NJ: Princeton University Press.

Jaynes, E. T. (2003). *Probability theory: The logic of science*. New York: Cambridge University Press.

Jeffreys, H. (1931). *Scientific inference*. New York: Cambridge University Press.

Jescheniak, J. D. & Levelt, W. J. M. (1994). Word frequency effects in speech production: retrieval of synactic information and of phonological form. *Journal of Experimental Psychology: Learning, Memory and Cognition*, 20, 824–43.

Judson, H. (1980). *The eighth day of creation*. New York: Simon & Schuster.

Kahneman, D., Slovic, P., & Tversky, A. (eds.). (1982). *Judgment under uncertainty: Heuristics and biases*. Cambridge: Cambridge University Press.

Kamin, L. J. (1967). "Attention-like" processes in classical conditioning. In M. R. Jones (ed.), *Miami symposium on the prediction of behavior: Aversive stimulation* (pp. 9–33). Miami: University of Miami Press.

Kamin, L. J. (1969). Selective association and conditioning. In N. J. Mackintosh & W. K. Honig (eds.), *Fundamental issues in associative learning* (pp. 42–64). Halifax, Canada: Dalhousie University Press.

Kehoe, E. J., Graham-Clarke, P., & Schreurs, B. G. (1989). Temporal patterns of the rabbit's nictitating membrane response to compound and component stimuli under mixed CS-US intervals. *Behavioral Neuroscience*, 103, 283–95.

Kelley, A. E., Baldo, B. A., Pratt, W. E., & Will, M. J. (2005). Corticostriatal-hypothalmic circuitry and food motivation: Integration of energy, action and reward. *Physiology & Behavior*, 86, 773–95.

Killeen, P. R. & Weiss, N. A. (1987). Optimal timing and the Weber function. *Psychological Review*, 94, 455–68.

King, A. P. & Gallistel, C. R. (1996). Multiphasic neuronal transfer function for representing temporal structure. *Behavior Research Methods, Instruments and Computers*, R28, 217–23.

King, B. M. (2006). The rise, fall, and resurrection of the ventromedial hypothalamus in the regulation of feeding behavior and body weight. *Physiology & Behavior*, 87, 221–44.

Kirkpatrick, K. & Church, R. M. (2000). Independent effects of stimulus and cycle duration in conditioning: The role of timing processes. *Animal Learning & Behavior*, 28, 373–88.

Knill, D. C., & Pouget, A. (2004). The Bayesian brain: The role of uncertainty in neural coding and computation. *Trends in Neuroscience*, 27, 712–19.

Koch, C. (1997). Computation and the single neuron. *Nature*, 385, 207–10.

Koch, C. (1999). *Biophysics of computation: Information processing in single neurons*. Oxford University Press, Oxford.

Koch, C. & Hepp, K. (2006). Quantum mechanics in the brain. *Nature*, 440, 611–12.

Koch, C. & Poggio, T. (1987). Biophysics of computation: Neurons, synapses and membranes. In G. M. Edelman, W. E. Gall, & W. M. Cowan (eds.), *Synaptic function* (pp. 637–97). New York: John Wiley.

Koltermann, R. (1971). 24-Std-Periodik in der Langzeiterrinerung an Duft- und Farbsignale bei der Honigbiene. *Z. Vergl. Physiol.*, *75*, 49–68.

Konorski, J. (1948). *Conditioned reflexes and neuron organization.* Cambridge: Cambridge University Press.

Krantz, D., Luce, R. D., Suppes, P., & Tversky, A. (1971). *The foundations of measurement.* New York: Academic Press.

Lashley, K. S. (1950). In search of the engram. In *Symposium of the society of experimental biology*, no. 4: *Psychological mechanisms in animal behavior* (pp. 454–82). Cambridge: Cambridge University Press.

Latham, P. E. & Nirenberg, S. (2005). Synergy, redundancy, and independence in population codes, revisited. *J Neurosci*, *25*(21), 5195–206.

Laughlin, S. B. (2004). The implications of metabolic energy requirements for the representation of information in neurons. In M. S. Gazzaniga (ed.), *The cognitive neurosciences* (vol. 3, pp. 187–96). Cambridge, MA: MIT Press.

Leslie, A. M. (in press). Where do integers come from? In P. Bauer & N. Stein (eds.), *Festschrift for Jean Mandler.*

Leslie, A. M., Gelman, R., & Gallistel, C. R. (2008). The generative basis of natural number concepts. *Trends in Cognitive Sciences*, *12*, 213–18.

Lewis, F. D. (1981). *Theory of computing systems.* New York: Springer.

Lindauer, M. (1957). Sonnenorientierung der Bienen unter der Aequatorsonne und zur Nachtzeit. *Naturwissenschaften*, *44*, 1–6.

Lindauer, M. (1959). Angeborene und erlente Komponenten in der Sonnesorientierung der Bienen. *Zeitschrift für vergleichende Physiologie*, *42*, 43–63.

LoLordo, V. M. & Fairless, J. L. (1985). Pavlovian conditioned inhibition: The literature since 1969. In R. R. Miller & N. E. Spear (eds.), *Information processing in animals* (pp. 1–50). Hillsdale, NJ: Lawrence Erlbaum.

Lòpez-Moliner, J. & Ma Sopena, J. (1993). Variable binding using serial order in recurrent neural networks. In *Lecture notes in computer science* (vol. 686, pp. 90–5). Berlin: Springer.

Lorente de No, R. (1932). Analysis of the activity of the chains of internuncial neurons. *Journal of Neurophysiology*, *1*, 207–44.

Maas, W. & Sontag, E. D. (1999). Analog neural nets with gaussian or other common noise distributions cannot recognize arbitrary regular languages. *Neural Computation*, *11*, 771–82.

Major, G., Baker, R., Aksay, E., Mensh, B., Seung, H. S. & Tank, D. W. (2004). Plasticity and tuning by visual feedback of the stability of a neural integrator. *Proceedings of the National Academy of Science (USA)*, *101*, 7739–44.

Marcus, G. F. (2001). *The algebraic mind: Integrating connectionism and cognitive science.* Cambridge, MA: MIT Press.

Markram, H., Lübke, J., Frotscher, M., & Sakmann, B. (1997). Regulation of synaptic efficacy by coincidence of postsynaptic APs and EPSPs. *Science*, *275*, 213–15.

Marr, D. (1982). *Vision.* San Francisco: W. H. Freeman.

Mather, J. (1991). Navigation by spatial memory and use of visual landmarks in octopuses. *Journal of Comparative Physiology A*, *168*, 491–7.

Matsuzawa, T. & Biro, D. (2001). Use of numerical symbols by the chimpanzee (*Pan troglodytes*): Cardinals, ordinals, and the introduction of zero. *Animal Cognition*, *4*, 193–9.

Mattell, M. S. & Meck, W. H. (2000). Neuropsychological mechanisms of interval timing behavior. *Bioessays*, *22*, 94–103.

McCulloch, W. S. & Pitts, W. (1943). A logical calculus of the ideas immanent in nervous activity. *Bulletin of Mathematical Biophysics, 5*, 115–33.

Mel, B. W. (1994). Information processing in dendritic trees. *Neural Computation, 6*, 1031–85.

Menzel, R., Greggers, U., Smith, A., Berger, S., Brandt, R., Brunke, S., et al. (2005). Honey bees navigate according to a map-like spatial memory. *Proceedings of the National Academy of Sciences (USA), 102*, 3040–5.

Miall, R. C. (1989). The storage of time intervals using oscillatory neurons. *Neural Computation, 1*, 359–71.

Miall, R. C. (1992). Oscillators, predictions and time. In F. Macar, V. Pouthas, & W. J. Friedman (eds.), *Time, action and cognition: Towards bridging the gap* (NATO Advances Science Institutes Series D, no. 66, pp. 215–27). Dordrecht: Kluwer Academic.

Miall, R. C. (1996). Models of neural timing. In M. A. Pastor & J. Artieda (eds.), *Time, internal clocks and movement. Advances in psychology* (vol. 115, pp. 69–94). Amsterdam: North-Holland/Elsevier Science.

Miller, R. R. & Escobar, M. (2002). Laws and models of basic conditioning. In C. R. Gallistel (ed.), *Stevens handbook of experimental psychology*, vol. 3: *Learning and motivation* (3rd edn., pp. 47–102). New York: John Wiley.

Mistlberger, R. E. (1994). Circadian food-anticipatory activity: Formal models and physiological mechanisms. *Neuroscience and Biobehavioral Reviews, 18*, 171–95.

Mustaca, A. E., Gabelli, F., Papine, M. R., & Balsam, P. (1991). The effects of varying the interreinforcement interval on appetitive contextual conditioning. *Animal Learning and Behavior, 19*, 125–38.

Newell, A. (1980). Physical symbol systems. *Cognitive Science, 4*, 135–83.

Nieder, A., Diester, I., & Tudusciuc, O. (2006). Temporal and spatial enumeration processes in the primate parietal cortex. *Science, 313*, 1431–5.

Nirenberg, S. & Latham, P. E. (2003). Decoding neuronal spike trains: How important are correlations? *Proceedings of the National Academy of Sciences, USA, 100*(12), 7348–53.

Pearl, J. (2000). *Causality: Models, reasoning, and inference.* Cambridge: Cambridge University Press.

Perlis, A. J. (1982). Epigrams in programming. *SIGPLAN Notices, 17*(9).

Piattelli-Palmarini, M. (1994). *Inevitable illusions: How mistakes of reason rule our minds.* New York: John Wiley.

Port, R. (2002). The dynamical systems hypothesis in cognitive science. In L. Nadel (ed.), *Encyclopedia of cognitive science* (vol. 1, pp. 1027–32). London: MacMillan.

Potter, M. C., Staub, A., & O'Connor, D. H. (2004). Pictorial and conceptual representation of glimpsed pictures. *Journal of Experimental Psychology: Human Perception and Performance, 30*, 478–89.

Pylyshyn, Z. W. (1986). *Computation and cognition: Towards a foundation for cognitive science.* Cambridge, MA: MIT Press.

Redish, A. D. & Touretzky, D. S. (1997). Cognitive maps beyond the hippocampus. *Hippocampus, 7*, 15–35.

Rescorla, R. A. (1968). Probability of shock in the presence and absence of CS in fear conditioning. *Journal of Comparative and Physiological Psychology, 66*, 1–5.

Rescorla, R. A. (1969). Pavlovian conditioned inhibition. *Psychological Bulletin, 72*, 77–94.

Rescorla, R. A. (1972). Informational variables in Pavlovian conditioning. In G. H. Bower (ed.), *The psychology of learning and motivation* (vol. 6, pp. 1–46). New York: Academic Press.

Rescorla, R. A. & Wagner, A. R. (1972). A theory of Pavlovian conditioning: Variations in the effectiveness of reinforcement and nonreinforcement. In A. H. Black & W. F. Prokasy (eds.), *Classical conditioning* (vol. 2, pp. 64–99). New York: Appleton-Century-Crofts.

Richter, C. P. (1922). A behavioristic study of the activity of the rat. *Comparative Psychology Monographs, 1.*

Rieke, F., Bodnar, D. A., & Bialek, W. (1995). Naturalistic stimuli increase the rate and efficiency of information transmission by primary auditory afferents. *Proceedings: Biological Sciences, 262,* 259–65.

Rieke, F., Warland, D., de Ruyter van Steveninck, R., & Bialek, W. (1997). *Spikes: Exploring the neural code.* Cambridge, MA: MIT Press.

Roche, J. P. & Timberlake, W. (1998). The influence of artificial paths and landmarks on the foraging behavior of Norway rats (*Rattus norvegicus*). *Animal Learning and Behavior, 26*(1), 76–84.

Rosenwasser, A. M., Pelchat, R. J., & Adler, N. T. (1984). Memory for feeding time: Possible dependence on coupled circadian oscillators. *Physiology and Behavior, 32,* 25–30.

Rozin, P. (1976). The evolution of intelligence and access to the cognitive unconscious. In A. N. Epstein & J. M. Sprague (eds.), *Progress in psychobiology and physiological psychology* (vol. 6, pp. 245–80). New York: Academic Press.

Rumbaugh, D. M. & Washburn, D. A. (1993). Counting by chimpanzees and ordinality judgments by macaques in video-formatted tasks. In S. T. Boyese & E. J. Capaldi (eds.), *The development of numerical competence: Animal and human models* (pp. 87–106). Hillsdale, NJ: Lawrence Erlbaum.

Rumelhart, D. E. & McClelland, J. L. (1986). On learning the past tenses of English verbs. In J. L. McClelland, D. E. Rumelhart, & The PDP Research Group (eds.), *Parallel distributed processing: Explorations in the microstructure of cognition. Vol. 2: Psychological and biological models* (pp. 216–71). Cambridge, MA: MIT Press.

Rumelhart, D. E. & McClelland, J. L. (eds.). (1986). *Parallel distributed processing.* Cambridge, MA: MIT Press.

Rumelhart, D. E. & Todd, P. M. (1993). Learning and connectionist representations. In D. E. Meyer & S. Kornblum (eds.), *Attention and performance* (vol. 14, pp. 3–30). Cambridge, MA: MIT Press.

Samsonovich, A. & McNaughton, B. L. (1997). Path integration and cognitive mapping in a continuous attractor neural network model. *Journal of Neuroscience, 17,* 5900–20.

Scapini, F., Rossano, C., Marchetti, G. M., & Morgan, E. (2005). The role of the biological clock in the sun compass orientation of free-running individuals of *Talitrus saltator. Animal Behavior, 69,* 835–43.

Schneidman, E., Berry, M. J., Segev, R., & Bialek, W. (2006). Weak pairwise correlations imply strong correlated network states in a neural population. *Nature, 440,* 1007–13.

Shannon, C. E. (1948). A mathematical theory of communication. *Bell Systems Technical Journal, 27,* 379–423, 623–56.

Sherrington, C. S. (1947 [1906]). *The integrative action of the nervous system.* New Haven: Yale University Press.

Siegel, S. (1999). Drug anticipation and drug addiction. *Addiction, 94,* 1113–24.

Siegel, S. & Allan, L. G. (1998). Learning and homeostasis: Drug addiction and the McCollough effect. *Psychological Bulletin, 124,* 230–9.

Simmons, P. J. & de Ruyter van Steveninck, R. (2005). Reliability of signal transfer at a tonically transmitting, graded potential synapse of the locust ocellar pathway. *Journal of Neuroscience, 25,* 7529–37.

Skaggs, W. E., Knierim, J. J., Kudrimoti, H. S., & McNaughton, B. L. (1995). A model of the neural basis of the rat's sense of direction. In G. Tesauro, D. S. Touretzky, & T. Leen (eds.), *Advances in neural information processing* (vol. 7). Cambridge, MA: MIT Press.

Skinner, B. F. (1938). *The behavior of organisms.* New York: Appleton-Century-Crofts.

Skinner, B. F. (1957). *Verbal behavior.* New York: Appleton-Century-Crofts.

Skinner, B. F. (1990). Can psychology be a science of mind? *American Psychologist, 45*, 1206–10.

Smolensky, P. (1986). Information processing in dynamical systems: Foundations of harmony theory. In D. E. Rumelhart & J. L. McClelland (eds.), *Parallel distributed processing: Foundations* (vol. 1, pp. 194–281). Cambridge, MA: MIT Press.

Smolensky, P. (1988). On the proper treatment of connectionism. *Behavioral and Brain Sciences, 11*, 1–74.

Smolensky, P. (1990). Tensor product variable binding and the representation of symbolic structures in connectionist systems. *Artificial Intelligence, 46*, 159–216.

Smolensky, P. (1991). Connectionism, constituency and the language of thought. In B. Loewer & G. Rey (eds.), *Meaning in mind: Fodor and his critics* (pp. 201–27). Oxford: Blackwell.

Sougné, J. (1998). Connectionism and the problem of multiple instantiation. *Trends in Cognitive Sciences, 2*, 183–9.

Staddon, J. E. R. & Higa, J. J. (1993). Temporal learning. In D. Medin (ed.), *The psychology of learning and motivation* (vol. 27, pp. 265–94). New York: Academic Press.

Stein-Beling, I. v. (1935). Über das Zeitgedächtnis bei Tieren. *Biological Reviews, 10*, 18–41.

Stevens, S. S. (1951). Mathematics, measurement and psychophysics. In S. S. Stevens (ed.), *Handbook of experimental psychology* (pp. 1–49). New York: John Wiley.

Strong, S. P., de Ruyter van Steveninck, R. R., Bialek, W., & Koberle, R. (1998). On the application of information theory to neural spike trains. *Pacific Symposium on Biocomputation*, 621–32.

Sujino, M., Masumoto, K. H., Yamaguchi, S., van der Hors, G. T., Okamura, H., & Inouye, S. T. (2003). Suprachiasmatic nucleus grafts restore circadian behavioral rhythms of genetically arrhythmic mice. *Current Biology, 13*, 664–8.

Sun, R. (1992). On variable binding in connectionist networks. *Connection Science, 4*, 93–124.

Sutton, R. S. & Barto, A. G. (1981). Toward a modern theory of adaptive networks: Expectation and prediction. *Psychological Review, 88*, 135–70.

Sutton, R. S. & Barto, A. G. (1990). Time-derivative models of Pavlovian reinforcement. In M. Gabriel & J. Moore (eds.), *Learning and computational neuroscience: Foundations of adaptive networks* (pp. 497–537). Cambridge, MA: Bradford/MIT Press.

Tautz, J., Zhang, S. W., Spaethe, J., Brockmann, A., Si, A., & Srinivasan, M. (2004). Honeybee odometry: Performance in varying natural terrain. *PLoS Biology, 2*, 915–23.

Trommershäuser, J., Maloney, L. T., & Landy, M. S. (2003). Statistical decision theory and rapid, goal-directed movements. *Journal of the Optical Society, A(20)*, 1419–33.

Tulving, E. (1972). Episodic and semantic memory. In E. Tulving & W. Donaldson (eds.), *Organization of memory* (pp. 381–403). New York: Academic Press.

Tulving, E. (1989). Remembering and knowing the past. *American Scientist, 77*, 361–7.

Turing, A. M. (1936). On computable numbers, with an application to the Entscheidungsproblem. *Proceedings of the London Mathematical Society 2nd series, 42*, 230–65.

Vander Wall, S. B. (1990). *Food hoarding in animals.* Chicago: University of Chicago Press.

von Frisch, K. (1967). *The dance-language and orientation of bees.* Cambridge, MA: Harvard University Press.

Wagner, A. R., Logan, F. A., Haberlandt, K., & Price, T. (1968). Stimulus selection in animal discrimination learning. *Journal of Experimental Psychology, 76*, 171–80.

Wahl, O. (1932). Neue Untersuchungen über das Zeitgedächtnis der Bienen. *Zeitschrift für vergleichende Physiologie, 16*, 529–89.

Watson, J. D. & Crick, F. H. (1953). A structure for deoxyribose nucleic acid. *Nature, 171*, 737–8.

Wehner, R., Lehrer, M., & Harvey, W. R. (eds.). (1996). Navigation: Special issue of *The Journal of Experimental Biology*, *199*(1). Cambridge: The Company of Biologists, Ltd.

Wehner, R. & Srinivasan, M. V. (1981). Searching behavior of desert ants, genus *Cataglyphis* (*Formicidae*, Hymenoptera). *Journal of Comparative Physiology*, *142*, 315–38.

Wehner, R., & Srinivasan, M. V. (2003). Path integration in insects. In K. J. Jeffery (ed.), *The neurobiology of spatial behaviour* (pp. 9–30). Oxford: Oxford University Press.

Weidemann, G., Georgilas, A., & Kehoe, E. J. (1999). Temporal specificity in patterning of the rabbit nictitating membrane response. *Animal Learning and Behavior*, *27*, 99–107.

Weiss, P. (1941). Self-differentiation of the basic patterns of coordination. *Comparative Psychology Monographs*, *17*, 1–96.

White, N. E., Kehoe, E. J., Choi, J.-S., & Moore, J. W. (2000). Coefficients of variation in timing of the classically conditioned eyeblink in rabbits. *Psychobiology*, *28*(4), 520–4.

Wiltschko, R., & Wiltschko, W. (2003). Avian navigation: From historical to modern concepts. *Animal Behaviour*, *65*, 257–72.

Glossary

action potentials Large pulse-like changes in membrane potential that propagate in the axons of neurons over long distances without degrading; the signals by which information is rapidly transmitted over long distances in nervous systems.

address bus The set of parallel wires carrying the bit pattern that specifies the address (location) in memory from or to which a symbol is to be read or written. A transcription factor that binds to ("is recognized by") a promoter plays the role in biological memory of the signal on an address bus, which is recognized by the hardware at the address it specifies.

addressable memory A memory whose contents may be retrieved by probing with symbols that encode for the address (location) of the memory. Examples are (1) the random access memory in a computer, in which the contents of a location are retrieved by probing with the address of that location, and (2) genes, which are activated by probing with a transcription factor that binds to the promoter for the gene.

algorithm A step-by-step process that determines the output of a function, given the input. Also called a **procedure**, particularly when the inputs and outputs are symbols.

analog principle The principle that analog symbols (and also digital symbols encoded without the use of combinatorial syntax) demand resources that are proportional to the number of potential messages for which they encode, making such symbols ultimately untenable for use in complex representing systems.

analog symbol/signal A symbol/signal that comes from a non-discrete (continuous), infinite, and orderable set of possible symbols/signals.

argument An entity chosen from the domain of a function. Also called the **input** to the function.

ASCII The American Standard Code for Information Interchange; a code for assigning bytes to common characters (letters, numbers, punctuation, etc.).

association A conductive connection between two mental or brain units, formed or altered by experience. The critical aspect of the requisite experience has traditionally been assumed to be the close temporal pairing of two "ideas" or sensations (in the doctrines of the empiricist philosophers of the eighteenth and nineteenth centuries) or of a stimulus and a response (in the Behaviorist tradition) or of a stimulus and a stimulus, or of a presynaptic action potential and a postsynaptic depolarization (in contemporary neurobiologically oriented theorizing).

atomic data The irreducible physical forms that can be distinguished in a representing system and used in the construction of data strings and symbols.

Bayes' law The analytic relation between two unconditional probabilities – $p(x)$ and $p(y)$ – and the corresponding conditional probabilities – $p(x|y)$ and $p(y|x)$: $p(y|x) = p(x|y) \, p(y)/p(x)$; the rule governing normative probabilistic inference from data (signals) to the states of the world that may have generated them.

bijection A function that is both one-to-one and onto.

bit A basic unit of measurement for information. Also, a symbol that comes from a set of two possible symbols.

bit pattern An ordered set (sequence) of bits.

blocking The phenomenon in classical and operant conditioning in which a previously learned association between one conditioned stimulus (CS) and an unconditioned stimulus (US) blocks the formation of an association between another (potential) CS and that same US when the new CS is always presented together with (in compound with) the old CS. It is one of the proofs that the temporal pairing of a CS and a US is not a sufficient condition for the development of an association.

Boolean algebra The mathematical system of logical functions and binary symbols.

byte A unit of measurement for information; a byte is eight bits.

Cartesian product The set of all possible pairwise (or triplewise, etc.) combinations of elements chosen from two or more sets, with one element from each set in each combination.

channel The medium (such as a wire, a band of radio frequencies, or an axon) that is used to carry a signal.

checksum Information contained within a signal that is not about the encoded message but rather about the signal itself; it is used to help verify that the signal received is the signal that was sent.

Church-Turing thesis The hypothesis that a Turing machine (and other formally equivalent systems, such as the lambda calculus or recursive functions) delimit the set of functions that may be computed (determined by a generative mechanism).

circadian clock An endogenous entrainable biochemical cycle with a period of approximately 24 hours that times the daily variations in the activity and physiology of an organism, organ, tissue, or cell. To say that it is *entrainable* is to say that external signals from another cycle with roughly the same period (most often the cyclical variation in solar illumination) adjust the phase of the cycle so that it maintains a constant phase relation to the source of the external signal (called the *Zeitgeber*, or *time-giver*).

classical conditioning An experimental protocol in which the temporal contingency between the conditioned stimulus and the unconditioned stimulus does not depend on the subject's behavior.

code The rules that specify the encoding process by which messages are converted into symbols/signals. More generally, it is the relationship between the set of possible messages and the set of possible symbols/signals.

codomain The set of distinct (and possibly infinite) elements of which the outputs (also values) of a particular function are members. For the function $f : D \rightarrow C$, it is the set C.

codon A sequence of three nucleotides that codes for an amino acid or for the punctuation that marks the start and end of a gene, which specifies the sequence of amino acids in a protein or polypeptide (the molecular building blocks of organic structure).

cognitive map A data structure in the brain that records the locations (coordinates) of experienced points of interest in the environment, together with addresses that permit the retrieval of information pertinent to those locations, such as compass-oriented views.

combinatorial explosion The effect that results from a set of combinations in which the number of combinations grows exponentially with the number of different elements entering into each combination.

combinatorial syntax Syntax created by combining symbols based on their form and their ordering (relative positions). Using combinatorial syntax results in compact symbols, as one can produce d^n symbols from d atomic symbols and strings of length n.

compact (compressed) code A code is compact to the degree by which it minimizes the average number of bits that are needed to encode for a set of messages. As this number of bits is reduced, the code is said to be more *efficient*. A code is maximally compressed (efficient) when the average number of bits in the signal or symbol equals the source entropy.

compact procedures Procedures for which the number of bits required to communicate them (the bits required to encode the algorithm) is many orders of magnitude smaller than the number of bits required to communicate the look-up table for the function realized by the procedure.

compact symbols Symbols that are constructed using combinatorial syntax. Such symbols require physical resources that grow logarithmically in the number of entities for which they may encode.

composition of functions The construction of a new function by taking the output of one function and making it the input to another function. Where ∘ denotes composition, $f_a \circ f_b = f_a(f_b(x))$. This creates a new function that has the range of f_a and the domain of f_b.

computable numbers Those numbers for which there exists a procedure that will determine their symbolic representation to an arbitrary level of precision (out to arbitrarily many decimal places). Most real numbers are *not* computable.

computation The effecting of a procedure so as to determine the output of a function, given an input. A computation usually implies that the input and output are symbols.

conditioned stimulus A stimulus that does not elicit an anticipatory behavior in a naïve subject.

conditioning Jargon for the learning that occurs in simple experimental paradigms designed originally to reveal the laws of association formation. From a modern computational perspective, the term implies a state-memory (rewiring) conception of the learning process, in that experience is conceived of as altering the condition (processing state) of the nervous system, so that the animal behaves differently as a result of the learning experience. In this conception of learning, there is no symbolic memory. The alternative conception is that experience imparts information, which is carried forward in a symbolic memory to inform subsequent behavior.

connectionism The elaboration of psychological models built on neural nets, which model psychological phenomena without recourse to a symbolic memory, except as implemented via recurrent connections that allow self-sustaining activity mediated by signals traveling round and round in loops. Part of the justification for such models is their putative neurobiological plausibility.

content-addressable memory A memory in which locations may be found not by probing with their address but rather with partial contents. When a location matches the partial probe, it returns either: (1) its address, or (2) the rest of the contents.

countable A set is countable if it can be placed in one-to-one correspondence with the set of natural numbers, $\mathbb{N}$, that is, if its members can be listed in such a way that if the list were continued indefinitely any specified member of the set would eventually appear in the list. Famous proofs by Cantor show that the rational numbers are countable but the real numbers are not. The computable numbers are countable, although they include many non-rational numbers, such as *pi*, *e*, and $\sqrt{2}$.

data bus The set of parallel wires carrying a bit pattern signal from or to a location in memory, depending on whether the information in the signal is to be read from or written to that location.

data strings The ordered symbolic forms composed of one or more atomic data. For example, a sequence of bits, a sequence of numerals, a sequence of digits, or a sequence of nucleotides.

data structures Often called *expressions* in the philosophical and logical literature, data structures are symbol strings (or, possibly, structures with a more complex topology than that of a one-dimensional string) that have referents by virtue of the referents of the symbols out of which they are composed and the arrangement of those symbols. For example, the point on the plane represented by the vector <12, −4> is a data structure, as its referent is determined by the referents and arrangement of the symbols for the numbers 12 ('12') and −4 ('−4'). Data structures often encode for propositions, statements such as "All men are mortal," that express relationships.

dead reckoning The integration of velocity with respect to time (or the summing of successive small displacements) to obtain the net change in position (aka, *path integration*).

decode To reconstitute a message from a symbol/signal.

delta rule Formal description of a process for adjusting the strength of associations that has first-order kinetics. The change in strength is proportional to the difference between the sum over all current associations to that element (node) and a quantity representing the value to which the sum must converge in the limit under stable conditions.

digital symbol/signal A symbol/signal is digital if it comes from a discrete and finite set of possible symbols/signals.

dimer Two molecules (temporarily) bound together in a form with a functionality that the combining molecules do not alone have. Dimerization may implement at the molecular level the logic functions from which all other functions may be realized by composition (for example, NOT and AND).

direct addressing Accessing a memory location (a variable) via a symbol that encodes for the address of the memory location. Using a simple variable in a traditional programming language is an example of direct addressing.

domain A set of distinct (and possibly infinite) elements from which the inputs (arguments) to functions are chosen.

effective procedure See **procedure**.

effector A device that converts signals within an information processing device into external behaviors.

encode To convert a message into a symbol or signal. One then says that the symbol/signal codes for this message.

encoding symbols Symbols related to their referents by generative principles (a compact procedure).

entropy The amount of uncertainty regarding which message in a set of possible messages will obtain. Given a discrete or continuous probability distribution on the set of possible messages, it is the sum or integral of $p\log p$ with respect to p. Typically measured in bits.

EPSP An Excitatory PostSynaptic Potential; a temporary depolarization of the postsynaptic membrane that can result in the initiation of an action potential.

finite-state automaton A computing machine with state memory but without symbolic memory; a Turing machine without a tape to which it can write.

flip-flop A bi-stable memory device that provides the minimal functionality for the read/write memory of a Turing complete computing device. It also makes state memory possible.

function A deterministic mapping between elements of one set of distinct entities, called the **domain,** to elements from another set of distinct entities, called the **codomain.**

grandmother neuron A neuron that is selectively tuned to a combination of stimulus elements from among an essentially infinite set of possible combinations, implying that there would have to be an infinite number of such neurons to represent the entire set.

halting problem The problem of determining whether a computer program, given a particular input, will halt. This problem is not computable, that is, there is no machine that can give the answer in a finite amount of time in all cases.

Hebbian synapse A synapse whose conductance is altered by the temporal pairing of a presynaptic signal and a postsynaptic depolarization (**EPSP**).

homomorphism A structure preserving mapping from one set of entities and functions to another set of entities and functions.

Huffman code A code made efficient by using the probabilities of each message in the set of potential messages to produce the code.

immediate addressing A misnomer: utilizing a value by embedding it directly within the computational device itself in non-symbolic form. Such values are not accessible for general purpose computation. Using a literal (constant) in a traditional programming language is an example of immediate addressing.

indirect addressing Accessing a memory location (a variable) by probing an address that contains the address of the location sought. Using an array in a traditional programming language is an example of indirect addressing. A transcription factor that binds to the promoter of the gene encoding another transcription factor plays the analogous role in biological memory.

indirect code A code is indirect with respect to intrinsic properties of an entity to the extent that it produces symbols whose physical form does not reflect these intrinsic properties in any simple way.

infinitude of the possible The infinite number of possible values that could obtain for a variable. For example, the (essentially) infinite number of different pictures that a digital camera can take.

information The reduction in the entropy of the receiver's probability distribution (over a set of possible messages) effected by a signal. Typically, the signal was received in the indeterminate past, so the reduction it effected must be carried forward in time by a symbol. The information carried by a symbol is the difference between the receiver's uncertainty about the relevant state of the world, given that symbol, and the receiver's uncertainty about that same state of the world, absent that symbol (assuming that the receiver can decode the symbol).

information source A producer of messages that are to be communicated.

input An entity chosen from the domain of a function. Also called the **argument** of the function.

integers Signified by $\mathbb{Z}$, this is the infinite set $\{0, -1, 1, -2, 2, \ldots\}$.

intractable function A function whose determination requires exponential growth in spatial or temporal resources as the size of the encoding of the input grows linearly (linearly in the cardinality of the domain). Intractable functions cannot be computed efficiently.

ionotropic receptor A molecular structure embedded in the postsynaptic membrane of a neuron, which allows some species of ions (usually, sodium, or chloride, or calcium or potassium) to flow through it when in the open configuration but not when in the closed configuration. The configuration is controlled by the binding of external signal-transmitting substances (neurotransmitters) to portions of the molecular structure on the outside of the membrane.

IPSP An Inhibitory PostSynaptic Potential; a temporary hyperpolarization of the postsynaptic membrane that can prevent the occurrence of an action potential. An effect opposite in sign to the effect of an excitatory postsynaptic potential (**EPSP**).

joint distribution A function specifying for the Cartesian product of two sets of messages (that is, for each possible combination of two messages, one from each set) the probability of that combination. Being a probability distribution, the set of all the joint probabilities must sum to 1.

likelihood A probability distribution read backward. When read forward, a probability distribution is taken as the given and we read from it the probability of different possible signals (data) that we might observe. When read backward, the data are taken as given (already observed) and we read from an hypothesized probability distribution (for example, a distribution with an assumed mean and standard deviation) the likelihood of our having observed those signals if that were the distribution from which they came. In the first case, we infer from the distribution to the probability of the data; in the second case, we infer from the data back to the likelihood of a source distribution.

likelihood function The function specifying for different possible source distributions (e.g., normal distributions varying in their mean and standard deviation) their relative likelihood given some data (observed signals). Because likelihoods, unlike probabilities, are not mutually exclusive and exhaustive, likelihood functions rarely integrate (sum) to 1, unlike probability distributions, which always do. The likelihood function plays a central role in Bayesian inference: it represents the data, specifying their implications regarding the possible states of the world, that is, regarding which messages from among a set of messages are and are not likely in the light of the data.

linked list A linear data structure that is created using a virtual "next to" relationship by specifying along with each symbol the address of the next symbol. If the data structure also maintains the address of each previous symbol, then it is called a doubly linked list.

logic function An elementary two-argument function in digital processing (and in symbolic logic), specifying for each of the four possible combinations of the two values of two binary variables that serve as inputs or arguments (00, 01, 10, and 11) the value of the output (0 or 1). This specification is called a truth table. For example, the AND function has the truth table: $00\rightarrow0$, $01\rightarrow0$, $10\rightarrow0$, $11\rightarrow1$, while the OR function has the truth table: $00\rightarrow0$, $01\rightarrow1$, $10\rightarrow1$, $11\rightarrow1$, and the NAND function has the truth table: $00\rightarrow1$, $01\rightarrow1$, $10\rightarrow1$, $11\rightarrow0$. More complex functions are constructed from these elementary functions by composition. The one-argument NOT function ($0\rightarrow1$, $1\rightarrow0$) is generally included among the logic functions.

look-up table A table structure that defines and determines a function by giving the explicit mapping of each input to its respective output. Look-up tables demand spatial resources that grow linearly in the number of potential inputs (the cardinality of the domain), making them unusable for functions that have large domains.

LTP Long-term potentiation: an enduring increase in the conductance of a synapse, that is, an enduring change in magnitude of an EPSP produced by a presynaptic action potential. Widely considered to be the physical basis of associative memory.

marginal distribution The distribution obtained by summing or integrating over one or more of the parameters or variables that define a distribution. If one imagines a joint distribution as a probability "hill," then the marginal distributions are the distributions that one gets using a bull-dozer that piles up all the probability mass onto one or the other of the two orthogonal vertical planes.

memory (symbolic) The mechanism that carries information forward in time in a computationally accessible form. Often used in a much more general sense, to include the innumerable processes that organize the information (form it into data structures), revise it, and retrieve it.

message One member from a set of possibilities, typically, possible states of the world that are to be communicated to a receiver.

metabotropic receptor A molecular structure embedded in the postsynaptic membrane of a neuron, whose configuration is altered by the binding of a neurotransmitter substance to a portion of the receptor on the outside of the membrane. The change in configuration alters the structure of a G protein to which the inside portions of the structure are coupled, setting in motion an intracellular signal cascade. These receptors allow signals external to a neuron to affect its internal signal system.

mutual information The sum of the entropies of two marginal distributions minus the entropy of the joint distribution. If the two distributions are the source distribution and the signal distribution, then this is the fraction of the source information contained in the signal. It is the upper limit on the information about the source that a signal can transmit to a receiver.

natural numbers Signified by $\mathbb{N}$, this is the infinite set $\{0, 1, 2, \ldots\}$.

neural net A schematic arrangement of abstract neuron-like elements with many connections between the elements (nodes). The connections are thought to have functional properties somewhat like the functional properties of the synapses by which signals pass from one neuron to another within a nervous system. Neural net theorists investigate the ability of such nets to mimic behavioral or mental phenomena. The nets are commonly imagined to have three layers, an input layer, a hidden layer, and an output layer, corresponding roughly to sensory neurons, interneurons, and motor neurons. In a recurrent net, the pattern of connections allows for signals to flow round and round in loops.

noise sources All factors other than the message that contribute to variation in a signal. Noise sources tend to corrupt the signal and make decoding more difficult.

nominal symbol A symbol that maps to its referent in an arbitrary way using a look-up table; a mapping that is not constrained by any generative principles and cannot be determined by a compact procedure.

nucleotide The basic building block of the double-helical DNA molecules that carry inherited information forward in time. Each nucleotide contains one of four nitrogenous bases (adenine, thymine, cytosine, and guanine or ATCG for short), which pair to form the cross links within the double helix. The hereditary data strings are sequences of these four data elements. Because adenine can link only with thymine, and cytosine only with guanine, the two helical strands have complementary antiparallel sequences. This enables the code to be copied (replicated).

one-to-one function A function where distinct members of the domain get mapped to distinct members of the codomain, that is, $f(a) = f(b)$ implies $a = b$.

onto function A function where the range is the same as the codomain, that is, if every element in the codomain is the output for (is paired with) one or more elements in the domain.

operant conditioning An experimental protocol in which there is an experimenter-imposed contingency between the subject's behavior and some event, such as the delivery of food.

output An entity from the codomain of a function resulting from a particular input. Also called the **value** of the function.

overshadowing The phenomenon in classical and operant conditioning in which presenting two (potentially) conditionable stimuli together (in compound) leads to the formation of an association to one or the other but not both. It is one of the proofs that the temporal pairing of a CS and a US is not a sufficient condition for the development of an association.

Pavlovian conditioning See **classical conditioning.**

place coding A proposed encoding scheme by which different states of the world are represented by the firing of different neurons. Thus, the state of the world is encoded by the location of activity within neural tissue.

plasticity Neurobiological jargon for the presumed capacity of neural tissue to make enduring changes in its processing state in response to experience; an allusion to the presumed capacity for the rewiring of neural connections.

posterior probability The probability of a source message in the light of both the data (signals received), the likelihood function, and the prior probability. The posterior probability is the probability after taking both prior probability and the data into account.

predicate A function that maps one or more arguments to a binary output (*True-False* or 1, 0).

prefix code A code that produces variable length symbols/signals that, when strung together linearly, are unambiguously distinguishable. It achieves this by making sure that no encoding appears as the prefix of another. For example, the code that produces English words is not a prefix code, as it has words such as "fast" and "fasten."

prior probability The probability of a source message, the probability based on information other than the information contained in a specified signal.

probability density The rate at which probability mass accumulates as one moves past a given point on the parameter axis of a continuous probability distribution, that is, the point slope (derivative at a point) of the cumulative probability function. Because it is a derivative (rate of change of probability) rather than an amount (mass), it may have any positive value.

probability distribution A function specifying for each of a set of possible values (messages) of a variable (set of possible messages) a probability. Because one and only one message can obtain at any one time (because the possibilities are mutually exclusive and exhaustive), the set of all the probabilities must sum to 1.

problem of the infinitude of the possible This problem recognizes that the possible number inputs that many functions might take are effectively infinite. As such, it is not possible to implement such functions using non-compact procedures (**look-up tables**).

problem of pre-specification This problem recognizes that if one uses a non-compact procedure (a look-up table architecture) to implement a function, then one must specify in advance – and allocate physical resources to – all of the possible outputs that one might hope to get back from the function.

procedure A step-by-step process (**algorithm**) that determines the output of a function, given the input. This term is used most often within a computational framework, where the inputs and outputs of the function are symbols. One says that a procedure, when effected as a computation, *determines* a function, and that the procedure, as a physical system, *implements* a function. As a physical system, the word *process* is often used as synonymous with procedure.

productivity The ability of a computational mechanism (a procedure that implements a function) to map an essentially infinite number of possible input arguments to outputs – an ability lacking in a look-up table, because the table must contain in its physical structure elements unique to all possible inputs and outputs.

promoter A stretch of DNA to which a transcription factor binds and, in so doing, promotes the transcription (reading) of a gene. The promoter plays the same role in the retrieval of genetic information that an address probe plays in the retrieval of information from a random access computer memory

property A predicate of one argument.

proposition See **data structures**.

RAM Random Access Memory; addressable, read/write memory in a conventional computer.

rate coding A proposed encoding scheme in which different rates of firing of a neuron code for different states of the world.

real numbers Signified by $\mathbb{R}$, the real numbers are those that can encoded by an infinite decimal representation. Real numbers include the natural, rational, irrational, and transcendental numbers. Geometric proportions are isomorphic only to the proportions represented by real numbers in that every geometric proportion (for example, the proportion between the side of a square and its diagonal or the diameter of a circle and its circumference) maps to a real number and every real number maps to a geometric proportion. This is not true for infinitesimal subsets of the real numbers, like, the rational numbers.

receiver A physical system that operates on (decodes) a signal to reconstitute a communicated message.

recurrent (reverberating) loop A putative connection between a neuron and itself or between a sequence of neurons leading back to the first neuron. Such loops are widely supposed to carry information forward in time by continuously cycling the information without noise.

register A multi-bit read/write memory device in a conventional computer.

reinforcement A motivationally important outcome of some sequence of stimuli and/or responses that alters the subject's future responses. The term presupposes an associative theory of learning and memory in that it implies that the altered behavior is the consequence of the strengthening of some connection (association).

relation A predicate of more than one argument.

relative validity A conditioning protocol in which it is observed that the best predicting CS among three different partially predictive CSs is the only CS to which an association apparently forms. It is one of the proofs that the temporal pairing of a CS and a US is not a sufficient condition for the development of an association. It is also a strong indication of the computational sophistication of the process that mediates the formation of putative associations.

representation A representation consists of a represented system, a representing system, and structure-preserving mappings between the two systems. The latter map between entities and functions in the represented system and symbols and procedures in the representing system in such a way that (at least some) formal properties of the functions in the represented system are preserved in the symbols and procedures to which they map and that map back to them. This preservation of formal structure is what enables the representing system to anticipate relations in the represented system.

ribosomes The intracellular molecular machine that assembles proteins following the instructions transmitted from an activated gene by messenger RNA.

Shannon-Fano code A code made efficient by using the relative probabilities (probability rankings) of the set of messages to produce the code.

shift register A memory register that preserves a sequence of binary inputs by shifting the bit pattern down by one bit as each successive bit is received, preserving the newly received bit as the top bit in the register.

signal A fluctuation in a physical quantity carrying information across space. Signals always come from a set of possible signals.

solar ephemeris The compass direction of the sun as a function of the time of day. In traditional navigation, it refers to *both* the compass direction (azimuth) *and* elevation (angular distance above the horizon) as functions of the time of day and the date, but there is no evidence that animal navigators make use of the elevation.

spike trains The sequences of action potentials that function as the universal currency by which information is transmitted from place to place within neural tissue.

state memory Memory implicit in the effect of the past on the current state of the symbol processing machinery, with no encoding of the information into computationally accessible symbolic form.

sun compass A mechanism that uses the sun (and a learned solar ephemeris) to maintain a constant orientation with respect to the earth's surface.

symbol A physical entity that carries information forward in time. Symbols in a representing system encode for entities in a represented system. Symbols always come from a set of possible symbols. Often used as a general term to refer to both symbols and signals.

synaptic conductance The scale factor relating the magnitude of a presynaptic signal to its postsynaptic effect; the magnitude of the postsynaptic effect produced by a given presynaptic signal. Changes in synaptic conductance are commonly assumed to be the neurobiological mechanism by which associations form.

syntax The rules that govern the mapping from the structure of symbol strings or data structures to their referents. The rules are based on the form of the constituent symbols and their spatial and/or temporal context. For example, the rule that specifies that whether a given power of 2 does or does not form part of the sum that must be computed to get the numerical referent of a bit string depends on the bit at the corresponding position when counting from the right of a bit string (if there is a '1' at that position, that power of 2 is to be included in the sum; if there is a '0', it is not).

transcription factor A molecule that binds to a promoter or repressor region of DNA to promote or repress the transcription (reading) of a gene. Plays roughly the same functional role as a bit pattern on the address bus in random access computer memory.

transduce To convert a sensory (proximal) stimulus into a sensory signal, typically into streams of spikes in sensory axons.

transition table A table specifying for a computing machine what state to transition to given the current state of the machine and any potential inputs, internal or otherwise. The table often includes other actions to be taken, such as producing an output or writing a symbol to memory.

transmitter A physical system that operates on a message to create a signal that can be sent across a channel. The transmitter encodes the message.

transmitter substance A substance released from a presynaptic ending that diffuses across the very narrow synaptic cleft and binds to postsynaptic receptors, thereby affecting signaling in the postsynaptic neuron.

Turing computable A function is Turing computable if, given an encoding of the inputs and outputs, there is a Turing machine that can determine the function.

Turing machine An abstract computing machine that consists only of a symbolic memory tape (which may be arbitrarily large), a read/write head, and a transition table.

two senses of knowing This refers to the distinction between straightforward, transparent symbolic knowledge (information accessible to general purpose computation), and the indirect, opaque "knowing" that is characteristic of finite-state machines, which lack a symbolic read/write memory.

unconditioned stimulus A stimulus that elicits some behavior in a naïve subject. In conditioning experiments, this is the stimulus that is predicted by a conditioned stimulus. A subject that experiences this predictive relation comes in time to make a US-anticipatory response (a conditioned response) to the conditioned stimulus.

universal Turing machine A Turing machine TM_1 that is capable of computing the function computed by any other Turing machine TM_2 on an input x by taking an appropriate encoding of TM_2 and x. A universal Turing machine is a mathematical model for a general-purpose computer.

value (1) The output of a function for a particular input (argument). (2) The message that currently obtains for a given variable (set of possible messages).

variable A set of possible messages; the messages in the set constitute the possible values of the variable. Physically speaking, the symbol for a variable is the symbol for the address where the current value resides.

variable binding problem The problem of how to locate, retrieve, and set the symbol specifying the current value of a variable. This is a problem for connectionist architectures only. In a conventional computing architecture, this ability derives transparently from the addressability of the values in memory.

vector In its most general sense, an ordered set (string) of numbers (or symbol elements, as in a binary vector). In a narrower sense, only such strings as may be validly subject to vector operations (vector addition and vector subtraction and multiplication by, for example, rotation matrices). To say that the set is ordered is to say that the sequence matters; different sequences of the same elements constitute different vectors. The Cartesian coordinates specifying a location (point) are examples of vectors in the narrow sense. The words in a computer (binary strings, e.g., <00011010111001111>) are an example of vectors in the more general sense.

window of associability The elusive temporal window implied by the hypothesis that temporal pairing is what drives association formation. Its determination would specify what constitutes temporal pairing. Attempts to determine it experimentally have repeatedly failed.

word The size of the primitive memory unit used in a conventional computer, typically 32 or 64 bits. The size of a word determines the number of different possible messages in the set of possible messages that may be encoded by the form (bit pattern) of the word.

Index